Intrinsic Motivation and Self-Determination in Exercise and Sport

Martin S. Hagger, PhD
University of Nottingham

Nikos L.D. Chatzisarantis, PhD
University of Plymouth

Human Kinetics

Library of Congress Cataloging-in-Publication Data

Intrinsic motivation and self-determination in exercise and sport / [edited by] Martin Hagger, Nikos Chatzisarantis.
   p. ; cm.
   Includes bibliographical references and index.
   ISBN-13: 978-0-7360-6250-3 (hard cover)
   ISBN-10: 0-7360-6250-5 (hard cover)
   1. Sports--Psychological aspects. 2. Exercise--Psychological aspects. 3. Intrinsic motivation. I. Hagger, Martin. II. Chatzisarantis, Nikos.
   [DNLM: 1. Exercise--psychology. 2. Physical Fitness--psychology. 3. Motivation. 4. Sports--psychology. QT 255 1618 2007]
   GV7006.4.I592 2007
   796'.01--dc22
                          2006038971

ISBN-10: 0-7360-6250-5
ISBN-13: 978-0-7360-6250-3

Acquisitions Editor: Myles Schrag; **Developmental Editor:** Maggie Schwarzentraub; **Assistant Editor:** Maureen Eckstein; **Copyeditor:** Joyce Sexton; **Proofreader:** Erin Cler; **Indexer:** Marie Rizzo; **Permission Manager:** Dalene Reeder; **Graphic Designer:** Nancy Rasmus; **Graphic Artist:** Yvonne Griffith; **Photo Manager:** Laura Fitch; **Cover Designer:** Nancy Rasmus; **Photographer (interior):** Photo on page 21 © Digital Vision; photo on page 141 © StockByte; **Art Manager:** Kelly Hendren; **Illustrator:** Al Wilborn; Illustration on inside front cover courtesy of Martin S. Hagger; **Printer:** Edwards Brothers

Printed in the United States of America   10 9 8 7 6 5 4 3 2 1

Human Kinetics
Web site: www.HumanKinetics.com

United States: Human Kinetics
P.O. Box 5076
Champaign, IL 61825-5076
800-747-4457
e-mail: humank@hkusa.com

Canada: Human Kinetics
475 Devonshire Road Unit 100
Windsor, ON N8Y 2L5
800-465-7301 (in Canada only)
e-mail: orders@hkcanada.com

Europe: Human Kinetics
107 Bradford Road, Stanningley
Leeds LS28 6AT, United Kingdom
+44 (0) 113 255 5665
e-mail: hk@hkeurope.com

Australia: Human Kinetics
57A Price Avenue
Lower Mitcham, South Australia 5062
08 8372 0999
e-mail: liaw@hkaustralia.com

New Zealand: Human Kinetics
Division of Sports Distributors NZ Ltd.
P.O. Box 300 226 Albany
North Shore City
Auckland
0064 9 448 1207
e-mail: info@humankinetics.co.nz

To my parents, Lazaros and Despoina Chatzisarantis; my grandparents, Dimitris and Evanthia Chatzisaranti; my wife, Madalina Cruceru; and Marika and Nikos Syriopoulou.

Nikos Chatzisarantis

To the Hagger clan: Elinor, Mike, Damian, and Mary-Jane.

Martin Hagger

CONTENTS

CONTRIBUTORS

Anthony J. Amorose, PhD
Illinois State University

Stuart J.H. Biddle, PhD
Loughborough University

Julie C.S. Boiché, PhD
Université Joseph Fourier

Céline Blanchard, PhD
University of Ottawa

Nikos L.D. Chatzisarantis, PhD
University of Plymouth

J. Douglas Coatsworth, PhD
Pennsylvania State University

David E. Conroy, PhD
Pennsylvania State University

Edward L. Deci, PhD
University of Rochester

Joan L. Duda, PhD
University of Birmingham

Jemma K. Edmunds, PhD
University of Birmingham

Andrew J. Elliot, PhD
University of Rochester

Michelle Fortier, PhD
University of Ottawa

Marylène Gagné, PhD
Concordia University

Fiona Gillison, MSc
University of Bath

Martin S. Hagger, PhD
University of Nottingham

Vello Hein, PhD
University of Tartu

David K. Ingledew, PhD
University of Wales, Bangor

Andre Koka, PhD
University of Tartu

John Kowal, PhD
Ottawa Hospital General Campus

Kendy K. Kuczka, PhD
AIA Academy

Pierre-Nicolas Lemyre, PhD
Norwegian University of Sport and Physical Education

Willy Lens, PhD
University of Leuven

David Markland, PhD
University of Wales, Bangor

Nikos Ntoumanis, PhD
University of Birmingham

Luc G. Pelletier, PhD
University of Ottawa

Wendy M. Rodgers, PhD
University of Alberta

Richard M. Ryan, PhD
University of Rochester

Philippe Sarrazin, PhD
Université Joseph Fourier

Bart Soenens, MSc
University of Leuven

Martyn Standage, PhD
University of Bath

Darren C. Treasure, PhD
Competitive Advantage International Performance Systems

Robert J. Vallerand, PhD
Université du Québec à Montréal

Maarten Vansteenkiste, PhD
University of Leuven

Chee Keng John Wang, PhD
Nanyang Technological University

Philip M. Wilson, PhD
Brock University

PREFACE

Social scientists, sport psychologists, coaches, exercise professionals, fitness industry managers, physical education teachers, and athletes are all fascinated by the factors that motivate and determine behaviors in the physical domain. It is therefore no coincidence that motivation is central to the study of behavior in the exercise and sport domain. In everyday life the word *motivation* is often used in an eclectic, unstructured manner that may mask its true value and utility as an important predictor of behavior. Formally, motivation can be considered an internal state that energizes and drives action or behavior and determines its direction and persistence. Motivation has been central to many social psychological theories that aim to explain behavior and is central to self-determination theory, one of the most influential theories of human motivation developed in the last three decades. It naturally follows that motivation is central to this book, which seeks to examine the contribution of self-determination theory to motivation and behavior in the domains of exercise and sport.

Self-determination theory is a dialectic, organismic theory of human motivation that draws from the seminal work by humanist researchers in motivation such as White (1959) and deCharms (1968). The theory focuses on the extent to which behaviors are autonomous or self-determined, which researchers study through the methods of social psychology and personality. Self-determination theory is actually a meta-theory that comprises four subtheories: cognitive evaluation theory, organismic integration theory, causality orientations theory, and basic needs theory. Each subtheory has its own set of detailed hypotheses that cover the major predictions of the meta-theory.

At the heart of self-determination theory is the premise that individuals are active in their pursuit to satisfy three basic and universal psychological needs for autonomy, competence, and relatedness. These needs determine the direction and persistence of an individual toward engaging in goal-directed behaviors that are likely to result in satisfying these needs. Cognitive evaluation theory, the first of the subtheories to be developed, focuses on intrinsic motivation as the epitome of self-determined motivation. Cognitive evaluation theory outlines the environmental contingencies that support or thwart intrinsic motivation. Organismic integration theory outlines how behaviors that are not intrinsically motivated can be internalized and integrated into an individual's behavioral repertoire that satisfies psychological needs. Causality orientations theory examines individual differences in personal tendencies to pursue and engage in self-determined behaviors. Basic needs theory examines relations between psychological needs, their origins, and behavior and salient outcomes. Together, the component theories of the self-determination meta-theory have provided an effective, comprehensive, and integrative framework for the understanding of motivation.

Self-determination theory has demonstrated efficacy in explaining the motivational processes underlying exercise and sport behavior. Narrative and meta-analytic reviews have highlighted that self-determination theory can effectively predict exercise behavior and sport performance, as well as a plethora of salient outcome variables. Given the proliferation of this research, the breadth of applications, and the concomitant success of self-determination theory, the purpose of this book is to bring together contributions from leading authors responsible for the development and application of the theory in the domains of exercise and sport over the past two decades. In this book we have sought to provide a contemporary, up-to-date compendium of applications of self-determination theory to these domains. Each author is an acknowledged expert in the area with considerable experience in applying the theory to the domain of exercise and sport. Each author will visit a specific theoretical or applied aspect of the theory and provide a showcase for his or her own research and what it brings to the literature in terms of the understanding of motivation in exercise and sport.

The book begins with an introductory chapter in which the founding fathers of self-determination theory, Ed Deci and Rich Ryan, provide a detailed overview of the theory and its constituent subtheories and chart its history with respect to exercise and sport, highlighting classic studies and seminal works along the way. Both the novice and experienced reader will find that this introduction masterfully provides sufficient theoretical grounding and serves as an excellent prologue to subsequent chapters. The chapters from the contributors to this book are organized into two parts that visit key theoretical and applied topics using the theory in the exercise (part I) and sport (part II) domains. The contributions into separate parts on exercise and sport were segregated on the basis that research in the exercise domain tends to focus on different types of behaviors and outcomes from that in the sport domain. The chapters that adopt self-determination theory in an exercise context are oriented toward health-related activities and outcomes such as psychological well-being, while the chapters that report research in sport contexts tend to direct attention to competitive and performance-related behaviors and outcomes. However, not surprisingly, there are some commonalities, and we visit these in the final chapter. The authors of the chapters in each part expertly define the context of their specific approach to motivation using self-determination theory, provide an overview of previous research relevant to their topic, introduce recent evidence from their own research, and then outline future directions for research using self-determination theory in this domain. In addition, each author has provided recommendations and guidelines that practitioners and professionals in exercise and sport can adopt to enhance the motivation of the people they work with. The aim of these practical suggestions is to provide clear and pragmatic guidance in terms of the actual behaviors and activities that practitioners can take away and use in their own practice sessions or interventions. Each set of recommendations are based on practices that have been shown to be effective in empirical research using self-determination theory in the sport or exercise domain.

In the concluding chapter we have not only provided an executive summary of the contributions, but also attempted to draw together some of the commonalities from the two sections and provide some global action points in terms of guidelines for practitioners and directions for future research. We are grateful to the tireless effort the authors have committed in making their contributions to this volume; they truly practice what they preach when it comes to their commitment to the self-determined approach and require little external cajoling from the likes of us! We hope that readers will be inspired, as we were, by the wealth of information, research, and philosophy that these contributions yield to knowledge of motivation in exercise and sport.

ACKNOWLEDGMENTS

We would like to extend our gratitude to Professor Stuart Biddle, our friend and mentor over the past decade; all of the contributors for their tireless commitment and intense interest; our colleagues and students for helping us and presenting us with (optimal!) challenges; and our family and relatives for their ceaseless patience and noncontingent support.

Active Human Nature

Self-Determination Theory and the Promotion and Maintenance of Sport, Exercise, and Health

Richard M. Ryan, PhD, and Edward L. Deci, PhD
University of Rochester

Whether considering an exerciser in a spinning class pumping pedals for an hour, a jogger persisting over miles of lonely roads, or a rugby player grunting his way through a crowded scrum, no one can doubt that sport and exercise require motivation. In fact, sport and exercise epitomize motivation—people being moved to act—for these activities require exertion, energy, focus, and sometimes a great deal of discipline.

What is most intriguing, however, is that, for most athletes and exercisers, the rewards and contingencies that drive their motivation are not all that apparent. Certainly the motivators of sport and exercise are typically not those externally separable rewards and reinforcements that behaviorists imagined controlled all behaviors, nor are they the trophies and ribbons that seem so often tethered to organized versions of the activities (Frederick & Ryan, 1995; Pedersen, 2002). Indeed, it is the very fact that people so frequently play sports or exercise their bodies without any externally supplied impetus or pressure that makes sport and exercise motivation not only intriguing, but critically important as a domain of study. As we understand more and more about what drives sport and exercise, we move closer to what is a central mystery in behavioral science—our active human nature and what sustains it. Perhaps it is for this reason that self-determination theory (Deci & Ryan, 1985b; Ryan & Deci, 2000b) has become so important in the domain of sport and exercise, as it is the only major theory of human motivation that both acknowledges spontaneous, intrinsically motivated activity and pinpoints the factors that either enhance or debilitate it.

In what follows we do not intend to comprehensively review this fast-expanding literature, but instead to highlight the basic tenets of self-determination

---

Correspondence concerning this article should be addressed to Richard M. Ryan, Department of Psychology, University of Rochester, P.O. Box 270266, Rochester, NY 14627. E-mail: ryan@psych.rochester.edu

theory as it applies to sport and exercise. Specifically, we outline the differentiation of intrinsic and extrinsic motivation in self-determination theory and consider how these two forms of motivation apply to sport and exercise activities. Then we review research on the determinants of intrinsic motivation and internalized extrinsic motivation and discuss how it has been applied in the field, the park, and the gym. Finally, we take a very brief look at current and future directions in self-determination theory research in the fields of sport and exercise, including new research on mindfulness, vitality, and health.

Intrinsic Motivation and Our Active Nature

In her classic comparative study of young chimpanzees and humans, Ladygina-Kohts (2002) remarked, "Active play with live creatures represents an essential need for the Chimpanzee. . . . That is why movement for the sake of movement is his unalterable, unquenchable desire . . . he can engage in it for hours, from dawn to sunset, day in and day out" (p. 134).

This recognition of the natural propensity of chimpanzees not only to explore, exercise skills, and seek challenges but also to subjectively enjoy doing so is pervasive among observers of other mammalian behaviors. Oddly, however, theories of perhaps the most active and curious of all animals, namely *Homo sapiens*, often seem to be without an account of this intrinsic bent. Behaviorist, cognitive, and other reductionistic theories of human behavior all try to give an *external account* of action, without any appreciation that the "causes" of much human activity are spontaneous in the true sense of that term: They emanate from within the organism, latching on to whatever opportunities the environment supplies. Be it a playground or a cardboard box, a fine china doll or a clothespin manikin, humans will find a way to play on it, in it, or with it. Throw in a ball, a goal box, and other "live creatures," and the motivation latent in the human spirit becomes manifest as sport.

This inherent propensity to actively develop skills, engage challenges, and take interest in new activities even in the absence of external prompts or rewards is what in self-determination theory is termed *intrinsic motivation*. The term intrinsic motivation was, we believe, coined by Harlow (1950), the great primatologist, as he recognized that the active, exploratory behavior of his chimps occurred independently of external rewards or prompts. Subsequently, White (1959) linked Harlow's ideas with his concept of *effectance motivation*, the innate propensity to develop competencies. Building on these seminal ideas, self-determination theory uses the concept of intrinsic motivation as a cornerstone of its theoretical foundations.

Specifically, intrinsic motivation refers to doing an activity "for its own sake," for the satisfactions inherent in the activity (Ryan & Deci, 2000a). The concept was defined, in part, in opposition to the ideas that behavior was always (a) under the control of reinforcers in the environment, as Skinner (1953) had argued; and (b) motivated by reinforcements linked directly or derivatively to primary drives, as Hull (1943) had argued. *Intrinsic motivation* thus has a dual meaning: It concerns an innate propensity of the organism, rather than being externally propelled and directed, as Skinner had maintained; and it refers to the fact that the rewards for an activity are inherent in the activity—that is, in the spontaneous internal condition prompted by the activity—rather than being instrumental to the reduction of biological drives, as Hull had proposed. In fact, White (1959) suggested that, rather than being tied to biological needs, intrinsically motivated actions were energized by *psychological* satisfactions, specifically feelings of effectance or competence. Later deCharms (1968) added that the feeling of being an origin or an initiator of one's own action was central to intrinsic motivation.

As we shall explicate, self-determination theory incorporates both views: Self-determination theory, and specifically its component theory, called cognitive evaluation theory (Deci & Ryan, 1980, 1985b), propose that experiences of *competence* and *autonomy* are both necessary conditions for the maintenance and enhancement of intrinsic motivation. Environmental conditions that support feelings of competence and autonomy are thus expected to facilitate intrinsic motivation, whereas any factor that diminishes feelings of autonomy or competence is theorized to undermine intrinsic motivation. Finally, self-determination theory suggests that intrinsic motivational processes are most able to take root in contexts where the need for *relatedness* is supported—that is, contexts where people feel a sense of connectedness and belonging. Although the support for relatedness need not be so proximal as support for autonomy and competence, it is nonetheless essential in order for intrinsic motivation to thrive. In contrast, when people feel relationally insecure or alienated, they are more inhibited and defensive and less likely to experience interest or enjoyment in their activities (Deci & Ryan, 2000). In other words, feeling rejected and unloved tends to undermine intrinsic motivation.

This multidimensional approach to the underpinnings of intrinsic motivation provides a more complete picture than do various other theories that emphasize just one necessary antecedent of intrinsic motivation. For example, self-efficacy theory denies any significance to the issue of autonomy (Bandura, 1989), placing importance only on competence, whereas self-determination theory holds that efficacy without perceived autonomy will not foster intrinsic motivation. Even a very highly competent, but controlled, performer will not manifest the behavioral or experiential features of intrinsic motivation. Similarly, Csikszentmihalyi (1990) suggests that *flow*—the subjective experience associated with intrinsic motivation—will occur when there is a balance between skills and opportunities for action. However, although self-determination theory has long emphasized the importance of just such an *optimal challenge* (Deci, 1975), an optimal challenge that is not accompanied by feelings of autonomy will not prompt intrinsic motivation. Indeed, optimal challenges surround us, but only those that can be autonomously engaged and, ideally, will connect us with others are likely to be pursued as interests and to be reflective of sustained intrinsic motivation (Kowal & Fortier, 2000; Krapp & Ryan, 2002). Thus self-determination theory research has uniquely focused on the additional and interactive roles of autonomy and relatedness satisfactions in fostering flow and intrinsic motivation.

Insofar as self-determination theory makes predictions about how perceptions of autonomy, competence, and relatedness will affect intrinsic motivation, it does so by implicating social environments. In the language of self-determination theory, elements in the social context can facilitate or undermine intrinsic motivation as a function of the degree to which they support versus thwart satisfaction of the three psychological needs. This locution reflects our organismic view that environments do not cause motivation, which is a property of the living organism, but rather either nurture or diminish it. Nonetheless, the fact that social environments and reward structures affect intrinsic motivation has significant applied ramifications. It suggests that attempts to motivate people through controlling means such as the use of contingent rewards, threats of punishments, evaluative pressures, and conditional regard will often backfire. Although they may produce immediate compliance, such "motivators" can undermine feelings of autonomy and diminish intrinsic motivation. Alternatively, supports for competence, autonomy, and relatedness are conducive toward the enhancement of intrinsic motivation. Thus, studies have shown how such factors as offering true choice, minimizing external pressures, providing empathic support, and supplying optimal challenges and informational feedback all enhance intrinsic motivation (Deci, Koestner, & Ryan, 1999; Ryan & Deci, 2000a).

Intrinsic Motivation in Sport and Exercise

It is noteworthy that virtually all investigators concur that sport is, for most participants, intrinsically motivated. For example, Frederick and Ryan (1993) surveyed people regarding why they engaged in individual sport and exercise activities. Although people frequently cited intrinsic motives for both exercise and sport, participation in sport was on average significantly more intrinsically motivated than was exercising; exercisers were significantly more likely to be motivated by extrinsic motives such as improving one's appearance. Moreover, the more amateur the level of sport, the more likely it was that the motives for engaging in it were intrinsic. Sports are, therefore, more often played for interest and enjoyment than for extrinsic goals. Because of this, controlling coaching climates, contingent reward motivators, and evaluative pressures are all environmental factors that are at serious risk for undermining sport participation, as a relatively large literature, both experimental and descriptive, has shown (see, e.g., Fortier, Vallerand, Brière, & Provencher, 1995; Vallerand & Losier, 1999). Moreover, contexts fostering perceived competence and autonomy enhance enjoyment and sustained motivation (e.g., Goudas, Biddle, & Fox, 1994; Goudas, Biddle, & Underwood, 1995; Hagger, Chatzisarantis, Culverhouse, & Biddle, 2003).

Despite the fact that, on average, sport is more intrinsically motivated than exercise, it turns out that intrinsic motivation may be among the most important factors in maintaining exercise over time. In other words, even though most people engage in exercise for extrinsic reasons (e.g., improved fitness, appearance, or health), if they do not enjoy the activity or discover its inherent satisfactions they are unlikely to persist at it (Ryan, Frederick, Lepes, Rubio, & Sheldon, 1997; Wankel, 1993). In fact we assert that sustained exercise is most likely when a person has both intrinsic motivation *and* well-internalized extrinsic motivation, as both facilitate what is, normatively speaking, a precarious endeavor (Matsumoto & Takenaka, 2004; Ntoumanis, 2000; Vlachopoulos, Karageorghis, & Terry, 2000; Wilson, Rodgers, & Fraser, 2002). That is, although most people do not adhere to exercise goals or programs, when they exercise because they find both intrinsic satisfaction *and* instrumental value in the activities they are likely to be much more persistent, a point to which we will return.

Luckily, many forms of exercise can be made more intrinsically motivating. For example, people can be given choices about when and how they engage in the activity; exercise goals can be made optimally challenging; an atmosphere of relatedness can be created; and so on. Moreover, insofar as exercise is guided or led, it can be guided using methods that are autonomy supportive (Hagger et al., 2003; Mandigo & Holt, 2002; Wilson, Rodgers, Blanchard, & Gessell, 2003).

Competition and Intrinsic Motivation

A particularly interesting and controversial issue is the impact of competition on intrinsic motivation. According to cognitive evaluation theory, competitive contexts have both *informational* and *controlling* aspects (Deci & Ryan, 1985b). The informational component is linked to the idea that competitive environments can offer optimal challenge and competence feedback, resulting in feelings of efficacy and enhancing intrinsic motivation. On the other hand, competition often includes controlling components, as people feel pressure to win, either from others or from their own *ego involvement* (Ryan, 1982). Thus competitive settings with such pressures to win are typically expected to undermine intrinsic motivation, whereas those that focus on task involvement and mastery regardless of the outcome can maintain or even enhance intrinsic motivation. This was demonstrated by Reeve and Deci (1996), who showed that participants pressured to win lost intrinsic motivation even when they won, whereas those competing in the absence of such pressure did not. These effects of context were mediated by their impact on feelings of competence and autonomy, as predicted by self-determination theory.

Another problem with too much focus on winning is that under such conditions, those who lose are especially at risk for losing intrinsic motivation. Indeed, a number of studies have confirmed that losing undermines subsequent intrinsic motivation relative to winning (e.g., McAuley & Tammen, 1989; Reeve, Olson, & Cole, 1985; Vallerand & Reid, 1984). Yet, even in this context, cognitive evaluation theory has a more differentiated idea. In the absence of controlling pressures to win, and combined with a focus on accomplishment, intrinsic motivation can be maintained even for those who do not come out on top. Vansteenkiste and Deci (2003), for example, demonstrated that losers' motivation could be maintained provided that they received noncontrolling positive competence feedback.

Such findings are particularly important in the arena of youth and amateur sport. Insofar as the goal of many sport programs is to engage youth in physical activity that they can maintain over time, cultivating intrinsic motivation is critical. Unfortunately, too often coaches, physical education teachers, and parents can lose sight of this, creating an atmosphere that is too controlling, too critical, or too focused on winning (Mandigo & Holt, 2002). Controlling, pressuring settings lead to diminished interest, especially among those who might benefit most from engagement in physical activity. That is, in their focus on performance and the extrinsic goal of winning, adults can often drive students and youth away from sport rather than toward it, especially those who might benefit most from participating.

Beyond Intrinsic Motivation: Internalization and Extrinsic Forms of Motivation

It is clear that intrinsic motivation is a critical topic within the scientific study of sport and exercise. But at the same time, whether we are speaking of sport or exercise, there is much more than intrinsic motivation at work. First, as we already indicated, people have many extrinsic reasons for engaging in sport or exercise activities, from health reasons to desire for recognition. Second, let's admit it, while both sport and exercise have their "moments" of flow and intrinsically motivated engagement, these moments are often separated by long periods of hard work. In sport, practice and skills building, which are essential to high performance, can often be repetitive rather than novel and interesting. Moreover, performance requires body work and disciplined exercise, from sprints for the football player to weightlifting for the gymnast. Third, even if sport and exercise were highly intrinsically motivating, the social context (e.g., that provided by parents and coaches) often supplies both direct extrinsic incentives and interpersonal contingencies that shape the athletes' attributions, motivations, and subjective experiences.

Accordingly, any complete motivational theory of sport and exercise must address the nonintrinsically motivated aspects of those pursuits. Within self-determination theory there are two broad classes of nonintrinsic motivation. The first is *extrinsic motivation*, which concerns all instrumental behavior—that is, behavior motivated by expected outcomes or contingencies not inherent in the activity itself. The second, termed *amotivation*, concerns the various forms of not having either intention or energy directed toward action.

Extrinsic Motivation and the Continuum of Autonomy

In the early literature on intrinsic motivation, many theorists pitted intrinsic motivation against extrinsic motivation in an either/or fashion. For example, in deCharms' (1968) view, intrinsic motivation had an internal perceived locus of causality (and was autonomous), whereas extrinsic motivation had an external perceived locus of causality (and was nonautonomous). Similarly, Harter's (1981) well-known motivation scale pitted intrinsic motives against extrinsic motives in a bipolar fashion.

In contrast, self-determination theory departs from this intrinsic *versus* extrinsic conceptualization in two ways. First, people are viewed as typically having multiple motives, both intrinsic and extrinsic, that are simultaneously in play, all of which must together be assumed to determine the overall quality of motivation (Ryan & Connell, 1989). Moreover, self-determination theory incorporates a differentiated view of extrinsic motives in terms of how much they emanate from or reflect one's self (or do both)—that is, how autonomous they are. Specifically, we uniquely argue within self-determination theory that extrinsic motivations vary in their relative autonomy, with some forms of extrinsic motivation being highly volitional or autonomous, and others representing forces that are experienced as external to the self of the actor but are nonetheless compelling. This thinking and resulting research led to *organismic integration theory* (OIT; Deci & Ryan, 1985b), another mini-theory within self-determination theory that describes the various forms of extrinsic motivation, along with their antecedents and consequences. The basic tenets of this mini-theory and its relations to causality orientations theory and cognitive evaluation theory are illustrated in figure I.1. (Figure notes: [1]*Basic psychological needs* of autonomy, competence, and relatedness are shown as indicators of global basic psychological needs according to the hypothesis that optimal motivational function is achieved with the satisfaction of all three needs; the needs form the starting point of the motivational process and reflect top-down individual differences in psychological need satisfaction and affect motivation in many contexts. [2]*Cognitive evaluation theory* describes the environmental contingencies that lead to the adoption of intrinsically- or extrinsically-motivated behavior; it is illustrated in the figure as the distinction between intrinsic and extrinsic motivation, and the motivational contingencies for these two fundamental forms of motivation are given in the defining features descriptions. [3]*Organismic integration theory* identifies the quality of motivation on a perceived locus of causality ranging from highly autonomous to highly controlling. It provides a framework to describe how externally-referenced contingencies can be internalized and integrated, such that they become more autonomous in nature because they service internal rather than external goals.)

Organismic Integration Theory: Extrinsic Motivation and Internalization

In the view of self-determination theory there are various types of extrinsic motivation, ranging from those that are controlled externally to those that are self-endorsed and personally valued and are therefore volitional and autonomous. In the former case, exercise is motivated through *external regulation*, as

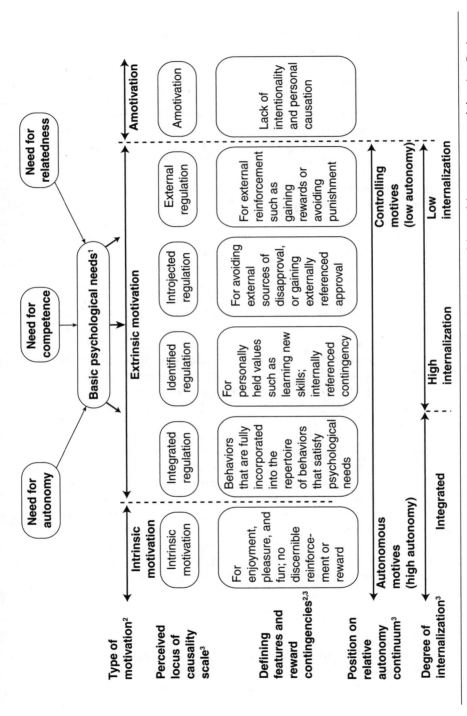

Figure I.1 Schematic representation of self-determination theory illustrating the features of three of the component subtheories: Basic psychological needs theory, cognitive evaluation theory, and organismic integration theory.

Courtesy of Martin S. Hagger

8

when a member of the women's soccer team plays hard because she expects to be rewarded for reaching an externally defined goal. Here the source of motivation is alien to the self of the actor, so her motivation is dependent on the continued presence of external monitoring and reinforcement for its maintenance. Accordingly, external regulation is considered within self-determination theory to be a highly controlled form of extrinsic motivation.

A person could also be motivated out of *introjected regulation*. Here, rather than having other people controlling the actor's behavior with rewards and punishments, the actor controls him- or herself with internal contingencies of reward and punishment (Ryan, 1982). For example, a lacrosse player whose motivation for playing is introjected extrinsic motivation will reward himself for meeting standards or reaching goals with pride and self-aggrandizement and will punish himself for failure with shame and anxiety and, at a somewhat more sophisticated level (Green-Demers, 2004), with guilt. In other words, introjection is based on self-esteem-related contingencies and ego involvements (Ryan, 1982; Ryan, Koestner, & Deci, 1991). Thus both external and introjected forms of regulation represent controlling forms of motivation in which the self is controlled by pressures and contingencies.

Extrinsic motivation can, however, be relatively autonomous, as when a person behaves through *identified regulation*. In identified regulation the person engages in the extrinsic action because he or she identifies with its purpose and value. Thus, a woman who exercises because she personally believes this enhances her energy and health is extrinsically motivated (the behavior is instrumental), but also autonomous (the behavior is self-endorsed and valued). At a still more autonomous level of functioning this woman could fully coordinate and assimilate the regulation of exercise into her overall life goals and style of living; we call this *integrated regulation*. Here the value for behaving is reflectively brought into congruence with other values and needs and thus becomes not only volitional, but also stable and well anchored within the personality.

There is considerable evidence that these forms of regulation typically represent a continuum ranging from less to more autonomy (see figure I.1 for an illustration). Presentation of this evidence began with Ryan and Connell's (1989) demonstration of a quasi-simplex pattern for motive assessments, such that those types of regulation most adjacent along the hypothetical continuum were most highly correlated, and those more distant from each other on the conceptual scale were less positively or more negatively correlated. Ryan and Connell's approach to conceptualizing and measuring motives (viz., the self-regulation questionnaire, or SRQ) has spawned a family of domain-specific assessments, including measures for sport (e.g., Pelletier, Fortier, Vallerand, Tuson, Briere, & Blais, 1995) and exercise (e.g., Mullan, Markland, & Ingledew, 1997; Wilson, Rodgers, & Fraser, 2002) that have well-established validities. Moreover, the basic structure of motives has been supported in numerous cross-cultural studies spanning the East and West, in many domains (e.g., Chirkov, Ryan, Kim, & Kaplan, 2003; Tanaka & Yamauchi, 2000) including sport and exercise (Bagoien & Halvari, 2005; Doganis, 2000; Matsumoto, Takenaka, & Takaya, 2003).

It is important to specify, however, that this is not a developmental continuum or a stage model (Mullan & Markland, 1997), but rather a conceptual continuum concerning degrees of self-determination or volition. People do not necessarily begin with external regulation and move toward integration of a particular behavioral regulation. Rather, depending on the social conditions in which they acquire a new regulation, people can begin anywhere along this continuum. In an autonomy-supportive setting, for example, a novice athlete might readily identify with the value of practice and personally commit to it. Alternatively, an experienced athlete with a great work ethic and value for training might be converted to introjected regulation by a coach who applies contingent regard, or to external regulation by a coach who employs contingent rewards and punishments as incentives. In fact, although self-determination theory acknowledges individual differences in motivational orientations, it also predicts within-person variations in motivation, largely as a function of the social climate.

Amotivation

All of the types of regulation—both intrinsic and extrinsic—that we have discussed thus far represent forms of motivation. Self-determination theory also identifies the state of amotivation in which one is literally without motivation for an activity. Theoretically there are several sources of amotivation, which can have different consequences. One can be amotivated when feeling incompetent to do an activity or because it does not lead to a desired outcome (Pelletier, Dion, Tuson, & Green-Demers, 1999). Further, one can feel that the act has no value, either instrumental or intrinsic, and thus be amotivated. Recently, Vansteenkiste, Lens, Dewitte, De Witte, and Deci (2004) have shown that people can even be autonomous in their lack of motivation for pursuing a socially endorsed activity, as when one chooses not to play golf even though all one's friends spend their weekends on the course.

At the same time, in many research studies amotivation has been associated with very negative experiences and consequences (e.g., Vallerand & Bissonnette, 1992). The reason is that researchers have often focused on settings where an activity may or may not be voluntary (e.g., mandatory physical education classes), or on activities whose benefits are clear; and in these situations, lacking motivation is likely to be costly (e.g., health-relevant behaviors; school). In such contexts, amotivation is clearly a suboptimal state and thus often falls at the low end of the continuum of relative autonomy (e.g., Pelletier et al., 1995).

Supporting and Undermining Internalization

According to organismic integration theory, people are inherently oriented to assimilate and internalize social regulations (Chandler & Connell, 1987), but that inherent tendency must have certain environmental supports. Specifically, people will accept and internalize a new behavioral regulation or guiding value to the extent that they feel support for relatedness, autonomy, and competence in the context of behaving. Ample evidence from both experimental (e.g., Deci, Eghrari, Patrick, & Leone, 1994) and field studies (e.g., Grolnick & Ryan, 1989; Williams, Rodin, Ryan, Grolnick, & Deci, 1998) supports this formulation and highlights practices that are entailed in need support.

In terms of supports for internalization, a premise of organismic integration theory is that one must experience *competence* to be motivated in any fashion, be it external, introjected, identified, integrated, or intrinsic. Otherwise one will be amotivated. However, to be introjected, one must feel not only competence, but also some *relatedness* (or at least a desire for relatedness). Indeed, it is typically the concern with relatedness, and the dynamics of self and other approval that relatedness engenders, that leads people to introject behaviors that may or may not fit with their interests and values. However, for a behavior to be regulated through identification or integration, more than relatedness and competence supports is necessary. A person must also experience *autonomy*—a sense of choicefulness and self-endorsement. Controlling environments tend to undermine these more internalized bases for acting because they thwart satisfaction of the need for autonomy. Thus, the more internalized forms of regulation result from, and in turn provide, satisfaction of all three needs—competence, relatedness, and autonomy (Deci & Ryan, 2000).

Extrinsic Motivation and Internalization in Sport and Exercise

Numerous findings in the fields of sport and exercise support the formulations of organismic integration theory in terms of both the structure of motives and their antecedents and consequences (of which there are far too many to adequately review here). As already noted, research groups from diverse countries, in both the East (e.g., Matsumoto, Takenaka, & Takaya, 2003) and West (e.g., Mullan, Markland, & Ingledew, 1997; Wilson, Rodgers, Fraser, & Murray, 2004), have replicated the self-determination theory taxonomy of motives, its continuum of relative autonomy, and its predicted consequences, supporting the underlying model and its cross-cultural validity. More importantly, studies of social contexts have clarified how supports for autonomy, competence, and relatedness affect motivation. We shall not provide a comprehensive review but instead give a few illustrative examples. Other chapters in this book provide many more examples.

Pelletier, Fortier, Vallerand, and Brière (2001) surveyed elite swimmers from across Canada, asking them to rate their coaching climate (autonomy supportive versus controlling) and their personal motivation using an SRQ type of assessment as described earlier. The authors then followed the swimmers over a 22-month period, assessing continuing participation. They found that whereas controlling climates were associated with external and introjected regulation, autonomy-supportive coaching was associated with more integrated extrinsic motivation and intrinsic motivation. As expected, they also found that more internalized motivation predicted greater persistence over time, while controlled motives were associated with faster dropout. Indeed, dropout over time followed an ordered pattern such that the more internalized and autonomous the regulation, the more the athlete manifested persistence.

In another illustrative study, Hagger and colleagues (2003) tested a *trans-contextual model* in which the motivational climate in physical education classes was expected to affect motivation for leisure-time activity outside the educational context. Autonomy-supportive teaching was associated with more autonomous motivation, which in turn enhanced intentions to be active, which predicted behavior. This study is unique in showing how motivational inputs in one context affect internalization processes that shape ongoing lifestyles.

Parish and Treasure (2003) examined adolescent physical education students. In a developmental context in which physical activity was declining with age, these researchers showed that perceptions of a mastery-oriented teaching climate were associated with more situational self-determination for physical activity, whereas perceptions of a performance climate were associated with less self-determination. Degree of self-determination and perceived competencies, were, in turn, associated with more physical activity. The findings support a mastery rather than a performance focus when the goal is increased physical activity.

Gaumond (2000) examined the role of parental influences on adolescents' motivation and physical activity. They showed not only that more physically active parents had more active offspring, but also that parents who were more autonomy supportive had children who were more active as well as more self-determined in their activities. This research complements studies showing coaching and teaching influences on motivation.

Beauchamp, Halliwell, Fournier, and Koestner (1996) accomplished one of the few intervention experiments in the literature. They applied a cognitive-behavioral teaching program to novice golfers, comparing them with a physical skills group and a control group. The intervention group showed enhanced intrinsic motivation and diminished introjection. These motivational changes related to performance differences in follow-up assessments.

As noted previously, we have simply selected a few illustrative studies from a burgeoning and multifaceted literature. The research suggests the promise of the internalization model not only for predicting motivation and its consequences, but also as a target for intervention.

Causality Orientations

Regulatory styles—that is, intrinsic motivation and types of extrinsic motivation—are typically assessed with respect to an activity or domain (e.g., for participating in aerobics or for playing sports). Thus, it is possible that people might be quite controlled for some activities and more autonomous for others. The concept of causality orientations (Deci & Ryan, 1985a) relates to a more general sense of being autonomous or controlled across domains. In other words, it is an individual difference in autonomous and controlled motivation (as well as amotivation) at a relatively general level. Links between generalized causality orientations and components from the other mini-theories from self-determination theory are illustrated in Figure I.1. Thus, with respect to Vallerand's (1997; this volume) hierarchical model, causality orientations would be at the most global level, whereas regulatory styles (assessed with the SRQ) would be at a less global, domain-specific level.

Considerable research has related the autonomy orientation to effective performance and well-being. For example, one study of participants in a very-low-calorie weight loss program (Williams, Grow, Freedman, Ryan, & Deci, 1996) showed that people high in autonomy orientation participated in the program for more fully internalized reasons and that this predicted maintained weight loss over two years. Somewhat less research has been done using the General Causality Orientations Scale (GCOS) in studies of sport and exercise, so it is an area that could be more fully examined. In this vein, Rose, Markland, and Parfitt (2001) have modified the GCOS to form the Exercise Causality Orientations Scale, which is now being used in studies of sport and exercise.

Basic Needs Theory: Self-Determination Theory and the Facilitating Environment

It should be clear to the reader by this point that whether we are discussing intrinsic motivation or the more autonomous forms of extrinsic motivation, the social environment supplies specific nutriments that facilitate the occurrence of autonomous motivation. Within self-determination theory these basic or fundamental nutriments are referred to as *basic psychological needs*, and there are but three: autonomy, competence, and relatedness (Deci & Ryan, 2000). As we have already suggested, when these basic needs are supported within a context, both intrinsic motivation and internalization are facilitated. By contrast, whenever the social context thwarts or neglects one of these needs, intrinsic motivation and internalization, as well as positive experience, wither.

After recognizing the invariant role these supports play in sustaining motivation and in promoting well-being across studies of motivation in multiple domains, we felt it important to clarify the meaning of the concept of needs as used within self-determination theory. Specifically we define needs as *nutriments essential to growth, integrity, and well-being* (Deci & Ryan, 2000; Ryan, 1995). As essential supports, needs are expected to have a functional impact whether or not they are valued, and whether or not they are specifically sought after. That is, even if people do not value a need, they will show negative effects in terms of motivation and wellness if they do not satisfy it and will show enhancement if they do satisfy it. Self-determination theory thus specifically posits the *universal* and *cross-developmental* significance of need satisfaction for optimal functioning, even while recognizing that cultural values and practices associated with needs vary greatly.

This assertion of universality has been a controversial notion, especially since some cross-culture researchers (e.g., Markus, Kitayama, & Heiman, 1996) and some gender theorists (e.g., Jordan, 1997) have hypothesized that autonomy does not have any significance in non-Western cultures or for females. Taken on their surface, such claims would suggest that people in the East, women, and other human subgroups would suffer no motivational harm when controlled or coerced, and would experience no benefit when supported to act in accord with their abiding interests and values.

But it is our view that when examined more deeply, these "cultural-relativist" perspectives conceptually conflate issues of independence, separateness, or uniqueness with the issue of autonomy. Self-determination theory has long held that autonomy, both as we use the term and as it is typically defined in the philosophical literature (e.g., Friedman, 2003), concerns the self-endorsement of one's actions, or the sense of volition. It cannot therefore be equated with independence or uniqueness (Ryan & Lynch, 1989). A person can be autonomously dependent, as when volitionally relying on others, or can be autonomously conformist, as when truly valuing a particular group's practices. Similarly, as studies have shown, people can be autonomous or controlled in pursuing either collectivistic or individualistic goals, and the relative autonomy of one's goals is strongly related to adjustment and health (e.g., Chirkov et al., 2003; Chirkov & Ryan, 2001).

In our view, then, researchers claiming to show that autonomy is unimportant in a particular group have typically confused it with independence or uniqueness, neither of which is considered a need within self-determination theory, or they have measured differences in values or mean levels of satisfaction rather than functional impact per se. The fact that numerous studies, many using either indigenous measures or surveys carefully crafted to ensure the cross-cultural comparability of construct measurements (Little, 1997), show the same import of autonomy within Eastern samples as in the Western ones (e.g., Chirkov et al., 2003; Matsumoto, Takenaka, & Takaya, 2003; Tanaka & Yamauchi, 2000) is particularly problematic for those espousing a cultural-relativist view.

Another controversial aspect of the needs model is our claim that all three needs are essential, such that neglect of any one will have negative functional effects. Again, we cannot review the rather substantial literature on this issue here, but extensive reviews are available (e.g., Deci & Ryan, 2000). Simply stated, the claim has been well supported, and in our view it is especially well tested using within-person methodologies (Brown & Ryan, 2005). For example, Reis, Sheldon, Gable, Roscoe, and Ryan (2000) looked at daily fluctuations in well-being at a within-person level of analysis and found that each need contributed independently to rises or falls in wellness.

Basic Needs in Sport and Exercise

Although support for the basic needs theory within self-determination theory research as a whole is apparent, studies using this framework are just beginning to emerge with sport and exercise. Gagné, Ryan, and Bargmann (2003) provided an illustrative case in their study of gymnasts' experiences of motivation and well-being from practice to practice. Specifically, these researchers followed female gymnasts over a four-week period. Using multilevel analyses, they showed that athletes with more autonomous forms of motivation had, on average, more positive experiences in sport and higher well-being. Moreover, at a within-person level of analysis, the data revealed that changes from pre- to postpractice well-being were directly related to basic need satisfaction within practice. Athletes who experienced supports for relatedness, autonomy, and competence showed more positive affect, more vitality, higher state self-esteem, and less negative affect.

In another relevant study, Kowal and Fortier (2000) related need satisfaction to "flow" experiences in a sport context. They found that satisfaction of all three basic needs independently contributed to situational motivation and flow. Such studies extend our understanding of what constitutes a facilitating environment for both persistence and positive experience.

Intrinsic and Extrinsic Goals and the Effects of Goal Framing

Beginning in the '90s, self-determination theory researchers began to classify goals in terms of their intrinsic and extrinsic foci. Specifically, Kasser and Ryan (1996) showed that aspirations for fame, money, and attractiveness tended to form a common factor and to stand in contrast or opposition to goals such as growth, intimacy, health, or community, which also tended to covary. They labeled these separate factors *extrinsic goals* and *intrinsic goals*, respectively, suggesting that the former were typically unrelated to or even problematic for need fulfillment, whereas the latter would tend to be directly satisfying of basic needs and therefore be conducive to well-being. Numerous subsequent studies showed the stability of this distinction and its predicted effects on well-being (Kasser, 2002). Specifically, people who place higher value on extrinsic goals tend to have poorer mental health, whereas those more oriented to intrinsic goals show more positive outcomes. Grouzet and colleagues (in press), using a circumplex modeling strategy, recently confirmed that this intrinsic–extrinsic goal distinction held across 15 diverse cultural groups in both poor and developed nations.

Extending this framework, Vansteenkiste and his colleagues (see Vansteenkiste, Soenens, & Lens, this volume) have done experimental studies of goal framing, including studies in sport and exercise contexts, in which they framed activities in terms of either intrinsic or extrinsic goals. For example, Vansteenkiste, Simons, Soenens, and Lens (2004) studied Belgian students of high school age who were exposed to *tai bo*, an Asian sport activity, in the context of a physical education class. As part of their introduction to this activity the students read descriptions that framed the benefits of tai bo in terms of either extrinsic (attractiveness) or intrinsic (health and fitness) goals. Results revealed that the intrinsic framing positively affected effort expenditure and long-term persistence, whereas extrinsic goal framing undermined these outcomes. In another study, Vansteenkiste, Simons, Braet, Bachman, and Deci (2005) followed obese 11- to 12-year-old children exposed to either intrinsic or extrinsic goal framing within a school-based program for eating healthier food. Intrinsic goal framing led to eating a significantly better diet and also, interestingly, led to the children's exercising more regularly. The improved diet and exercising in turn led to greater maintained weight loss over two years.

Motivation, Vitality, and Health: When Self-Regulation Is Not Depleting

In recent years self-determination theory researchers have taken interest in both the determinants and consequences of subjective energy, or vitality. This began when, as a part of their studies of sport and exercise motivation, Frederick and Ryan (1993) asked people in both interview and survey formats why they exercised or engaged in sport. Among the many answers given, one common term mentioned was "vitality." People often felt as if vigorous physical activity not only did not deplete subjective energy, but also added to it. People, that is, appeared to feel more vital and alive after exercising. This led to the development of an assessment of vitality and to theorizing about what maintains and enhances vitality.

In their validation work on this construct, Ryan and Frederick (1997) specifically showed that subjective vitality was associated with physical and psychological health. On the physical end, factors such as diet, exercise, and smoking all affect vitality. On the psychological side, vitality is associated with need fulfillment: The more one feels competence, relatedness, or autonomy, the more vitality is reported. Following up on this, Nix, Ryan, Manly, and Deci (1999) had people do an activity under conditions in which their actions were either externally controlled or autonomously organized. Results showed that this same activity was differentially associated with changes in energy, with controlled regulation being more energy draining than autonomous regulation.

Such results stand in contrast to some recent claims by Baumeister and his colleagues (e.g., Baumeister, Bratslavsky, Muraven, & Tice, 1998) that self-regulation and choice are *ego depleting*, a term that refers to a drainage of energy and vitality. In several studies Baumeister and others showed that regulating one's actions, and even making choices, deplete energy available for subsequent tasks. Because self-determination theory suggests that only controlled forms of regulation should be draining, Moller, Deci, and Ryan (2006) replicated Baumeister's regulation tasks in an experimental setting, but varied the degree to which the "choices" people made represented true, autonomous choice or alternatively were subtly controlled (as they had been in the work by Baumeister et al.). The results showed that the autonomy–control distinction moderated the ego depletion effect as predicted by self-determination theory. Choices that were made under subtly controlling conditions led participants to manifest significantly less energy compared to choices that represented true autonomy.

The study of vitality and energy is relatively new, but its implications for sport and exercise practitioners are manifold. First, vitality is a positive psychological state and thus has inherent value. Second, however, the dynamics of subjective energy have relevance to behavioral persistence and performance, especially in activities in which effort expenditure or endurance is of central importance. Third, we believe, as did Selye (1976), that the subjective sense of energy and "aliveness" may be a marker of health and may relate to both immunological status and physical resilience, as well as to one's capacities for psychological coping and wellness (Ryan & Frederick, 1997).

Conclusions, Musings, and Future Directions

As we noted, this discussion was not intended to be a comprehensive review; rather, our goal was to highlight the basic tenets of self-determination theory as they apply to the domains of sport and exercise. We specifically discussed the construct of intrinsic motivation, as well as cognitive evaluation theory, which specifies how supports for autonomy, competence, and relatedness affect intrinsic motivation. We then discussed extrinsic motivation and the continuum of autonomy associated with the taxonomy of extrinsic motives articulated within organismic integration theory. We noted that the continuum of autonomy has been cross-culturally replicated in many domains, including sport and exercise, as have the positive effects of autonomy, even in collectivistic cultural contexts. We argued that cultural-relativist perspectives often confuse autonomy with concepts such as independence or uniqueness, whereas self-determination theory takes a more differentiated view. Moving beyond organismic integration theory, with its focus on regulatory styles that are assessed in relation to specific behaviors or domains, we discussed causality orientations, which are the more global individual differences in autonomous and controlled motivations. Together these mini-theories: causality orientations, basic psychological needs theory, cognitive evaluation theory, and organismic integration theory, comprise the organismic, dialectical meta-theory that is self-determination theory. Relations among the concepts developed by three of these theories are represented schematically in Figure I.1.

After showing how both intrinsic motivation and more internalized forms of extrinsic motivation are facilitated by supports for autonomy, competence, and relatedness, we outlined the self-determination theory approach to basic psychological needs. Needs are defined as necessary nutriments for growth, integrity, and wellness in any domain, and sport proves to be no exception. Optimal motivation and positive experience, including flow, require that competence, autonomy, and connectedness be afforded. The theory of basic needs was also the basis for our distinction between intrinsic and extrinsic aspirations or goals. Intrinsic goals are those that directly relate to need satisfaction, whereas extrinsic goals tend to be either unrelated to need satisfaction or, sometimes, even antithetical to it. Accordingly, studies have shown that intrinsic goals are more conducive to well-being. Based on this, new studies of goal framing show that introducing new activities with intrinsic versus extrinsic goal rationales differentially predicts interest, persistence, and quality of experience. Finally we discussed new research in the dynamics of subjective energy or vitality, arguing that need support is positively associated with energy and that need-satisfying activities are energizing rather than draining, even when they demand effort.

Looking across these areas of study, we find it impressive how much solid research has been done in the field of sport and exercise to test these self-determination theory formulations and elaborate upon them. This body of research, whose surface we merely scratched in this overview, has great applied significance for understanding factors that promote versus undermine sport and exercise participation, and is important at both interpersonal and policy levels. Clearly, as we look at the increasing prevalence of sedentary lifestyles in modern cultures and their health implications, engaging people in physical activity is a critical issue. Traditional approaches based on rewarding only top performers, using contingent rewards, and focusing on performance evaluation and competition are viewed within self-determination theory as not only risky, but often counterproductive. Especially in amateur and youth contexts, where our principal goal is to foster sustained lifelong interest in physical activity, we should be especially wary of such controlling strategies of motivation and instead be trying to enhance intrinsic and autonomous motives for participation.

Because our focus in this review was on motivating participation, we did not address the relations between motivation and performance. Many have argued, on the basis of anecdotal evidence, that to get top performance out of athletes, pressure and control by coaches or trainers are often efficacious. However, there is much evidence, both anecdotal and empirical, to suggest that whereas controlling pressure can disrupt flow and attention, autonomy support and promotion of task rather than ego involvement are more optimal (see Treasure, Lemyre, Kuczka, & Standage, this volume). In the main, we agree with Orlick (1996) and others who suggest that athletes' performance at all levels can "benefit from a greater sense of fun, passion and enjoyment in their pursuits" (p. 15), especially when these are combined with value and commitment. Our own formulation is that athletes are likely to be at their best when motivated by both identified (or integrated) and intrinsic regulations, rather than operating out of introjected ego involvement or external regulation.

In highlighting the benefits of intrinsic and autonomous extrinsic motivation, we are not suggesting that extrinsic incentives, controlling pressures, and evaluation do not motivate. They do, albeit typically in ways that are perceived as controlling. In some contexts this type of motivation may even produce results, although we suggest that such results are often short-term and unstable. There may also be some interesting differences by sport in terms of how debilitating controlling contexts may be. For example, an American football coach screaming at a defensive end may indeed activate his adrenalin and foster more aggressive play in a context in which that helps performance. However, the same intervention with a tennis player may backfire, activating "inner chatter," negative affect, and mental distraction (Deci & Ryan, 1985b). The interaction between motivation and performance at different sports, at both amateur and elite levels, thus warrants attention in future research. However, in saying this we reiterate that even in those contexts in which sport is a "business," our goals ought to be fostering interest, engagement, and involvement over time as well as fostering the athletes' well-being. As Newburg and Rotella (1996) pointed out, even gifted athletes are often victimized by the high expectations and desires of their coaches and colleagues, whose controlling investment in their performance can lead to injury, stress, and burnout (see Sarrazin, Boiché, & Pelletier, this volume).

Related to the theme of autonomous versus controlled regulation in sport is emerging work within self-determination theory on the relations between mindfulness (i.e., present-centered awareness) and motivation. Brown and Ryan (2003) developed an assessment of both trait and state mindfulness, showing that mindfulness is associated with more autonomous motivational orientations, reduced stress, and greater well-being. Studies are suggesting that mindfulness can be beneficial as well for sustained motivation and performance and can be enhanced under need-supportive conditions (Brown & Ryan, 2005). Although the role of mindfulness in sport performance has yet to be well understood, the fact that mindfulness, like flow, appears to be facilitated by need supports suggests directions for further research and intervention studies.

We began by arguing that humans are inherently physically active, curious, challenge-seeking creatures. But we also pointed out that this human potential is actualized only under certain conditions, largely shaped by the social environments. Self-determination theory posits that under conditions that support relatedness, competence, and autonomy, our active human nature is most robust, and both psychological wellness and biological health are most likely to accrue. Without such nutriments, however, our vulnerabilities will be all too apparent, resulting in diminished performance and well-being.

Intrinsic Motivation and Self-Determination in Exercise

The chapters in part I examine the contribution of self-determination theory to the explanation of participation in and adherence to health-related exercise, as well as examine the motivational antecedents and contingencies that give rise to exercise behavior and health-related outcomes (e.g., psychological well-being).

In the opening chapter David Markland and David Ingledew introduce the role of participation motives in explaining a number of these outcomes as well as exercise behavior. This discussion is complemented in chapter 2 by Jemma Edmunds, Nikos Ntoumanis, and Joan Duda, who look at more global antecedents from basic psychological needs theory and perceived autonomy support as influences on exercise behavior. Our chapter (chapter 3) and the chapter by Martyn Standage, Fiona Gillison, and Darren Treasure (chapter 4) examine physical education as a unique context and adopt an integrative approach to explain how perceptions of autonomous forms of motivation lead to the adoption of health-related exercise intentions and behavior in school-aged adolescents. David Markland and Maarten Vansteenkiste in chapter 5 provide a self-determination theory reading of the popular technique known as motivational interviewing, which has been shown to be very effective in enhancing exercise behavior in cardiac rehabilitation and exercise referral contexts.

Chapter 6, by Philip Wilson and Wendy Rodgers, summarizes empirical research and offers some unique findings regarding the positive effects of self-determination theory constructs on psychological well-being and exercise behavior. Michelle Fortier and John Kowal (chapter 7) make important links between the "flow" state and the premises of self-determination theory and also look at how self-determination theory can predict change in exercise behavior. Finally, Vello Hein and Andre Koka (chapter 8) provide insight into the efficacy of feedback plans based on self-determination theory in enhancing intrinsic motives and exercise behavior in a physical education context.

This collection of articles demonstrates that self-determination theory is an effective and versatile theory for explaining health-related exercise involvement and outcomes. The wealth of practical recommendations provided by each author for enhancing autonomous forms of motivation in exercise contexts also illustrates the utility of the theory as a guide for practice.

Exercise Participation Motives

A Self-Determination Theory Perspective

David Markland, PhD, and David K. Ingledew, PhD
University of Wales, Bangor

The term *participation motives* has traditionally been used in exercise psychology to refer to the reasons that individuals give for engaging in physical activity. In the 1980s and early 1990s, researchers in the then-emerging field of exercise psychology were largely preoccupied with documenting and profiling the types of participation motives held by people and with examining group differences such as those between males and females or across different age bands. This research was essentially descriptive (Biddle & Mutrie, 2001) and rightly criticized by a number of authors for being atheoretical (e.g., Rodgers & Brawley, 1991). Despite the fact that a number of researchers have since adopted theoretically grounded approaches to the study of participation motives, the charge of atheoreticism has lingered. For example, even quite recently Biddle and Mutrie (2001) seemed to condemn with faint praise the study of participation motives by stating that they "can offer a useful 'surface' analysis of motivation as long as it is recognised that this is all you get" (p. 36).

In this chapter we aim to show that self-determination theory offers a strong theoretical rationale for positing that different types of participation motive will exert differential effects on exercise behavior and well-being, as well as an understanding of how these differential effects come about. We briefly describe the major ways in which participation motives have been measured. We will show that the literature on the relationships between participation motives and exercise behavior, well-being, body image, and autonomous and controlled motivation is consistent with a self-determination theory perspective. Finally, we offer some caveats about assuming that certain motives are inherently maladaptive and discuss some applied implications for exercise

Correspondence concerning this article should be addressed to David Markland, School of Sport, Health and Exercise Sciences, University of Wales, Bangor, George Building, Bangor, Gwynedd LL57 2PZ, United Kingdom. E-mail: d.markland@bangor.ac.uk promotion. We restrict our discussion primarily to the contexts of recreational and health-related exercise among healthy adults.

The Theoretical Status of Participation Motives

Participation motives are similar to what in self-determination theory are termed *goal contents*, these being the goals to which people aspire (Ryan, Sheldon, Kasser, & Deci, 1996). Goal contents describe *what* goals people adopt. In self-determination theory, these goals contribute to determining an individual's motivational orientation, whether it is autonomous or controlled (Deci & Ryan, 2000; Ryan, Sheldon, Kasser, & Deci, 1996). Goal contents have been distinguished according to the extent to which they represent intrinsic or extrinsic aspirations, with these being held to have differential effects on well-being. Goal contents that reflect intrinsic aspirations, such as social affiliation or personal growth, will enhance well-being because they are more likely to facilitate satisfaction of the basic psychological needs for autonomy, competence, and relatedness (Deci & Ryan, 2000). Conversely, extrinsically oriented goal contents, such as the pursuit of wealth, fame, or good looks, are less likely to lead to need satisfaction because, being based upon external or internally imposed pressures, they will tend to be experienced as controlling (Ryan et al., 1996). Thus such goals are likely to lead to less adaptive outcomes. A number of studies support these propositions (e.g., Kasser & Ryan, 1993, 1996; Ryan et al., 1999; Sheldon, Ryan, Deci, & Kasser, 2004; Vansteenkiste, Soenens, & Lens, this volume). The goal contents examined in self-determination theory research are relatively general life aspirations, and the focus has been on their effects on well-being. Furthermore, these general life aspirations can be satisfied through engagement in a wide variety of specific behaviors.

In parallel with this body of life goals research, we have proposed that different types of exercise participation motive can be conceptualized as intrinsically or extrinsically oriented and will carry different functional significances for exercise behavior (Ingledew, Markland, & Medley, 1998; Markland & Hardy, 1993; Markland & Ingledew, 1997; Markland, Ingledew, Hardy, & Grant, 1992), as have other researchers (e.g., Duda & Tappe, 1989b; Frederick-Recascino, 2002; Frederick & Ryan, 1993, 1995; Gill, Gross, & Huddleston, 1983; Ryan, Vallerand, & Deci, 1984). Motives such as enjoyment, personal challenge, and social affiliation are likely to be experienced as autonomous, and reflect intrinsic motivation to exercise. When intrinsically oriented motives predominate, participation is likely to be accompanied by a sense of volition and freedom from pressure and therefore long-term commitment is to be expected, and engagement will be accompanied by positive exercise-related cognitions and affect. Motives such as losing weight, improving appearance, or pleasing others, however, are more likely to be experienced as internally controlling (e.g., as when one tells oneself "I *must* exercise to lose weight"), and reflect extrinsic motivation. When one is regulated in a controlling fashion, long-term commitment to an activity is less probable and will be accompanied by feelings of tension and pressure to act (Pelletier, Fortier, Vallerand, & Brière, 2001; Ryan & Connell, 1989; Ryan, Deci, & Grolnick, 1995; Ryan, Rigby, & King, 1993).

In self-determination theory, the effects of goal contents on well-being are held to be more than a function of the extent to which the underlying regulatory processes are controlling or autonomous (Deci & Ryan, 2000). Sheldon and colleagues (2004) outlined several other ways in which extrinsic goal contents could influence well-being, two of which are particularly relevant in the context of exercise motives. First, when people pursue extrinsic goals, their self-worth may become contingent on the achievement of these goals. If individuals are focused on exercising to look good or to be slim, failure to attain these ideals could leave them feeling worthless, and indeed helpless, leading to behavioral disengagement. Second, pursuing such extrinsic goals could lead people to make more frequent social comparisons. In an exercise context, this might mean that the individual is never satisfied with him- or herself, because there are always plenty of people who look better. Thus it is important to consider what goals people pursue, in addition to whether they pursue the goals for autonomous versus controlled reasons (Ryan et al., 1996; Sheldon et al., 2004). Hence, from a self-determination theory perspective, the study of participation motives is theoretically valid and worthwhile. It should be noted that there is potential for confusion in linking participation motives with goal contents in self-determination theory, because in the self-determination theory literature the reasons individuals engage in a behavior, in terms of their degree of autonomy versus control, are often referred to as "motives" (e.g., Sheldon et al., 2004). However, we have noted that outside of self-determination theory, the term *motives* is widely used to refer to the goals that people pursue through their behavior—that is to say, to goal contents (e.g., Ingledew & Ferguson, in press). Furthermore, in exercise psychology the terms *participation motives* and *reasons for exercising* have tended to be used interchangeably and to refer to exercise goals such as losing weight or getting fitter. Thus any such confusion is terminological, not conceptual.

Measurement of Participation Motives

Several standardized instruments have been developed to allow a systematic approach to the study of participation motives, as opposed to the ad hoc measures often used in earlier research. Although there are similarities among these instruments, they can be distinguished according to their level of generality or degree of differentiation of the motives they assess and consequently the number of subscales they include. At the least differentiated level, instruments assess a relatively small number of motives or collapse a number of discrete but related motives into broader factors. The most widely used of these are the Reasons for Exercise Inventory (REI; Silberstein, Striegel-Moore, Timko, & Rodin, 1988) and the Motivation for Physical Activities Measure (MPAM; Frederick & Ryan, 1993) and its revised version (MPAM-R; Ryan, Frederick, Lepes, Rubio, & Sheldon, 1997). The original REI comprises seven subscales: weight control, fitness, health, body tone, physical attractiveness, mood, and enjoyment. Alternative factor structures have been found by other researchers (e.g., Davis, Fox, Brewer, & Ratusny, 1995). The REI does not appear to have been developed with any particular theoretical perspective in mind. The MPAM/MPAM-R was specifically developed within a self-determination theory framework to examine motives for both sport and exercise participation. The later version assesses five domains: interest/enjoyment, competence, fitness, appearance improvement, and social motives.

Two very similar instruments assessing motives at the more differentiated level are prominent in the literature: the Personal Incentives for Exercise Questionnaire (PIEQ; Duda & Tappe, 1987, 1989a, 1989b), derived from personal investment theory (Maehr & Braskamp, 1986), and our revised version of Markland and Hardy's (1993) original Exercise Motivations Inventory (EMI-2; Markland & Ingledew, 1997). Like the MPAM-R, the EMI-2 was developed to address research questions drawn from self-determination theory, but it comprises 14 subscales: challenge, enjoyment, revitalization (i.e., feeling good after exercising), stress management, positive health (i.e., promotion of well-being), health pressures (i.e., pressures arising from some specific medical advice or medical condition), ill-health avoidance, affiliation, competition, social recognition, strength and endurance, nimbleness, weight management, and appearance. An important consideration in the development of the original EMI was that it should assess individuals' personal reasons for exercising and not just their opinions on whether an item was a good reason for anybody to exercise, and the item stems were worded accordingly. In order to make the EMI-2 applicable to both current exercisers and nonexercisers, it was further refined by rewording the item stems to refer to why individuals exercise or why they *might* exercise.

The advantage of adopting a more differentiated approach to assessing participation motives is that this allows a more fine-grained analysis of individuals' reasons for exercising. The disadvantage is that very large sample sizes are needed if one wants to conduct multivariate analyses with so many variables. Consequently, in some of our more recent work with the EMI-2 we have collapsed the 14 subscales into broader categories based on higher-order factor analyses (e.g., Ingledew & Markland, 2005; Markland, Taylor, & Adams, in preparation). These analyses have shown a fairly consistent pattern of three major second-order factors representing health and fitness motives, social engagement, and weight and appearance management.

Participation Motives and Engagement in Various Types of Activity

One approach to determining the role of various types of participation motives has been to examine whether they differ according to the types of activity in which individuals engage. One would expect individuals who participate in

activities or exercise contexts that emphasize outcomes to endorse more extrinsic motives, and those who exercise in contexts that de-emphasize outcomes
or focus more on the process of engagement to report more intrinsic motives
(Frederick-Recascino, 2002). Frederick and Ryan (1993), using the MPAM,
compared participants in activities assumed to be focused on the outcome of
improving physical appearance (e.g., weight training, aerobics) with participants in individual-sport activities (e.g., tennis, sailing), who were expected to
be more associated with engagement in the activity per se. As predicted, the
sport participants showed higher interest/enjoyment and competence motives
and lower body-related motives. Similarly, in the first of two studies reported
by Ryan and colleagues (1997), aerobics class participants scored lower on the
enjoyment and competence motives of the MPAM and higher on body-related
motives than participants in a tae kwon do class.

In an early study employing the original EMI (Markland et al., 1992), we
used similar reasoning to examine differences between participants in community-based aerobics classes and individuals enrolled in a weight-watching
program. We hypothesized that because the weight watchers had to attend an
exercise class twice a week as a condition of their enrollment in the program,
and because their engagement was specifically focused on the outcome of weight
reduction, they would experience exercise participation as more controlled and
accordingly would report more extrinsic motives for taking part. While we
expected body-related motives to also be highly salient for the aerobics class
participants, these individuals at least had a degree of choice about where and
when they exercised and a more diverse social context for their classes. We
therefore expected them to hold more intrinsic motives. The results supported
these expectations. Weight management was the most important motive for
both groups. However, the aerobics group could be significantly discriminated
from the weight watchers by a dimension representing an emphasis on more
intrinsic motives for exercise, namely enjoyment, affiliation, fitness, personal
development, stress management, and revitalization. Furthermore, the aerobics
group also scored significantly higher on a measure of autonomous motivation
for exercise, the Locus of Causality for Exercise Scale (Markland & Hardy,
1997), as well as on perceptions of competence and several other indicators
of intrinsic motivation. Thus, there was at least indirect evidence that certain
types of participation motive are indeed associated with more autonomous
engagement in physical activity.

Participation Motives and Exercise Behavior

Although the studies just discussed indicate an association between different
motives and involvement in particular types of activity, they provide only weak
support for the proposition that different motives hold different functional
significances for exercise behavior. For one thing, they rely on assumptions
about the extent to which certain activities provide more or less controlling

environments. In addition, their cross-sectional nature leaves the question of the direction of causality open. Do the types of motive lead people to adopt certain activities, or do activity contexts prompt people to adopt certain motives? Intuitively, one would expect that both of these are likely to be the case. From the perspective of promoting engagement in regular physical activity, however, a more important question is whether participation motives are predictive of exercise behavior.

In their studies, Frederick and Ryan (1993) and Ryan and colleagues (1997) also examined the relationships between motives and self-reported exercise behavior. Frederick and Ryan (1993) found that interest/enjoyment and competence motives were positively associated with time spent exercising per week. Body-related motives were positively associated with weekly frequency of exercise but negatively associated with the actual time spent exercising. Ryan and colleagues (1997, study one) found that competence and enjoyment motives prospectively predicted both dropout and class attendance over a 10-week period. Body-related motives, however, were not associated with adherence. In a second prospective study using the MPAM-R, Ryan and colleagues (1997) found that competence, enjoyment, social, and fitness motives were positively associated with attendance over 10 weeks at a fitness center. The appearance improvement motive was not associated with attendance. In addition, competence and enjoyment were associated with longer duration of exercise sessions.

Ingledew and colleagues (1998) examined whether participation motives differed across the stages of change for exercise (Prochaska & Marcus, 1994) and whether motives could predict movement from one stage of change to the next. British government employees completed the EMI-2 and a stage of change measure at baseline and at three-month follow-up. Examination of the relative strength of intrinsic and extrinsic motives across the stages at baseline showed that in the precontemplation stage, extrinsic motives (appearance and weight management) dominated over intrinsic motives (enjoyment and revitalization). In contemplation, this dominance was less marked, and in preparation it had disappeared. In the action stage, however, the extrinsic motives again dominated over the intrinsic motives. Finally, in maintenance, the situation was reversed, with intrinsic motives dominating over the extrinsic motives. Looking at how the motives varied across the stages, the authors found that the intrinsic motives received relatively little emphasis in precontemplation, increased in salience through contemplation to preparation, decreased in action, and increased again in maintenance. The extrinsic motives started at a moderate level in precontemplation, increased through contemplation to action, and dropped in maintenance.

Overall, then, extrinsic motives were more prominent in the early stages and became less so in maintenance, while intrinsic motives followed the opposite pattern. However, there was a "blip" in the action stage where intrinsic motives became less salient and extrinsic motives more important. Indeed, extrinsic motives reached their highest levels during this stage. The action stage is the period of initial regular involvement in exercise; and we suggested that the explanation for the increase in extrinsic motives and concomitant decrease in intrinsic motives was that for previously inactive people, the early days of exercising may not be experienced as very enjoyable. It could be that the increase in the appearance and weight management motives represented a renewed focus on the extrinsic benefits of exercising that would provide people with incentives to help them through this difficult period. Another noteworthy finding from the baseline results was that health pressures (an extrinsic motive reflecting exercising because of medical advice or conditions) were moderately important in the contemplation stage and became more so in preparation but became de-emphasized in the action stage and were not salient in maintenance. This suggests that the motive of health pressures might play a part in one coming to the decision to exercise but does not contribute to turning intentions into action. However, these findings were cross-sectional. More importantly in supporting a potential causal role for motives on exercise behavior, analyses of change over time indicated that progress from lower to higher stages of change was associated with greater levels of intrinsic motives but not with extrinsic motives.

Participation Motives and Well-Being

Self-determination theory concerns not merely the extent to which motivation influences the quantity of behavior, but also the quality of the experience of motivated behavior. As noted previously, intrinsic motives are held not only to engender greater behavioral persistence but also to have more positive effects on well-being than extrinsic motives, whereas an emphasis on extrinsic motives is likely to result in reduced well-being and negative affect. Some research supports this position with respect to exercise motives. In Frederick and Ryan's (1993) study, interest/enjoyment and competence motives were positively related to feeling satisfied with the activities that individuals engaged in. Body-related motives, however, were negatively associated with body-related self-esteem and positively associated with anxiety and depression. Maltby and Day (2001), using the EMI-2, found that among individuals who had been exercising regularly for less than six months, extrinsic motives were positively related to somatic symptoms, anxiety, social dysfunction, and depression and inversely related to self-esteem. Extrinsic motives were also positively associated with scores on the time pressure, health concerns, and inner concerns subscales of the Hassles Scale (Lazarus & Folkman, 1989). Among those who had been exercising for more than six months, intrinsic motives were positively associated with self-esteem and negatively related to somatic symptoms, anxiety, social dysfunction, and depression, as well as to time pressure, health concerns, and inner concerns from the Hassles Scale.

Participation Motives and Body Image

Given the physical nature of exercise, it would be surprising if body perceptions did not influence the participation motives that individuals adopt; and
research shows consistent associations between body-related exercise motives
and a negative body image. McDonald and Thompson (1992), using the REI,
found that among both females and males exercising for weight management,
attractiveness and body tone were related to a greater drive for thinness, and
body tone reasons were associated with more body dissatisfaction whereas
health motives were positively related to self-esteem. Among females, weight
management was also associated with greater body dissatisfaction. Among
males, weight management correlated with bulimic symptoms, and exercising
for attractiveness was related to lower self-esteem and higher body dissatisfaction. Crawford and Eklund (1994) found that scores on the REI subscales of
body tone and attractiveness were negative predictors, and fitness motives a
positive predictor, of social physique anxiety among females. Cash, Novy, and
Grant (1994), also using the REI, found that exercising for appearance/weight
management was associated with less body satisfaction and greater body image
disturbance among women, independently of actual body size as assessed by
body mass index. Similarly, Smith, Handley, and Eldredge (1998) found that
weight-related motives were associated with body-related negative affect in
women but not in men, while body mass index was not associated with the
weight-related motive in either gender.

Ingledew, Hardy, and de Sousa (1995) found a gender difference in the
relationships between perceived, ideal, and actual body size and participation
motives. Men were more likely to exercise for weight management reasons if
they were actually overweight; women were more likely to exercise for weight
management if their perceived and ideal body sizes were discrepant, regardless
of whether they were actually overweight. Ingledew and Sullivan (2002) found
that this gender difference arose during adolescence. It is during adolescence
that boys naturally gain more muscle, facilitating attainment of an idealized
muscular male body image, and girls naturally gain more fat, thwarting attainment of an idealized slim female body image (Striegel-Moore, Silberstein, &
Rodin, 1986), while society pressures individuals toward the respective idealized
body images (Rolls, Federoff, & Guthrie, 1991). From the self-determination
theory perspective, one would expect that being driven to exercise because of
body-related concerns would ultimately undermine exercise adherence because
it would be experienced as controlling. We found support for this in a recent
study in which body-related motives (weight management and appearance) were
shown to mediate a negative relationship between discrepant perceived and ideal
body size and low- to moderate-intensity exercise among women (Markland,
Taylor, & Adams, in preparation). Thus being more dissatisfied with one's body
was associated with less engagement in exercise, and this was explained by an
increasing focus on exercising for weight management and appearance.

Participation Motives and Autonomy: Beyond the Intrinsic–Extrinsic Dichotomy

The research base shows that intrinsic motives are invariably associated with positive outcomes while extrinsic motives, particularly body-related motives, are consistently associated with lower well-being and self-esteem, more negative affect, and body image disturbances. Thus, there is compelling indirect evidence that exercising for intrinsic reasons is experienced as autonomous while exercising for weight and appearance reasons is experienced as internally controlling. Markland (1999) found more direct evidence for this in an examination of the effects of intrinsic motives (enjoyment and affiliation) and extrinsic motives (weight management, appearance, and health pressures) on the degree of autonomy for exercise, assessed by the Locus of Causality for Exercise Scale (Markland & Hardy, 1997). Not surprisingly, enjoyment was positively related to autonomy, although affiliation was unrelated to autonomy. More significantly, all three extrinsic motives had negative effects on autonomy. In addition, autonomy mediated the relationship between the motives and interest/enjoyment of exercise. Thus it appears that the average functional significance (Deci & Ryan, 1985) of body-related and health pressure motives is to undermine the experience of autonomy and intrinsic motivation.

So far we have discussed participation motives in terms of the intrinsic–extrinsic dichotomy and have equated intrinsic and extrinsic motives with autonomous and controlled regulation of behavior, respectively, as is the convention in much of the exercise participation motives literature and in the self-determination theory research on goal contents. However, one of the major contributions of self-determination theory to the understanding of motivation is that it has gone beyond the intrinsic–extrinsic dichotomy to describe how extrinsic motivation can be better conceptualized as a continuum representing the extent to which people have internalized externally driven behavioral regulations in order to engage autonomously in their activities (Deci & Ryan, 1985; Ryan & Deci, 2000). Extrinsic motivation can be controlling, as when people are regulated externally or by internally controlling, introjected forces; but it can also be autonomous, as when the individual identifies with and values the outcomes of the behavior or has integrated that identification with his or her other core values and beliefs. Thus, being extrinsically motivated per se is not necessarily a bad thing (Ryan et al., 1997).

Recently, we examined the effects of different motives on external, introjected, identified, and intrinsic behavioral regulations (Ingledew & Markland, 2005), assessed by Markland and Tobin's (2004) Behavioural Regulation in Exercise Questionnaire-2. This was part of a larger model that tested the mediating role of participation motives and behavioral regulations on the relationship between personality characteristics and exercise behavior. Motives were assessed using the EMI-2 but were collapsed into the three higher-order factors mentioned previously: health/fitness, social engagement, and weight/appearance. Of relevance to the present discussion, we found that health/fitness was unrelated to external regulation, had small positive associations with introjected and intrinsic regulation, and showed a strong positive relationship with identified regulation. Social engagement was also unrelated to external regulation, had a strong positive relationship with intrinsic regulation, and had small positive relationships with both identified and introjected regulation. Weight/appearance had a small positive relationship with external regulation, had a stronger positive relationship with introjection, had a small positive relationship with identified regulation, and was unrelated to intrinsic regulation.

These findings show a more complex picture of participation motives than we have hitherto presented and attest to the limitations of the intrinsic–extrinsic dichotomy. The "intrinsic" motive of social engagement was indeed most strongly related to intrinsic regulation but was also related to identified regulation and introjection. Health/fitness, the other motive that would typically be considered "intrinsic," was actually only slightly related to intrinsic regulation and was most strongly associated with identification, and again had some element of introjection. Relatively speaking, then, both of these motives were more autonomous but not strictly speaking intrinsic. Although the "extrinsic" motive of weight/appearance was, uniquely among the three, associated with external regulation and even more strongly related to introjection, it too also had a small association with identified regulation. The net indirect effects of the motives on exercise behavior were that both social engagement and health and fitness increased participation while weight and appearance had no effect, reflecting the findings of Ingledew and colleagues (1998) and Ryan and colleagues (1997).

Conclusions and Implications for Exercise Promotion

The literature suggests that more intrinsic motives are associated with positive psychological outcomes and greater exercise adherence. Clearly, intrinsic motives should be encouraged whenever possible. A focus on extrinsic motives, in particular body-related motives, is generally experienced as controlling and has a detrimental effect on well-being. Furthermore, body dissatisfaction is associated with a greater emphasis on such motives. On its face, this would suggest that extrinsic motives should be discouraged. On the other hand, extrinsic body-related motives such as weight management and appearance seem to be important determinants of the decision to adopt exercise during the early stages of change, and they may be particularly valuable incentives to persist during the pivotal action stage when exercising might not be felt to be very enjoyable or intrinsically motivating in its own right (Ingledew, Markland, & Medley, 1998). Furthermore, even long-term exercisers are likely to be extrinsically motivated to some degree. Thus, it would be a mistake to automatically disparage body-related motives or deny their potentially useful functional significance, particularly during the deliberation and adoption stages of exercise.

Theoretically, there are two ways in which any negative effects of extrinsic motives might be mitigated. First, self-determination theory suggests that when extrinsic motives are well internalized, they will be experienced as autonomous and positive outcomes will ensue. Second, extrinsic motives might not be harmful when individuals hold intrinsic motives at the same time, especially when the intrinsic motives are overall more dominant. In the self-determination theory research on goal contents, researchers have argued that it is critical to examine the *relative* importance of intrinsic and extrinsic goal contents because extrinsic goals can serve to facilitate the satisfaction of psychological needs to some extent. It is when they become so strong that they are out of balance with intrinsic goals that detrimental effects on well-being are likely to result (Sheldon et al., 2004). Similarly, Amabile's (1993) motivational synergy model proposes that extrinsic goals can complement intrinsic motivation when they serve to orient people toward involvement in the task itself and provide positive competence information. Markland and colleagues' (1992) study provides some support for this, in that even though the most strongly endorsed motive for both aerobics participants and weight watchers was weight management, the groups were significantly differentiated by a range of more intrinsic motives and also by levels of autonomy and competence. Thus for the aerobics group, a strong endorsement of weight management as a motive did not appear to be detrimental to autonomous engagement in exercise.

Self-determination theory is based on the fundamental assumption that individuals have an inherent tendency to internalize and integrate extrinsic motives to come to autonomously self-regulate their behaviors (Deci & Ryan, 1985; Ryan & Deci, 2000). This tendency is facilitated when the social environment provides supports for the three basic psychological needs for autonomy, competence, and relatedness. Thus the message for those involved in promoting exercise is that providing such supports will encourage individuals to identify with and personally value the extrinsic benefits of exercising so that their behavioral regulation becomes less controlled and more autonomous (see "Recommendations for Practitioners Aiming to Foster Exercisers' Participation Motives"). Motivational interviewing (see Markland & Vansteenkiste, this volume) offers considerable promise in this regard. Furthermore, an awareness of the functional significance of individuals' participation motives would allow practitioners to address and implement the more abstract and conceptual theoretical principles of self-determination theory with their clients in more concrete and personally meaningful terms. Thus we contend that, from both theoretical and applied perspectives, the study of participation motives offers much more than merely a surface analysis of exercise motivation.

Recommendations for Practitioners Aiming to Foster Exercisers' Participation Motives

- Key practitioners, like exercise promoters in exercise referral schemes and personal trainers, are encouraged to enhance intrinsic motivation as a reason for engaging in exercise, but should recognize that stressing fun and enjoyment of exercise is unlikely to be accepted by individuals who are not yet considering exercising. It is therefore important to investigate reasons for participating and to encourage potential exercisers to identify their own reasons for exercising. These may very well include extrinsic outcomes like "losing weight," but provided that they are personally relevant and also linked to other motives such as improving time and effort in the chosen activity, this is acceptable.

- During the early days of adoption, practitioners are advised to acknowledge individuals' conflict of goals and empathize with the difficulties involved, but to do so in the context of highlighting their autonomous reasons for engaging in exercise. For example, an exercise specialist might say to a person trying to lose weight, "Although it might be hard now, you will begin to reach those goals that are important to you as you get fitter, like losing weight and feeling healthier."

- Exercise practitioners can also recognize that extrinsic motives are not necessarily inherently detrimental and may be very important in helping people in the early days of adoption of exercise. For example, an exercise promoter might design a poster campaign that highlights some extrinsic reasons for exercising, but do so in an autonomy-supportive manner and stress the importance of the extrinsic goal to the individual. In this way the extrinsic goal is more likely to be internalized over time and perhaps be integrated into the personal repertoire of need-satisfying pursuits.

- Practitioners' support of individuals' autonomy, competence, and relatedness will help people to come to identify with and value the rewards of exercising so that it becomes less of a chore and more freely chosen. This is through the processes of internalization and integration. For example, a personal trainer may provide clients with novel training sessions by presenting exercise to them in an autonomy-supportive manner (e.g., adopting a questioning approach, using cooperative learning, giving participants opportunities to lead drills and practices, acknowledging competence); this, over time, is likely to result in the participants' internalizing the sessions and incorporating them into their own training programs.

Perceived Autonomy Support and Psychological Need Satisfaction in Exercise

Jemma K. Edmunds, PhD
Coventry University

Nikos Ntoumanis, PhD, and Joan L. Duda, PhD
University of Birmingham

The links between exercise and improved physical and psychological health have been well documented (Biddle & Mutrie, 2001). Despite this evidence, however, physical inactivity is the predominant lifestyle pattern observed among people living in contemporary industrialized societies (U.S. Department of Health and Human Services [USDHHS], 1996). To increase the number of people that engage in, and derive the benefits associated with, regular physical activity, it is imperative to understand the factors that underpin exercise adoption and maintenance. Exercise engagement is influenced by a variety of biological, environmental, social, and psychological variables (Biddle & Mutrie, 2001). Of these, the social-environmental and psychological determinants of exercise behavior appear to be those factors that practicing health and fitness professionals may most easily target with intervention strategies. However, before exercise-focused behavioral interventions are designed and implemented, the psychological processes that contribute to active engagement must be better understood, as well as the social-environmental conditions that foster their development.

The Self-Determination Perspective in Exercise

Self-determination theory holds promise for elucidating the specifically motivational factors influencing physical activity participation and the associated psychological and emotional benefits (Deci & Ryan, 1985; Ryan & Deci, this volume). A growing body of research evidence is emerging to suggest support for self-determination theory's propositions within the exercise setting. For

Correspondence concerning this article should be addressed to Jemma K. Edwards, Applied Research Centre of Health and Life Sciences, Faculty of Health & Life Sciences, Whitefrairs Building, Coventry University, Priory Street, Coventry, CV1 5FB, UK, E-mail: j:edmunds@coventry.ac.uk example, autonomy support from friends (e.g., Wilson & Rodgers, 2004) and satisfaction of the basic psychological needs (Wilson, Rodgers, Blanchard, & Gessell, 2003; Wilson, Rodgers, & Fraser, 2002) have been shown to be positively associated with the most self-determined forms of motivational regulation. Autonomous regulation has also been associated with the action and maintenance stages of change for exercise (Landry & Solomon, 2004; Mullan & Markland, 1997), more frequent self-reported exercise behavior (Wilson, Rodgers, & Fraser, 2002), greater physical fitness (Wilson et al., 2003), more positive attitudes toward exercise (Wilson et al., 2003), behavioral intentions to continue exercising (Wilson & Rodgers, 2004), and exercise-related self-esteem (Wilson & Rodgers, 2002).

This chapter presents a series of studies that extend previous research examining the utility of the basic theoretical propositions of self-determination theory in the exercise domain. The chapter focuses specifically on the role of autonomy support and psychological need satisfaction in fostering adaptive motivational regulations and, subsequently, optimal behavioral, cognitive, and affective aspects of the exercise experience. First, we discuss the relationships between autonomy support, psychological need satisfaction, autonomous regulation, and adaptive exercise behavior as determined from research that used mediational models to test and explain the processes involved in these relationships. Next, we present data on the role of thwarted need satisfaction and controlling forms of regulation in the prediction of maladaptive exercise engagement. We also examine the applicability of the basic needs and motivational regulations proposed by self-determination theory in predicting variations in cognitive and affective responses across different ethnic groups in group exercise settings.

In addition, we present the results of the first experimental study in the area of exercise that has addressed the effect of an experimentally induced autonomy-supportive instructor style on exercise class participants' psychological need satisfaction, motivational regulations, exercise program attendance, and important cognitive and affective outcomes. Drawing from this work, we present directions for future physical activity research based on self-determination theory. The potential contribution of self-determination theory toward the design of behavioral interventions is also discussed. We conclude the chapter by proposing recommendations for practicing health and exercise professionals.

Autonomy Support, Psychological Needs, and Autonomous Regulation

A number of studies examining self-determination theory's propositions in the exercise domain have focused on the conditions that are conducive to the autonomous regulation of exercise behavior (e.g., Wilson & Rodgers, 2004; Wilson, Rodgers, & Fraser, 2002). For example, Wilson and Rodgers (2004) reported that perceived autonomy support from friends was positively associated with intrinsic motivation and identified regulation. However, self-determination theory suggests that the relationship between autonomy support and autonomous regulation is mediated by the satisfaction of the three basic psychological needs (see Hagger, Chatzisarantis, Barkoukis, Wang, & Baranowski, 2005; Hagger, Chatzisarantis, Culverhouse, & Biddle, 2003).

With an eye toward extending previous studies in the exercise domain, we assessed the direct effects of an autonomy-supportive exercise environment on psychological need satisfaction, as well as on the different forms of motivational regulation proposed by self-determination theory (Edmunds, Ntoumanis, & Duda, in press). In addition, we examined whether psychological need satisfaction mediated the relationship between an autonomy-supportive environment and the autonomous regulation of exercise behavior.

A sample of 106 participants (35.2% male, 64.8% female) ranging in age from 16 to 62 years, who reported engaging in regular exercise classes, completed measures of perceived autonomy support provided by their exercise instructor (measured utilizing the six-item version of the Health Care Climate Questionnaire; Williams, Grow, Freedman, Ryan, & Deci, 1996), psychological need satisfaction (via an amended version of the Basic Need Satisfaction at Work Scale; Deci et al., 2001), and motivational regulations for exercise (via the Behavioural Regulation in Exercise Questionnaire; Mullan, Markland, & Ingledew, 1997).

Supporting self-determination theory's propositions, hierarchical regression analyses revealed that perceived autonomy support from the exercise instructor positively predicted autonomy, relatedness, and competence need satisfaction, as well as intrinsic motivation. In addition, competence need satisfaction partially mediated the relationship between perceived autonomy support and intrinsic motivation. The effect of autonomy support on intrinsic motivation dropped significantly when the effect of competence need satisfaction was controlled for, suggesting partial mediation (see figure 2.1).

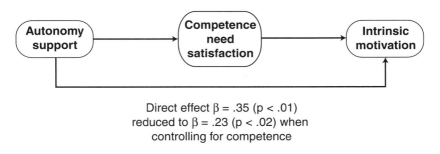

Figure 2.1 The relationship between autonomy support and intrinsic motivation as mediated by competence need satisfaction.

Psychological Needs, Autonomous Regulation, and Exercise Behavior

Research in the exercise setting has also begun to address the utility of the theoretical constructs embedded in self-determination theory in the prediction of self-reported exercise behavior. For example, Wilson and colleagues (2002), using a sample of 500 university students and staff partaking in exercise classes, found psychological need satisfaction to be positively correlated with intrinsic motivation and identified and introjected regulations. In turn, these forms of regulation were positively associated with self-reported exercise behavior. However, a more complete examination of self-determination theory's theoretical propositions would suggest that greater need satisfaction may predict behavioral responses not only directly but also indirectly, via the motivational regulations (Ryan & Deci, 2000b; Vallerand, 1997).

We tested these propositions on a sample of 369 individuals (47% male, 53% female) ranging in age from 16 to 64 years (Edmunds, Ntoumanis, & Duda, 2006; see also Hagger, Chatzisarantis, & Harris, 2006, for other investigations examining these relationships in the physical domain). As reported previously, participants completed measures of exercise-specific psychological need satisfaction, motivational regulations for exercise, and self-reported exercise behavior (in terms of mild, moderate, and strenuous intensities), as well as total exercise behavior, using the Leisure Time Exercise Questionnaire (Godin & Shephard, 1985).

The results of hierarchical regression analyses supported the importance of motivation-related variables in understanding variability in self-reported exercise behaviors. Specifically, external regulation emerged as a negative predictor of strenuous exercise behavior. In contrast, competence need satisfaction and introjected and identified regulations positively predicted strenuous exercise behavior. Introjected regulation also emerged as a positive predictor of total exercise. Identified regulation was found to partially mediate the relationship between competence need satisfaction and strenuous exercise behavior (see figure 2.2).

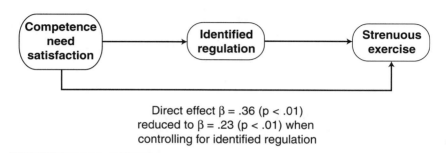

Figure 2.2   The relationship between competence need satisfaction and strenuous exercise as mediated by identified regulation.

Of particular interest was the finding that competence need satisfaction had direct and indirect (via identified regulation) effects on behavioral investment. The indirect effect indicates that feelings of competence result in increased exercise behavior by reinforcing the personal importance of exercise. Collectively, these results suggest that competence is a particularly relevant need in the exercise domain, and that exercise instructors and health professionals should pay special attention to ensuring that this need is met.

Identified and introjected regulations also emerged as significant positive predictors of exercise behaviors. Valuing the benefits associated with an activity (i.e., identified regulation) constitutes a self-determined form of extrinsic motivation that should, according to self-determination theory, be associated with more adaptive outcomes. Given that many forms of exercise (e.g., working out on the step machine) are commonly construed as boring or not inherently enjoyable, this finding appears to support the suggestion that identification is essential to the regulation of valuable, but uninteresting, activities (Koestner & Losier, 2002).

Introjected regulation, however, is a more controlling form of extrinsic motivation that reflects feelings of guilt and compulsion or contingent self-esteem and pride (Ryan & Deci, 2000b). The observed positive association between introjection and exercise behavior should not be interpreted as advocacy for instilling feelings of guilt or contingent self-worth in individuals in an attempt to facilitate active lifestyles. Indeed, there is evidence demonstrating that introjected regulation has negative implications for sustained involvement in sporting activities (e.g., Pelletier, Fortier, Vallerand, & Brière, 2001; Vansteenkiste, Soenens, & Lens, this volume). In addition, research in the educational and political domains has shown introjected regulation to be related to poor emotional functioning (Koestner & Losier, 2002). Thus, this form of regulation may also have a detrimental impact on the psychological well-being of the exerciser. Future longitudinal research is warranted to examine the role of autonomous versus controlling forms of regulation not only in relation to sustained behavioral engagement, but also in terms of the psychological and emotional responses associated with physical activity participation.

Contrary to the propositions of self-determination theory, intrinsic motivation did not emerge as a significant predictor of exercise behavior in the study by Edmunds and colleagues (2006). In interpreting this finding, one should note that intrinsic motivation and identified regulation were not marked by multicollinearity; that is, they were not very highly correlated. Thus, it is unlikely that the observed effect of intrinsic motivation on behavior was severely attenuated by identified regulation. This finding adds credence to the claims of Mullan and colleagues (1997), who suggested that "individuals may be unlikely to maintain regular exercise behavior, with all the organization and commitment it entails, purely for the intrinsic reasons of fun and enjoyment" (p. 745).

However, before dismissing the importance of intrinsic motivation in the exercise domain, we should acknowledge research findings suggesting that intrinsic motivation fosters exercise persistence. For example, Mullan and Markland (1997) demonstrated that, in conjunction with identified regulation, individuals in the later stages of change (i.e., action and maintenance) reported higher levels of intrinsic motivation compared to those individuals in the earlier stages of change (i.e., precontemplation and preparation). It is therefore suggested that longitudinal methodologies be adopted to delineate the role of intrinsic motivation in *sustaining* exercise engagement. In addition, future work may benefit from being more specific regarding the type of exercise under examination. It is conceivable that different types of physical activity may be guided by different regulatory styles. For example, individuals playing a sport, which may typically be an inherently interesting activity, are likely to be far more intrinsically motivated toward their exercise endeavor than those engaging in a vigorous gym workout involving exercise equipment (e.g., running on the treadmill).

Similar to findings from previous research (e.g., Wilson, Rodgers, & Fraser, 2002), in our study the motivational regulations considered by self-determination theory were more strongly correlated with strenuous and total exercise behaviors than with moderate and mild ones (Edmunds, Ntoumanis, & Duda, 2006). This is probably the case because mild and moderate forms of exercise commonly constitute more habitual modes of physical activity, such as walking and easy cycling. Future researchers might examine whether the motivational regulations proposed by self-determination theory are more important for predicting structured, as opposed to incidental (e.g., walking to work or to the shops), forms of exercise.

Predicting Maladaptive Exercise Engagement

Despite the well-documented benefits associated with regular physical activity, researchers (e.g., Hausenblas & Symons Downs, 2002a, 2002b) have suggested that, if allowed to become excessive, exercise can result in serious detrimental physical (e.g., depressed immune response, menstrual irregularity) and psychological (e.g., anxiety and depression) consequences. Researchers examining the negative consequences associated with excessive physical activity have focused primarily on the occurrence of exercise dependence, a condition in which moderate to vigorous physical activity becomes a compulsive behavior (Hausenblas & Symons Downs, 2002a).

Limited research has dealt with the etiological factors of exercise dependence (Loumidis & Roxborough, 1995). However, there is evidence to suggest that certain motives for exercise can be potential antecedents of this condition (Ogles, Masters, & Richardson, 1995). For example, research adopting a self-determination theory approach has highlighted the difference between obsessive and harmonious passions with respect to pastimes like exercise (Vallerand et al., 2003). Obsessive passion is characterized by an internal pressure that compels individuals to participate in a "passionate" activity, while harmonious passion is defined by an individual's choosing to participate in an activity. Hamer, Karageorghis, and Vlachopoulos (2002) recently examined the relationship between motivational regulations from self-determination theory and exercise dependence among endurance athletes. Introjected regulation emerged as a positive predictor of exercise dependence, supporting self-determination theory's propositions that more controlling forms of regulation will be associated with maladaptive outcomes. However, Hamer and colleagues (2002) did not consider the relationship between satisfaction of the three psychological needs proposed by self-determination theory and the regulation and level of exercise dependence. Furthermore, their study was limited in that it utilized a unidimensional measure of exercise dependence that does not consider the *Diagnostic and Statistical Manual of Mental Disorders* (DSM-IV) criteria for dependence (American Psychiatric Association, 1994). With these limitations in mind, we conducted a study to more comprehensively examine the "darker side" of introjected regulation (see Ryan & Deci, 2000a, for review) in the exercise domain (Edmunds, Ntoumanis, & Duda, 2005a). That is, we aimed to determine whether a thwarting of the psychological needs and an emphasis on introjected regulation were pertinent to the prediction of exercise behavior among individuals classified as exercise dependent.

A sample of 351 male and female exercisers, ranging in age from 16 to 62 years, completed measures of exercise-specific psychological need satisfaction (Deci et al., 2001), motivational regulations (Li, 1999; Mullan, Markland, & Ingledew, 1997), and exercise behavior (Godin & Shephard, 1985). In addition, participants completed the Hausenblas and Symons Downs (2002b) Exercise Dependence Questionnaire. This measure was chosen as it allows individuals to be classified, on the basis of DSM-IV criteria (American Psychiatric Association, 1994; i.e., tolerance, withdrawal, intention effects, lack of control, time, reduction in other activities, and continuance), into three groups. These are (a) at risk for exercise dependence, (b) nondependent symptomatic (i.e., not classified as exercise dependent but showing some symptoms), or (c) nondependent asymptomatic (i.e., showing no symptoms of exercise dependence). However, despite repeated attempts to recruit "at-risk" individuals, only 12 of the 373 participants were classified as suffering from this pathological condition, and thus these individuals were excluded from any further analyses. Therefore only nondependent symptomatic (56.4%; 52.5% male, 46.5% female) and nondependent asymptomatic (40.1%; 39% male, 59.6% female) individuals were compared with respect to the psychological needs and motivational regulations underpinning their reported exercise behavior.

The results of regression analyses revealed that among nondependent symptomatics, introjected regulation was a marginally significant predictor of strenuous exercise behavior. In contrast, in the case of asymptomatic individuals, identified regulation predicted strenuous exercise behavior. These findings add further support to the applicability of self-determination theory within the exercise domain. That is, introjected regulation, proposed by self-determination theory to represent a harshly evaluative and pressured regulatory style linked to maladaptive outcomes (Koestner & Losier, 2002), predicted a pattern of excessive exercise engagement associated with detrimental behavioral and psychological consequences. On the other hand, autonomous regulation (i.e., identified regulation) was associated with more adaptive patterns of exercise, a finding that is consistent with previous exercise research grounded in self-determination theory (Edmunds, Ntoumanis, & Duda, 2006; Wilson & Rodgers, 2002, 2004; Wilson et al., 2003).

Considering the findings of the studies discussed thus far, it appears that to participate in a regular exercise regime, individuals have to place some value on exercise behavior and to recognize its importance in terms of health and well-being. However, to understand long-term engagement, researchers should examine not only whether one values exercise, but also the cognitive and affective responses associated with exercise. A particularly attractive facet of self-determination theory, adding to its appeal and relevance in the exercise domain, is that besides considering the behavioral regulations underpinning a particular activity, it provides a theoretical explanation for observed variations in thoughts and feelings about a given activity. That is, self-determination theory hypothesizes that psychological need satisfaction and more self-determined forms of motivational regulation should give rise to more adaptive cognitions and affect.

A limited number of investigations have begun to address cognitive and affective responses to exercise from a self-determination theory perspective. For example, Wilson and Rodgers (2004) demonstrated that autonomous motives (i.e., identified regulation and intrinsic motivation) were most strongly correlated with behavioral intentions to exercise relative to controlling forms of regulation (i.e., introjected and external regulation). Also, Wilson and Rodgers (2002) found autonomous motives to play an important role in explaining variability in physical self-esteem. While these studies add support to the applicability of self-determination theory to the exercise domain, they overlook the role that psychological need satisfaction plays in facilitating desired cognitive and affective outcomes. Consequently, we conducted a study to examine the role of the motivational regulations and psychological need satisfaction in predicting important cognitive and affective outcomes (Edmunds, Duda, & Ntoumanis, 2005b), as discussed in the next section.

Ethnic and Cultural Group Considerations

A further aspect of self-determination theory that has received little attention in the exercise domain relates to its predictive utility across ethnic and cultural groups. Deci and Ryan (2000) argued that although the specific means of expressing and satisfying the three basic needs in self-determination theory may vary considerably by context and culture, all needs are functionally relevant across these surface variations. That is, all of the psychological need constructs embedded within self-determination theory are relevant to the quality of human engagement in diverse activities, regardless of ethnicity or cultural background (Ryan et al., 1999). However, some authors (e.g., Markus & Kitayama, 1991) have questioned the assumed cross-cultural applicability of contemporary psychological frameworks such as self-determination theory. Such criticism is based on the observation that individuals from Western cultures (e.g., in North America and Europe) tend to stress attending to and asserting the self and appreciating one's difference from others, whereas collectivistic cultures (e.g., in Southeast Asia and much of South America and Africa) emphasize the importance of the self to the group and harmonious interdependence. Consequently, it has been suggested that different cultural groups engender different needs, motives, and values, which in turn are assumed to be differently associated with psychological well-being (Ryan et al., 1999). Considering such distinctions, it has been suggested that autonomy will be more important for individualistic cultures, whereas relatedness may be more pertinent in collectivistic ones (e.g., Iyengar & Lepper, 1999). However, research has shown that autonomy is important in the prediction of behavior in both collective and individualist contexts, even though levels of autonomous motivation tend to be higher among individuals in individualist cultures (Chirkov & Ryan, 2001; Chirkov, Ryan, Kim, & Kaplan, 2003).

Given the suggestion in recent reports that participation rates in regular physical activity are lower for some ethnic groups than among the population as a whole (USDHHS, 2003), establishing whether the tenets of self-determination theory are equally applicable across diverse ethnic groups appears to constitute an important research direction in the exercise domain. Thus, addressing the aforementioned issues, we conducted a study to explore the predictive utility of self-determination theory in explaining cognitive and affective aspects of the group exercise experience across members of three different ethnic groups (Edmunds, Duda, & Ntoumanis, 2005). (Please note: This study also measured the psychological need constructs proposed by Optimal Distinctiveness Theory [ODT; Brewer, 1991, 1993], but the results pertaining to these variables are not presented in this chapter.) Importantly, such ethnic groups are likely to endorse different cultural orientations in line with their cultural background, although this may be partially mitigated if they have lived for a prolonged period in a culture that has values that vary from those of their traditional cultural background.

Female exercise class participants ($N = 260$) of white (i.e., British, Irish, or other white background; 38%), Asian/Asian British (i.e., Indian, Pakistani, Bangladeshi, or any other Asian background; 33%), and black/black British (i.e., Caribbean, African, or any other black background; 29%) ethnic origin completed measures of psychological need satisfaction (Sheldon & Bettencourt, 2002) and motivational regulations specific to the group exercise experience (Li, 1999; Mullan, Markland, & Ingledew, 1997). In addition, their commitment toward the group (Scanlan, Carpenter, Schmidt, Simons, & Keeler, 1993) and behavioral intention (Wilson & Rodgers, 2004) toward the group, as well as their affect (Watson, Clark, & Tellegen, 1988) and subjective vitality (Ryan & Frederick, 1997) derived from the group exercise experience, were assessed.

Separate regression analyses for each ethnic group revealed that more self-determined forms of regulation predicted adaptive outcomes for female exercisers of white and black/black British ethnic origin. Specifically, for white female exercise class participants, intrinsic motivation corresponded to greater positive affect and commitment and lower negative affect. Moreover, integrated regulation positively predicted subjective vitality. For black/black British female exercise class participants, intrinsic motivation was linked to positive affect, subjective vitality, and commitment, whereas integrated regulation predicted low negative affect. These findings are in line with the tenets of self-determination theory.

However, the utility of self-determination theory in predicting exercise-related cognitions and affect among Asian/Asian British female exercise class participants was not supported. None of the needs proposed by self-determination theory predicted any of the motivational regulations or targeted cognitive and affective responses for this group. A couple of issues are worthy of consideration to explain this finding. Diener (2000) demonstrated that variables that have typically been viewed as tapping well-being, including positive and negative affect (Watson, Clark, & Tellegen, 1988) and subjective vitality (Ryan & Frederick, 1997), may be more culture bound than originally believed (e.g., Diener & Diener, 1995). Moreover, the extent to which individuals from different cultures have become integrated into Western society may vary, and thus the extent to which the different ethnic groups retained their traditional values and norms may have influenced the observed findings. Further studies in the exercise domain need to address these issues in order to provide a more conclusive answer regarding the relevance of self-determination theory to Asian/Asian British groups.

Promoting Autonomy Support in the Exercise Domain

While the findings discussed thus far suggest that self-determination theory-based behavioral interventions would be beneficial in enhancing exercise engagement and the quality of the exercise experience, all of the studies presented to this point have been nonexperimental in design. As a result, causality cannot be inferred from the findings described thus far. Cause-and-effect relationships can be confirmed only when the variables under investigation are manipulated experimentally (Ellsworth & Gonzalez, 2003).

To address this shortcoming in the literature, we conducted a field experiment (Edmunds, Ntoumanis, & Duda, 2005b) to determine the effects of an exercise instructor's adopting an autonomy-supportive teaching style, versus a realistically controlling one, on exercise class participants' need satisfaction;

motivational regulations; and important behavioral, cognitive, and affective responses. Two "cardio-combo" exercise classes, incorporating a mix of step aerobics and kick boxing, were selected for the study. Each class was part of a 10-week Active Lifestyle Program run at a large U.K. university and was held at a similar time of day, in the same facility, and by the same (female) instructor. One class comprised the autonomy-supportive condition and included 25 females ranging in age from 18 to 53 years, the majority of whom were of white ethnicity (96%). The other class made up the realistically controlling condition and included 31 females who ranged in age from 18 to 38 years. Again, the majority of participants were white (74.2%), while 19.3% were Asian/Asian British and 6.5% were Chinese. It is important to note that the participants were university students and staff who had chosen to sign up for a given class, and thus they were not randomly assigned in a strict experimental sense to a specific condition (although they were not aware of the nature of the intervention).

Following the guidelines of Reeve (2002), we manipulated autonomy support in conjunction with structure and interpersonal involvement. To create the autonomy-supportive condition, the exercise instructor took the perspective of the exercise class participants into account, acknowledged their feelings, and provided them with pertinent information and opportunities for choice. In this condition, the use of pressure, demands, and extrinsic rewards was minimized (Black & Deci, 2000). These strategies are in line with the theoretical propositions of self-determination theory and previous experimental studies in other domains (Deci & Ryan, 1985; Deci, Eghrari, Patrick, & Leone, 1994). The provision of structure involved the exercise instructor's offering clear expectations, optimal challenge, and timely and informative feedback (Reeve, 2002). Interpersonal involvement was manipulated via encouraging the exercise instructor to dedicate psychological resources to the exercise class participants, such as time, energy, and affection (Reeve, 2002). Table 2.1 provides practical examples illustrating how autonomy support, structure, and involvement were manipulated.

The realistically controlling condition utilized a treatment style similar to that commonly observed in health care settings and patient–practitioner interactions (Sheldon, Williams, & Joiner, 2003). This condition was intended to replicate the style of teaching regularly observed in the exercise setting, whereby exercise instructors seek to maintain control over large groups of individuals in order to ensure that they are all exercising safely and effectively. Autonomy support, structure, and interpersonal involvement were kept to a minimum. Choices, rationale, and explanations were limited; instead, direct instruction guided the various activities. Goals were not set; minimal feedback was provided; and personal distance from participants prior to, during, and after the class was maintained by the instructor.

Attendance was logged weekly. At the start, at the halfway point, and at the end of the 10-week course, measures were taken of perceived autonomy support, structure, and interpersonal involvement (Markland & Tobin, 2004a);

Table 2.1   Examples of the Autonomy-Supportive Teaching Styles
Used in the Intervention

Dimension	Characteristic	Application
Autonomy support	Provide choice	Provide options about pace, frequency, and type of exercise when possible
	Be supportive and praise quality	Praise improvement in techniques and fitness
	Acknowledge and take into account exercisers' feelings and perspectives	Be open to complaints and respond to them in a positive manner
	Provide meaningful rationale	Explain why each activity is beneficial, what muscle groups are working, and what aspects of fitness will improve
Structure	Demonstrate good leadership	Discuss plans and set goals at the start of class
	Answer questions well and directly	As described
	Provide optimal challenge	Work at level that pushes participants maximally but accommodate for those less able; provide easy versus harder options
Interpersonal involvement	Dedicate resources to participants	Spend time chatting at the start of class, learn names, show affection and enjoyment
	Ensure close proximity	Mix with class—don't dominate at front

psychological need satisfaction (Markland & Tobin, 2004a); motivational regulations (Markland & Tobin, 2004b; Li, 1999); exercise behavior (Godin & Shephard, 1985); commitment to the class (Scanlan et al., 1993); behavioral intention to continue exercising in the class (Wilson & Rodgers, 2004); enjoyment (Markland & Tobin, 2004a); and positive and negative affect (Watson, Clark, & Tellegen, 1988).

Manipulation checks, completed by two independent observers who were unaware of the purpose of the study, the exercise instructor, and the exercise class participants, revealed that the autonomy-supportive condition was perceived as providing higher levels of autonomy support, structure, and involvement as compared to the realistically controlling condition. A significant difference in attendance emerged, with those exercisers in the autonomy-supportive condition attending more frequently than those in the realistically controlling condition. Further, multilevel modeling analysis showed that, compared to what occurred in the realistically controlling condition, competence and relatedness need satisfaction, class enjoyment, and positive affect experienced while exercising significantly increased over time in the autonomy-supportive condition. Both groups demonstrated a significant increase in introjected regulation over time and a significant decrease in amotivation, behavioral intention, and commitment; there were no group differences on these variables. For all other study variables, no significant rates of change were observed (table 2.2).

Table 2.2   Descriptive Statistics Demonstrating Changes in Self-Determination Theory Constructs Across the Intervention Conditions Over Time

Variable M	Range	AUTONOMY SUPPORTIVE			REALISTICALLY CONTROLLING		
		Wk 1	Wk 6	Wk 10	Wk 1	Wk 6	Wk 10
Autonomy	1-7	4.85	5.42	5.39	5.56	5.61	5.59
		(1.44)	(1.07)	(1.06)	(1.28)	(1.16)	(1.35)
Relatedness	1-7	4.60	5.38	5.72	5.11	5.44	5.40
		(1.51)	(0.79)	(0.84)	(1.27)	(1.07)	(1.28)
Competence	1-7	3.80	5.18	5.61	4.54	5.22	5.33
		(1.44)	(0.90)	(0.69)	(1.30)	(1.23)	(1.08)
Amotivation	0-4	0.37	0.27	0.13	0.45	0.13	0.03
		(0.57)	(0.45)	(0.17)	(0.70)	(0.29)	(0.08)
External regulation	0-4	0.68	0.70	0.71	0.50	0.35	0.58
		(0.85)	(0.90)	(0.83)	(0.66)	(0.39)	(0.98)
Introjected regulation	0-4	1.76	2.04	1.89	1.34	1.61	2.10
		(0.78)	(1.03)	(1.00)	(0.91)	(0.75)	(1.03)
Identified regulation	0-4	2.75	3.10	3.13	3.15	3.48	3.30
		(0.68)	(0.69)	(0.81)	(0.55)	(0.45)	(0.72)
Integrated regulation	0-4	2.21	2.37	2.38	2.49	2.48	2.87
		(0.66)	(1.15)	(1.25)	(0.86)	(0.63)	(0.92)
Intrinsic motivation	0-4	2.78	3.05	3.04	3.25	3.48	3.38
		(0.59)	(0.37)	(0.50)	(0.67)	(0.54)	(0.81)
Total exercise	–	45.92	51.93	57.92	43.32	44.31	58.88
		(22.96)	(28.96)	(30.23)	(18.91)	(16.90)	(20.07)
Behavioral intention	1-7	6.48	6.47	5.67	6.44	6.33	4.67
		(0.79)	(0.55)	(1.33)	(0.74)	(0.75)	(1.52)
Commitment	1-5	3.96	4.07	3.63	3.98	4.10	3.50
		(0.49)	(0.45)	(0.53)	(0.64)	(0.75)	(0.67)
Enjoyment	1-5	3.65	3.73	3.79	3.87	3.90	3.58
		(0.73)	(0.67)	(0.41)	(0.69)	(0.95)	(0.71)
Positive affect	1-5	3.48	3.59	3.72	3.79	3.88	3.67
		(0.50)	(0.55)	(0.51)	(0.59)	(0.76)	(0.57)
Negative affect	1-5	1.38	1.17	1.18	1.37	1.21	1.52
		(0.38)	(0.25)	(0.20)	(0.40)	(0.22)	(0.69)

Note. Statistics are mean scores with standard deviations in parentheses.

Although increases in need satisfaction and adaptive outcomes were observed as a consequence of the autonomy-supportive condition manipulations, no group differences emerged with regard to the most autonomous form of extrinsic motivation (i.e., identified regulation) as would be hypothesized by self-determination theory. The fact that the teaching style did not significantly affect identified regulation suggests that the participants in both classes acknowledged the importance of exercise. This is not surprising given that the participants voluntarily enrolled in the exercise classes sampled. With regard to the nonsignificant difference in intrinsic motivation, it is possible that this was seen because the type of class targeted (i.e., a structured aerobics class that incorporated step and kick boxing choreography) was not perceived as inherently pleasant. These findings suggest that interventions may be more successful when exercise behaviors are nonvoluntary or have yet to be internalized by the exerciser.

Summary and Avenues for Future Research

The research presented in this chapter adds to a growing body of literature supporting the utility of the propositions of self-determination theory in predicting behavioral investment and the quality of the exercise experience. Drawing from this work, a number of potential avenues for future exercise-focused research, grounded in self-determination theory, appear worthy of consideration.

The results of the field experiment described earlier provided preliminary support for interventions based on self-determination theory. A next step in validating the effectiveness of self-determination theory-based interventions would be to conduct larger randomized controlled trials of a patient–practitioner exercise consultation. Such trials may benefit from targeting low-income groups, in which physical activity participation rates are particularly problematic (Department of Culture, Media and Sport, 2004), or individuals who do not value exercise (i.e., have low levels of identified regulation).

Researchers may also attempt to further explore the influence of relatedness need satisfaction on intrinsic motivation and the autonomous regulation of exercise behavior. While exercise-focused studies have addressed the importance of relatedness at a proximal level, that is, within the exercise domain specifically, Ryan and Deci (2000b) also highlight the importance of a secure relational base at a more distal level. Future studies should consider the role of relatedness need satisfaction across general motivational contexts including physical activity.

Researchers may also benefit from integrating self-determination theory's propositions and constructs with other theoretical perspectives in an attempt to better understand physical activity engagement and responses to the exercise experience. For example, Skinner (2002) suggests that the basic psychological needs are central in shaping how we cope with stress. Given the increasing number of individuals that are now classified as obese or overweight (National

Audit Office, 2001), and the associations between obesity and stress (Williams et al., 1996), Skinner's propositions may have significant implications for those trying to deliver behavioral interventions for persons who are obese. Essentially, Skinner's work implies that through the design of interventions that facilitate psychological need satisfaction, obese individuals will appraise weight loss-related stressors more adaptively. As a result, they will utilize more effective coping mechanisms. The use of these adaptive coping strategies is expected to be associated with more advantageous outcomes such as investment in, and more positive perceptions and experiences of, physical activity.

Implications for Exercise Practitioners

Although further intervention studies are needed, the findings of the research presented in the current chapter have implications for behavioral interventions and health promotion programs aiming to increase physical activity. For example, research findings suggest that to optimize the exercise experience and facilitate exercise adherence, health and exercise professionals should endeavor to ensure that the basic psychological needs of exercise participants are met. Studies have indicated that competence need satisfaction is especially important to the prediction of autonomous regulation and exercise behavior. Showing novice exercisers that individuals of a similar ability level have previously managed to master exercise-related tasks and achieve desired outcomes, designing well-structured exercise programs that allow for gradual and continual improvement, setting appropriate goals, and providing positive feedback are all strategies that may satisfy the need to feel competent in the exercise domain.

To achieve satisfaction of all three basic needs and the facilitation of autonomous forms of motivation, exercise programs and consultations should be delivered in an autonomy-supportive manner. Three contextual factors are central to an autonomy-supportive leadership style, namely the provision of choice, a meaningful rationale, and acknowledgment of the feelings and perspectives of others (Deci et al., 1994). Thus, the available literature suggests that it would appear beneficial for health and exercise professionals to provide participants with choices and options about the type and content of their exercise programs. For example, the health professional or exercise instructor could discuss with the individual what types of exercise best fit with his or her current preferences and commitments. Moreover, the health professional or exercise instructor may provide a detailed description of the benefits associated with a particular form of exercise, as well as its relevance to the needs of the individual. The health professional or exercise instructor should also acknowledge any negative feelings that an individual or group has about exercise or encounters during the exercise experience, provide reassurance, and take these concerns into consideration when designing and delivering the exercise program.

On the basis of the tenets of self-determination theory and research adopting this theory, exercise specialists should also provide structure whereby expectations and goals are made clear to the individual and praise is given for effort and improvement. Structure needs to be delivered in an autonomy-supportive manner (Reeve, 2004). Instructors may achieve this by involving the exerciser in the goal-setting process and providing a rationale for their specific expectations about the individual's progress and improvement.

It is also imperative to ensure that health professionals or exercise instructors are perceived as supportive and as investing personal resources in exercisers. While maintaining their professionalism, exercise instructors should be warm and open, showing exercisers that they are dedicated to and care about their progress and exercise experience.

Practical Recommendations for Exercise Professionals

• Practitioners like physical education teachers and those prescribing exercise in primary care are encouraged not to pressure exercisers into engaging in a specific type of activity and not to use controlling language including words like "should" and "must." When instructing exercisers, health professionals are advised to involve them in the decision-making process and allow them to choose which forms of exercise would best suit their personal needs and preferences. For example, a person may be given a definition of the general type of health-related activity required (e.g., "sustained activity of 20 minutes or more using large muscle groups") and then encouraged to choose an activity that fits with this requirement.

• When choice cannot be provided because of limited facilities, constraints on the type of activity, or safety considerations, for example, it is suggested that practitioners offer a rationale for participating in the exercise. Even when choices are available, it is important to explain to the individual why the activity or activities offered will be beneficial and to explain how the activity will bring about desired changes (e.g., increased fitness). For example, it may be important to highlight the immediate personal benefits of exercise (e.g., "If you exercise for 20 minutes at a time, three times a week for one month, you are likely to reach your goal of losing 2 kilograms [4 pounds], which is important to you").

• Practitioners are advised to be responsive to the thoughts and feelings of exercisers at all times and to ask regularly for their comments and feedback. For example, a personal trainer might ask a client, "What did you like and dislike about this activity? What would you like to change about the exercise program?" Practitioners need to recognize and address any issues, concerns, or negative feelings the individual has about the exercise experience without compromising goals.

• It is suggested that practitioners make every effort to ensure that people develop a sense of competence and that activities are tailored to meet individuals' current experience and ability levels. Realistic and achievable goals need to be set and effort- and persistence-based feedback provided. For example, an exercise specialist who is training personal trainers might encourage them to inquire about a client's background and ask for the client's help in determining goals that are suitable for his or her level of experience. These goals would be personally relevant to the client and therefore likely to be engaged in with a sense of autonomy.

• It is also important for exercisers to perceive that the professional is personally interested in the exercise program and cares about each exerciser's improvement and development. Professionals are encouraged to facilitate interaction between the individual and other exercisers or members of an exercise group. For example, an exercise advisor might tell clients that they are more likely to attain their goals if they identify someone of like ability and experience with whom to exercise and agree on times and places to exercise. This will enhance their sense of relatedness and autonomy because they have made the choice to commit to a mutually beneficial routine.

The Trans-Contextual Model of Motivation

Martin S. Hagger, PhD
University of Nottingham

Nikos L.D. Chatzisarantis, PhD
University of Plymouth

Considerable evidence suggests that the health problems associated with low levels of physical activity have their origins in youth. Given this, along with epidemiological research that has identified elevated levels of the risk factors of cardiovascular disease, a rising incidence of obesity, and low levels of regular, vigorous physical activity of a sustained nature among young people in Western nations, it is not surprising that the promotion of physical activity in youth and adolescents is receiving elevated priority among governments, health educators, and researchers interested in stemming the tide of potential health risks presented by physical inactivity. Health psychologists, exercise promoters, education professionals involved in curriculum development, and researchers interested in the motivational factors that underpin behavior have suggested that the use of existing networks to deliver health-related physical activity messages to young people is a key strategy to affect behavior change in favor of increasing youth physical activity levels.

Prominent among these networks is physical education, and researchers have sought to utilize the "captive audience" in physical education settings to convey messages about increasing physical activity levels to young people. However, while research has addressed the social cognitive antecedents that underpin young people's motivation in physical education and the factors that influence such motivation, few studies have sought to establish whether these antecedents, and interventions based on these antecedents, will have an influence on the motivational factors that underpin physical activity and actual physical activity behavior among young people outside of school in their

Correspondence concerning this article should be addressed to Martin S. Hagger, School of Psychology, University of Nottingham, University Park, Nottingham, NG7 2RD, United Kingdom. E-mail: martin.hagger@nottingham.ac.uk free "leisure" time. This is clearly paramount to achieving the health aims of interventions, as the activities that young people perform in physical education lessons are too brief and infrequent to provide lasting health benefits, and the long-term goal of health promoters is to permit young people to regulate their own physical activity behavior so that omnipresent health messages are not required to maintain that behavior.

This chapter outlines a series of studies we have conducted using a multi-theory model of motivation that attempts to address the question whether support for autonomous forms of motivation and motivational orientations toward physical activities presented in a physical education context can be transferred into autonomous motivational orientations, intentions, and actual physical activity behavior in a leisure-time context among young people. The proposed model, known as the *trans-contextual model*, incorporates three prominent theories of motivation to provide a comprehensive framework that outlines the transfer of motivation from an educational context to a leisure-time context. These theories are Deci and Ryan's (1985, 2000; Ryan & Deci, this volume) self-determination theory, Ajzen's (1985, 1991) theory of planned behavior, and Vallerand's (1997) hierarchical model of intrinsic and extrinsic motivation. Each theory lends an integral element to the model, which is both comprehensive in outlining the key mechanisms that underlie the transfer of motivation across contexts and parsimonious in its aim to minimize redundancy in the theoretical constructs from the models.

The model proposes a motivational sequence that begins with perceived autonomy support; such perceptions have shown concurrent validity with autonomy supportive behaviors that have been shown to foster autonomous or self-determined forms of motivation (Reeve & Jang, 2006). Perceived autonomy support is depicted as the strongest influence on autonomous forms of motivation in a physical education context, which in turn influence autonomous motivation toward physical activity in a leisure-time context (Hagger, Chatzisarantis, Barkoukis, Wang, & Baranowski, 2005; Hagger, Chatzisarantis, Culverhouse, & Biddle, 2003; Hagger et al., 2006). These motives are proposed to influence the proximal decision-making constructs from the theory of planned behavior that precede intentional behavior, intentions toward future physical activity engagement, and actual physical activity behavior. We first present the theoretical background to each component theory, then outline the conceptual arguments behind the integration of the three theoretical approaches, and next report four empirical studies that were aimed at testing the motivational sequence proposed by the model.

The Trans-Contextual Model: Component Theories

Integration of the component theories of the trans-contextual model is based on the hypothesis that they provide complementary explanations of the network of motivational processes involved in the transfer of motivation across contexts leading to intentional behavior. Means to support self-determined or autonomous forms of motivation and young people's autonomous motivational orientations form the origin of motivation and the trans-contextual transfer of motives into intentional behavior. The theory of planned behavior maps the process by which motivational constructs from self-determination theory are translated into action. The hierarchical model, on the other hand, provides a framework that describes the top-down links between the generalized, context-tied self-determination theory constructs such as autonomous motivation and the specific, situational constructs like intentions from the theory of planned behavior. In the following we present the hypotheses of the three theories before outlining three bases for their integration.

- *Self-determination theory.* Self-determination theory and the self-determination continuum are central to the trans-contextual model and provide a basis for the development and influence of contextual-level autonomous forms of motivation that affect intentional behavior across contexts (Ryan & Connell, 1989; Ryan & Deci, this volume). Research in self-determination theory has shown that persistence in behavior is associated with autonomous forms of motivation (Chatzisarantis & Biddle, 1998; Hagger, Chatzisarantis, & Biddle, 2002a; Williams, 2002; Williams, Gagné, Ryan, & Deci, 2002); and social contexts that support autonomous motivation, such as the behaviors of significant others (e.g., physical education teachers), promote autonomous motivation and behavioral persistence in a number of life contexts (Gagné, 2003; Williams, Freedman, & Deci, 1998; Williams, Saizow, Ross, & Deci, 1997), particularly education (Black & Deci, 2000; Deci, Vallerand, Pelletier, & Ryan, 1991; Reeve, 2002; Vansteenkiste, Simons, Lens, & Sheldon, 2004).

- *The theory of planned behavior.* The purpose of the theory of planned behavior is to identify and explain the proximal interpersonal determinants of specific, consciously enacted behaviors. Central to the theory is the premise that a person's intention or stated plan is the most proximal predictor of behavior. Intention is influenced by three sets of belief-based social cognitive constructs, namely attitudes, subjective norm, and perceived behavioral control. Attitudes are a person's beliefs that the target behavior will result in certain desirable outcomes and are conceptually similar to the outcome expectancies cited by Bandura (1997). Subjective norms reflect a person's beliefs that significant others desire him or her to perform the target behavior. Perceived behavioral control represents a person's beliefs that he or she has the capacities, faculties, abilities, and resources to engage in the target behavior, and has been overtly compared with Bandura's (1997) self-efficacy construct (Ajzen, 1991). Intention is hypothesized to mediate the effects of these belief-based constructs on actual behavior. The hypothesized relationships among the theory of planned behavior constructs have been supported in meta-analytic studies across a variety of behaviors (e.g., Armitage & Conner, 2001; Sheeran & Orbell, 1998; Sheeran & Taylor, 1999), including physical activity (Hagger, Chatzisarantis, & Biddle, 2002b).

• *The hierarchical model of motivation.* Vallerand (1997) deepened and extended hypotheses from self-determination theory regarding the relative level of generality of the motivational constructs, their antecedents, and their impact on outcomes. His hierarchical model of intrinsic and extrinsic motivation hypothesized that the forms of motivation from self-determination theory could be viewed as operating at three levels of generality: global, contextual, and specific. Motivation at the global level represents generalized tendencies to be autonomously motivated and is expected to have an effect on behavioral engagement across a number of contexts. Contextual-level motivation reflects autonomous motivation to participate in a variety of behaviors in a given context. Contexts refer to behavioral categories encompassing a number of given behaviors or actions, such as physical education or leisure-time physical activity. At the situational level, motivation is conceptualized as motives to engage in specific bouts of a given behavior, and as such, motivation at this level cannot be transferred across behaviors or contexts. In Vallerand's model, motivation is proposed to flow top-down, from the global to situational levels, and there is little evidence to support the presence of bottom-up effects (Guay, Boggiano, & Vallerand, 2001). Finally, a key aspect of the model is that motivation at each level affects cognitive, emotional, and behavioral outcomes specific to that level (Vallerand, 1997).

The Trans-Contextual Model: Three Premises for Theoretical Integration

The integration of these three theories in the trans-contextual model is based on the hypothesis that self-determination theory and the theory of planned behavior can offer complementary explanations of motivated behavior, with the hierarchical model acting as a unifying framework that provides a basis for the model relationships. We have proposed (e.g., Hagger et al., 2005; Hagger et al., 2003; Hagger et al., 2006) three premises for the integration of these theories:

1. When forming the social cognitive judgments in the theory of planned behavior, individuals draw from their motivational orientations as outlined by self-determination theory.

2. The context-level motivational orientations from self-determination theory affect judgments regarding future behavioral engagement from the theory of planned behavior because such judgments reflect situational-level social cognitive (e.g., attitudes, perceived behavioral control) and motivational constructs (e.g., intention).

3. At the empirical level, measures of the motivational orientations from self-determination theory are designed to reflect an individual's *current* perceived motivational status, while the theory of planned behavior

constructs are measured as expectancies regarding *future* behavioral engagement.

Next we briefly outline each premise and present the hypotheses of the trans-contextual model.

With respect to the first premise, Deci and Ryan (2000) suggest that self-determination theory constructs, reflected by the perceived locus of causality, should provide a basis for the formation of social cognitive judgments toward specific behaviors. This is based on the proposition that such motivational orientations need to be channeled into intentions in order for the appropriate need-satisfying behavior to be enacted (Elliott, McGregor, & Thrash, 2002). Autonomous motivation should therefore act as the impetus in the formation of judgments and expectations regarding future behavioral engagement. Similarly, Ajzen (1991) suggested that the formation of the social cognitive constructs from the theory of planned behavior draws from dispositional constructs like personality as well as beliefs regarding the behavior. Therefore, generalized autonomous motives should act as an impetus when people form judgments and expectations regarding future behavior. Ajzen therefore predicted that the theory of planned behavior constructs would mediate the effects of external variables on intentions and behavior, a hypothesis that has been verified on numerous occasions (Conner & Abraham, 2001; Hagger, Chatzisarantis, & Harris, 2006; Rhodes, Courneya, & Jones, 2002). Thus it is expected, in a model that integrates these theories, that the theory of planned behavior constructs of attitudes, subjective norm, and perceived behavioral control will mediate the effects of motivational orientations from self-determination theory on intentions and behavior, as seen in previous research (Chatzisarantis, Hagger, Biddle, & Karageorghis, 2002; Hagger, Chatzisarantis, & Biddle, 2002a). This is illustrated on the right-hand side of figure 3.1 in the solid lines emanating from autonomous motivation in leisure time to attitudes, subjective norms, and perceived behavioral control. The broken lines from this construct to intention and behavior represent the direct, unmediated effect, which should, according to the theory, be zero.

The second premise for integration states that the motivational constructs from the perceived locus of causality reflect context-level motivational orientations while the theory of planned behavior constructs are located at the situational level. This distinction is based on hypotheses from Vallerand's (1997) hierarchical model of motivation. The perceived locus of causality constructs reflect motivation in terms of a given context, such as physical education or leisure-time physical activity. The theory of planned behavior constructs, on the other hand, make reference to a specific bout of behavior, defined in terms of the specific action itself, the context in which the action will be performed, the target of the action, and the time frame in which the action will be performed. Such constraints or *boundary conditions* (Chatzisarantis & Biddle, 1998) make these social cognitive variables more akin to the situational

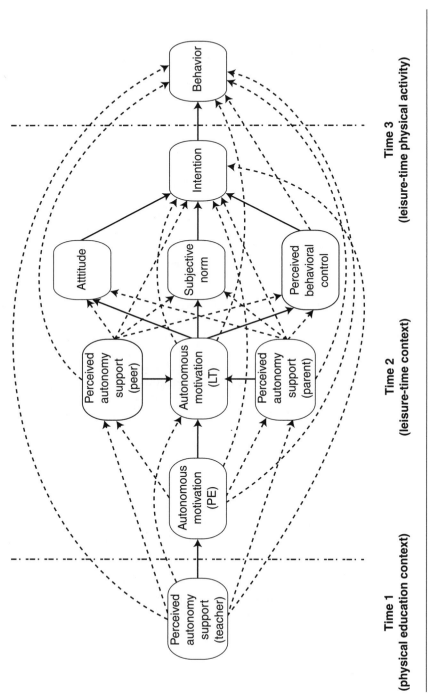

Time 1
(physical education context)

Time 2
(leisure-time context)

Time 3
(leisure-time physical activity)

Figure 3.1 The trans-contextual model.

The original version of the model presented by Hagger and colleagues (2003) did not include the influences of perceived autonomy support from peers and parents, and the model depicted here represents the augmented model as described later (Hagger et al., 2006). Broken lines indicate paths that were tested empirically in the three-wave prospective studies of the trans-contextual model, but hypothesized to be zero.

level in Vallerand's model. Further, since Vallerand specifies that the effects of motivational constructs flow from a higher level of generality (e.g., contextual level) to a lower level of generality (e.g., situational level), it is expected that the motivational orientations will influence the theory of planned behavior in that direction. Finally, and most importantly for the trans-contextual model, Vallerand hypothesized a cross-contextual interplay between motivation at the contextual level, suggesting that motives in one context can affect motivation in others. This provides a basis for the transfer of autonomous motivation across contexts from physical education to leisure time, a central hypothesis in the trans-contextual model. This is depicted on the left-hand side of Figure 3.1 by the broken lines from autonomous motives in a physical education context to autonomous motives in a leisure-time context.

The third and final premise for the integration of the constructs makes reference to the methods of measurement of the constructs from self-determination theory and the theory of planned behavior. Specifically, motivational orientations from self-determination theory such as the perceived locus of causality are typically measured as current internal motivational states of the individual with respect to the context in question. Such perceptions are supposed to reflect the person's general tendency to act in accordance with those perceptions in any behavior relevant to that context. However, measures of the theory of planned behavior constructs are conceptualized in terms of future behavioral engagement. Such judgments do not reflect an individual's current internal state per se, but his or her level of attitude, subjective norm, perceived behavioral control, and intention toward engaging in the target behavior at some future point in time given the current available information regarding the behavior. Therefore these constructs differ in terms of their focus and can therefore be presumed to exhibit discriminant validity, but may offer complementary explanations of the processes that lead to intentional behavior.

Perceived Autonomy Support

Central to the trans-contextual model are the effect of perceived autonomy support on autonomous motivation in a physical education context and the effect of perceived autonomy in physical education on autonomous motivation in a leisure-time physical activity context via the mediation of autonomous motivation in physical education. Research has shown that perceived autonomy support is fostered through the provision of autonomy support by significant others in motivational contexts (Reeve, 2002; Reeve, Bolt, & Cai, 1999). In addition, studies in a number of contexts have shown that perceived autonomy support is an influential variable in the prediction of autonomous forms of motivation, and that these forms of motivation influence behavioral engagement and persistence (e.g., Williams, Frankel, Campbell, & Deci, 2000; Williams, Freedman, & Deci, 1998; Williams, Rodin, Ryan, Grolnick, & Deci, 1998). It is important to note that motivational orientations are hypothesized to mediate the effect of perceived autonomy support on behavioral outcomes, suggesting that motivational orientation is necessary to translate perceptions regarding autonomy support from significant others into behavior.

The trans-contextual model takes this premise a step further and proposes that perceived autonomy support in an educational context will affect motivation and intentional behavior in a related but separate context via the mediation of motivation in the educational context. Specifically, the model hypothesizes that school pupils' perceived autonomy support from physical education teachers affects autonomous motivation in physical education, but also autonomous motivation in a leisure-time context via the mediation of autonomous motivation in physical education. Furthermore, the model predicts that perceived autonomy support will have a significant total effect on intention to participate in leisure-time physical activity and actual physical activity behavior via the mediation of the proposed motivational sequence. These processes are shown on the far left side of Figure 3.1 by the solid lines emanating from perceived autonomy support in physical education to autonomous motivation in physical education, and by the broken line from perceived autonomy support in physical education to autonomous motivation in leisure time. The total effect is illustrated by the broken line from perceived autonomy support in physical education directly to intention and behavior.

Testing the Trans-Contextual Model

In this section we present a series of studies that have provided empirical tests of the trans-contextual model. We first report on an initial three-wave prospective study that supports the hypotheses of the model followed by a study of identical design supporting the effects of the model across cultures. A third study extends the model to include the influences of sources of autonomy support other than physical education teachers, namely, peers and parents. This model is also tested across cultural groups. This is followed up by an experimental test of the model in the field, which aims to change autonomy support and examine its effects across physical education and leisure-time contexts. Finally, we present a meta-analytic cumulation of the effects of the trans-contextual model across these studies.

A Three-Wave Prospective Study

We provided an initial test of the hypothesized relationships among the trans-contextual model constructs using a prospective, three-wave design (Hagger et al., 2003). The model was tested in a representative sample of 295 British secondary school pupils aged 12 to 14 years. On the first data collection occasion, participants completed a measure of perceived autonomy support from physical education teachers, derived from Deci and Ryan's (1987) perceived autonomy support scale, and a measure of autonomous motivation in a physical education context, which comprised a modified version of Ryan and Connell's

(1989) perceived locus of causality questionnaire. One week later the same participants completed Mullan, Markland, and Ingledew's (1997) Behavioural Regulation in Exercise Questionnaire, a measure of autonomous motivation in a leisure-time physical activity context, and measures of attitudes, subjective norms, perceived behavioral control, and intentions from the theory of planned behavior (Ajzen, 1985, 2003; Ajzen & Driver, 1991) with respect to future participation in leisure-time physical activity. The one-week lag between these measures was to allay the potentially confounding effects of common-method variance that may arise from the use of similar measures of autonomous motivation in two different contexts. At a final point of data collection five weeks later, participants completed a self-report measure of physical activity (Godin & Shephard, 1985).

After initial confirmation of the discriminant validity of the attitude and intention constructs with the constructs from the perceived locus of causality, results of a path analysis representing the motivational sequence showed that perceived autonomy support in a physical education context influenced autonomous forms of motivation in physical education (intrinsic motivation and identified regulation), consistent with previous research in the area (Ntoumanis, 2005; Standage, Duda, & Ntoumanis, 2003). Autonomous forms of motivation in physical education were also found to affect autonomous motivation in a leisure-time context. This trans-contextual transfer of motivation is based on the third premise for theoretical integration from Vallerand's (1997) hierarchical model indicating that such effects occur at the contextual level. Autonomous forms of motivation in leisure time were also found to influence intention and behavior via the mediation of the proximal determinants of intentions, namely attitudes, subjective norms, and perceived behavioral control. These effects were based on the three premises outlined previously and previous empirical support for the integration of these theories (Chatzisarantis et al., 2002; Hagger, Chatzisarantis, & Biddle, 2002a; Wilson & Rodgers, 2004). Overall, the significant correlation between perceived autonomy support in physical education and leisure-time physical activity behavior was accounted for by the proposed motivational sequence, supporting the premise that the motivational constructs from the model were necessary to understand the mechanisms behind the influence of perceived autonomy support in physical education on leisure-time physical activity behavior.

Cross-Cultural Invariance

We subsequently tested whether the hypothesized relationships among the constructs in the trans-contextual model were replicable and consistent among young people from different cultures (Hagger et al., 2005). It was anticipated that the proposed motivational sequence in the trans-contextual model would be invariant (i.e., the pattern and size of the effects would be equal) across samples from different cultures because research has supported the universal nature of the effects of self-determined motivation on emotional and behavioral outcomes. For example, studies in occupational psychology have shown that intrinsic motivation predicts adaptive outcomes among people from eastern European nations that are traditionally more collectivistic in cultural orientation than western European and North American nations (Chirkov, Ryan, Kim, & Kaplan, 2003; Deci et al., 2001). Furthermore, research in educational contexts has shown consistent effects of self-determined motivation on subjective well-being (Chirkov & Ryan, 2001), adaptive coping in the classroom (Hayamizu, 1997), and learning outcomes (Yamauchi & Tanaka, 1998) in cultures that tend to endorse more collectivistic values (e.g., Japan, Russia) compared with cultures that tend to be more individualistic (e.g., Great Britain, United States; Triandis, 1989).

On the basis of this premise, we conducted a test of the trans-contextual model in samples of school pupils aged 12 to 16 years from Britain (N = 295), Greece (N = 93), Poland (N = 103), and Singapore (N = 133). The study design was identical to that adopted in the previous test of the model (Hagger et al., 2003). Initial multisample confirmatory factor analyses suggested that the attitude, perceived behavioral control, and intention constructs achieved discriminant validity with the perceived locus of causality constructs and were also invariant at the measurement level across samples. The path analytic strategy adopted in the previous study was again used to test the efficacy of the proposed model across cultures. The only exception was that constructs from perceived locus of causality were collapsed to form a single index of autonomous motivation, known as the self-determination index or the relative autonomy index (see Pelletier & Sarrazin, this volume), to maximize parsimony and minimize model parameterization. Results from path analyses of the trans-contextual model supported the general pattern of relationships among the model constructs across samples, with many of the key relationships invariant. Perceived autonomy support in a physical education context affected autonomous motivation in a leisure-time context in all samples, the Polish sample excepted. However, the mediation of the relationships between perceived autonomy support and autonomous motives in leisure time by autonomous motivation in physical education was not consistent across samples. Autonomous motivation in a leisure-time context had consistent effects on physical activity intentions and behavior via the mediation of attitudes and perceived behavioral control across samples, although some of the effect sizes were not invariant across samples. These results provide some support for the cross-cultural invariance of the proposed motivational sequence of the trans-contextual model in several cultures with differing levels of collectivist and individualist orientations.

The Influence of Alternative Sources of Perceived Autonomy Support

It must be noted that the tests of the trans-contextual model conducted by Hagger and colleagues (2005, 2003) involved no attempt to control for the effects of autonomy support from significant others apart from physical education teachers. This is an important omission, as research in self-determination theory has highlighted that autonomy support from significant others like friends or peers and parents has pervasive effects on autonomous motivation and behavioral engagement in educational contexts (Deci, Driver, Hotchkiss, Robbins, & Wilson, 1993; Deci, Schwartz, Sheinman, & Ryan, 1981). One problem this raises is whether the effect of perceived autonomy support from such significant others is likely to account for the majority of the variance in autonomous motivation toward leisure-time physical activity relative to the perceived autonomy support from physical education teachers. This may be the case, since the perceived autonomy support offered by these significant others is substantially closer in proximity, as it occurs in a leisure-time context, compared to the autonomy support perceived to be provided by teachers, which occurs in a relatively more distal context.

Acknowledging this potential limitation, we set ourselves the task of testing a more elaborate model that controlled for effects of perceived autonomy support from these other sources (Hagger et al., 2006). It was expected that while perceived autonomy support for physical activity from peers and parents in a leisure-time context would have significant effects on autonomous motivation in a leisure-time context, the effect of perceived autonomy support from physical education teachers would not be completely attenuated when such sources were included. It was therefore expected that perceived autonomy support from physical education teachers would have a unique effect on autonomous motivation in leisure time, albeit via the mediation of autonomous motivation in physical education. It was anticipated that such evidence would not only provide a more robust test of the hypotheses of the trans-contextual model, but also provide additional evidence to support the promotion of physical activity to pupils in physical education lessons in order to foster their continued participation in physical activity outside of school.

We therefore conducted a test of an augmented trans-contextual model using the same three-wave prospective design in three samples of schoolchildren, aged 12 to 16 years, from different cultural groups: Great Britain (N = 210), Estonia (N = 268), and Hungary (N = 235). The methods and measures adopted in the previous studies were followed, with the exception that two further measures were provided for the pupils in the second wave of data collection. These measures were modifications of the perceived autonomy support scale (Deci & Ryan, 1987) to reflect peer and parental influences (see Hagger et al., in press). Preliminary analyses supported the discriminant validity of the perceived autonomy support constructs from the three sources: physical education teachers, peers, and parents. Path analyses revealed that while perceived autonomy support from peers and parents had significant effects on autonomous motivation in a leisure-time physical activity context, there were still significant indirect effects of perceived autonomy support from physical education teachers on autonomous motivation in leisure time in all three samples. Autonomous motivation in physical education mediated the effect of perceived autonomy support from physical education teachers on autonomous motivation in leisure time, as expected. The remaining hypotheses from the trans-contextual model were also supported. This evidence provided additional support for the trans-contextual model by eliminating the potential confounding effects of perceived autonomy support from other sources. It supported the grand purpose of the model of targeting physical education as a means to promote leisure-time physical activity.

Experimental Manipulation of Autonomy Support

While there appears to be substantial support for the trans-contextual model in the previously cited studies, the evidence is derived from data that are correlational, and therefore true causal effects cannot be inferred. Furthermore, the focus of the studies was on perceived autonomy support rather than *actual* autonomy support. If the true value of autonomy-supportive behaviors displayed by teachers for autonomous motivation toward physical activity in a leisure-time context is to be gleaned, evidence should be presented in the form of the effects of actual autonomy support. We therefore conducted an experimental study, in which we instructed physical education teachers to adopt autonomy-supportive behaviors in accordance with the recommendations of proponents of self-determination theory (Reeve, 2002; Reeve, Bolt, & Cai, 1999) and the trans-contextual model (Hagger et al., 2005, 2003), in order to observe the effects of such a manipulation on perceived autonomy support, autonomous motivation, intentions to engage in physical activity, and actual physical activity behavior in a leisure-time context. These were compared with the effects of an additional experimental condition in which teachers adopted teaching behaviors based on participants' salient beliefs about leisure-time physical activity, derived from studies using the theory of planned behavior (Hagger, Chatzisarantis, & Biddle, 2001), and a control condition that merely provided information about physical activity in a leisure-time context. Teachers were asked to strictly follow these behaviors for a week. Measures of the trans-contextual model constructs were administered before the teaching sessions and one week later, after the intervention. Five weeks after the beginning of the experiment, self-reported physical activity behavior was measured.

Results suggested that participants in the trans-contextual model condition had significantly higher levels of autonomous motivation, perceived autonomy support, attitudes, and intentions compared with those in the control condition. However, participants in the theory of planned behavior condition also had significantly higher levels of attitudes and intentions, on a par with those of the trans-contextual model experimental group. We concluded that the effects of the two types of manipulation accessed different mechanisms in the promotion of intentional physical activity behavior. The trans-contextual model manipulation had effects on the distal motivational constructs as well as the proximal constructs, providing support for the effects of autonomous motivation on theory of planned behavior constructs like attitudes. The theory of planned behavior constructs, on the other hand, had pervasive effects on attitudes and intentions, in keeping with Ajzen's (1985, 1991) theory and previous meta-analyses on theory of planned behavior interventions (Hardeman et al., 2002). This suggests that those involved with promoting physical activity in a physical education context may look to "hybrid" interventions that incorporate multiple treatments from different theoretical models of motivation to promote physical activity behavior, a notion that has recently become popular in research on intentional behavior (Koestner, Lekes, Powers, & Chicoine, 2002; Prestwich, Lawton, & Conner, 2003).

A Meta-Analysis

As previously reported, we have conducted numerous tests of the hypothesized relationships among the trans-contextual model variables in some eight independent samples, and the results suggest that the general pattern of the relationships holds across samples. However, we have also noted some variations in the size of the effects across samples. In the cross-cultural studies this has been attributed to differences in cultural background of the samples from different national groups. However, there may also be a substantial contribution to this variation from methodological artifacts. While we have taken care to measure the constructs with some degree of precision in each study, many of the samples used were convenience samples that were relatively small. (It is important to note that when sample sizes were very small [i.e., fewer than 100 participants; Hagger et al., 2005], we conducted bootstrap resampling procedures [Efron, 1982] with the path analyses testing the trans-contextual model. This provides stronger evidence for the robustness of the model through repeated tests of the hypothesized model in many simulated samples equal in size to the actual sample [Hagger et al., 2005]). Meta-analysis is a useful statistical method to establish whether the set of results is consistent across studies while simultaneously eliminating the potential bias due to sample size (Hedges & Olkin, 1985; Hunter & Schmidt, 1990; Rosenthal & Rubin, 1982). Meta-analysis is a quantitative research synthesis technique that aims to "objectively assimilate and quantify the size of effects across a number of independent empirical studies while simultaneously eliminating inherent biases in the research" (Hagger et al., 2006, p. 103). In a meta-analysis, effect sizes (e.g., zero-order correlations) between constructs of interest in a study are weighted for their sample size, such that studies with larger, ostensibly more representative samples are given greater weight and then averaged across studies. In addition, measures of spread of the effect size across the studies, usually in the form of corrected standard deviations, are given and are used to calculate *credibility intervals*. These enable the researcher to test the hypothesis that the effect is significantly different from zero and to determine whether the majority of the variation in the statistic across the studies is due to the artifact of sampling error or other extraneous variables or *moderators*.

We therefore conducted a meta-analysis of the effect sizes of our tests of the hypothesized relationships from the trans-contextual model (k = 8). While this is a relatively small sample of studies, Hunter and Schmidt (1990) suggest that meta-analysis should not be confined only to cumulating studies across an entire body of literature after an exhaustive literature search, but is also "valid for 'convenience' samples of studies that just happen to lie at hand" (p. 83). However, since the sample of studies was small, we used the random effects meta-analysis model proposed by Hunter and Schmidt, as this has been shown to provide more accurate estimates of true effect sizes in simulation studies (Field, 2001, 2003). The corrected correlations for the trans-contextual model constructs from the current set of studies are given in table 3.1. The most important relationships in the model were all significant, particularly those between perceived autonomy support, autonomous motivation in both contexts, attitudes, perceived behavioral control, intentions, and physical activity behavior. Furthermore, many correlations (correlations between perceived autonomy support and autonomous motivation in both contexts, attitudes, perceived behavioral control, intention, and behavior; correlations between autonomous motivation in both contexts and attitude; and the correlation between autonomous motivation in leisure time and intentions) represented a homogeneous case; that is, sampling error accounted for the majority of the variance in these effect sizes across this sample of studies.

Using these correlations as input for a path analytic model that tested the multivariate relationships within the trans-contextual model (see figure 3.1) in a simultaneous process resulted in a model that was not significantly different from the independence model ($\beta^2 = 11.70$, $p = .02$) and therefore fit the data well. Beta coefficients from the meta-analytic path analysis are provided in table 3.2. The hypotheses of the trans-contextual model were supported in the model. Perceived autonomy support in a physical education context predicted autonomous motivation in leisure time, but the total effect ($\beta = .26$, $p < .01$) was partially mediated by autonomous motives in physical education (indirect effect, $\beta = .13$, $p < .01$) as hypothesized. Autonomous motivation influenced intentions, but the total effect ($\beta = .40$, $p < .01$) was decomposed into indirect effects via the mediation of attitudes ($\beta = .15$, $p < .01$) and perceived behavioral control ($\beta = .08$, $p < .01$) and direct effects ($\beta = .17$, $p < .01$). Finally, intentions predicted behavior ($\beta = .50$, $p < .01$); and the total effects of perceived autonomy support ($\beta = .24$, $p < .01$) and autonomous motivation in leisure time ($\beta = .28$, $p < .01$) on behavior were directed through the motivational sequence proposed by the model, as evidenced by the very small direct effects of these constructs on behavior (perceived autonomy support, $\beta = .11$, $p < .01$; autonomous motivation in leisure time, $\beta = .08$, $p < .01$). Overall, the model accounted for 42.7% and 33.3% of the variance in leisure-time physical activity intentions and behavior, respectively. In sum, the results of this multivariate analysis, based on the synthesis of results across eight studies, not only support the pattern of the proposed trans-contextual model but also corroborate the hypothesized mechanisms involved, such as the mediational relationships in the hypothesized

Table 3.1 Correlations Among the Trans-Contextual Model Components Derived From Meta-Analysis (k = 8)

Variable	1	2	3	4	5	6	7	8
1. Perceived autonomy support (PE)	—							
2. Autonomous motivation (PE)	.35*†	—						
3. Autonomous motivation (LT)	.26*†	.41*	—					
4. Attitudes	.26*	.32*†	.48*†	—				
5. Subjective norm	.16*†	.09	.16	.21	—			
6. Perceived behavioral control	.12*†	.08	.34*	.43*	.30*	—		
7. Intention	.22*†	.28*	.46*†	.58*	.23*	.46*	—	
8. Physical activity behavior	.24*†	.22*	.34*	.40*	.16	.32*	.56*	—

PE = PE context; LT = leisure-time context.

*Correlation significantly different from zero ($p < .01$); †no significant difference between variance accounted for by sampling error and total error variance in effect size across studies.

Table 3.2 Beta Coefficients From Meta-Analytic Path Analysis of the Trans-Contextual Model

	Beta
Perceived autonomy support (PE) → autonomous motivation (PE)	.35**
Perceived autonomy support (PE) → autonomous motivation (LT)	.13**
Perceived autonomy support (PE) → attitude	.12**
Perceived autonomy support (PE) → subjective norm	.13**
Perceived autonomy support (PE) → PBC	.06*
Perceived autonomy support (PE) → intention	.02
Perceived autonomy support (PE) → physical activity behavior	.11**
Autonomous motivation (PE) → autonomous motivation (LT)	.36**
Autonomous motivation (PE) → attitude	.11**
Autonomous motivation (PE) → subjective norm	−.01
Autonomous motivation (PE) → PBC	−.09**
Autonomous motivation (PE) → intention	.06*
Autonomous motivation (LT) → attitude	.40**
Autonomous motivation (LT) → subjective norm	.13*
Autonomous motivation (LT) → PBC	.36**
Autonomous motivation (LT) → intention	.17**
Autonomous motivation (LT) → physical activity behavior	.08**
Attitude → intention	.37**
Subjective norm → intention	.05*
PBC → intention	.22**
Intention → physical activity behavior	.50**

PE = PE context; LT = leisure-time context; PBC = perceived behavioral control.
*p < .05. **p < .01.

motivational sequence. With this, coupled to the cross-cultural support for the trans-contextual model and the bootstrap analyses, researchers attempting to replicate the findings of this model can be confident that they will likely obtain the same results in schoolchildren aged 12 to 16 years.

Conclusions, Recommendations for Future Research, and Practical Considerations

The series of studies reviewed in the present chapter supports the premise that the promotion to young people of autonomous forms of motivation toward physical activity in a physical education context can influence their autonomous motivation toward physical activity in a leisure-time context. Four studies, three prospective and correlational and one experimental in design, with a total sample size of 1424 participants, corroborated the proposed model and its motivational sequence. Further, a meta-analytic synthesis of these studies, presented here for the first time, suggests that the hypotheses of the trans-contextual model are consistent across these studies and indicates a high likelihood that the model will be replicated in subsequent studies of young people in this age group.

Future studies will provide further experimental evidence to support the motivational sequence in the trans-contextual model. In particular, experimental studies are needed that model in detail the synergy between interventions based on the trans-contextual model and on the theory of planned behavior. This is in keeping with the recent trends toward hybrid or interactive models of intervention at the different stages of the motivational sequence (Koestner et al., 2002; Prestwich, Lawton, & Connor, 2003). Such evidence will mean that practitioners, particularly physical education teachers and those involved with curriculum development, may be able to arrive at the most optimal set of contextual conditions promoting physical activity messages to school pupils to maximize their physical activity participation in leisure time. Such fine-tuning will come only from studies that examine the effects of such manipulations on the different motivational constructs in the trans-contextual model. In addition, it may be useful to look at the effects of these manipulations, which tend to operate at the predecisional phase in the decision-making process toward engaging in physical activity, in conjunction with other intervention strategies that operate at the postdecisional or implemental phase (which is the most proximal phase outlined in the trans-contextual model). Implementation intentions (Gollwitzer, 1999) is a good example of such a postdecisional intervention strategy and may provide an additional means for interventions that span both school-based and home-based modes of administration. Another interesting avenue may be to examine, or at least control for, the effects of basic psychological need satisfaction on the motivational orientations in the model, which may explain the distal origins of the motivational constructs in the model as shown in recent studies (Hagger, Chatzisarantis, & Harris, 2006).

Practical recommendations arising from the tests of the trans-contextual model suggest that physical education teachers can have a pervasive influence on the physical activity participation of their pupils in their free time outside of school. Physical education teachers therefore need to frame the activities they teach in their lessons in terms of (a) information about how pupils might implement them in their leisure time; (b) a rationale for doing the activities outside of school; (c) the provision of choice of, and opportunities to try out, activities that could be done in free time; (d) acknowledging the conflicts and difficulties that pupils might encounter; and (e) highlighting intrinsic goals and helping pupils set their own personally valued goals for their activities outside of school. The informational aspects of these recommendations could be cast in terms of the salient beliefs about the advantages of physical activity from theory of planned behavior-based elicitation studies (e.g., Hagger, Chatzisarantis, & Biddle, 2001), and acknowledgement of conflict could be gleaned from the disadvantages listed in such studies. These recommendations are summarized in "Practical Recommendations for Physical Education Teachers Based on the Trans-Contextual Model." In conclusion, physical education seems to be an appropriate existing network for health psychologists and professionals, curriculum developers, and teachers to provide health-related physical activity messages that may have a lasting impact on young people's motivation, intentions, and behavior toward physical activity in a leisure-time context.

Practical Recommendations for Physical Education Teachers Based on the Trans-Contextual Model

- Physical education teachers should adopt autonomy-supportive behaviors to promote physical activity for health reasons among young people in physical education lessons. Such behaviors include listening to pupils, providing choice of activities within the curriculum or at least involving pupils in the decision-making process, providing informational feedback, offering encouragement and hints, being responsive to questions, and acknowledging understanding.

- Teachers should provide pupils with information and opportunities to try out new activities that are likely to fulfill needs for autonomy, competence, and relatedness in physical education lessons. Such choice is possible if teachers are innovative in varying their lesson plans, even within a relatively rigid curriculum. For example, a physical education teacher may develop varied practice sessions that focus on a variety of warm-up exercises, drills, match practice or time-trial work (for team and individual sports, respectively), and skill-related tests (e.g., shooting penalties in soccer, practicing taking rebounds in basketball) within a single lesson.

- Providing choice, giving a rationale, and acknowledging conflicts are standard techniques that have been shown to foster autonomous forms of motivation (Deci, Eghrari, Patrick, & Leone, 1994). If physical education teachers can do this with reference to the salient beliefs children have regarding physical activity, then the intervention is more likely to be effective (Hagger, Chatzisarantis, & Biddle, 2001). For example, a physical education teacher might suggest that students choose the type of practice they focus on while giving them a reason for doing each type of practice—for example, to work on weaknesses or to acquire sufficient stamina.

- Physical education teachers can assist pupils in setting personally relevant, intrinsic goals for their chosen activity or for activities that they can then pursue in their leisure time, outside of school. For example, a physical education teacher might tell pupils to select one of the activities included in lessons to pursue outside of school and try to match their personal bests, such as their 100-meter time or the number of press-ups they can do.

Self-Determination and Motivation in Physical Education

Martyn Standage, PhD, and Fiona Gillison, MSc
University of Bath

Darren C. Treasure, PhD
Competitive Advantage International Performance Systems

Past work has shown that younger children are, in general, physically active relative to adolescents and adults (Department of Health, 2004; Joint Health Surveys Unit, 1998). It is when children make the transition into the adolescent years that marked decrements in levels of physical activity have been reported, which have serious consequences for cardiovascular, skeletal, and psychological health (Anderssen, Wold, &, Torsheim, 2005; Biddle, Gorely, & Stensel, 2004; Sallis, 2000; Sallis & Owen, 1999). In view of the age of this identified cohort, it is not surprising that school physical education has been advanced as an arena in which to combat the reported reductions in physical activity participation (e.g., Hagger & Chatzisarantis, this volume; National Audit Office, 2001; Shephard & Trudeau, 2000).

Clearly, an important avenue of work for researchers interested in optimizing the motivation of young people in physical education settings, as well as potentially influencing physical activity levels and well-being among the general population, is an understanding of the diverse motivational processes that account for varying levels of student investment in physical education (Standage, Duda, & Ntoumanis, 2003). A broad theoretical framework addressing the personal and situational factors that elicit differing types of motivation in all life domains is self-determination theory (Deci & Ryan, 1985, 1991; Ryan & Deci, 2000a, 2002).

Self-determination theory (Deci & Ryan, 1985, 1991; Ryan & Deci, 2000a, 2002, this volume) has evolved over the past 30 years; and although initial applications of tenets from self-determination theory in physical education were largely rooted in the achievement goal literature (e.g., motivational regulations

Correspondence regarding this article should be directed to Dr. Martyn Standage, Sport and Exercise Science Research Group, School for Health, University of Bath, Bath BA2 7AY, United Kingdom. E-mail: m.standage@bath.ac.uk employed as dependent variables), the theory has increasingly provided the conceptual foundation for contemporary research on student motivation in physical education. Indeed, recent work in physical education has begun to provide a more complete examination of self-determination theory (e.g., Ntoumanis, 2001, 2005; Standage, Duda, & Ntoumanis, 2003; Standage, Duda, & Pensgaard, 2005; Standage, Duda, & Ntoumanis, in press).

In this chapter, we review the major directions that work grounded in self-determination theory has taken in the context of school physical education. To facilitate this objective, we have adopted an approach akin to the motivational sequence identified by Vallerand (1997) of social factors → psychological mediators → types of motivation → consequences, which is commensurate with the logical pattern of associations proposed by self-determination theory (see also Sarrazin, Boiché, & Pelletier, this volume). Specifically, we discuss each link identified in figure 4.1 with regard to empirical findings and theory.

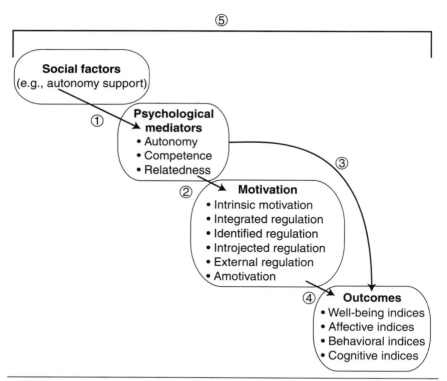

Figure 4.1   A model of empirically supported links among self-determination theory constructs and psychological, social, and outcome variables in physical education. (1) Links between social factors (both autonomy support and other social contexts that have been explored) and need satisfaction; (2) influence of need satisfaction on motivation; (3) impact of need satisfaction on indices of well-being; (4) links between the various motivational types and outcome variables; (5) a complete test of the proposed sequence of motivational processes.

Next, we discuss various practical implications that past work grounded in self-determination theory has for physical education teachers and educational administrators. After synthesizing and discussing pertinent empirical findings, we advance recommendations for future research. The chapter concludes with a number of summary remarks and practical recommendations.

Autonomy Support in Physical Education

Fundamental to self-determination theory is the assumption that the nature of the social context influences an individual's motivation (i.e., autonomous vs. controlled), well-being, and level of functioning. To this end, according to Deci and Ryan (1985, 1991), autonomy-supportive environments (i.e., social contexts that support choice, initiation, and understanding) as opposed to controlling environments (i.e., social contexts that are authoritarian, pressuring, and dictating) facilitate self-determined motivation, healthy development, and optimal psychological functioning.

Akin to previous work in classroom education (e.g., Deci, Nezlek, & Sheinman, 1981), past work in physical education has shown a direct and positive association between an autonomy-supportive environment and self-determined forms of motivation (Hagger, Chatzisarantis, Culverhouse, & Biddle, 2003; Hagger, Chatzisarantis, Barkoukis, Wang, & Baranowski, 2005). As part of a study adopting a prospective design, Hagger and colleagues (2003) found support for the positive association between perceptions of autonomy support in physical education and the students' reported levels of identified regulation and intrinsic motivation. More recently, Hagger and colleagues (2005) have provided support for this relationship in samples from Britain, Greece, and Poland. Corroborating the findings of Hagger and colleagues (2003, 2005), indirect effects obtained via structural equation modeling (SEM) analyses have also shown that perceptions of autonomy support positively predict self-determined forms of motivation through the needs of autonomy, competence, and relatedness (e.g., Standage, Duda, & Ntoumanis, 2003, 2006). Taken collectively, this emerging body of work supports the theoretical tenets of self-determination theory and past work from classroom-based education (cf. Reeve, Deci, & Ryan, 2004) showing that an autonomy-supportive environment fosters adaptive forms of motivation. Such findings make conceptual sense, as autonomy-supportive environments permit students to have a perceived internal locus of causality with regard to their learning.

According to self-determination theory, self-determined learning and healthy functioning are not direct functions of social factors, but are dependent on the satisfaction of three innate psychological needs, namely for autonomy, competence, and relatedness (Deci & Ryan, 1991, 2000). In a series of studies, my colleagues and I (Standage & Gillison, 2005; Standage, Duda, & Ntoumanis, 2003, 2006) have examined the impact that perceptions of an autonomy-supportive environment have on the basic needs proffered by Deci and Ryan (1991, 2000). A consistent finding to emerge across all these studies has been a positive association between autonomy support and each of the innate psychological needs. Based on this initial work, it appears that consonant with the theorizing of self-determination theory, autonomy-supportive environments foster self-determined motivation by nurturing the three basic needs (Deci & Ryan, 2000).

Findings from research based in physical education and other life domains, such as classroom-based education (cf. Deci & Ryan, 2002; Reeve, Deci, & Ryan, 2004), support the assertion that students in physical education benefit from interactions with autonomy-supportive teachers. We would argue, however, that there is a need for researchers to develop a valid and reliable physical education-specific instrument of autonomy support if we are to better understand students' perceptions of this interpersonal context.

Other Influential Social Context Factors

Psychological need satisfaction only in part determines self-determined forms of motivation in physical education, according to the self-determination theory perspective, social factors have an important role in determining motivational involvement. Central to this is the environment in physical education in which the child acts that has the potential to support or thwart self-determined forms of motivation. The subsequent sections will outline how goal perspective theory and need supporting contexts based on self-determination theory and autonomy support influence motivation and behavior in physical education.

Goal Perspective Frameworks

During the past 20 years, much of the research on social factors in physical education has been grounded in goal perspective frameworks of motivation (e.g., Ames, 1992; Nicholls, 1989). Through use of the umbrella term perceived motivational climate to encompass the perceptions of the overall situationally emphasized goal structure, two dimensions of the motivational climate have been examined, namely mastery and performance structures (cf. Ames, 1992). Mastery (or task involving) climates refer to structures that support hard work, learning, cooperation, and task mastery and are based on the principle that involving students is an essential part of the learning process. Conversely, performance (or ego involving) climates refer to situations that foster normative comparisons, focus on interpersonal competition, and entail the punishment of mistakes.

The main objective of this line of work has been to examine how these social contexts influence the achievement-related cognitions, behaviors, and affective responses of students in physical education. Results have consistently documented the adaptive achievement patterns of students perceiving a mastery, as opposed to a performance, climate (Biddle, 2001; Ntoumanis & Biddle, 1999), although recent 2 × 2 conceptualizations of achievement goals suggest that performance goals can be beneficial to motivation provided that they are not contingent with avoidance or low competence (Elliot & McGregor, 2001). In addition, research has suggested that performance climates engendered by competition may undermine intrinsic motivation and persistence. However, it is important to note the suggestion in recent research that winners in competition receive self-affirming information about their competence and are therefore more intrinsically motivated. More importantly, the effects of losing a competition can be ameliorated if other compensatory competence-enhancing information is given concurrently (Vansteenkiste & Deci, 2003). Therefore, although performance climates may be detrimental to intrinsic motivation in general, competitive climates may not always lead to reduced motivation provided that sufficient competence-affirming information is available.

Drawing from the goal perspective literature, researchers originally proposed and subsequently examined how perceptions of task- and ego-involving information affected individuals' levels of intrinsic motivation (Butler, 1987; Ryan, 1982). As Ryan and Deci (1989) pointed out, to foster intrinsic motivation in educational contexts, "both perspectives would advocate the use of feedback and other procedures that minimize ego involvement and facilitate a fuller, more task-involved engagement with academic endeavors" (p. 268). Support for these proposed interrelationships has emerged in past physical education work. Specifically, intrinsic motivation has been consistently associated with perceptions of a mastery climate, whereas perceptions of a performance climate have generally been found to be unrelated to intrinsic motivation (e.g., Cury et al., 1996; Goudas & Biddle, 1994; Papaioannou, 1994). More recently, researchers have examined how these social factors influence the various types of motivation embraced by self-determination theory. In a study designed to examine the influence of the motivational climate on physical activity and situational motivation in a sample of male and female adolescent physical education students, Parish and Treasure (2003) found perceptions of a mastery climate to be strongly related to more self-determined forms of motivation. In contrast, perceptions of a performance climate were found to be strongly related to less self-determined forms of situational motivation. In addition to providing empirical support for the utility of examining multidimensional situational motivation in the context of physical education, the conceptually coherent pattern of relationships suggests that social conditions, in this case perceptions of the motivation climate, may play an important role in determining motivation in physical education.

In an initial attempt to test the sequence of motivational processes encompassed by self-determination theory, Ntoumanis (2001) hypothesized that the cooperation, improvement, and choice (i.e., opportunities to plan one's own activities) facets of a mastery environment would predict relatedness, competence, and autonomy, respectively. Through use of SEM to analyze the responses of British secondary school students, results supported the hypothesized relationships. Support for the interrelationships among goal perspective social context dimensions and need satisfaction has been demonstrated in lab-based work. Standage, Duda, and Pensgaard (2005) randomly assigned participants to one of four conditions and manipulated the social context in which college-aged physical education students performed a novel physical coordination task. Supporting their reasoning, the results showed that students who engaged in a coordination task within a task-involving (mastery) condition reported higher levels of need satisfaction than those participating in an ego-involving (performance) setting.

In a study designed to incorporate the research on self-determination theory and goal perspective, we (Standage, Duda, & Ntoumanis, 2003) examined the impact of mastery and performance climates (in addition to perceptions of autonomy support) on satisfaction of the basic needs. Results revealed that only the path between mastery climate and autonomy was supported. While this finding bears out the notion that students report higher levels of personal autonomy when they perceive the environment to support elements of self-referenced progress and learning, the nonsignificant links between a mastery climate and relatedness and competence departed from our study hypotheses. These null findings were, in part, attributed to the measure employed to assess the participants' overriding perceptions of the physical education class climate. However, as these links can be justified theoretically (cf. Standage, Duda, & Ntoumanis, 2003), it appears that the dimensions constituting mastery and performance climates in physical education have yet to be clearly established and consistently examined (Biddle, 2001). To this end, akin to the situation with autonomy support in physical education, there is a call to generate new items, refine existing items, and better align inventories to theory in order to more accurately capture the underpinning tenets of mastery and performance dimensions in school physical education (Standage, Duda, & Ntoumanis, 2003). Such empirical undertakings would allow for a better understanding of how the goal perspective literature may complement or add to contemporary self-determination theory work.

Need-Supporting Environments

Contemporary physical education research has begun to examine what has been termed a *need-supporting* context (Standage, Duda, & Pensgaard, 2005). Such an approach has built on the notion that, when accompanied by an autonomy-supportive environment, support for competence and relatedness promotes self-determined motivation (Deci, Koestner, & Ryan, 2001; Deci, Vallerand, Pelletier, & Ryan, 1991). As Ryan and Deci (2000a) note, "[I]n schools, the facilitation of more self-determined learning requires classroom conditions that allow satisfaction of these three basic human needs that support the innate needs to feel connected, effective, and agentic as one is exposed to new ideas and exercises new skills" (p. 65). Although lab-based work has addressed various supports for relatedness and competence (cf. Deci et al., 1991), assessments of students' overall perceptions of classroom and physical education contexts have, for the most part, focused only on the effects of *autonomy-supportive* versus *controlling* environments (Black & Deci, 2000; Vallerand, Fortier, & Guay, 1997; Standage, Duda, & Ntoumanis, 2006). Commenting that such an approach may overlook social factors that could contribute to the satisfaction of the other two important psychological needs, my colleagues and I (Standage, Duda, & Pensgaard, 2005) examined the predictive utility of a multifaceted environment encompassing perceptions of *autonomy support, competence support*, and *relatedness support* on students' psychological need satisfaction. The results confirmed our hypotheses, revealing perceptions of a need-supportive environment to be a strong positive predictor of students' perceptions of need satisfaction. Moreover, indirect effects showed *all three* social support elements to have strong positive impacts on overall need satisfaction. Thus we were able to identify additional situational elements that contribute to the amount of variance accounted for in need satisfaction above and beyond that explained independently by autonomy support.

Identification of the social contexts fostered by teachers that promote, rather than forestall, need satisfaction, autonomous motivation, and adaptive responses represents an important avenue of inquiry. Researchers may wish to examine numerous social environments alongside autonomy support as we attempt to increase our understanding of what contributes to "healthy" physical education class environments. Research on these dimensions of the social context may include an examination of how Deci and Ryan's (1991) proposed dimensions of *structure* (degree of feedback, clear expectations, and understandable behavior-outcome contingencies) and *involvement* (degree to which significant others such as physical education teachers devote time, energy, and interest to the relationship) complement student perceptions of autonomy support.

Basic Psychological Needs

Fundamental to self-determination theory and the central tenet of *basic needs theory* (Ryan & Deci, 2000a) is that satisfaction of the universal and innate needs of autonomy, competence, and relatedness represents the essential nutriments for psychological health and well-being. When these basic psychological needs are satisfied, self-determined motivation, psychological growth, and well-being are promoted (cf. Ryan & Deci, 2002). Conversely, when these needs are not nurtured, autonomous motivation, well-being, and optimal functioning are diminished (Deci & Ryan, 2000). Studies have demonstrated that basic psychological needs are consistent across cultures and predict salient outcomes such as psychological well-being, integration of regulations, and intentional behavior (e.g., Hagger, Chatzisarantis, & Harris, 2006; Kasser & Ryan, 1999; Ryan, 1995; Ryan & Deci, 2000b; Sheldon, Elliot, Kim, & Kasser, 2001).

Several studies have examined the utility of psychological need satisfaction for predicting motivational and well-being responses in physical education. These studies have addressed the three needs independently (e.g., Ntoumanis, 2001; Standage & Gillison, 2005; Standage, Duda, & Ntoumanis, 2003, 2006) and as a composite variable labeled *psychological need satisfaction* (Ntoumanis, 2005; Standage, Duda, & Pensgaard, 2005; Hagger, Chatzisarantis, & Harris, 2006). With this composite approach in mind, Hagger, Chatzisarantis, and Harris (2006) have recently corroborated this methodology by revealing that the shared variance among the psychological needs factors can be explained by a higher-order factor that captures all three basic needs in a single latent construct. Returning to the predictive utility of the needs, in general, past work has shown the three needs to predict self-determined forms of motivation, both independently (Standage, Duda, & Ntoumanis, 2003, 2006) and when combined (Ntoumanis, 20005; Standage, Duda, & Ntoumanis, 2006). Although work has alluded to the predictive utility of the needs independently of one another (i.e., determining which need is the best predictor), it is important to note that self-determination theory does not consider the basic needs to have a hierarchical structure; rather all three must be met so as to allow for continual psychological growth and integrity—a hypothesis of complementarity of needs (Hagger, Chatzisarantis, & Harris, 2006; Ryan & Deci, 2000a).

Research has also shown need satisfaction to have indirect effects on psychological well-being, cognitive responses, and reported behavioral outcomes (Standage, Duda, & Ntoumanis, 2003; Standage, Duda, & Pensgaard, 2005; Standage, Duda, & Ntoumanis, 2006). For example, Standage and colleagues (2005) found that reported need satisfaction had positive indirect effects on adaptive physical education outcomes (i.e., concentration, preference for challenge, positive affect, and lower unhappiness) in secondary school students. In a further study, Standage and colleagues (2006) found competence, autonomy, and relatedness to have significant (albeit weak) positive indirect effects through self-determined motivation on ratings of motivated behavior by the students' physical education teacher.

A further postulation of self-determination theory is that the innate needs are universal to all cultures, across gender, and throughout all developmental periods. Although Ryan and Deci (2002) recognize that there are numerous vehicles and expressions through which the needs may be fulfilled, they propose that the underlying core characteristic of all the needs is that they are unchanging. To test this precept, my colleagues and I (Standage, Duda, & Pensgaard, 2005) recently examined the invariance of a self-determination theory model across gender by using SEM multisample invariance testing procedures. Our results supported the tenets of self-determination theory by revealing the proposed psychological processes to be largely invariant across male and female students. Similarly, and also via multisample invariance testing procedures, Hagger and colleagues (2005) have found support for hypotheses drawn from self-determination theory across different cultures in their work pertaining to the trans-contextual model (see Hagger & Chatzisarantis, this volume).

Motivational Regulations and Related Consequences

Self-determination theory adopts a multidimensional perspective to motivation, proposing and distinguishing between different reasons "why" individuals are impelled to act. Rather than merely viewing intrinsic versus extrinsic motivation as a dichotomy, Deci and Ryan (1985, 1991) have identified three types of motivation: *intrinsic motivation* (self-determined behavior), *extrinsic motivation* (controlled behavior), and *amotivation* (nonintentional behavior) (see Ryan & Deci, this volume).

Self-determination theory proposes that intrinsic motivation and autonomous types of extrinsic motivation (i.e., identified and integrated regulations) lead to positive functioning, effective personal adjustment, improved learning, and enhanced psychological health and well-being (Deci & Ryan, 1991, 2000). Empirical work has supported this proposition by showing that self-determined forms of motivation positively correspond to a number of desirable responses in physical education. These correlates include higher levels of reported positive affect (Standage, Duda, & Pensgaard, 2005; Ntoumanis, 2005), greater concentration (Standage, Duda, & Pensgaard, 2005), higher effort (Ntoumanis, 2001), increased interest (Goudas, Biddle, & Fox, 1994), a preference for attempting challenging tasks (Standage, Duda, & Pensgaard, 2005), and an intention to be physically active in leisure time (Standage, Duda, & Ntoumanis, 2003; Hagger et al., 2003). Conversely, nonautonomous forms of motivation (i.e., amotivation or external regulation or both) have been shown to positively correspond with student boredom and unhappiness (Ntoumanis, 2001; Standage, Duda, & Pensgaard, 2005). Moreover, a negative link has emerged between amotivation toward physical education and students' intentions to be physically active in their own leisure time (Standage, Duda, & Ntoumanis, 2003). Accordingly, because amotivation represents little or no motivation, one would not expect children who do not perceive any viable reason for engaging in physical education to display an intention to pursue similar activities within their leisure time.

Data from sources other than the students themselves are available to corroborate the benefits of self-determined motivation. For example, students' ratings of autonomous motivation have been shown to positively predict teacher ratings of effort and persistence in physical education (Ferrer-Caja & Weiss, 2000; Standage, Duda, & Pensgaard, 2005). Ntoumanis (2005) assessed persistence through a prospective design to examine whether motivation toward compulsory physical education could predict participation in optional physical education during the following school year, measured through enrollment in an optional physical education course. Results revealed that students who enrolled in optional physical education reported higher levels of self-determined motivation and lower levels of amotivation than those who chose not to participate.

Overall, research guided by self-determination theory has shown that autonomous forms of regulation positively correspond with desirable motivational indices. In contrast, nonautonomous motivational regulations have been shown to undermine adaptive student responses. Thus, research to date provides clear support for self-determination theory by demonstrating that students benefit from being autonomously motivated with respect to their engagement in physical education.

Tests of the Motivational Sequence

Akin to classroom-based research (e.g., Vallerand, Fortier, & Guay, 1997), a number of studies have tested the complete sequence of motivational processes (as displayed in figure 4.1) through SEM (e.g., Standage, Duda, & Ntoumanis, 2003; Standage, Duda, & Pensgaard, 2005; Standage, Duda, & Ntoumanis, 2005; Ntoumanis, 2001). Strong support for the theoretical predictions of self-determination theory has emerged via this work. Specifically, research has confirmed the presence of the "social factors → psychological mediators → types of motivation → consequences" pattern of associations by showing that data obtained from students fit well with the proposed covariance structures put forward to explain motivational processes in physical education (e.g., Ntoumanis, 2001, 2005; Standage, Duda, & Ntoumanis, 2003; Standage, Duda, & Pensgaard, 2005; Standage, Duda, & Ntoumanis, 2006).

Practical Implications in Physical Education

Contexts such as physical education, which encompass activities that are desirable but not always intrinsically interesting to *all* students, pose a particular challenge to education professionals in motivating students toward uninteresting tasks. Practical steps toward this process are proposed in Deci, Eghrari, Patrick, and Leone's (1994) conceptualization of internalization and its subsequent applications. As outlined by Ryan and Deci (this volume), internalization is a progressive process by which external regulations are transformed into internal regulations as the person "takes in" the value and integrates the activity into his or her repertoire of need-satisfying behaviors. In physical education, many students will be at the preinternalization stage. Accordingly, they engage in physical education activities solely because they are told to do so by the physical education teacher (i.e., they are externally regulated). To facilitate the internalization process, Deci and colleagues (e.g., Deci et al., 1994; Deci & Ryan, 1991; Deci & Vansteenkiste, 2004; Ryan & Deci, 2002) have identified various social preconditions. In what follows we discuss these prerequisites and their practical implications.

- The interpersonal context in which the behavior is performed must be supportive of the basic needs so as to facilitate autonomous regulation and integration. To facilitate autonomy, a physical education teacher may provide students with the required information regarding a skill or tactic, but then provide choice regarding the way in which students execute the task, or the scope regarding tactics or game plan decisions, or both. Additionally, the physical education teacher may establish peer learning groups (e.g., students demonstrate skills to one another, referee games, and establish tactics). Students' perceptions of competence may be facilitated through the promotion of environments in which self-referenced standards and indicators of improvement are adopted as opposed to competitive situations in which evaluated outcomes are contingent upon the performance of others (Ames, 1992). Finally, relatedness may be met if physical education teachers use small-group activities and set reward structures that support cooperation (e.g., group-level outcomes).

• A meaningful rationale must be provided, especially when the activity is not interesting to the student. For example, one may convey the health benefits of a physical activity (e.g., cross country running) to an uninterested student in an attempt to promote the personal value of self-regulation.

• There should be some expression of empathy or acknowledgment of the concerns that the student faces with regard to the requested behavior. For example, if a physical education teacher says, "I know that doing sit-ups is not much fun," this will legitimize students' perceptions of the activity and allow them to feel understood and accepted, as well as to believe that their perceptions are not incongruent with the requested behavior.

• The physical education teacher should be careful about how the rationale (point 2) and acknowledgment of empathy (point 3) are conveyed to the student. That is, to facilitate internalization, the teacher should try to avoid the use of externally controlling language (e.g., "You must . . ."; "You have to . . ."; "You should . . ."). Rather, requests should portray choice and support (e.g., "You may want to . . ."; "You can try to . . .").

These recommendations are appropriate if a teacher has the self-awareness to adopt these techniques. However, the question may arise: *What about teachers who intuitively adopt a controlling style toward their teaching?* Fortunately, past work in classroom-based education has shown teaching styles to be malleable (cf. Reeve, Deci, & Ryan, 2004). For example, field-based work by Reeve (1998), using a sample of preservice teachers, revealed that participants exposed to just an 80-minute training session reported significant and enduring changes in their interpersonal teaching style as compared with a control group (i.e., they became more autonomy supportive). This is especially important in a school context, because although autonomy support is important in all interpersonal situations, self-determination theory holds that the saliency of the interpersonal context is accentuated in an unequal power situation (e.g., physical education teacher and physical education student) (Sheldon, Williams, & Joiner, 2003). Given the burgeoning body of empirical work that has documented the adaptive motivation and well-being responses of students who interact with autonomy-supportive teachers, physical education teacher education programs would seemingly benefit from integrating educational information pertaining to autonomy-supportive contexts within pedagogical curricula. To this end, teacher training contexts provide an ideal platform for educating and translating theory into practice.

Avenues for Future Self-Determination Theory Work in Physical Education

As suggested at the outset of this chapter, physical education has been advanced as a vehicle to promote physical activity levels. Accordingly, we believe that future field-based research should examine how motivation-related processes toward physical education predict actual physical activity patterns. Drawing from self-determination theory, researchers may begin to examine how important socializing agents (e.g., physical education teachers) can structure and promote physical education activities in a manner that facilitates and encourages autonomous engagement and long-term persistence (Hagger et al., 2003, 2005). Clearly, such work could significantly contribute to the development of cost-effective interventions that may be readily implemented in physical education settings on a scale that could positively affect public health. Of course, such an objective is fraught with many difficulties; but on the basis of past self-determination theory work, we feel that interpersonal contexts that promote intrinsic goal pursuits (see Vansteenkiste, Soenens, & Lens, this volume) and internalization (see Deci et al., 1994), and that support the basic needs of autonomy, competence, and relatedness, hold much promise in applied physical education settings.

Continuing with the applied theme, further research is needed to provide understanding of how to design and implement intervention programs to enhance autonomous motivation, facilitate learning, and foster healthy participation in physical education settings. To inform such programs, a variety of research designs and methods would yield fruitful information. Longitudinal work would give researchers an understanding of the dynamic and temporal patterns of social contexts, basic needs, and motivational regulations while providing further information regarding their interrelationships with more enduring dependent variables (e.g., persistence, ongoing performance, psychological functioning, indicators of change, etc.). Lab-based experimental investigations would allow researchers to isolate and test key relationships (e.g., the effect of differing social context factors on basic needs) in a controlled fashion prior to examination of their application to physical education settings. Finally, qualitative work would allow for greater insight into the experiences of children in physical education. As with recent work on *amotivation* in physical education from an idiographic approach (Ntoumanis, Pensgaard, Martin, & Pipe, 2004), we feel that a qualitative analysis of *introjected regulation* would provide rich and detailed insight into the characteristics of this controlling form of regulatory style often cited as a reason for engagement (e.g., "PE is something that I have to do"). This would be especially pertinent in that introjected regulation has not received much attention in the literature and has been shown to exhibit a problematic structure in factor analytic studies aimed at developing valid measures of this construct.

Another avenue for future work rests with Deci and Ryan's proposition of the universal psychological needs for autonomy, competence, and relatedness. In alignment with recent investigations in the field of applied social psychology (e.g., Reis, Sheldon, Gable, Roscoe, & Ryan, 2000), particularly sport (Gagné, Ryan, & Bargmann, 2003), researchers may wish to examine between-person (individual differences) and within-person (i.e., daily fluctuation) variations of need satisfaction through multilevel modeling. Using both diary procedures and questionnaires before and after physical education classes, longitudinal work adopting this approach would offer insight into the functioning role of psychological needs in predicting indices of student motivation and well-being in physical education.

In addition to addressing the isolated physical education setting, it would be insightful for future research to examine the impact of multiple social agents (e.g., peers, parents) in addition to, and in conjunction with, the perceptions of the teacher-created social context. In view of empirical work and the theoretical tenets of basic needs theory, such research would allow us to tease out which characteristics of each socializing agent best support levels of need satisfaction and subsequently the associated indices of student well-being in physical education.

Finally, if we are to accurately examine the fundamental tenets of self-determination theory in physical education settings, it would seem important for future research to focus on the development of context-specific measures designed to assess the basic needs and perceptions of autonomy support. It would be beneficial in future work to involve physical education students in all stages of the questionnaire development process (e.g., focus groups, item development, item meaning, etc.) to ensure that we are capturing all the processes that operate within the child or adolescent population and physical education context that may be pertinent to self-determination theory.

Conclusion

The evidence presented here from reviews of contemporary physical education research has reinforced a number of the theoretical tenets advanced by self-determination theory. Indeed, the extant literature corroborates the motivational benefits of teacher-created contexts that support basic need satisfaction; work has supported the veracity of a needs-based approach to motivation and well-being; and research has documented the many positive cognitive, behavioral, and affective consequences yielded by autonomous forms of motivation. As also evident from this chapter, there are many important directions that future work guided by self-determination theory could take in physical education settings. Using a variety of methods, the directions for future work offered in this chapter and others in this edited volume will only serve to expand and enhance our conceptual understanding of the theoretical tenets offered by Deci and Ryan (1985, 1991; Ryan & Deci, 2000a, 2002). Finally, as in work in other life domains (cf. Deci & Ryan, 2002), researchers should attempt to use the vast accumulated evidence from self-determination theory to inform and guide applications and interventions in physical education settings.

Summary of Practical Recommendations for Physical Educators

- To promote adaptive student learning, effort, self-determined motivation, and well-being, physical education teachers might aim to facilitate physical education class environments that support the basic psychological needs of autonomy, competence, and relatedness. Teachers can do this, for example, by adopting the appropriate autonomy-supportive discourse to appeal to each of these needs (e.g., "OK, class, you can discuss among yourselves [relatedness] and agree on your choice(s) [autonomy] of the practice(s) you do today, and remember, you can improve your personal goals by choosing the practices that will improve important parts of your game/event [competence]").

- Physical education teachers may also seek to increase students' informed opportunities for choice (e.g., offer a wide variety of practices, with reasons for doing them and information about how they will improve the students' game), provide increased opportunities for student input (e.g., ask students to discuss which practices will help them most), empathize with the students' perspective (e.g., acknowledge that some practices involve hard work or some field positions may involve sacrificing personal accolades for the benefit of the team), and demonstrate or establish peer learning groups (e.g., encourage students to demonstrate skills to one another, referee games, and decide on tactics).

- It is recommended that physical education teachers promote environments in which self-referenced standards and indicators of improvement are adopted (i.e., task-involving situations like setting a number of on-target pitches to complete in baseball or targeting a number of topspin forehands that land on the final third of the tennis court). Such an approach is much more motivationally adaptive than competitive situations (i.e., ego-involving settings) in which students are judged and evaluated contingent on their relative physical education ability.

- Physical education teachers may use small-group activities and develop reward structures that support cooperation (e.g., the formulation of group-level goals such as maintaining possession of the ball in hockey or soccer).

• Physical education teachers are advised to try use the appropriate discourse to portray choice and support (e.g., "You may want to . . ."; "You can try to . . .") as opposed to controlling language (e.g., "You should . . ."; "You have to . . .").

• Physical education teachers are advised to promote *structure* so that they are promoting student choice within the specific rules and limits of the physical education class. For example, structure-providing behaviors involve giving informational feedback (e.g., "Excellent, you completed a personal best number of passes, you achieved your personal goal"), clear expectations (e.g., "If you put forth sustained effort . . ."), and understandable behavior-outcome contingencies (e.g., "If you are able to read when your opponent opens his body you will be able to anticipate a cross-court rather than down-the-line forehand correctly every time").

• Teaching styles have been shown to be malleable. On the basis of the past three decades of self-determination theory research, we feel that it would be prudent to formally educate physical education teachers about the importance of germinating and satisfying these needs so that they are structuring motivationally adaptive physical education classes. The importance of such a teacher training endeavor is reinforced by recent work that has revealed a positive association between perceptions of the physical education class and wider leisure-time physical activity patterns (see Hagger & Chatzisarantis, this volume).

• When a student is not inherently interested in the activity, the physical education teacher is advised to (a) provide a meaningful rationale expressing why it is important to partake in the activity effectively (e.g., health benefits that can be derived from certain activities); (b) acknowledge the student's feelings and perspective about the activity; and (c) use language that conveys choice rather than control.

Self-Determination Theory and Motivational Interviewing in Exercise

David Markland, PhD
University of Wales, Bangor

Maarten Vansteenkiste, PhD
University of Leuven

Recognition of the importance of regular exercise for health and well-being has led to increasing attention to how individuals can be encouraged to adopt and maintain a physically active lifestyle. For instance, in the United Kingdom the government has set a target to increase the proportion of the adult population that participates in at least 30 minutes of moderate physical activity five or more times a week to 50% by the year 2011 (Department of Culture, Media, and Sport, 2002). Comparable targets have been set by the governments of many Westernized nations, such as the United States (e.g., U.S. Department of Health and Human Services, 2000). The challenge presented by such targets for governments and, more importantly, for individuals in society is evident when one considers that current figures for England, for example, indicate that only 37% of men and 24% of women typically meet these activity levels (Department of Health, 2004). Similarly, recent data show that only 33% of adults in the United States regularly engage in 30 minutes or more of moderate physical activity at least five times a week (U.S. Department of Health and Human Services, 2004).

Until quite recently there was a tendency for health promotion agencies to emphasize the provision of advice and education about the benefits of physical activity and the risks of being sedentary (e.g., Department of Health, 1996; Health Education Authority, 1994), and to exhort individuals to "keep physically active" (Chief Medical Officer, 1999) as a means of encouraging greater uptake of exercise. However, advice giving and direct persuasion alone are not effective means of promoting sustained behavior change (Miller, Benefield, & Tonigan,

Correspondence concerning this article should be addressed to David Markland, School of Sport, Health and Exercise Sciences, University of Wales, Bangor, George Building, Bangor, Gwynedd LL57 2PZ, United Kingdom. E-mail: d.markland@bangor.ac.uk

1993; Miller & Rollnick, 1991; Rollnick & Miller, 1995). Although advice can be a key component of behavior change interventions, the manner in which it is given is of critical importance (Rollnick, Kinnersley, & Stott, 1993; Rollnick & Miller, 1995). Pressuring or directive communications often engender resistance in people (Miller, 1983; Miller, Benefield, & Tonigan, 1993) or at best render them passive recipients of the advice giver's point of view (Markland, Ryan, Tobin, & Rollnick, 2005; Rollnick & Miller, 1995), making change less likely. From a self-determination theory perspective, pressuring communications are likely to undermine voluntary engagement in an activity, because when individuals are regulated in this way they do not experience their involvement as self-initiated or autonomous (Deci, Koestner, & Ryan, 1999; Vansteenkiste, Simons, Soenens, & Lens, 2004). Stressing the dire consequences of not exercising, in particular, is likely to be experienced by individuals as highly authoritarian or *controlling*, and under such conditions they are unlikely to come to value physical activity as something that is personally important to them.

Fortunately, more recent approaches to the promotion of physical activity have moved away from the general persuasion model and now adopt a more person-centered approach that considers individuals' needs and available resources and aims to engage them in the process of adopting an active lifestyle. For example, in the United Kingdom, guidelines for the quality assurance of exercise referral schemes (Department of Health, 2001) explicitly state that such schemes should enable participating individuals to become more autonomous in their physical activity choices. Furthermore, the guidelines stipulate that health and exercise professionals working in referral schemes should employ an accepted model of behavior change and have the necessary motivational counseling skills to deliver behavior change objectives. Thus motivational considerations are central to the guidelines, and there is a clear recognition of the need for both a sound theoretical basis to physical activity interventions and practical skills and strategies for translating theory into action.

Motivational interviewing, a counseling approach that is specifically designed to avoid coercive tactics and promote client autonomy in order to enhance motivation, has become increasingly popular among exercise practitioners (Breckon, 2005; Miller & Rollnick, 1991, 2002). Several authors, including ourselves, have proposed that motivational interviewing can be conceptualized and understood in terms of self-determination theory (Foote et al., 1999; Ginsberg, Mann, Rotgers, & Weekes, 2002; Markland et al., 2005; Vansteenkiste & Sheldon, in press). In this chapter we aim to show that the practice of motivational interviewing and the principles of self-determination theory complement each other to provide a comprehensive account of the processes required to achieve successful behavior change. We first outline the background to motivational interviewing and its basic principles. We discuss the fundamental assumption, shared by motivational interviewing and self-determination theory, that humans have an inherent tendency for growth toward psychological integration and the resolution of intrapersonal conflicts, although the motivational processes facilitating these outcomes have been somewhat differently conceptualized in the two approaches. Furthermore, we show that there is considerable overlap in the social-environmental facilitating factors proposed by motivational interviewing and self-determination theory, and that the efficacy of motivational interviewing can be understood in terms of the provision of supports for the satisfaction of psychological needs as outlined in self-determination theory.

We discuss the principles of motivational interviewing in light of the differentiated conceptualization of extrinsic motivation in self-determination theory. In so doing we suggest that an understanding of the tenets of self-determination theory can inform the practice of motivational interviewing by emphasizing the need to promote freedom from internally imposed pressure and control, not just the need to avoid coercion and pressure from others. Finally, we draw upon these considerations to present some suggestions for helping exercise practitioners promote autonomous motivation for exercise among their clients.

The Principles of Motivational Interviewing

Motivational interviewing evolved originally from clinical experience in the treatment of problem drinking and was first described by Miller (1983). Its principles and clinical procedures were expanded upon in two influential volumes edited by Miller and Rollnick (1991, 2002). Motivational interviewing and its briefer adaptations have been extended to a wide range of behavior change contexts, and it has become a widely accepted approach among health professionals to enhancing treatment motivation (Resnicow et al., 2002). Reviews of the efficacy of motivational interviewing and its derivatives have shown relatively consistent positive effects across a variety of contexts, particularly those involving alcohol and substance abuse (e.g., Burke, Arkowitz, & Dunn, 2002; Resnicow et al., 2002).

Miller and Rollnick (2002) defined motivational interviewing as a "client-centered, directive method for enhancing intrinsic motivation to change by exploring and resolving ambivalence" (p. 25). In motivational interviewing, intrinsic motivation to change is considered to be motivation arising from within the person as opposed to motivation that is imposed or pushed upon the person by others (Miller, 1994; Miller & Rollnick, 2002). Thus, in motivational interviewing, intrinsic motivation is equated with *autonomous* motivation, that is, motivation initiated by the person rather than being forced by external contingencies. In contrast, self-determination theory distinguishes between different types of autonomous motivation, which vary in their degrees of autonomy. By this view, intrinsic motivation represents only one type of internally derived motivation, as we will discuss in more detail later. Nevertheless, both motivational interviewing and self-determination theory acknowledge that in order for lasting behavior change to be realized, motivation cannot be coerced or forced by external agents but must be generated by individuals themselves and for their own reasons. Critical to achieving this outcome is the resolution of ambivalent feelings toward the behavior.

When individuals are considering a change in their behavior, they typically hold conflicting motivational orientations. On the one hand they can see good reasons to change, but on the other hand they are aware that changing will also carry costs or losses. For example, people might understand and desire the health and fitness benefits associated with becoming physically active but at the same time fear that this will require too much effort and that they will not be able to find the time. This internal conflict can result in people's being "stuck" in a permanent state of contemplation in which they are constantly weighing the pros and cons of changing but never actually getting started, or alternatively are yo-yoing between engagement and relapse. Motivational interviewing suggests that attempting to directly overcome this ambivalence by the force of argument in favor of the benefits of change is, paradoxically, likely to have the reverse effect. The reason is that direct persuasion often leads the person to adopt the opposite stance, arguing against the need for change and thereby entrenching the "negative pole" of the conflicting motivational orientations, with the consequence of a reduced likelihood of change (Miller & Rollnick, 1991; Rollnick & Miller, 1995). Instead, motivational interviewing accepts that ambivalence is a normal part of the change process and seeks to guide individuals themselves to increasingly emphasize the "positive pole" of their ambivalence in order to tip the balance in favor of change.

Four interrelated general principles stem from the definition of motivational interviewing and underpin its specific techniques and strategies: the expression of empathy, the development of discrepancy, rolling with resistance, and support for self-efficacy. The importance of *empathy expression* by a counselor is a fundamental and defining feature of motivational interviewing (Miller & Rollnick, 1991, 2002). Firmly grounded in Rogers' (1957) client-centered approach to therapy, motivational interviewing holds the position that successful discussion of behavior change is possible only when the client feels personally accepted and valued. Counselor empathy is seen as crucial because it provides a safe and supportive environment within which clients can openly explore conflicting feelings and difficult issues about change in order to reach a satisfactory resolution themselves (Miller & Rollnick, 1991, 2002).

Development of discrepancy involves allowing people to articulate their ambivalence by exploring the perceived benefits and disadvantages of changing their behavior compared with not changing, in order to generate or intensify an awareness of the incongruity between their existing behaviors and their broader goals and values. Discrepancy development goes hand in hand with the third principle of motivational interviewing, *rolling with resistance*, which entails not trying to counter a client's arguments against change with persuasion in favor of the benefits of changing. Instead, the intention is to encourage the clients themselves to make the case for change by eliciting and selectively reinforcing what is termed "change talk" or "self-motivating statements." These are declarations by clients that reflect the positive pole of their ambivalence, demonstrating a recognition that change is needed and that change would be a good thing, an optimism that change is possible, and ultimately an intention to change (Miller & Rollnick, 2002). The final general principle of motivational interviewing is the need to *support self-efficacy* for change. It is acknowledged that even if clients are motivated, change can occur only if they also believe that they have the resources and capabilities to overcome barriers and successfully implement new ways of behaving.

Self-Determination Theory

The tenets of self-determination theory are described in detail elsewhere in this volume, so we will cover only issues germane to the comparison between self-determination theory and motivational interviewing. The theory begins with the fundamental assumption that people have an innate organizational tendency toward growth, integration of the self, and the resolution of psychological inconsistency (Deci & Ryan, 1985; Ryan & Deci, 2000). The theory proposes that one can understand the process of integration by considering motivated behaviors as lying along a motivational continuum, known as the self-determination continuum, that represents the extent to which people have internalized externally driven behavioral regulations and integrated them into their sense of self in order to engage autonomously in their activities. This continuum is delineated by four types of extrinsic motivation of varying degrees of autonomy—external regulation, introjected regulation, identified regulation, and integrated regulation—as well as the prototypical form of self-determined motivation, intrinsic motivation. For a detailed discussion of the self-determination continuum, see Ryan and Deci (this volume).

The theory further states that the natural integrative tendency and process of internalization can be facilitated or thwarted to the extent that the person's social environment provides support for three fundamental psychological needs. These are the need to experience a sense of volition and choicefulness rather than coercion and pressure to engage in an activity (a need for *autonomy*), the need to feel effective in dealing with and mastering one's environment (a need for *competence*), and the need to feel a sense of connectedness with others and to have mutually satisfying and supportive social relationships (a need for *relatedness*). According to self-determination theory, these psychological needs are innate and universal; and their satisfaction is required for optimal motivation, adaptive functioning, and well-being (Ryan & Deci, 2000). When the social environment provides support for the satisfaction of these needs, the person will move toward integration and develop the personal resources for engaging in adaptive and autonomous regulation of his or her behavior (Deci & Ryan, 1991, 2000). If the social environment is controlling, confrontational, or uninvolved, internalization and autonomous motivation will be forestalled, leading to defensive behaviors and psychological withdrawal (Deci & Ryan, 2000; Ryan, Deci, & Grolnick, 1995).

Three interrelated dimensions of a motivationally facilitative social environment correspond to the psychological needs for autonomy, competence, and relatedness: autonomy support, structure, and involvement (Deci & Ryan, 1991; Ryan, Deci, & Grolnick, 1995). *Autonomy support* concerns encouraging individuals to recognize that they can exercise choice regarding their behavior. In autonomy-supporting contexts, pressure to engage in specific behaviors is minimized and people are encouraged to initiate actions for themselves, based on their personal goals and values. Reeve (1998, 2002) has described several specific behaviors associated with autonomy support. These include helping the person to embrace a personally meaningful rationale for engaging in the behavior, minimizing external controls, providing opportunities for participation and choice in making decisions, and acknowledging difficulties associated with engaging in the behavior.

The *structural* dimension of the facilitative environment supports individuals' perceptions of competence by helping them to adopt clear and realistic expectations about behavior change and to formulate realistically achievable goals, encouraging them to believe that they are capable of engaging in the appropriate behaviors, and providing positive feedback regarding progress. Of course, for this structure and guidance to be effective, it needs to be provided in an autonomy-supportive fashion. If, for instance, individuals are assigned a realistic goal for exercising but they do not personally accept it, this structuring facet of the social environment is unlikely to yield a beneficial effect.

The *involvement* dimension entails demonstrating a genuine interest in people and their well-being and an understanding of the difficulties they are facing, as well as showing that significant others can be trusted to provide material or emotional support (Connell & Wellborn, 1991; Deci & Ryan, 1991; Grolnick & Ryan, 1987). Notably, just as in the case of structure, a counselor can display interest in a controlling fashion. That is, counselors can make their praise and their interest in and acceptance of the client contingent upon achieving particular outcomes. Thus, in order to be effective, counselors need to be genuinely involved and truly accepting of the person's opinions and goals (Assor, Roth, & Deci, 2004; Soenens, Vansteenkiste, Luyten, Duriez, & Goossens, 2005).

Self-Determination Theory and Motivational Interviewing

Miller (1983) described motivational interviewing as based on the principles of experimental social psychology, drawing on the concepts of causal attributions, cognitive dissonance, and self-efficacy. Motivational interviewing has also been closely associated with the transtheoretical model of behavior change (Miller & Rollnick, 1991). However, Miller (1994, 1996, 1999; Miller & Rollnick, 2002) has acknowledged that so far the emphasis in motivational interviewing research has been on the development and assessment of effective clinical procedures while relatively little attention has been paid to building a satisfactory theoretical explanation of how and why motivational interviewing can be effective

(Hagger & Chatzisarantis, 2005). We believe that self-determination theory can provide such an explanation by offering a framework in which the motivational processes involved in a successfully applied motivational interviewing approach can be more accurately defined, and by presenting basic psychological need satisfaction as an explanation for how motivational interviewing can yield beneficial change effects.

At the most fundamental level, self-determination theory is capable of providing such additional insights into motivational interviewing because the two approaches share the same underlying philosophical position concerning the person's innate capacity for self-direction and propensity for personal growth toward integration and cohesion. Miller (1994) has portrayed motivational interviewing in just such terms, describing it as a process of movement toward integration and internal harmony whereby the client's behaviors, attitudes, and beliefs become consistent with the values that are core to his or her personal identity. Moreover, the resources needed to motivate this process are considered to reside within the individual (Miller & Rollnick, 2002). Thus both approaches assume that individuals possess a powerful internal potential for change (Vansteenkiste & Sheldon, 2006). In addition, both self-determination theory and motivational interviewing hold that the inherent tendency to move toward integration cannot be forced or imposed by others but can be facilitated through provision of the appropriate interpersonal conditions.

More specifically, one can understand the efficacy of motivational interviewing in terms of the provision of support for satisfaction of the three psychological needs that, according to self-determination theory, are essential for optimal psychological growth and well-being. Autonomy support permeates all of the principles of motivational interviewing. One promotes autonomy by avoiding confrontation and coercion; acknowledging clients' perspectives; developing the discrepancy between clients' current behavior and how they would like to act so that they present the case for change themselves; and exploring behavioral options and encouraging clients to choose their preferred courses of action, rather than imposing solutions (Deci et al., 1994; Miller, Benefield, & Tonigan, 1993). One supports competence by providing clear but neutral information and advice to clients; helping them to embrace realistic expectations; encouraging them to self-select appropriate goals and strategies to achieve the goals; affirming their efforts; and giving them positive, nonjudgmental feedback. Such support will both enhance clients' confidence in their capacity to make progress and equip them to effectively cope with setbacks (Grolnick, 2003; Markland et al., 2005). Finally, the empathic style of motivational interviewing and the genuine interest and understanding demonstrated by the counselor will satisfy the need for relatedness. Thus, the key principles of motivational interviewing can be easily reconciled with self-determination theory's notion of need satisfaction as a mechanism by which the social environment can facilitate the process of internalization. Furthermore, the insights gained from clinical experience in the use of motivational interviewing, as well as the methods and techniques drawn from its key principles, can provide self-determination theory with a deeper and more complete understanding of the specific behaviors that counselors can adopt in order to promote autonomous motivation for change in therapeutic contexts (Vansteenkiste & Sheldon, 2006).

It is important not to consider any of the three dimensions of the facilitative environment in self-determination theory, or the four principles of motivational interviewing, as isolated factors. According to self-determination theory, the satisfaction of all three basic needs is required in order to promote internalization and optimal motivation (Hagger, Chatzisarantis, & Harris, 2006). A sense of secure relatedness is seen as providing essential but not sufficient conditions for the internalization of extrinsic motives (Ryan & Deci, 2000). Support for relatedness (and competence) can be enough to promote introjected regulation or identified regulations that are not well integrated with the individual's other behaviors and values. However, for behavioral regulation to be fully integrated so that the person acts with an authentic sense of self-direction, the need for autonomy must also be satisfied (Deci & Ryan, 2000). Similarly, in motivational interviewing an empathic stance by the counselor is seen as critical in providing the baseline conditions in which clients can feel safe to explore their internal conflicts and resolve their ambivalence. However, Miller and Rollnick (2002) point out that expressing empathy alone is not enough to mobilize the change process. Discrepancy development, along with rolling with resistance and supporting self-efficacy, is also required to promote change.

Intrinsic Motivation in Motivational Interviewing: A Conceptual Refinement

We noted earlier that in motivational interviewing the term *intrinsic motivation* is used differently from the way it is used in self-determination theory. In motivational interviewing, intrinsic motivation refers to motivation that arises from within the person rather than being imposed by others (Miller & Rollnick, 2002). Thus the distinction is between "internal" motivation (i.e., change is initiated by the person) and "external" motivation (i.e., change is driven by factors external to the person). Strictly speaking, however, intrinsic motivation refers to one particular type of autonomous motivation, that is, the tendency to engage in an activity for the pleasure and satisfaction inherent in doing so. This is contrasted with extrinsic motivation, in which the rewards of participation are outcomes that are separable from the activity itself. In self-determination theory, the terms "intrinsic" and "extrinsic" are not synonymous with "internal" and "external" (Vansteenkiste, Soenens, & Vandereycken, 2005). While intrinsic motivation is one form of internal, autonomous motivation, extrinsic motivation can also be internal to the individual and experienced as autonomous and volitional, as when a behavioral regulation is identified or integrated (Ryan & Deci, 2000). Thus motivational interviewing might be better defined as a method of promoting autonomous motivation for change, rather than intrinsic motivation (Markland et al., 2005; Vansteenkiste & Sheldon, 2006).

This issue is more than just a matter of semantics and important for two reasons. First, in the behavior change contexts where motivational interviewing would typically be used, it is often unrealistic to expect clients to become truly or only intrinsically motivated to engage in a new behavior. For example, research suggests that long-term participation in regular physical activity is more likely when individuals are intrinsically motivated (e.g., Ingledew, Markland, & Medley, 1998; McAuley, Wraith, & Duncan, 1991; Mullan & Markland, 1997). However, the extrinsic rewards of physical activity, such as losing weight or improving health, are also important and powerful motivators for exercise; and initial adoption, at least, is likely to be prompted by such factors (Ingledew, Markland, & Medley, 1998; see also Markland & Ingledew, this volume; Vansteenkiste, Soenens, & Lens, this volume). Indeed, it is unlikely that even the most committed exercisers are not motivated by some extrinsic factors (Markland, Ingledew, Hardy, & Grant, 1992). This is not problematic from the self-determination theory point of view, provided that individuals have internalized and fully endorse their reasons for participation so that their extrinsic motives are experienced as autonomous and exercise is experienced as volitional rather than controlled. When using motivational interviewing to promote the adoption of physical activity, while one would seek to enhance intrinsic motivation, one would also want to explore the personally valued extrinsic motives held by the individual in order to harness his or her power to tip the balance of the scales of ambivalence in favor of change.

A second reason for the importance of an emphasis on autonomous rather than intrinsic motivation is that in motivational interviewing as currently formulated, any motivation arising from within the individual is seen as a good thing. In self-determination theory, however, the critical motivational distinction is not between internal and external regulation of behavior per se but between controlled and autonomous regulation. Introjected motivation, which does arise from within the individual, represents a controlled form of behavioral regulation because it is associated with pressuring self-demands, shame, or guilt. When one is regulated in a controlling fashion, commitment to the behavior in the long term is not robust, regardless of whether the demands are imposed by others or driven by internally controlling, introjected forces (Deci & Ryan, 1985; Pelletier, Fortier, Vallerand, & Brière, 2001). Furthermore, introjected regulation has been shown to be associated with a variety of maladaptive responses and outcomes, including poorer coping mechanisms, decreased learning and achievement, psychological distress, and reduced well-being (Ryan & Connell, 1989; Ryan, Rigby, & King, 1993; Vansteenkiste, Simons, Lens, Soenens, & Matos, 2005). Thus health professionals, psychologists, and counselors would want to avoid the promotion of introjected regulation, even though it is internal to the individual, just as much as they would avoid external control and pressure.

This consideration highlights a potential danger in the strategy of developing discrepancy if it is not skillfully and sensitively applied (Markland et al., 2005). Ideally, developing discrepancy promotes change by helping clients to become more aware of inconsistencies between their current behaviors and their core values, thereby leading them to articulate and endorse well-internalized motives for change. However, merely raising awareness of such discrepancies risks leading people to become introjected in their regulation, especially if this awareness engenders feelings of guilt or shame at not living up to the demands or expectations of significant others. Thus developing discrepancy could forestall the broader therapeutic aim of helping the individual to move toward integration and internal harmony. The self-determination theory perspective helps to underscore the central importance of supporting autonomous motivation, not just intrinsic motivation. Furthermore, it reinforces Rollnick and Miller's (1995) warnings that it is a mistake to adopt a purely mechanical approach to motivational interviewing and to become overly focused on its technical components. Instead, the emphasis should be on motivational interviewing as an interpersonal style, especially with regard to helping clients express the case for change themselves and for personally valued reasons.

Conclusions and Applied Implications

In this chapter we have discussed how self-determination theory can offer a comprehensive theoretical rationale for understanding the efficacy of motivational interviewing. It was argued that motivational interviewing and self-determination theory are predicated on the same fundamental assumption that humans have an innate propensity for personal growth. This tendency can be harnessed to the extent that the social environment supports the satisfaction of the needs for autonomy, competence, and relatedness. The principles and strategies of motivational interviewing correspond with these social-environmental factors. The tenets of self-determination theory can inform the practice of motivational interviewing by emphasizing the need to adopt an application of its strategies that is sensitive to the motivational importance of promoting freedom from pressure and control, regardless of whether that pressure arises from within the person or is imposed by others. In turn, the clinical insights gained from motivational interviewing can further inform and enhance the self-determination theory conception of the motivationally facilitative environment.

A detailed consideration of the specific strategies of motivational interviewing is beyond the scope of this chapter. Indeed, to become skilled in the use of motivational interviewing requires specialist training and much practice. Nevertheless, as Rollnick and Miller (1995) have pointed out, the style of motivational interviewing is not restricted to formal counseling. Therefore we can offer some suggestions for practitioners that are grounded in the spirit of motivational interviewing (Rollnick & Miller, 1995) and in the self-determination theory perspective on motivation. Figure 5.1 presents these ideas in schematic form.

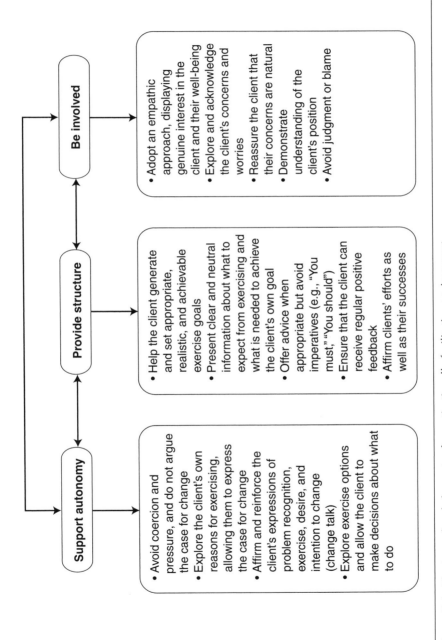

Figure 5.1 The interrelated elements of a motivationally facilitative environment.

Adapted from D. Markland et al., 2005, "Motivational interviewing and self-determination theory," *Journal of Social and Clinical Psychology*, 24: 785-805.

Above all, it is important for practitioners to have in the forefront of their minds that motivating people cannot be a prescriptive process. Attempts to cajole, persuade, or frighten people into adopting and maintaining a physically active lifestyle are likely to lead to nonautonomous forms of motivational regulation and are ultimately doomed to failure. Instead, practitioners should trust that their clients possess the inner resources to motivate change for themselves. The task is to elicit and mobilize these resources. In our view an assimilation of the style of motivational interviewing, allied with an understanding of the principles of self-determination theory, can equip practitioners with the ability to promote self-direction and truly autonomous motivation among their clients who are struggling with the difficult business of incorporating regular exercise into their lives.

Practical Recommendations for Motivational Interviewers Adopting a Self-Determination Theory Approach

- Interviewers would do well to recognize and accept that clients will have conflicting motivational orientations with respect to changing their physical activity behavior. Interviewers should therefore be trained to strictly apply the strategies appropriate to individuals in the early stages of behavior change (e.g., exploring conflicts) in order to investigate the personally relevant motives or reasons for change and to arrive at self-directed reasons for change. Self-directed change options provide choice and personal agency, which are prerequisites for autonomous forms of motivation. For example, an interviewer might ask a client to "think about why you might like to change your behavior in favor of more exercise."

- Direct persuasion and argumentation for change are likely to undermine clients' autonomy and lead them to adopt the opposite stance, arguing against change. Interviewers are therefore encouraged to avoid a controlling approach and to focus on autonomy-supportive strategies likely to encourage client-centered choice in favor of change. For example, an interviewer might encourage a client to engage in a self-reflective exercise to identify the reasons for change: "Now could you identify the good and the bad things about changing your lifestyle in favor of exercise?" and "Could you think of times in your daily life when you could fit in more exercise?"

- It is suggested that interviewers try to encourage clients to articulate their own reasons for changing their physical activity behavior. Such personal reasons have been shown to be linked to more self-determined forms of motivation. For example, the interviewer might say to the client,

"Tell me what you think are the most important reasons for your doing more exercise in the future."

- Other key strategies are exploring options with clients for changing their sedentary behavior and allowing them to decide what to do and how to do it. With use of these strategies, interviewers will be providing a sense of choice for the individual, a hallmark of self-determined forms of motivation. In such cases the interviewer might suggest to the client types of activities that he or she might find feasible and enjoyable. One might ask the client when he or she would be able to fit in more exercise and then suggest potential solutions: for example, "OK, so you have told me that you think you could spare about 20 minutes, but no more, before work. How about getting off the bus two stops early and briskly walking the rest of the way to work?"

- Practitioners would do well to think in terms of *negotiating* change rather than *prescribing* change to clients toward changing their exercise behavior. Negotiating change supports the need for relatedness with the interviewer and negates the sense that the interviewer is controlling the proceedings. The negotiation should focus on the reasons suggested by the client, but produce a contract or an agreement between the interviewer and client based on these suggestions. The interviewer might summarize the contract like this: "OK, so you mentioned that you were prepared to stop at the gym on Tuesdays and Thursdays after dropping the kids off at school and do 20 minutes on the step machine or 10 laps in the swimming pool. How about trying that for a couple of weeks and see if that works out?"

Self-Determination Theory, Exercise, and Well-Being

Philip M. Wilson, PhD
Brock University

Wendy M. Rodgers, PhD
University of Alberta

Dan and Dave are two high school friends who, like other teen-agers developing during adolescence, enjoy pizza, video games, and music. Dan is the captain of the school rugby team, represents his district in athletics, and has been invited for trials with the local professional football team. He excels in environments where he is challenged physically, and feels alive, energetic, and self-fulfilled when he pushes his capabilities. Dave, on the other hand, is unath-letic, overweight, and considered indolent by his physical education teacher. He cringes at the thought of physical exertion, failed the fitness tests prescribed by the local high school as part of a national health campaign, and struggles to find pleasure or value in physical challenges because they isolate him from more athletically gifted peers. Given his predilection toward inactive pastimes, Dave is reminded of how unfit he is when physical activity beckons, and feels embarrassed in environments that evoke the opportunity for comparison with Dan's physical prowess.

This scenario may sound familiar to any youth sport coach, physical edu-cator, or parent who sees that children's physical capabilities evolve with considerable variability. Martens (1978) recognized this paradox when he suggested that physical activities can promote both joy and sadness. This situ-ation is perplexing for public health advocates given the importance of physical activity for offsetting disease, managing symptoms, and enhancing longevity (Blair & Connelly, 1996). Moreover, physical activity participation appears useful in offsetting depression (Craft & Landers, 1998) and anxiety (Long & van Stavel, 1999) while fostering positive changes in quality of life, vitality, and

Correspondence regarding this chapter should be addressed to Philip M. Wilson, Department of Physical Education and Kinesiology, Faculty of Applied Health Sciences, Brock University, 500 Glenridge Ave., St. Catharines, Ontario, L2S 3A1, Canada. E-mail: phwilson@brocku.ca self-esteem (Ryan & Deci, 2001; Fox, 1997). Considering this evidence, one puzzling question concerns how to cultivate long-term activity involvement when the effects of engagement on personal well-being seem idiosyncratic.

This chapter examines research pertaining to well-being in the context of exercise from the perspective of self-determination theory (Deci & Ryan, 1985, 2002), with a particular emphasis on the role of basic psychological needs as fundamental inputs to a healthy self-system. A brief synopsis of the self and well-being is offered using basic psychological needs as a guiding framework. Evidence from the exercise domain is presented that addresses some of self-determination theory's propositions concerning the relationship between psychological need satisfaction and well-being. The chapter closes with implications and recommendations, presented with an eye to advancing our understanding of the role of psychological need satisfaction in promoting well-being in exercise domains using self-determination theory.

The Self and Well-Being

It is hard to imagine a more important topic in contemporary psychology than the self, even though systematic investigation of this topic has emerged only recently with the demise of behaviorism (Leary & Tangney, 2003). Despite the relative infancy of this line of inquiry, there appear to be good reasons for continued investigation of the self and related emotional qualities that provide an index of psychological well-being. For example, Fox (1997) notes that self-esteem symbolizes emotional stability and adjustment, with links to well-being indices such as vitality, integration, and satisfaction with life. Moreover, self-esteem and related self-perceptions have been linked with a broad array of health behaviors including physical activity and dietary practices (Crocker et al., 2003; Martin Ginis & Leary, 2004).

The lion's share of research concerning the self and well-being in physical activity domains has used the model of self-perception proposed by Shavelson, Hubner, and Stanton (1976) and popularized by the work of Fox and Marsh (see Fox, 1997, for a review). In this model, global self-esteem sits at the apex of the self-perception hierarchy, immediately above perceived physical self-worth, and represents an omnibus indicator of psychological well-being. Physical self-worth, in turn, is underpinned by discrete perceptions of *competence* regarding the body's appearance and function in strength and endurance activities. Research in physical activity domains has supported the structure of this self-perception model and revealed that self-perceptions predict various health behaviors across the life span (Fox, 1997; Hagger, Biddle, & Wang, 2005), although evidence for causal flow between self-perceptions is equivocal (Kowalski, Crocker, Kowalski, Chad, & Humbert, 2003).

Research examining the self in relation to well-being has conceptualized the criterion as either a generalized trait or as a day-to-day estimate of how one is feeling relative to a baseline (Reis, Sheldon, Gable, Rosco, & Ryan, 2000).

Well-being can be characterized as the experience of more positive than negative affect in any given moment along with one's overall estimate of one's experiences as being more positive than negative. Well-being is generally inferred from assessment of positive affect or related constructs such as satisfaction, vitality, and self-esteem. Exercise is pertinent to both types of well-being because at the generalized level, exercisers enjoy a "positive stereotype," rating their well-being as higher compared to nonexercisers (Martin Ginis, Latimer, & Jung, 2003), and because at the person level, individual bouts of exercise facilitate more positive affect (Blanchard, Rodgers, & Gauvin, 2003).

A Self-Determination Perspective on the Self and Well-Being

Self-determination theory proposes an organismic dialectical model of the self in social contexts as a foundation for understanding well-being. Consistent with this view, the self does not represent an appraisal system reliant on perceived *competence* alone as the foundation for well-being. Self-determination theory views the self as an active agent engaged in an ongoing process of integration with ambient cultural and environmental inputs (Deci & Ryan, 1991, 2002). This integrative process is a natural endeavor that is supported (or thwarted) by the degree to which social environments provide opportunities to satisfy basic psychological needs for *competence, autonomy,* and *relatedness* (Deci & Ryan, 2002). In this formulation, the satisfaction of basic psychological needs nourishes the self to assimilate and develop within his or her social world.

Self-determination theory asserts the existence of three basic psychological needs that warrant satisfaction for the self's development and well-being. In this view, psychological needs represent innate and universal inputs required by the self to function effectively and support well-being as opposed to acquired goals, values, or motives (Deci & Ryan, 2002; Ryan & Deci, this volume). According to self-determination theory, the psychological needs for *competence, autonomy,* and *relatedness* qualify as essential inputs to the self's function that appear culturally invariant in terms of their influence on growth, integration, and well-being promotion (Deci & Ryan, 2002). *Competence* concerns feeling effective in mastering challenging tasks and exercising personal capacities within a given domain (White, 1959). The concept of *autonomy* builds upon the work of deCharms (1968) and concerns the extent to which a person feels volitional and agentic in behavioral pursuits as opposed to a pawn of outside forces. Finally, *relatedness* involves perceiving a meaningful connection to others or communities (Baumeister & Leary, 1995). Although not without controversy, the concept of basic psychological needs specified within self-determination theory provides a unified framework for understanding the social conditions that nurture (or derail) the self's development and psychological well-being (Deci & Ryan, 2002). Moreover, emerging evidence supports the dynamic and positive effects across cultures of the satisfaction of these psychological needs (Sheldon, Elliot, Kim, & Kasser, 2001).

Is the Evidence Consistent With Theory?

Despite the intuitive appeal of self-determination theory's basic psychological needs, Vallerand (2001) noted that research in exercise domains has been slow to consider the effects of satisfying *autonomy* and *relatedness* needs compared with the attention bestowed on perceived *competence* as a facilitator of integration and well-being. Building upon Markland's work (Mullan, Markland, & Ingledew, 1997; Mullan & Markland, 1997; Markland, 1999; Markland & Hardy, 1997; Markland & Ingledew, this volume), our research program has attempted to address the complementary nature of need satisfaction along with the links between need satisfaction and indices of internalization such as motivational endorsement and psychological well-being in exercise contexts (Deci & Ryan, 2000; Hagger, Chatzisarantis, & Harris, 2006). Using theoretical arguments as a starting point, we assumed that people experiencing need satisfaction engage in activities volitionally and feel alive and vital while doing so. To the extent that people perceive the environment as denying opportunities for psychological need satisfaction, they either will disengage or will persist under duress to satisfy others or to support a contingent self-worth.

One plausible reason for the status of research on psychological need satisfaction in exercise settings concerns the lack of an established instrument measuring this aspect of self-determination theory's framework. Our work has utilized three different instruments to capture psychological need satisfaction (see table 6.1). The first instrument, adapted from the *self-concordance model* (Sheldon & Elliot, 1999), comprised three single items each measuring one of the need satisfaction constructs. Given the concern around construct representation with single-item indicators, we adapted the Activity Feeling Scale (AFS; Reeve & Sickenius, 1994) to assess psychological need satisfaction in a longitudinal study of prescribed exercise training in a controlled lab setting (Wilson, Rodgers, Blanchard, & Gessell, 2003). This study illustrated psychometric concerns with AFS scores that may be attributable to a lack of item-content relevance of certain AFS items in exercise contexts. The final measure used in our research program is the Psychological Need Satisfaction in Exercise (PNSE) scale, which was developed initially from theoretical specifications of domain clarity and phenomenological accounts of need-satisfying experience provided by exercisers. Using an iterative approach to construct validation (Messick, 1995), our work suggests that PNSE scale scores appear psychometrically sound and predict indices of internalization and well-being in accordance with theoretical arguments.

Self-determination theory's nomological network (Cronbach & Meehl, 1955) concerning psychological need satisfaction provides a platform for testing the

Table 6.1   Measurement of Psychological Need Satisfaction in Exercise

Study	Measure	Stem and list of items
Wilson et al. (2002b) Wilson et al. (2002a)	Single items	Stem: "To what extent do you typically have these experiences in your exercise classes?" *Competence* ("I feel competent and capable in the exercise I attempt") *Autonomy* ("I feel autonomous and choiceful in the exercises I do") *Relatedness* ("I feel related and connected to the people I exercise with")
Wilson et al. (2003)	AFS	Stem: "Participation in exercise makes me feel . . ." *Competence* ("capable," "competent") *Autonomy* ("free"; "I want to do this"; "my participation is voluntary") *Relatedness* ("involved with friends," "part of a team," "brotherly/sisterly")
Wilson et al. (2003) Wilson & Rodgers (2003) Wilson (2004)	PNSE	Stem: "The following statements represent different experiences people have when they exercise. Please answer the following questions by considering how YOU TYPICALLY feel while you are exercising." *Competence* (6 items; sample item: "I feel capable of completing exercises that are challenging to me") *Autonomy* (6 items; sample item: "I feel like I am the one who decides what exercises I do") *Relatedness* (6 items; sample item: "I feel a sense of camaraderie with my exercise companions because we exercise for the same reasons")

Single items were adapted from the work of Sheldon and Elliot (1999). AFS = Activity Feeling Scale (Reeve & Sickenius, 1994). The items dropped were "achieving" (*competence* item) and "offered a choice what to do" (*autonomy* item). PNSE = Psychological Need Satisfaction in Exercise Scale (Wilson, 2004).

following propositions pertaining to internalization and well-being in exercise contexts:

• Proposition 1: The processes of satisfaction of needs for competence, autonomy, and relatedness are complementary psychological processes. Self-determination theory asserts that ongoing satisfaction of basic psychological needs provides the foundation for optimal development, well-being, and the internalization of social values and practices (Deci & Ryan, 2002). Despite the appeal of this framework, the universal and innate nature of self-determination theory's psychological needs has not gone unchallenged, with one major criticism concerning the compatibility of autonomy and relatedness. Self-determination theory proponents have been very clear about this issue and have indicated that the manner in which need satisfaction unfolds is not exclusionary (Deci & Ryan, 2002). Deci and Ryan propose the notion of complementarity in psychological need satisfaction, such that the satisfaction of autonomous needs can occur only in the light of satisfaction for competence and relatedness. Empirically, there is some support for this. For example, Hagger, Chatzisarantis, and Harris (2006) found that latent variables representing the needs for autonomy, competence, and relatedness could be explained by a single global psychological need satisfaction factor.

Our research on this issue has yielded some consistent general trends among the psychological need satisfaction constructs. Overall, the needs for autonomy and competence are generally positively related and of moderate strength, with less strong relationships between these constructs and relatedness. Our first studies of university-based exercise class attendees (Wilson, Rodgers, & Fraser, 2002a, 2002b) supported moderate relationships between perceived competence and autonomy and weaker relationships between satisfaction of these needs and perceived relatedness. A second study using participants enrolled in a 12-week supervised physical training program showed weak-to-moderate relationships between perceived autonomy and competence, which in turn was associated with perceived relatedness (Wilson et al., 2003). In our most recent work using the PNSE scale, a consistent pattern of findings emerged in university fitness class attendees aged 18 to 74 years, who reported greater satisfaction of competence and autonomy than relatedness needs in these exercise contexts (Wilson, 2004; Wilson & Rodgers, 2003).

• Proposition 2: Satisfaction of needs for competence, autonomy, and relatedness will result in greater internalization of behavioral regulations for exercise.

Our research on the link between psychological need satisfaction and exercise regulations extended from Markland's work applying cognitive evaluation theory to exercise, which demonstrated support for the mediating effect of perceived autonomy on the perceived competence–intrinsic motivation relationship (Markland & Hardy, 1997) and showed that perceived competence is less of a concern for people who feel volitional while exercising (Markland, 1999).

Building upon Markland's work, we have examined the links between psychological need satisfaction and self-determination theory's continuum of internalizations defining graded degrees of behavioral regulation. The first study of university students in structured exercise classes (Wilson, Rodgers, & Fraser, 2002b) demonstrated that perceived psychological need satisfaction was most positively associated with identified and intrinsic exercise regulations. Interestingly, however, perceived relatedness was less distinctively associated with more internalized exercise regulations than the other need satisfaction indices, supporting self-determination theory's contention that meaningful connections with others may only catalyze internalization processes (Deci & Ryan, 2002). In other words, relatedness will have a positive influence on people's internalization of certain extrinsically regulated behaviors and make these their own, personally relevant, need-satisfying behaviors.

Our second study (Wilson et al., 2003) examined need satisfaction and motivational dynamics across a 12-week prescribed and monitored cardiovascular training program involving university- and community-based adults. Consistent with findings from our previous work, perceived competence and autonomy showed stronger relationships with more internalized exercise regulations than did perceived relatedness, which was not associated with indices of internalization or perceived autonomy. Moderate-to-large changes in psychological need satisfaction and self-determined regulations were evident across the study. Perhaps of greater theoretical interest is that while participants became increasingly effective in their exercise capacities and experienced an enhanced sense of connection to their exercise companions, their level of perceived autonomy declined considerably across the 12-week period (Wilson et al., 2003). In line with self-determination theory (Deci & Ryan, 2002), these data suggest that perceptions of need satisfaction represent dynamic processes sensitized to environmental conditions and warrant consideration in health promotion endeavors where the landscape is dominated by "prescriptive" approaches.

Our third study (Wilson, 2004) addressed the influence of psychological need satisfaction on internalization over the course of a 10-week self-selected exercise class aimed at reducing the prescriptive nature of the social environment. Structural equation modeling analyses of time 1 data indicated that satisfaction of competence and autonomy needs predicted the endorsement of identified and intrinsic exercise regulations. Interestingly, satisfaction of relatedness needs was associated with both external and identified regulations when considered jointly with the other need satisfaction indices. This finding corroborates our preliminary work (Wilson, Rodgers, & Fraser, 2002b) and suggests that feeling a meaningful connection to others or to one's community may be of little importance to intrinsically motivated activity and more important to extrinsic regulation of behavior, whether it be autonomous (e.g., identified) or nonautonomous (e.g., introjected). Changes were evident across the 10 weeks, with increases in all three need satisfaction indices as well as more internalized exercise regulations. Analysis of residual change scores indicated that elevations in all three need satisfaction indices were correlated with increased levels of intrinsic motivation and elevations in perceived autonomy and competence, though not perceived relatedness, were correlated with identified regulation. Collectively, these data provide initial support for the joint influence of perceived psychological need satisfaction on the internalization of exercise regulations, and suggest that elevations in perceptions of need satisfaction covary with the internalization of exercise motivation in a manner consistent with self-determination theory (Deci & Ryan, 1985, 2002; Hagger, Chatzisarantis, & Harris, 2006).

• Proposition 3: Satisfaction of competence, autonomy, and relatedness needs will promote a greater sense of well-being in exercise contexts. The final proposition pertaining to the self and basic psychological needs articulated within self-determination theory concerns the link between need satisfaction and well-being. One of the hallmark characteristics of psychological needs from the viewpoint of self-determination theory is the direct relation between need satisfaction and well-being. Self-determination theory makes a distinction between hedonic well-being, which focuses on happiness and pleasure as defining features, and eudaemonia, which refers to the well-being of a fully functional organism not solely focused on obtaining desired outcomes (Ryan & Deci, 2001). Considering the importance of well-being in exercise contexts (Fox, 1997), and the appeal of self-determination theory's assertions regarding the role of need-satisfying experiences in well-being promotion, it is surprising that research in this area has been scarce. One explanation for this situation is the difficulty of measuring eudaemonic well-being, which has been indexed using various measures ranging from vitality to positive affect and self-esteem (Deci & Ryan, 2002). Notwithstanding this limitation, emerging lab-based experiments with university-aged adults have linked choice of exercise mode (Daley & Maynard, 2003; Parfitt & Gledhill, 2004), not intensity (Parfitt, Rose, & Markland, 2000), with elevations in exercise-specific perceptions of well-being.

Complementing these lab studies, two recent investigations in naturalistic settings have explored the influence of internalizations varying in their degree of perceived autonomy on perceived physical self-worth in Greek (Georgiadis, Biddle, & Chatzisarantis, 2001) and Canadian (Wilson & Rodgers, 2002) exercisers. Both studies noted that greater degrees of internalization with respect to exercise regulation were associated with elevated physical self-worth. Moreover, the study by Wilson and Rodgers indicated that more self-determined internalizations discriminated between females reporting high versus low physical self-worth in structured exercise classes, and the study by Georgiadis and colleagues indicated that more self-determined internalizations were stronger correlates of physical self-worth in recreational exercisers than task and ego orientations toward exercise competence.

While these studies clarify the role of internalization processes in motivating exercise behavior, neither study directly addressed the influence of psychological need satisfaction on well-being. Two additional investigations have dealt with this issue more directly. In the first (Wilson, Rodgers, Fraser, Murray, & McIntyre, 2004), hierarchical regression analyses supported the influence of need-satisfying experiences on physical self-worth and global self-esteem in females engaged in university-based exercise classes. Physical self-worth partially mediated the relationship between need satisfaction and global self-esteem; however, perceived autonomy retained a direct effect on global self-esteem, suggesting that the routes to global self-regard extend beyond the confines of perceived competencies articulated in most self-perception hierarchies (Fox, 1997).

In the second investigation (Wilson, Muon, Longley, & Rodgers, 2005), three separate studies addressed the influence of psychological need satisfaction on subjective well-being indices specific to exercise. The first study indicated that overall psychological need satisfaction was associated with greater positive well-being and less psychological distress in university-based exercisers. The second study indicated that satisfaction of each psychological need contributed to greater positive affect during typical exercise sessions, while greater autonomy was strongly associated with reduced negative affect during exercise. Finally, the third study noted that the contributions of perceived competence, autonomy, and relatedness to positive and negative affect remained robust after the influence of other candidate psychological needs (namely self-actualization, physical thriving, security, and popularity) was controlled for in patrons of a university fitness facility. While the results of these studies are tentative, they lend support to the theoretical links between satisfaction of competence, autonomy, and relatedness needs and well-being attainment in the sphere of structured exercise participation.

Summary and Recommendations

The focus of this chapter has been on the role of perceived psychological need satisfaction from the perspective of self-determination theory in the promotion of internalization and well-being in exercise. While the evidence is limited in scope and quality compared with that from research on self-determination theory's organismic integration subtheory, the available data appear promising and illustrate the importance of need satisfaction to well-being in exercisers. The available data suggest that perceptions of competence, autonomy, and relatedness form necessary inputs into a well-internalized self-system of behavior regulations and also promote a greater sense of "wellness" in exercise domains. Taken together with theoretical arguments (Deci & Ryan, 2002), the emerging evidence suggests that basic psychological needs may be a promising area for future researchers interested in understanding the roots of well-being in exercise from an "organismic" perspective. Given that professional practice resides on evidence-based decision making, physical activity proponents may wish to consider several guidelines based on these research findings for enhancing psychological well-being, summarized in the practical recommendations at the end of this chapter.

Although research on the nature and function of self-determination theory's basic psychological needs and their relative satisfaction in exercise contexts is unfolding, a number of areas warrant more careful attention in future research. Researchers should seek to move beyond nonexperimental designs and convenience sampling techniques. Instead, experimental and panel designs help to elucidate the direction of causal flow implied within self-determination theory between perceived psychological need satisfaction and indices of both internalization and well-being; such designs also establish the external validity of these relationships across cultures, people, settings, and time. Such approaches may consider time-series, prospective designs with sufficient time points, segmented according to meaningful time criteria, to establish the rate and nature of changes inherent in the need satisfaction variables integral to internalization. Additional attention to the measurement of well-being using the conceptual distinction between trait-like and state-like components of well-being described by Reis and colleagues (2000) would be helpful in determining the short- and long-term implications of need satisfaction on well-being.

In addition, there are measurement issues that need to be addressed in research on self-determination theory and the self in physical activity contexts. Attention to construct validation is an ongoing endeavor that is corroborated by the mosaic of evidence informing test score interpretation and use (Messick, 1995). While the available evidence supports select psychometric characteristics of PNSE scores, future researchers would do well to consider examining the stability of PNSE scores over meaningful epochs that are linked with natural transitions in exercise behavior, the sensitivity of PNSE scale scores to invariance across subgroups and contexts, and the susceptibility of PNSE scale scores to socially desirable response bias, to name just a few plausible directions. It seems that the utility of basic psychological needs concerns the broad range of exercise-related issues that can be addressed using this facet of the framework of self-determination theory. While much work remains to be done, the initial evidence is promising, and there is reason for optimism regarding the role afforded by basic psychological needs in the promotion of well-being in exercise.

Practical Recommendations Based on Research With Self-Determination Theory to Enhance Psychological Well-Being

- Practitioners such as health professionals, exercise promoters, and physical education teachers are advised to provide opportunities for individuals to maximize perceptions of *competence* focused on self-improvement, rather than social comparison and personal comparison with reference to unrealistic external standards and no contingency for other markers of competence. Feeling effective in one's environment is associated with the internalization of motives responsible for long-term persistence behavior and greater psychological health in exercise domains. For example, an exercise specialist might give a sedentary individual the choice of a number of novel activities and provide opportunities to try them out with other novices. This is a useful strategy for people initiating changes to engage in more regular exercise because it provides them with a sense of choice and helps them set their own goals for improvement, as there is no previous experience of low competence.

- A further recommendation is the provision of opportunities for people to gain a sense of *autonomy* over their participation. Feeling a sense of volition in exercise settings appears to be integral to the development of optimal motives regulating long-term investment, and also to the facilitation of psychological health and well-being. For example, an exercise professional might suggest to clients that they decide when, where, and how they are going to perform their chosen form of exercise, record these decisions, and then keep a diary to note whether they have carried out the chosen activities. Such an endeavor will provide exercisers with a sense of personal ownership over their actions, which is linked to autonomy.

- Practitioners are encouraged to provide opportunities for people to establish meaningful connections with others while engaging in exercise activities, or to feel that they belong to a larger community of exercisers, or both, to reduce the effects of social isolation. Such endeavors will likely lead to the initiation of the internalization process through enhanced relatedness and acceptance of the value of exercise, which will promote long-term exercise participation, internalized motivational structures, and feelings of psychological health and well-being. For example, physical education teachers are encouraged to get children working in small groups cooperatively to complete a sport or exercise skill. The cooperation should satisfy needs for relatedness.

- It is suggested that practitioners avoid creating the perception that support relies solely on the *outcomes* derived from exercise. Although outcomes can provide valuable information on competence, particularly in competitive environments, a reliance on such outcomes as the sole source of competence may result in the thwarting of psychological needs. Environments cultivating the feeling that support for exercise participation is contingent upon individuals' fitness or health outcomes are unlikely to satisfy basic psychological needs; they are more likely to hinder well-being and lead to possible disengagement from the activity. Exercise specialists can create environments that do not emphasize outcomes by encouraging clients to talk about their experiences of exercise and to investigate the reasons why they want to do more exercise.

- Practitioners are also encouraged to avoid overemphasizing the importance of environmental support (as in structuring realistic expectations or

(continued)

(continued)

involving others through genuine interest) in a manner that favors the satisfaction of one psychological need over another. Self-determination theory has been clear in asserting that the satisfaction of competence, autonomy, and relatedness needs in combination is fundamental to improved psychological health and well-being in any domain, including exercise. For example, health professionals interested in well-being promotion would be wise to organize exercise contexts to facilitate opportunities to satisfy each psychological need. Therefore, practices should focus on helping exercisers choose the right activities for them (to facilitate autonomy), select activities in which they can progress and learn (to help them demonstrate competence), and identify potential exercise partners (to facilitate relatedness).

The Flow State and Physical Activity Behavior Change as Motivational Outcomes

A Self-Determination Theory Perspective

Michelle Fortier, PhD
University of Ottawa

John Kowal, PhD
Ottawa Hospital General Campus

Although numerous motivational theories exist, self-determination theory (Deci & Ryan, 1985; Ryan & Deci, 2000) is a particularly useful approach for examining motivational outcomes because of its emphasis on human needs, motivational processes (e.g., self-regulation), and the social context. This theoretical framework has been well supported in a variety of contexts and in a wide range of populations (Deci & Ryan, 2002; Ryan & Deci, this volume; Sheldon, Williams, & Joiner, 2003; Vallerand, 1997), and this includes the physical activity domain (Frederick-Recascino, 2002; Vallerand, 2001; Vallerand & Losier, 1999). (Please note that in this chapter the term *physical activity* encompasses or includes sport, leisure-time physical activity, and structured exercise. This is in accordance with the widely used definition of physical activity as "any bodily movement produced by skeletal muscles that results in energy expenditure" [Caspersen, Powell, & Christenson, 1985, p. 126]. We also concur with these authors' definition of exercise as a subcategory of physical activity that is "planned, structured, repetitive, and purposive" [p. 128].)

Indeed, self-determination theory is being increasingly recommended and used in the physical activity context (Biddle & Nigg, 2000; Landry & Solomon, 2002). In terms of motivational consequences, autonomous motivation has been positively associated with attitudes about good sporting behavior (Vallerand & Losier, 1994), positive emotions (Frederick, Morrison, & Manning, 1996;

Correspondence concerning this article should be addressed to Michelle Fortier, School of Human Kinetics and Psychology, University of Ottawa, P.O. Box 450, Stn. A, Ottawa, Ontario, Canada, K1N 6N5. E-mail: mfortier@uottawa.ca

Li, 1999) and flow (Kowal & Fortier, 1999, 2000), and physical activity intentions (Kowal & Fortier, 2005; Standage, Duda, & Ntoumanis, 2003; Wilson & Rodgers, 2004), as well as with behavioral outcomes like sport persistence (Pelletier, Fortier, Vallerand, & Brière, 2001; Sarrazin, Vallerand, Guillet, Pelletier, & Cury, 2002), leisure-time physical activity (Hagger, Chatzisarantis, Culverhouse, & Biddle, 2003), exercise adherence (Fortier & Grenier, 1999; Ryan, Frederick, Lepes, Rubio, & Sheldon, 1997), stage of physical activity behavior change (Fortier, Sweet et al., 2006; Ingledew, Markland, & Medley, 1998; Mullan & Markland, 1997), and physical fitness (Wilson, Rodgers, Blanchard, & Gessell, 2003). It should be noted that the term *autonomous motivation* is used throughout this chapter and can be considered synonymous with self-determined motivation (see Ryan & Deci, this volume; Pelletier & Sarrazin, this volume). In terms of the perceived locus of causality or continuum of self-determination, autonomous motivation includes identified regulation, intrinsic motivation, or a combination of the two (Ryan & Deci, this volume).

Two motivational outcomes that have been of particular interest in our research program over the past decade are flow and physical activity behavior change. Indeed, we have conducted a number of investigations using self-determination theory as a conceptual framework for examining these consequences. Our aim in this chapter is to briefly review the extant literature on flow and physical activity behavior change from the vantage point of self-determination theory and to present our research findings in these areas. Theoretical implications are discussed, and future research directions are proposed. Practical applications are also outlined, especially in terms of fostering flow and physical activity behavior change.

Self-Determination Theory and Flow

A subjective human experience that has been closely examined over the past several decades is a positive psychological state known as *flow* (Csikszentmihalyi, 1975a, 1990). This highly enjoyable experiential state entails the "holistic sensation that people feel when they act with total involvement (in an activity)" (Csikszentmihalyi, 1975b, p. 36). Indeed, flow has been associated with peak physical activity performance (Jackson & Csikszentmihalyi, 1999; Kimiecik & Jackson, 2002). Research by Csikszentmihalyi and others (e.g., Jackson & Marsh, 1996) has identified numerous characteristics of flow, including concentration on the task at hand, a merging of action and awareness, a sense of control, a transformation of time, and a balance between perceived skills and challenges.

Csikszentmihalyi's conceptualization of flow was founded, at least in part, on the pioneering work of deCharms (1968), Deci (1971), and White (1959) on intrinsic motivation. For this reason, intrinsic motivation and flow have been considered conceptually similar (Csikszentmihalyi & Nakamura, 1989; Csikszentmihalyi & Rathunde, 1993), although they are not to be considered synonymous (see Ryan & Deci, this volume). Within the framework of self-determination theory, certain researchers have likened flow to an intrinsic motivation to experience stimulation (Pelletier et al., 1995; Pelletier & Sarrazin, this volume). Others have shown that flow and interest are two aspects of the subjective experience of intrinsic motivation (Waterman et al., 2003). In our own research, flow has been conceptualized as a positive psychological state experienced during engagement in an activity (i.e., a motivational outcome), whereas motivation has been conceptualized as the energy (i.e., internal or external forces or both) responsible for initiation, duration, and persistence of behavior (i.e., a determinant of flow).

One line of inquiry has addressed variables that might bring about this optimal psychological state. A consistent finding in work and leisure settings is that intrinsic motivation is associated with flow (Csikszentmihalyi & LeFevre, 1989; Graef, Csikszentmihalyi, & McManama-Gianinno, 1983). It has also been found that autonomous forms of extrinsic motivation (e.g., identified regulation) are related to the intensity of flow experiences (Mannell, Zuzanek, & Larson, 1988). Moreover, there is some evidence that flow is associated with teenagers' motivation to seek out opportunities to enhance their skills and abilities over time (Csikszentmihalyi, Rathunde, & Whelan, 1993).

In the context of sport and exercise, qualitative investigations have demonstrated that motivation plays an important role in athletes' flow experiences (Jackson, 1992, 1995). A task-involved goal orientation (a motivational orientation toward improving one's level of skill or mastering a given task) and perceived competence have both been positively associated with flow (Jackson & Roberts, 1992). Other studies, however, have failed to support relationships between situational motivational variables and this psychological state (Stein, Kimiecik, Daniels, & Jackson, 1995).

Although flow has been associated with motivational variables (e.g., autonomous forms of motivation and perceived competence), until recently, very few studies have used self-determination theory as a conceptual framework for examining this optimal psychological state. Indeed, self-determination theory is highly salient in this regard because it distinguishes between different forms of motivation based on the degree to which they are autonomous. Indeed, in a study of theater performers, flow was associated with intrinsic motivation to experience stimulation and intrinsic motivation to accomplish (Martin & Cutler, 2002). Self-determination theory is also useful for examining important phenomena such as the flow state because it describes motivation as a process beginning with determinants and ending with consequences.

Our own research has examined flow by conceptualizing it as a motivational outcome within the conceptual framework of self-determination theory. In particular, we were interested in examining the influence of situational motivational variables and situational autonomous motivation on flow, as well as the relationship between flow and contextual autonomous motivation over time. Our research has been conducted on a cross-sectional and a longitudinal basis.

In one of our studies (Kowal & Fortier, 1999), we assessed relationships among different types of situational motivation and flow, as well as among situational motivational determinants (perceptions of autonomy, competence, and relatedness) and the experience of this psychological state. Participants were Canadian masters-level swimmers (N = 203) who completed a situational questionnaire assessing motivational determinants, motivation, and flow immediately following a swim practice. In line with self-determination theory, swimmers who were motivated in an autonomous manner reported the highest levels of flow. Conversely, swimmers who reported being oriented toward more controlling forms of motivation (i.e., individuals who participated due to internal or external pressures or were amotivated to participate) reported the lowest levels of this psychological state. Perceptions of autonomy, competence, and relatedness were also found to be positively associated with flow, suggesting a mediational model between motivational style and flow.

In a follow-up longitudinal study (Kowal & Fortier, 2000), we tested a motivational model based on the hierarchical model of intrinsic and extrinsic motivation (Vallerand, 1997, 2001). This theoretical motivational model, based on self-determination theory, incorporates motivational constructs at multiple levels of generality (for a more detailed description, see Vallerand, 1997, 2001, this volume). We specifically examined relationships among situational and contextual motivational variables using flow as a situational motivational outcome. Canadian masters-level swimmers (N = 104) completed a psychological questionnaire on two separate occasions. At baseline, situational social variables (e.g., perceptions of the motivational climate), situational motivational mediators (perceptions of autonomy, competence, and relatedness), situational motivation, and flow at the situational level of generality were assessed immediately following a swim practice. Contextual-level measures of these same variables were assessed one week later, with the exception of flow. Data were analyzed using path analysis. Positive associations were obtained between situational perceptions of autonomy, competence, and relatedness and situational autonomous motivation. As well, contextual-level perceptions of relatedness predicted contextual autonomous motivation. Of particular interest, situational autonomous motivation was positively related to flow, suggesting that swimmers' reasons for engaging in a particular activity may facilitate flow experiences. A modest but positive relationship was also observed between flow and contextual-level motivation.

Theoretical Implications and Future Research on Flow and Self-Determination Theory

Collectively, results of our studies have supported many of the theoretical tenets of self-determination theory, and they concur with the results of past studies in which intrinsic motivation was positively associated with flow (e.g., Csikszentmihalyi & LeFevre, 1989; Graef, Csikszentmihalyi, & McManama-Gianinno, 1983; Haworth & Hill, 1992; Martin & Cutler, 2002). Our findings have also supported a wealth of investigations linking autonomous forms of motivation to positive outcomes (Deci & Ryan, 2002; Sheldon, Williams, & Joiner, 2003; Vallerand, 1997, 2001). Moreover, consistent with the hierarchical model of motivation (Vallerand, 1997, 2001) and with self-determination theory in general (Deci & Ryan, 2002), results have demonstrated that situational autonomous motivation is associated with situational motivational outcomes (i.e., flow).

One line of future inquiry would be to further examine associations between situational motivation and flow, particularly because certain studies have supported this relationship (Kowal & Fortier, 1999, 2000) whereas others have not (Stein et al., 1995). Additional research could further assess the link between flow and contextual motivation. Indeed, in our own research (Kowal & Fortier, 1999, 2000), we have conceptualized flow as a motivational outcome. It is also possible that the experience of flow could enhance autonomous motivation, and there is some initial evidence to support this (Csikszentmihalyi, Rathunde, & Whelan, 1993; Kowal & Fortier, 2000). As with many variables, it is likely that there is a reciprocal relationship between autonomous motivation and flow states. Regardless of one's initial motives for engaging in an activity, experiencing flow could lead one to engage in that activity out of choice (i.e., in an autonomous manner). As has been shown empirically, and consistent with self-determination theory, this could promote subsequent experiences of flow. A longitudinal, cross-lagged panel design could test these hypotheses.

Research has shown that perceptions of autonomy, competence, and relatedness are associated with flow (Kowal & Fortier, 1999; see also Jackson & Marsh, 1996; Waterman et al., 2003). These basic needs are central to self-determination theory and key to understanding optimal development within the framework of positive psychology (Deci & Vansteenkiste, 2004; see also Ryan & Deci, 2000). Whether these three fundamental needs are directly associated with flow or whether these relationships are mediated by autonomous motivation is an empirical question that could certainly be addressed in future studies. In a similar vein, social aspects of flow have received limited attention in past research. Feeling close to or connected with teammates, partners, or colleagues may play an important role in flow states (Jackson, 1995; Kowal & Fortier, 1999). Future studies may do well to assess the social nature of flow in group settings such as team sports or in interpersonal relations. Within self-determination theory, this could be accomplished via specific examination of the need for relatedness. Building on recent studies integrating flow theory and self-determination theory (Moneta, 2004), future studies could examine the potential moderating role of culture in athletes' flow experiences.

Practical Applications for Promoting Flow Experiences in Exercise and Sport

From an applied perspective, there is growing empirical evidence that engaging in sport and physical activity out of personal choice or for enjoyment (or both) may facilitate the experience of flow, which could also facilitate sport performance and physical activity maintenance. Autonomous forms of motivation could be fostered through enhancement of the fundamental needs for autonomy, competence, and relatedness (Hagger, Chatzisarantis, & Harris, 2006). Consistent with self-determination theory, these three basic needs could be fostered by coaches, parents, teachers, sport psychology consultants, and health care providers through provision of autonomy-supportive contexts that emphasize the acknowledgement of others' perspectives and feelings, the provision of choice (e.g., in terms of participation in physical activities, pre-competition planning and preparation, etc.), and the provision of a meaningful rationale (Sheldon, Williams, & Joiner, 2003). Providing social, emotional, and instrumental support and emphasizing personal growth and development, as well as encouraging mastery and the enhancement of skills, could also be useful in this regard.

Self-Determination Theory and Physical Activity Behavior Change

Numerous studies have demonstrated the utility of self-determination theory for understanding a wide range of health behaviors (Sheldon, Williams, & Joiner, 2003; Williams, 2002). In particular, self-determination theory has been supported in studies of weight loss and weight loss maintenance (Williams, Grow, Freedman, Ryan, & Deci, 1996), diabetes self-care and glycemic control (Sénécal, Nouwen, & White, 2000; Williams, McGregor, Zeldman, Freedman, & Deci, 2004), and smoking cessation (Williams, Cox, Kouides, & Deci, 1999; Williams, Gagné, Ryan, & Deci, 2002). In the physical activity context, a number of studies have examined the influence of self-determination on behavior. In the exercise domain, two earlier studies (Oman & McAuley, 1993; Ryan et al., 1997) investigated the link between exercise motivation and exercise adherence. Results revealed that intrinsic motives are an important determinant of exercise program participation.

Building on this work, we conducted a study in which 40 people who joined a fitness center were tracked for one month and their weekly minutes of exercise recorded and used as a measure of adherence. Autonomous exercise motivation emerged as an important predictor of exercise adherence (Fortier & Grenier, 1999). More recently, in the sport domain, Pelletier, Fortier, Vallerand, and Brière (2001) and Sarrazin and colleagues (2002) demonstrated that sport participants who were autonomously motivated were more likely to persist over time than those who were nonautonomously motivated. These findings have been replicated in two prospective studies on leisure-time physical activity, one with high school students (Hagger et al., 2003) and one with middle-aged adults (Wilson et al., 2003).

Although all these studies were pivotal in fostering a better understanding of the motivational underpinnings of physical activity behavior, they did not specifically investigate physical activity behavior change. This led us and others to further examine the link between self-determination and the physical activity behavior change process.

Self-Determination Theory and the Transtheoretical Model

Indeed, various cross-sectional and longitudinal studies, including some from our laboratory, have linked self-determination with the stages of physical activity behavior change. Most of these have used the transtheoretical model (Prochaska & DiClemente, 1983) and specifically Prochaska and DiClemente's (1986) stages of change model (Prochaska & Velicer, 1997). This model proposes five stages illustrating the chronological steps that individuals can move up or down while attempting to adopt and maintain a particular behavior. Specifically, someone who is not engaging in or does not intend to engage in physical activity is considered to be in the precontemplation stage. One who is not engaging in physical activity but is thinking about doing so is in the contemplation stage. An individual who begins to do physical activity, but not on a regular basis, is in the preparation stage. Once an individual is doing regular physical activity but has not done it for more than six months, he or she is in the action stage. Finally, someone who has participated in regular physical activity for a period of six months or more is considered to be in the maintenance stage.

The first study to integrate self-determination theory with the transtheoretical model was by Mullan and Markland (1997), who compared the exercise motivation of healthy adults in each stage of change and demonstrated that, as predicted, individuals in the higher stages of change were more autonomously motivated than those in the lower stages. Extending these findings, we conducted a cross-sectional study on motivational and barrier differences between the stages (Leblanc, 1999). This research, with male employees of a Canadian electric power commission (N = 74), revealed that two of the three types of intrinsic motivation (toward accomplishment and toward knowledge) were key in discriminating between active and less active participants.

More recently, Landry and Solomon (2004) conducted a study with African American women, an at-risk population, and revealed that participants in the later stages (i.e., preparation, action, and maintenance) were more autonomously motivated than those in the lower stages (i.e., contemplation and precontemplation). Other researchers (e.g., Ingledew, Markland, & Sheppard, 2004; Rose, Parfitt, & Williams, 2005) obtained similar results. These studies supported the notion that self-determination is important in the physical activity behavior change process; however, the fact that constructs were assessed at only one time point posed a serious limitation. In addition, even though Landry and Solomon (2004) targeted an at-risk population, there had been no investigations of self-determination in the regulation of physical activity behavior in a diseased population.

This was the purpose of Fortier and colleagues' (Fortier, Sweet et al., 2006) longitudinal study. Specifically, the aim of this research was to examine how exercise motivation, namely autonomous and nonautonomous motivation, changes as individuals with type 2 diabetes (N = 225) progress through the various stages of change from contemplation (baseline) to action (three months), and finally to maintenance (six months), using a randomized controlled trial for different exercise interventions, resistance (weight) training or aerobic (treadmill) training or a combination of the two. Hierarchical linear modeling revealed that autonomous motivation significantly increased as people progressed from contemplation to action, then leveled off at maintenance. Follow-up regression analyses showed that participants in the resistance group had, over time, a greater increase in autonomous motivation than the aerobic group, as well as the combined (resistance and aerobic training) and control groups. Of particular interest in this study was the gender-by-exercise condition moderation effects. For participants in the resistance conditions, there was a much steeper increase in autonomous motivation for females, while in the aerobic condition there was much steeper decrease in autonomous motivation over time for females. For males in both conditions, autonomous motivation seemed to increase from contemplation to action, then level off at maintenance. A similar trend was found between resistance and control. Finally, results showed a significant gender-by-condition interaction between the control and combined conditions, suggesting that for both conditions, females' motivation became more autonomous from contemplation to maintenance compared to that of their male counterparts. However, the interaction did not belie the fact that autonomous motivation was highest at the end of the trial (maintenance) for the resistance condition in both genders, but merely indicated that the effects of the manipulation appeared to be most apparent for females.

Although these studies contribute to an increasing understanding of the relationship between self-determination and physical activity behavior change, it should be acknowledged that some key researchers in this field (Armitage & Arden, 2002; Sutton, 2000) have suggested that the transtheoretical model is a pseudo-stage model that does not really exhibit true stage characteristics across psychological variables. Future research should consider using other stage models or different methodologies to test for nonlinear changes in psychological variables across stages.

Self-Determination Theory and the Theory of Planned Behavior

Recently, some researchers have integrated concepts from self-determination theory with concepts from the theory of planned behavior (Ajzen, 1985, 1991) in order to better understand direct and indirect pathways between physical activity motivation, intentions, and physical activity behavior and behavior change (Chatzisarantis & Biddle, 1998; Chatzisarantis, Biddle, & Meek, 1997; Chatzisarantis, Hagger, Biddle, & Karageorghis, 2002; Hagger et al., 2003, 2006; Hagger & Armitage, 2004; Hagger, Chatzisarantis, Barkoukis, Wang, & Baranowski, 2005; Hagger, Chatzisarantis, & Biddle, 2002; Wilson & Rodgers, 2004). Autonomous motivation has been associated with physical activity intentions (Ntoumanis, 2001; Standage, Duda, & Ntoumanis, 2003; Wilson & Rodgers, 2004), and physical activity intentions have been linked to physical activity behavior over time (Sarrazin et al., 2002). Global motives have been indirectly associated with physical activity intentions through perceived behavioral control, attitudes, and subjective norms (Hagger, Chatzisarantis, & Biddle, 2002). There is also evidence that autonomous and controlled motives mediate the relationship between perceived competence and physical activity intentions (Chatzisarantis, Hagger, Biddle, Smith, & Wang, 2003). Other studies have provided modest support for the moderating effect of motivation on the intentions–behavior link (e.g., Chatzisarantis, Biddle, & Meek, 1997; Sheeran, Norman, & Orbell, 1999).

Our own research has addressed relationships among intentions, motivation, and physical activity behavior change in middle-aged women by integrating concepts from the theory of planned behavior and self-determination theory. In one of our studies (Kowal & Fortier, 2005), we assessed the relative contributions of theory of planned behavior variables (attitudes, perceived behavioral control, and subjective norms) and self-determination theory variables (autonomous and controlled motivation) to intentions to increase physical activity. Participants in this cross-sectional study were French-speaking middle-aged women (N = 109) recruited from community-based facilities. In line with predictions, attitudes and perceived behavioral control were significantly associated with physical activity intentions. More interestingly, autonomous motivation uniquely contributed to physical activity intentions beyond and above attitudes, perceived behavioral control, and subjective norms.

In a second longitudinal study (Kowal & Fortier, 2005), the purpose was to assess physical activity behavior change over time by integrating concepts from the theory of planned behavior and self-determination theory. We specifically assessed mediating and moderating influences among motivation, intentions, and physical activity behavior change. Middle-aged English-speaking women (N = 149) completed a questionnaire assessing theory of planned behavior variables (attitudes, perceived behavioral control, subjective norms, and intentions), self-determination theory variables (autonomy-supportive and controlling interpersonal styles, autonomous and controlled motivation), and physical activity behavior. Six months later, physical activity was reassessed. Attitudes and subjective norms were significantly related to intentions to increase physical activity. Autonomous motivation was also significantly associated with physical activity intentions. Although intentions to increase physical activity were predictive of change in physical activity behavior over time, autonomous motivation was not. Autonomy-supportive and controlling interpersonal styles were also associated with autonomous and controlled motivation, respectively.

Self-Determination Theory Within the Ecological Model

Lastly, in a follow-up qualitative study (Humphries, 2005), middle-aged and older women's physical activity maintenance was explored using an ecological model (Sallis & Owen, 1999). Motivation, as conceptualized within the framework of self-determination theory, was the main factor explored at the intrapersonal level. Because little is currently known about the motivation of individuals who maintain physical activity (Deci & Ryan, 2002), this study explored not only what motivated these women to be physically active, but also how their motivation had changed over time to help them remain physically active.

In line with self-determination theory and past research (Landry & Solomon, 2004), some of the reasons cited by maintainers were autonomous in character. For example, many maintainers cited fun and enjoyment (e.g., "If you consider it a burden then you need some motivation, but to me it's not, its fun" [p. 5]) as the main reason they exercised, one that has been frequently associated with autonomous motives. Respondents also cited health reasons (e.g., "It just kind of grounds you. You need it to be physically, mentally and emotionally healthy" [p. 5]), positive feelings (e.g., "I think the way it makes you feel. There's nothing like it. Whether it's a good game or bad you are out there doing it and however this affects you, it's always a good thing" [p. 5]), and socializing with others (e.g., "Well I am in two pretty social sports . . . you do play in foursomes and the league I am in, the four ladies we get along really well. We met at the league but we continued on with each other during the winter as well. Curling is also very social" [p. 6]) as reasons for their participation. These reasons may be autonomous if they are perceived to serve autonomous goals and psychological needs, and future research should aim to establish where such reasons lie on the self-determination continuum.

With regard to changes in physical activity motivation over the life span, women indicated (retrospectively) that they were autonomously motivated, especially intrinsically motivated, in childhood (fun); that their motivation in adolescence was a combination of autonomous and nonautonomous (socializing); that in young adulthood or motherhood it was mainly nonautonomous (to get back in shape); that in middle adulthood it was a combination of autonomous and nonautonomous (appearance or weight control); and, finally, that in older adulthood it was mostly autonomous. A longitudinal approach would work well to further investigate changes in physical activity motivation over the life span. (It should be noted that types of reasons such as "to get back in shape" can be autonomous if they have been internalized and integrated into a person's repertoire of behaviors that satisfy psychological needs and thus can still result in persistence and continuity [see Hagger & Chatzisarantis, this volume; Standage, Gillison, & Treasure, this volume].)

Theoretical Implications

Our work, as well as that of others, has demonstrated that combining self-determination theory with other solid theories is a fruitful approach to enhance our understanding of the physical activity behavior change process. Indeed there has been a call for an integration of self-determination theory and stages of change theories given their resemblance with respect to the aim of understanding behavioral regulation over time (Abblett, 2002; Landry & Solomon, 2002). Another useful framework to combine with self-determination theory is the ecological framework (Sallis & Owen, 1999). Although self-determination theory has the potential for understanding relationships among psychological variables, social variables, and behavior (see Conner & Norman, 2005; Deci & Ryan, 2002), it does not typically include variables of a physiological, demographic, social-cultural, or policy-based nature, which have been found to influence physical activity (Sallis & Owen, 1999; Trost, Bauman, Sallis, & Brown, 2002) and are integrated in ecological approaches.

Future Research on Physical Activity Behavior Change and Self-Determination Theory

Future studies would do well to include self-determination theory within a broader ecological model to examine complex phenomena such as physical activity behavior change. Longitudinal, multiple-wave designs and sophisticated data analytic strategies, including hierarchical linear modeling, would be particularly useful in this regard. Integrating measures of flow as a mediator between motivation and physical activity behavior change to tie together these two areas of research would also be an interesting and worthy pursuit. In addition, we concur with Landry and Solomon (2004) that using complementary qualitative approaches would be valuable. This could serve, for instance, to further probe physical activity goal content and motivation (Sheldon, Ryan, Deci, & Kasser, 2004; Vansteenkiste, Simons, Lens, Sheldon, & Deci, 2004) and their links with physical activity behavior change. Using self-determination theory to understand other at-risk or diseased individuals' physical activity adoption and maintenance is another direction that needs to be explored.

Finally, another interesting research avenue would involve designing a self-determination theory-based intervention to foster physical activity behavior change, incorporating suggestions given in the following section, and testing its effectiveness. In response to this need, we are conducting a randomized controlled trial to test the effects of a self-determination theory-based physical activity counseling intervention on the self-determination, perceptions of competence, and physical activity behavior of primary care patients (Fortier, Hogg, et al., 2006; also see Tulloch, Fortier, & Hogg, in press, for background information). It is hypothesized that patients receiving brief autonomy-supportive physical activity counseling from their family physician plus intensive autonomy-supportive counseling from a physical activity counselor integrated into the primary health care team will show larger increases in their physical activity self-determination, perceived competence toward physical activity, and physical activity behavior, over a three-month period, than those patients receiving only brief autonomy-supportive physical activity counseling from their family physician.

Practical Applications for the Maintenance of Physical Activity Behavior

The findings of Fortier and colleagues (Fortier, Sweet et al., 2006) seem to indicate that resistance (weight training) exercise is a promising way to foster autonomous motivation for females particularly, as well as for males, and thus might possibly promote higher physical activity maintenance. More research is needed in this area, however. The results from Kowal and Fortier (2005) also lead to practical recommendations, specifically that autonomy support (i.e., the provision of choice, the encouragement of initiative, and the support of freedom) from significant others, such as a spouse or friend, should be encouraged to foster autonomous physical activity motivation. The findings from Humphries (2005) on the evolution of motivation over the life course could be used to tailor interventions to optimize self-determination and subsequently increase physical activity participation at different life phases for women.

Health practitioners should be informed about the importance of acting in an autonomy-supportive way by actively listening to and acknowledging individuals' perspectives and feelings about physical activity, as well as by involving individuals as much as possible in the physical activity decision-making process (Sheldon, Williams, & Joiner, 2003). They should also be educated to encourage individuals to participate in physical activities to make themselves feel good and in those that they enjoy. When participants are motivated in a nonautonomous way toward physical activity, helping them focus on the positive feelings and sensations that they get during and after doing physical activity could help them move along the self-determination continuum toward more integrated motivational regulations.

Conclusion

In conclusion, self-determination theory appears to be a key conceptual framework for understanding important motivational outcomes such as flow and physical activity behavior change. Future research would do well to build on existing literature to further examine these motivational outcomes in physical activity settings and across populations.

Practical Recommendations for Promoting Flow and Physical Activity Maintenance

- Interventions that focus on promoting autonomous goals, such as those that offer choice among activities and promote enjoyment and satisfaction by providing exercise participants with means to evaluate their progress (e.g., tracking their weight, rating their exertion), will enhance individuals' perception that their fundamental needs for autonomy, competence, and relatedness are being satisfied.

- One can foster autonomy by providing physical activity participants with choices as often as possible, acknowledging their perspectives and feelings, and involving them as much as possible in the decision-making process. One can do this while simultaneously avoiding pressuring and controlling language such as "should" and "must."

- Exercise practitioners are encouraged to foster physical activity participants' sense of competence by helping them set appropriate goals, encouraging them to engage in practices to meet these goals, and providing appropriate informational feedback and highlighting their progress relative to their goal.

- Practitioners can also foster a sense of relatedness by acting in a warm and caring manner and encouraging physical activity participants to seek and use their social support network. For example, practitioners might suggest that a client identify an "exercise buddy" or choose to join a club or exercise group.

Perceived Feedback and Motivation in Physical Education and Physical Activity

Vello Hein, PhD, and Andre Koka, PhD
University of Tartu

Feedback can be defined as information received by a learner, such as a pupil or athlete in a physical education context, about his or her performance during the teaching and learning process. This information may be available to the learner from two main sources, external and internal. *External* information includes feedback provided by the teacher, coach, or supervisor; and *intrinsic* information is received by the learner from his or her own perceptions of the performance of the exercise or sport skill and its outcome. However, learners may interpret feedback obtained from their teacher, coach, or supervisor differently; and various interpretations are likely to lead to different motivational states and behavioral outcomes. Indeed, research on motivation and learning has shown that learners' perceptions influence motivation as well as outcomes such as affect and skill acquisition (Bakker, 1999). Researchers have also suggested that students' reports of their thoughts are more accurate predictors of achievement than observers' estimates (Peterson & Swing, 1982; Peterson, Swing, Stark, & Waas, 1984). Therefore, it is insufficient for coaches to provide feedback in a blasé or ill-considered manner. An understanding of how the learner *perceives* the feedback provided by his or her teachers, coaches, and supervisors is essential if feedback is to result in optimal motivational and behavioral outcomes.

This chapter deals with the role of perceived feedback on learners' motivation in physical education in accordance with self-determination theory (Deci & Ryan, 1985). The feedback provided by coaches or teachers characterizes the behaviors they display toward their pupils or athletes. Consistent with self-determination theory, the behavior of the coach or teacher is viewed as an important social factor that may affect a learner's perceptions of autonomy and

Correspondence concerning this article should be addressed to Vello Hein, Faculty of Exercise and Sports Sciences, University of Tartu, Ülikooli 18, 50090 Tartu, Estonia. E-mail: vello@.ut.ee competence, which can consequently have a positive impact on the learner's motivation.

This chapter is divided into four sections. The first presents a view of perceived feedback as one of the antecedent social factors that influences perceived competence, which, in accordance with hypotheses from self-determination theory, is proposed to mediate the impact of these social factors on motivation. The second section introduces the methods used to measure the various types of perceived feedback in physical education and sport contexts. The third section reviews studies concerned with the role of perceived feedback on motivation in physical education; the fourth provides practical recommendations for instructors (e.g., teachers, coaches, and supervisors) for promoting self-determined motivation using feedback and also outlines future directions for research in this area.

Perceived Feedback as a Source of Competence

Based on theoretical and empirical evidence that highlights the importance of perceived competence in achievement contexts (see Conroy, Elliot, & Coatsworth, this volume), a further understanding of how students judge their competence in achievement contexts such as physical education and sport, and how competence relates to motivated behavior, is warranted. According to self-determination theory, individuals' level of intrinsic motivation toward a particular activity will vary as a function of the degree to which they perceive themselves to be competent at that activity and believe themselves to be self-determined with respect to their performance of that activity.

Much early research on the sources of competence and their effects on motivation in the physical education and sport domains adopted Harter's (1978, 1981) competence motivation theory. This theory has been utilized and extended in the development of comprehensive theoretical models of competence and its effect on motivation and behavioral outcomes (Ames, 1984; Dweck & Leggett, 1988; Nicholls, 1984, 1989). A central premise of these models is that the perception of competence is a function of the type of information that individuals use to judge their performance ability, and several different sources of information are identified. At a basic level, individuals often judge their competence by comparing their performance against set standards of performance, the performance of others, or their own previous performances. However, Horn, Glenn, and Wentzell (1993) have identified a total of 10 possible sources of competence information and produced a measure of these in the Physical Competence Information Scale. The sources are (a) teacher, coach, peer, and parental feedback; (b) self-comparison; (c) degree of skill improvement over time; (d) speed or ease of learning new skills; (e) amount of effort exerted; (f) enjoyment of or attraction to the sport; (g) performance statistics; (h) game outcome (win, lose); (i) achievement of self-set goals; and (j) game-related feelings.

In this chapter we focus on one of these sources of information, perceived feedback of significant others, as a source of competence. The starting point of our argument is the premise from Harter's (1978, 1981) competence motivation theory that positive, supportive behaviors from socializing agents in response to learners' independent mastery attempts at a given task will foster an intrinsic motivational orientation in the learner. Further, this orientation will lead to feelings of increased competence and control, positive affect, and motivated behavior in learners. On the other hand, negative behaviors and responses from significant others that reinforce perceptions of failure are expected to decrease perceived competence, decrease perceptions of control, and result in the learner avoiding further attempts to master the task. Following this premise, the chapter addresses how self-determination theory provides a theoretical framework to explain the processes behind competence-related feedback as a source of information, as well as its effects on self-determined motivation and adaptive outcomes among individuals in physical education and sport contexts.

Self-determination theory (Deci & Ryan, 1985, 1991) contains explicit hypotheses regarding the relationship between perceived competence and motivation. With respect to feedback as a specific source of competence information, the theory hypothesizes that the provision of feedback that is rich in information about a performer's competence and personal goals is likely to foster and promote intrinsic motivation, while the provision of feedback framed in terms of failure and focusing only on absolute performance according to external criteria is likely to generate perceptions of incompetence and to undermine an individual's intrinsic motivation for the given activity. Self-determination highlights the role of feedback as a social factor that influences motivation and behavioral outcomes. Central to the theory is the following motivational sequence: Social factors → psychological mediators → types of motivation → consequences. With respect to physical education and sport contexts, the motivational sequence suggests that social factors (e.g., coaches' or teachers' feedback, success or failure, competition or cooperation) influence performers' perceptions of competence, autonomy, and relatedness (i.e., the psychological mediators), which in turn determine their motivational orientation. This motivational orientation then leads to a host of consequences (e.g., persistence in physical activity, psychological well-being).

A review of the extant literature in exercise and sport contexts supports this theoretical proposition, and perceived feedback can be considered an important social factor that influences perceived competence (Allen & Howe, 1998; Amorose & Horn, 2000; Amorose & Smith, 2003; Amorose & Weiss, 1998; Black & Weiss, 1992). We have recently supported this finding in a physical education context (Koka & Hein, 2003). Although there were some variations in the terms used for the different types of feedback, these studies all showed that positive information-based feedback given in response to student performances resulted in increased perceptions of competence and a corresponding increase in intrinsic motivation.

Measurement of Types of Perceived Feedback

Several researchers investigating the effects on motivation of perceived feedback provided by coaches have used the Coaching Feedback Questionnaire (CFQ; Allen & Howe, 1998; Amorose & Horn, 2000; Amorose & Weiss, 1998; Black & Weiss, 1992). The CFQ was developed to serve as a questionnaire version of the Coaching Behavior Assessment System (CBAS; Smith, Smoll, & Hunt, 1977), which is an observational system developed to measure the frequency of coaching behaviors in 12 salient categories.

In developing the CFQ, Black and Weiss (1992) assessed adolescent swimmers' perceptions of coaches' feedback using 10 categories from CBAS: four categories that represented behavioral responses to athletes' successful performances or efforts (i.e., praise only, no response, information only, and praise combined with information) and six categories that represented behavioral responses to unsuccessful performances or errors (i.e., encouragement only, no response, criticism, corrective information, encouragement combined with corrective information, and criticism combined with corrective information). They also assessed the concurrent levels of perceived competence and intrinsic motivation of the performers. Their results revealed that perceptions of coaches' feedback had a significant impact on athletes' perceptions of competence and intrinsic motivation. Specifically, swimmers who perceived that their coaches provided information following successful performances, and encouragement combined with information following unsuccessful performances, demonstrated higher scores on perceived competence and intrinsic motivation scales than swimmers who perceived their coaches to exhibit lower levels of these information-based types of feedback.

Allen and Howe (1998) adopted an augmented questionnaire that included a further six items to measure two additional types of perceived nonverbal feedback and administered this questionnaire to adolescent female field hockey players. A factor analysis of scores from this inventory revealed seven interpretable factors: encouragement/information, praise/information, nonverbal criticism, critical information, information only, no response, and mistake-contingent nonresponse. However, only four factors (encouragement/information, praise/information, nonverbal criticism, and information only) attained acceptable internal consistency. In terms of the relationship between perceived feedback and competence, the authors found that more frequent encouragement and corrective coaching behaviors for skill-related errors were associated with lower levels of perceived competence. Similarly, Black and Weiss (1992) found that athletes receiving a high frequency of corrective feedback from the coach following a mistake, even when that feedback may include encouragement, are likely to interpret the feedback as an indication of failure, which in turn results in lower feelings of perceived competence. These findings suggest that positive feedback is not necessarily associated with increased competence; rather, if feedback is contingent with errors, it seems that competence is undermined.

The performer may be aware of the errors, and the encouragement may appear to be an acknowledgment of the error rather than informational toward correction of the error.

Amorose and Horn (2000) investigated the relationship between intrinsic motivation and perceived feedback among athletes from several different sports. The CFQ used in this study comprised 16 items representing eight different types of feedback. Three categories characterized the coach's responses to successful performances (i.e., praise/reinforcement, no reinforcement, reinforcement combined with technical instruction), and five characterized responses related to performance errors (i.e., mistake-contingent encouragement, ignoring mistakes, corrective instruction, punishment, and corrective instruction combined with punishment). A factor analysis revealed three perceived feedback dimensions (positive and informational feedback, punishment-oriented feedback, and nonreinforcement/ignoring mistakes), and the scales had satisfactory internal consistency. The authors reported that athletes with high levels of intrinsic motivation perceived that their coaches provided a high frequency of informational feedback and low frequencies of punishment-oriented and ignoring-mistake behaviors.

Although athletes' perceptions of their coach's feedback have been investigated in a number of studies, the perception of physical education teachers' feedback has received attention only recently (Koka & Hein, 2003). In order to measure perceptions of teachers' feedback in physical education, we developed the Perceptions of Teachers' Feedback questionnaire (PTF; Koka & Hein, 2003) based on the feedback categories in the Self-Assessment Feedback Instrument (SAFI; Mancini & Wuest, 1989) and the feedback categories previously adopted in the sport domain (Allen & Howe, 1998; Amorose & Horn, 2000; Amorose & Weiss, 1998).

In developing the new instrument, we initially conducted a pilot study using the SAFI (Mancini & Wuest, 1989). We recorded the frequency and types of feedback provided by two physical education teachers during 22 physical education lessons. Analyses of the more frequently used types of feedback allowed us to form six feedback categories: praise, instruction, instruction during performance, encouragement, criticism, and confirmation/reinforcement. Based on these initial findings, 12 items were developed to measure the perception of teacher's feedback. These 12 items were then administered to a small group of students (N = 21). Standardized instructions were given, and students completed the questionnaire. They were then interviewed informally and individually and asked whether or not they understood the items and what they thought the items meant. On the basis of these interactions, it was clear that students understood the concept of each question and did not report any difficulties completing the questionnaire.

The PTF questionnaire was then administered to a sample of 783 students aged 12 to 15 years. In order to establish the construct validity of the questionnaire, we randomly split the total sample of participants to produce two subsamples, one for an exploratory factor analysis (N = 391) and the other for a confirmatory factor analysis (N = 392). Three factors that emerged in the exploratory analysis were labeled as perceived positive specific feedback (e.g., "If my teacher gives me more instruction, I will acquire the exercise faster"), perceived positive general feedback (e.g., "My teacher often praises me"), and perceived knowledge of performance (e.g., "My teacher instructs me frequently during the performance"). The confirmatory factor analysis supported this three-factor structure. In addition, the three subscales exhibited satisfactory internal consistency and one-week test–retest reliability in a small subsample of students (N = 39).

The previously reviewed developments in measurement focused largely on verbal forms of feedback. However, theorists and researchers have indicated that in order to convey a clear and consistent message to students, it is important for teachers to use both verbal and nonverbal communication (Martens, 1987; Yukelson, 1998). Acknowledging the importance of nonverbal forms of feedback, we revised the PTF questionnaire to include subscales measuring perceived nonverbal feedback (Koka & Hein, 2005). Thus, items assessing both perceived positive (e.g., "In response to a good performance my teacher often smiles") and negative (e.g., "In response to a poor performance the teacher generally looks angry") nonverbal feedback were added to the inventory. These items were generated based on the questionnaire version of CBAS (Allen & Howe, 1998) and were modified for the physical education context (Koka & Hein, 2005).

In order to determine the construct validity of the revised PTF questionnaire, we adopted a procedure identical to that used in establishing the construct validity of the initial PTF. A total sample of 625 students aged 14 to 18 years completed the revised PTF questionnaire. Exploratory factor analysis yielded a four-factor solution, which was subsequently verified by confirmatory factor analysis. The resulting subscales, labeled perceived positive general feedback, perceived knowledge of performance, perceived positive nonverbal feedback, and perceived negative nonverbal feedback, exhibited acceptable levels of internal consistency for the majority of subscales. However, caution is warranted in interpretation of the positive nonverbal feedback subscale in future research, since its reliability was suboptimal. Also, modifications of this scale to include items assessing positive nonverbal teacher feedback should be considered in the future.

Relationship Between Perceived Feedback and Motivation in Physical Education

The relationship between perceived feedback and perceived competence (e.g., Allen & Howe, 1998) and between perceived feedback and intrinsic motivation (e.g., Amorose & Horn, 2000; Black & Weiss, 1992) has been extensively investigated in the sport domain. However, there is a relative dearth of research on the subject in the physical education domain. In order to address this gap in the literature, we investigated the relationship between perceived teacher feedback and intrinsic motivation among secondary school pupils in physical education lessons (Koka & Hein, 2003). A sample of 783 pupils aged 12 to 15 years completed the PTF questionnaire and the Intrinsic Motivation Inventory (IMI; McAuley, Duncan, & Tammen, 1989) for measurement of their intrinsic motivation, perceived competence, perceived interest, and perceived effort in physical education (see Pelletier & Sarrazin, this volume). Results indicated that both perceived positive general feedback and perceived knowledge of performance were positively related to intrinsic motivation, perceived competence, perceived interest, and perceived effort. More specifically, results demonstrated that perception of teachers' positive general feedback was a valid predictor of intrinsic motivation and its components such as perceived competence and perceived interest.

One criticism that could be leveled at this study is that general positive feedback with no contingency may not enhance intrinsic motivation. Furthermore, the manner in which the feedback is given could also affect the influence of general positive feedback on intrinsic motivation and perceived competence. For example, according to cognitive evaluation theory, even positive competence feedback can be given in a controlling way, and this may undermine intrinsic motivation. However, the PTF used to tap perceived general feedback in this study makes specific reference to intrinsically motivated behavior and the manner of presentation. For example, the questionnaire includes the items "If the teacher sees that I try very hard, I'll always get praise" and "In response to a good performance the teacher smiles." Therefore the perceived feedback inventory that was used incorporates both the manner in which the feedback is given (e.g., smiling and praise) and the contingency (e.g., through reference to behaviors that are linked with intrinsic motivation such as effort and good performance).

In a second study we examined the effects of both verbal and nonverbal types of perceived teacher feedback on students' intrinsic motivation (Koka & Hein, 2005). A sample of 625 students aged 14 to 18 years completed the revised PTF and a modified version of the Sport Motivation Scale (SMS; Hein, Müür, & Koka, 2004), which measured intrinsic motivation in a physical education context. Results indicated that after perceived knowledge of performance, perceived positive general feedback was the strongest predictor of students' intrinsic motivation in physical education. Nonverbal types of perceived teacher feedback, however, did not contribute to motivational differences. These findings are in line with previous studies in sport contexts (e.g., Amorose & Horn, 2000; Black & Weiss, 1992) and with self-determination theory (Deci & Ryan, 1985, 1991; Ryan & Deci, 2000), implying that high frequencies of perceived positive and informational feedback are related to higher levels of intrinsic motivation. Allen and Howe (1998) also demonstrated that nonverbal criticism did not contribute significantly to female adolescent field hockey players' perceived competence.

Both self-determination theory (Deci & Ryan, 1985) and Vallerand's (1997) hierarchical model of intrinsic and extrinsic motivation suggest that the influence on motivation of environmental factors, including the behavior of significant others in providing feedback, is mediated by the three basic psychological needs of perceived competence, autonomy, and relatedness. Considering the presence of significant relationships between perceived feedback and competence (e.g., Amorose & Horn, 2000; Koka & Hein, 2003), it follows that the impact of perceived feedback on motivation may be mediated by perceived competence.

On the basis of Vallerand's (1997) motivational model, we tested the mediation of the relationship between perceived positive informational feedback and perceived interest, a proxy measure of self-determined forms of motivation, by perceived competence in physical education. This analysis was conducted with data from the previously mentioned sample of students (N = 783). Figure 8.1 illustrates the results of the structural equation modeling analyses conducted to test the relationship. The results represented in figure 8.1*a* illustrate the full hypothesized model in which perceived competence acts as a mediator of the relationship between perceived positive informational feedback and perceived interest. When we eliminated the effect of perceived competence on perceived interest (i.e., fixing the effect of perceived competence on perceived interest to zero; see figure 8.1*b*) using the procedure advocated by other researchers (e.g., Hagger, Chatzisarantis, Barkoukis, Wang, & Baranowski, 2005a; Hagger, Chatzisarantis, & Harris, 2006; Hagger et al., 2005b), the effect of perceived positive informational feedback on perceived interest increased significantly, suggesting that the effect of perceived positive informational feedback on perceived interest was partially mediated by perceived competence (Baron & Kenny, 1986).

Overall, figure 8.1*a* shows that perceived positive informational teacher feedback as a social factor leads to positive motivational outcomes such as higher effort exertion among adolescent students in physical education. Although these results support the tenets of self-determination theory (Deci & Ryan, 1985) and Vallerand's (1997) hierarchical model of motivation, it must be stressed that this model does not include other important mediator variables like perceived autonomy and relatedness. Therefore, future modifications of this model may entail the addition of constructs like perceived autonomy and relatedness as mediators of the relationship between perceived positive informational feedback and perceived interest in physical education.

According to Deci and Ryan (2000) and Vallerand (1997), these motivational processes are likely to be consistent across individuals, suggesting that the processes are universal. Studies in physical education have confirmed this argument, demonstrating largely similar patterns of motivational processes across gender (e.g., Ntoumanis, 2001; Ferrer-Caja & Weiss, 2000, 2002) and culture

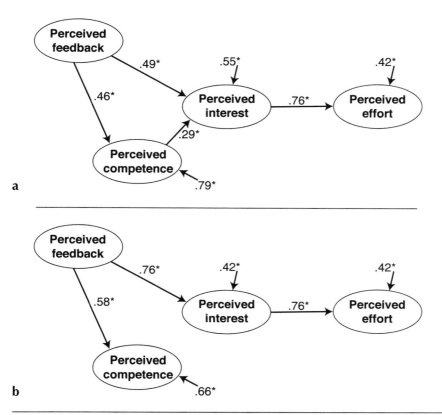

Figure 8.1   *(a)* Structural equation model illustrating the role of perceived competence as a mediator of the relationship between perceived positive informational feedback and perceived interest in physical education. *(b)* Alternative structural equation model in which the effect of perceived competence on perceived interest in physical education is fixed to zero in order to illustrate mediation of the relationship between perceived positive informational feedback and perceived interest.

* = .05

(e.g., Hagger et al., 2005a). We therefore conducted another study to test the assumption of universality across gender. Figure 8.2 shows mean differences in perceived positive informational feedback, perceived competence, perceived interest, and perceived effort in physical education according to gender (figure 8.2*a*), grade (figure 8.2*b*), and participation in leisure-time sport (figure 8.2*c*) in the same sample of secondary school students. Interestingly, boys scored significantly higher on each variable (figure 8.2*a*), suggesting that they tended to be more interested in physical education than girls and that they perceived their teachers to provide them with more positive informational feedback. This

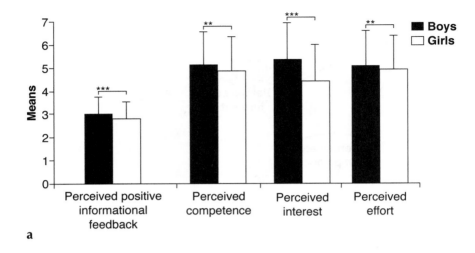

a

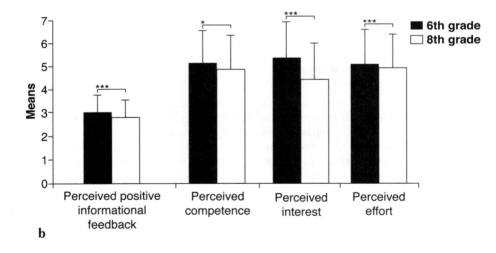

b

(continued)

Figure 8.2 Mean differences for perceived positive informational feedback, perceived competence, perceived interest, and perceived effort according to *(a)* gender, *(b)* grade, and *(c)* participation in leisure-time sport.

Scale responses ranged from 1 to 5 for perceived positive informational feedback and from 1 to 7 for perceived competence, perceived interest, and perceived effort.

$*p < .05$; $**p < .01$; $***p < .001$.

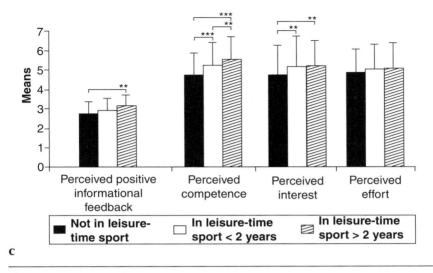

Figure 8.2   *continued*

was contrary to expectations. It is possible that in a physical context, boys perceived that they were more able to demonstrate competence and that teachers were more likely to offer positive feedback to boys compared to girls. This is congruent with research suggesting that physical education and the physical self are inherently "male" (Hagger, Biddle, & Wang, 2005). Such perceptions are likely to lead to girls' perceiving physical education as a more "controlling" environment because it is not an arena in which they perceive they are capable of demonstrating competence.

The results also suggest that as students grow older, their interest in physical education declines significantly (figure 8.2*b*). This is congruent with recent longitudinal (e.g., Prochaska, Sallis, Slymen, & McKenzie, 2003) and cross-sectional studies (e.g., Van Wersch, Trew, & Turner, 1992) showing that interest and enjoyment in physical education tend to decline with age. This has also been mapped in the self-esteem literature, and it has been suggested that changes in interests and a focus on academic work compared to physical education are responsible for such a decline (Marsh, 1989). Finally, older students perceived that they received much less positive informational feedback from their physical education teacher and did not feel that it was important to make an effort in physical education (figure 8.2*b*). These perceptions also mirror the changing interests of adolescents in terms of pastimes and academic work within school.

It is worth noting that students who participate in sport during their leisure time are more interested in physical education than students not involved in leisure-time sport (figure 8.2c). Similar findings were obtained by Anderssen (1993), who reported that students with sport experience tend to hold more favorable attitudes toward physical education than students lacking in experience. Furthermore, recent research suggests that schoolchildren reporting high levels of autonomous motivation in a physical education context also report high levels of autonomous motivation toward physical activity in a leisure-time context (Hagger et al., 2005a; Hagger, Chatzisarantis, Culverhouse, & Biddle, 2003). The significantly higher perceptions of competence in physical education among students with sport experience is not surprising, since they may already be familiar with the content of physical education as suggested by Goudas, Dermitzaki, and Bagiatis (2001).

Practical Recommendations and Future Directions for Research

In conclusion, research in this field has revealed that when learners such as athletes and physical education pupils perceive their coach or physical education teacher to be positive and informative in his or her responses to performance, their perceived competence and intrinsic motivation are likely to be enhanced. Studies demonstrate that although a voluntary sport context is considerably different from the compulsory context of physical education, the relationship between perceived positive informational feedback and intrinsic motivation is similar in the two contexts. Research has shown that perceived competence seems to have an important mediational role in the relationship between students' perceived positive informational feedback from teachers and perceived interest or intrinsic motivation in both sport and physical education contexts (Koka & Hein, 2003, 2005). Importantly, the content of the feedback must be informational, must be presented in an autonomy-supportive way, and should make reference to behaviors that are clearly related to intrinsic motivation such as effort and interest.

As our studies have been conducted in the physical education context alone, our recommendations are most relevant to physical education teachers. In order to create more stimulating learning environments and ultimately increase students' levels of intrinsic motivation, physical education teachers should aim to provide positive general and informational feedback during lessons (see practical recommendations at the end of the chapter). In addition, the positive feedback that teachers provide for students should comprise information about competence. In providing this type of information, teachers are likely to enhance students' interest in physical education, which means that students will be more likely to invest greater effort in their lessons. Since girls, older students, and students who do not participate in sport after school demonstrated significantly lower levels of interest in physical education, special attention should be dedicated to these groups. Positive interactions between teachers and pupils in these groups, such as the provision of positive and informational feedback, could increase their interest in physical education and reverse the downward developmental trends seen in motivation and interest levels among these groups. Finally, it is essential that such feedback be presented in an autonomy-supportive fashion without the use of controlling language such as "should" and "must."

Research in this field and in the physical education context has been cross-sectional, a design that does not permit the study of changes in the perceptions of the physical education teacher's feedback as students grow older or the investigation of any reciprocal relationships among these perceived feedback and motivational constructs over time. Therefore, longitudinal designs are needed to assess how students' perceptions of teacher feedback might change over time. Although there was support for mediation of the relationship between perceived positive and informational teacher feedback and perceived interest by perceived competence, the need to evaluate the potential mediating role of feelings of autonomy and relatedness in this system remains. Therefore, future studies in physical education contexts should test a model in which perceived competence, autonomy, and relatedness would mediate the effect of perceived teacher feedback on intrinsic motivation or interest.

Practical Recommendations for Coaches on the Use of Feedback

- Teachers and coaches are advised to provide positive and informational feedback in response to their pupils' and athletes' performances, as this has been shown to enhance perceived competence and intrinsic motivation. The type of feedback would be expected to contain positive statements about effort (e.g., "well done" or "excellent effort") but also make reference to personally relevant goals or to the goals of the task (e.g., "That's exactly how you wanted it"; "You performed the skill exactly as we discussed"; "You showed excellent technique during that play").

- The positive feedback provided for learners should comprise information about competence. For example, physical education teachers might say, "Well done, you performed the task well and in accordance with the techniques we discussed."

- Since perceived competence plays an important role in mediating the relationship between perceived positive informational feedback and intrinsic motivation, feedback that contains competence information is likely to have a potent effect on motivation and competence. Therefore,

(continued)

(continued)

positive feedback should make clear reference to personal competence-tied goals. For example, an exercise specialist might say, "Excellent job. You seem to be reaching your aim of hitting the ball on the rise and creating that extra topspin you were looking for."

• Girls, older students, and students not involved in voluntary sport activity need particular attention with respect to the provision of positive and informational feedback to increase their motivation toward physical activity. These groups need to be provided with opportunities that stimulate interest and assist in setting personal goals. This is often difficult among those who are not regular exercisers and for whom exercise does not feature in their repertoire of need-satisfying behaviors. Physical education teachers who work with students like this are encouraged to focus on novel activities to encourage and stimulate interest tied in with other interests, such as having people do exercise to music.

Intrinsic Motivation
and Self-Determination in Sport

The chapters in part II concern the role that self-determination theory plays in explaining motivational processes involved in competitive sport contexts. The opening chapter by Luc Pelletier and Philippe Sarrazin (chapter 9) focuses on measurement issues in the application of self-determination theory in sport contexts, with an emphasis on the Sport Motivation Scale as a leading measure of motivational types in sport. In chapter 10, Darren Treasure, Nicolas Lemyre, Kendy Kuczka, and Martyn Standage take a self-determination theory perspective in explaining participation and persistence in training and competition for elite athletes. Maarten Vansteenkiste, Bart Soenens, and Willy Lens take a different perspective in chapter 11, focusing on the intrinsic and extrinsic goals that people pursue in sport contexts, and explain the processes by which these goals motivate athletic pursuits. Competence motivation is the theme of chapter 12, in which David Conroy, Andrew Elliot, and Doug Coatsworth adopt a hierarchical model of achievement motivation alongside self-determination theory to illustrate the role that competence has to play in motivation in sport contexts. Theoretical integration is also central to John Wang and Stuart Biddle's chapter (chapter 13), which looks at achievement goals and perceptions of ability in order to provide understanding of the influences on sport behavior in young people.

Chapter 14 by Anthony Amorose deals with the often neglected area of coaching behaviors in sport contexts and with the role of such behaviors in motivating athletes. Philippe Sarrazin, Julie Boiché, and Luc Pelletier (chapter 15) examine the effects of intrinsic and extrinsic forms of motivation on athletes' dropout from sport. Echoing the chapter on well-being in exercise by Wilson and Rodgers in part I, Marylène Gagné and Céline Blanchard in chapter 16 focus on psychological well-being in athletes from a self-determination theory perspective. Finally, Robert Vallerand provides a detailed overview of his hierarchical model of motivation, which examines links between motivation, affect, cognition, and outcomes at three different levels: global, contextual, and situational.

Together these chapters summarize the state of the literature concerning self-determination theory in diverse areas of sport, including athletes' motivation and sport performance, goal content and orientations, dropout, psychological well-being, and the influence of coaching behaviors. The recommendations outlined at the close of each chapter should provide coaches, sport psychologists, sport promoters and managers, and physical educators with realistic, practical solutions to maximize sport performance, persistence in training, and, above all, enjoyment and well-being among athletes involved in sport.

Measurement Issues in Self-Determination Theory and Sport

Luc G. Pelletier, PhD
University of Ottawa

Philippe Sarrazin, PhD
Université Joseph Fourier

Self-determination theory proposes a differentiated view of motivation that translates into different regulatory processes through which the outcomes related to an activity are pursued. As described elsewhere (Ryan & Deci, this volume; Sarrazin, Boiché, & Pelletier, this volume), these regulatory processes include amotivation, four forms of regulation relating to extrinsic motivation (external, introjected, identified, and integrated regulations), and intrinsic motivation and are located on a self-determination continuum anchored in intrinsic motivation and amotivation. Higher levels of self-determination on the continuum are associated with enhanced psychological functioning. A number of studies in different life domains (Deci & Ryan, 2000; Ryan & Deci, 2000; Vallerand, 1997), and more specifically in sport and physical activity (Chatzisarantis, Hagger, Biddle, Smith, & Wang, 2003; Vallerand & Losier, 1999), have shown more behavioral effectiveness, conceptual understanding, intentional persistence, personal adjustment, positive coping, and overall enhanced well-being as one moves from amotivation to intrinsic motivation.

Most of the studies in sport and physical activity have assessed the various forms of motivation or regulatory processes using an approach initially developed by Ryan and Connell (1989) in which participants are asked why they engage in the specified activity. Typically, participants are provided with reasons that represent the various regulatory processes and asked to rate the extent to which each reason is true for them. Then they are assigned a score for each form of motivation that could be used separately to predict behavior

Correspondence concerning this article should be addressed to Luc G. Pelletier, School of Psychology, University of Ottawa, P.O. Box 450, Stn. A, Ottawa, Ontario, Canada K1N 6N5. E-mail: social@uottawa.ca or used in the calculation of a global score, referred to as the self-determination index (SDI) or the relative autonomy index (RAI).

In this chapter, we review the results of studies dealing with an instrument that originated in self-determination theory and was developed specifically in the context of sport, the Sport Motivation Scale (SMS; Pelletier et al., 1995). The SMS is probably the scale most widely used to measure the various regulatory styles proposed by self-determination theory in the context of sport. A few other scales that assess motivation in the context of physical activity (the Behavioural Regulation in Exercise Questionnaire [BREQ]; Mullen, Markland, & Ingledew, 1997), exercise (the Exercise Motivation Scale [EMS]; Li, 1999), and physical education (Goudas, Biddle, & Fox, 1994) are also available. These measures may have different emphases, but in large part they share the same underlying conception as the SMS (see Chatzisarantis et al., 2003, for a review of the studies on these scales and their construct validity).

This chapter is divided into two sections. First, we focus on the validity of the SMS in different languages and different cultures and examine the support that the various versions of the SMS provide for the self-determination continuum. Second, we examine several issues regarding the measurement of regulatory processes in the context of sport.

Versions of the Sport Motivation Scale

The SMS and its French version (l'Echelle de Motivation dans les Sports [EMS]; Brière, Vallerand, Blais, & Pelletier, 1995) were developed to assess the different types of regulatory processes proposed by self-determination theory in sport. Both the SMS and the EMS have 28 items that assess amotivation, external regulation, introjected regulation, identified regulation, and three types of intrinsic motivation (to know, to accomplish, and to experience stimulation). Both the French and the English versions were validated in a series of studies with Canadian athletes from different individual and team sports. Results from these investigations revealed that both versions had satisfactory internal consistency, a seven-factor structure that corresponds to the forms of motivation targeted by the scale, adequate construct validity, and moderate-to-high indices of temporal stability. The correlations among the seven subscales form a simplex-like pattern in which the scales that are theoretically closer are more strongly correlated. This has been corroborated in a recent meta-analysis of 21 studies adopting motivational styles from self-determination theory, including those adopting the SMS/EMS (Chatzisarantis et al., 2003). The analysis replicated the simplex-like pattern observed in individual investigations across this sample of studies.

Pelletier and colleagues (1995) also reported that correlations with various sport variables representing determinants (e.g., athletes' perceived competence, perceptions of coach's autonomy support, structure, and feedback of competence) and consequences (e.g., intentions to persist, perceived effort, concentration) were in agreement with self-determination theory, and showed that outcomes were decreasingly positive from intrinsic motivation to amotivation. Thus, the most positive outcomes were associated with the self-determined forms of motivation (intrinsic motivation and identified regulation), while negative outcomes were associated with the least self-determined forms of motivation (external regulation and amotivation).

Several other studies have addressed the relationships between the different forms of motivation assessed by the SMS and a variety of psychological constructs (see Sarrazin, Boiché, & Pelletier, this volume). These constructs include burnout (Cresswell & Eklund, 2005; Gould, Udry, Tuffey, & Loehr, 1996; Raedeke & Smith, 2001), exercise dependence among endurance athletes (Hamer, Karageorgis, & Vlachopoulos, 2002), perception of attraction- and entrapment-based commitment with gymnasts (Weiss & Weiss, 2003), fear of failing (Conroy, 2004), the perception of constraints (Alexandris, Tsorbatzoudis, & Grouios, 2002), persistence (Pelletier, Fortier, Vallerand, & Brière, 2001; Sarrazin, Vallerand, Guillet, Pelletier, & Cury, 2002), flow (Kowal & Fortier, 2000; Martin & Cutler, 2002), vitality and well-being (Gagné, Ryan, & Bargmann, 2003), interest-enhancing strategies (Green-Demers, Pelletier, Stewart, & Gushue, 1998), coping strategies (Amiot, Gaudreau, & Blanchard, 2004), cognitive-behavioral psychological skills training (Beauchamp, Halliwell, Fournier, & Koestner, 1996), orientations toward good sporting behavior (Vallerand & Losier, 1994) as well as good sporting behavior and aggression (Chantal, Robin, Vernat, & Bernache-Assolant, 2005) and task versus ego involvement orientations in achievement goals (Brunel, 1999; Ntoumanis, 2001; Petherick & Weigand, 2002). Overall, results of these studies, with athletes of different age categories and involved in a great variety of sports, showed consistently that more fully internalized forms of motivation as assessed by the SMS were associated with greater behavioral persistence, more effective performance, and better psychological functioning in sport.

Studies conducted in the United States have also dealt with the construct validity of the SMS. For instance, Martens and Webber (2002) tested the psychometric properties of the scales with 270 college athletes. Their results supported the reliability and the validity of the SMS with that population, although the results of their confirmatory factor analysis yielded relatively lower fit indices than those obtained by Pelletier and colleagues (1995). Li and Harmer (1996) tested the validity of the SMS with male and female college athletes (N = 857). Their results, using structural equation modeling, not only offered support for the structure of the scale but also supported the simplex-like pattern of the scale with both men and women. Support for the simplex-like pattern indicates that subscales situated closer to one another on the self-determination continuum are more strongly and positively associated, while subscales farther apart are negatively related (see also Chatzisarantis et al., 2003, for a test of the simplex-like order structure based on meta-analytic findings). The strong connection between intrinsic motivation and identified regulation shown in the studies by Li and Harmer (1996) and Chatzisarantis and colleagues (2003) indicates that the quality of motivation tapped by identified regulation is closely aligned with that of intrinsic motivation.

Other studies with English-speaking masters athletes, mainly from Australia and New Zealand (Jackson, Kimiecik, Ford, & Marsh, 1998) and from the United Kingdom (Hamer, Karageorghis, & Vlachopoulos, 2002; Ntoumanis, 2001), as well as French-speaking athletes from France (Sarrazin et al., 2002), offered more support for the construct validity and the reliability of the SMS and the EMS. Finally, support for the construct validity, reliability, and structure of the SMS also exists for translated versions of the scale in Bulgarian (Chantal, Guay, Dobreva-Martinova, & Vallerand, 1996), Chinese (Lin & Chi, 2003), and Greek (Alexandris, Tsorbatzoudis, & Grouios, 2002; Doganis, 2000; Georgiadis, Biddle, & Chatzisarantis, 2001).

In sum, the studies reviewed so far offer good support for the structure, reliability, and construct validity of the SMS with populations of different ages and cultural orientations and with participants drawn from different individual and team sports. Overall, these studies also support the existence of a differentiated view of motivation as proposed by self-determination theory. Cultures may vary greatly in the goals and values they transmit in general, and the goals and values pursued in sport more specifically. However, research using the SMS with participants from several different cultures supports the hypothesis in self-determination theory (Deci & Ryan, 2000) that the reasons athletes pursue those goals can be represented by functional and experiential forces operating across cultures, and that the underlying self-determination continuum representing those forces is universal.

Construct Measurement Issues

As in the assessment of any psychological construct, several issues have been raised over the years concerning the measurement of the various regulatory processes. In this section we examine two construct measurement issues—how to use the SMS and the assessment of integrated regulation.

How to Use the SMS

The simultaneous assessment of different forms of motivation raises a simple but important question: How should the SMS be used? We can consider four ways to use or combine the subscales. First, researchers could combine the subscales into an overall relative autonomy index (RAI) or self-determination index (SDI) (e.g., Blais, Sabourin, Boucher, & Vallerand, 1990; Vallerand, Fortier, & Guay, 1997; Vallerand & Losier, 1994). One does this by giving each subscale a specific weight according to its place on the self-determination continuum, multiplying the score on the scale by this weight, and adding the weighted scores on the subscales to obtain a single score. The higher the score on the index, the more self-determined the athlete's motivational profile. Because one obtains the score algebraically by weighting the self-determined forms of motivation positively and the nonautonomous forms of motivation negatively, a positive score implies that the participant considers self-determined forms of motivation more important in explaining why he or she practices an activity, while a negative score means the opposite. One could use the SDI as an individual difference measure by selecting participants who have a high or a low score on the index. As illustrated in the chapters on exercise persistence (Markland & Ingledew, this volume; Fortier & Kowal, this volume), it can also be used as a mediation variable to explain how specific determinants (e.g., coaches' interpersonal behaviors) may be related to various outcomes (e.g., effort or persistence).

Second, researchers could regroup the intrinsic subscales (possibly the integrated regulation subscale) and identified regulation subscales to form a global score of autonomous motivation and regroup the introjected regulation, external regulation, and amotivation subscales to form a global score of nonautonomous motivation (Amiot, Gaudreau, & Blanchard, 2004; Pelletier, Dion, Slovinec-D'Angelo, & Reid, 2004). The use of forms of motivation that are self-determined and forms of motivation that are not self-determined or are *nonautonomous* could be helpful when one is interested in the concurrent relations of the two forms of motivation to outcomes that may differ qualitatively, such as strategies of coping or intentions to perform behavior versus the maintenance of behavior.

Third, one could use each subscale to examine how it relates independently to a specific outcome, as has been the case in several of the correlation studies conducted to examine the construct validity of the SMS. Also, because motivation is dynamic and may change in itself as well as lead to changes in outcome variables, the use of individual subscales could be helpful in at least four other ways. For example, a subscale could be used to (a) identify which form of motivation is the best predictor of a specific behavior; (b) assess the impact of changes in an antecedent variable such as coaching style on specific forms of motivation over time; (c) examine the impact of the different forms of motivation on a specific outcome over time such as persistence (Pelletier et al., 2001; Sarrazin, Boiché, & Pelletier, this volume); or (d) examine how changes in specific motivation forms relate to specific outcomes or changes in these outcomes over time (Otis, Grouzet, & Pelletier, 2005).

Focusing on the various regulatory styles, rather than relying on an SDI or on two general forms of regulation (self-determined and nonautonomous), is important because this can lead to a better understanding of the distinct affective, cognitive, and behavioral consequences that characterize each type of motivation (Koestner & Losier, 2002). For example, although external regulation, introjected regulation, identified regulation, and intrinsic motivation should all be associated with involvement in an activity, external regulation should be characterized by a sense of activation and a desire to practice the activity as long as the source of external pressure (e.g., rewards, social comparison, threat) is present; introjected regulation should be characterized by a sense of compulsion and internal pressure; identified regulation should be characterized by a sense of personal importance and value; and intrinsic motivation should be characterized by positive emotions, interest, and fun. In other words, although the practice of an activity may appear the same from the outside, athletes who practice an activity for different reasons may approach the activity differently and may experience distinct emotions while engaging in the activity.

Another interesting example concerns the goal orientations of athletes with different regulatory styles. An athlete with an external regulatory style should try to gain social approval or external rewards; an athlete with an introjected regulatory style should experience conflicts between different reasons for participating such as fear of failure and the desire to please significant others; an athlete with an identified regulatory style should aim to achieve specific outcomes and long-term motives; and an athlete with an intrinsic regulatory style should concentrate on short-term motives related to the process of doing the activity. Once again, the different regulatory styles may be linked to different ways to approach (or avoid) an activity, to different goals, and especially to different affective consequences (see Conroy, Elliott, & Coatsworth, this volume). In addition, it is possible that the regulatory styles may not have a linear effect on activity engagement but instead interact with extrinsic factors such as rewards. Amabile (1996) suggests that it is the interpretation and subsequent value placed on such contingencies in a synergistic model that influence behavior rather than a standard linear effect.

Finally, a fourth and particularly helpful method of employing the SMS is to use cluster analysis to identify homogeneous groups of athletes, or clusters that share the same motivational characteristics (Härdle & Simar, 2003). For example, Ntoumanis (2002) used cluster analysis to identify the motivational profiles of physical education students and observed three types of motivational profiles. One, called "self-determined," included high intrinsic motivation and identified regulation, moderate introjected regulation, and low external regulation and amotivation; a second, called "moderate motivation," was characterized by moderate scores for all the different forms of motivation; and a third, called "controlling motivation and amotivation," was characterized by relatively high amotivation, relatively high external regulation, and low introjected regulation, identified regulation, and intrinsic motivation. These profiles provided very interesting insight into the complexities of participants' motivation. In agreement with self-determination theory and the self-determination continuum, the first and third clusters suggested that high and low levels of self-determined motivation were linked to low and high levels of nonautonomous motivation, respectively. However, in agreement with alternative approaches to motivation (e.g., achievement theory or goal-setting theory), the second cluster suggested that some participants were motivated by high levels of both intrinsic and extrinsic motivation at the same time (see Wang & Biddle, 2001). In sum, the presence of three motivational profiles raised intriguing questions. Are intrinsic and extrinsic motivation exclusive, as proposed by self-determination theory, or could these two forms of motivation be additive? Do athletes benefit more from the presence of both self-determined and non-self-determined forms of motivation, or are the benefits higher if athletes are mainly self-determined?

The Assessment of Integrated Regulation

Over the years, researchers have pointed out that the SMS deviates slightly from the hypothesized self-determined continuum because it does not include the construct of integrated regulation. Integrated regulation represents the fullest and most complete form of internalization of extrinsic motivation (Deci & Ryan, 2000). When a behavior is fully integrated it is considered not only important, but also in harmony with other behaviors considered important by the self, and it becomes coherent with our identity and values (Ryan, 1995). If a behavioral regulation is well integrated, the behavior is volitional; it is something the person fully values and is coherent with other behaviors that the person values; and the person experiences freedom. Integrated regulation, like intrinsic motivation, is characterized by a sense of autonomy and freedom and the absence of conflict. However, unlike the situation with intrinsic motivation, behavior flowing from integrated regulation is still instrumental with respect to an outcome that is separate from the behavior.

In response to this limitation, Pelletier and Kabush (2005) and Mallett (2003) have made an attempt to develop an integrated regulation subscale (the revised version of the SMS is available from the first author) based on items developed for the Client Motivation for Therapy Scale (Pelletier, Tuson, & Haddad, 1997), the Motivation for the Environment Scale (Pelletier, Tuson, Green-Demers, Noels, & Beaton, 1998), and the Motivation for the Regulation of Eating Behaviors Scale (Pelletier et al., 2004). This subscale incorporates items that encompass the essential characteristics of integrated regulation (e.g., "Participating in sport is an integral part of my life"; "Doing sport is a fundamental part of who I am"). Results from Pelletier and Kabush's (2005) and Mallett's (2003) studies showed that a confirmatory factor analysis of the modified version of the SMS supported the structure of the modified scale. More specifically, Pelletier and Kabush showed an acceptable level of internal consistency for the integrated regulation subscale (α = .83) and an acceptable level of test–retest reliability (r = .79). The integrated regulation subscale's location on the self-determination continuum was supported by positive and stronger correlations with the intrinsic motivation (r = .58) and identified regulation (r = .53) subscales than with the introjected regulation (r = .41), external regulation (r = .28), and amotivation (r = −.21) subscales.

Although the results of Pelletier and Kabush (2005) and Mallett (2003) supported the validity of the integrated regulation subscale, it is important to point out that these results are preliminary and that more studies may be necessary to determine more definitively whether or not the subscale provides a reliable assessment of the construct. Integrated regulation represents a complex latent construct that may be hard to assess with only a few items. There is reason to believe that the integrated regulation subscale reflects a higher form of internalization than the identification subscale; but if one wants to assess the extent to which the internalization of a behavior tends to be integrated, it may be valuable to consider several strategies in combination with use of the integrated regulation subscale.

First, researchers might consider that one indication of integrated regulation is positive correlations between behavior and self-reports of valuing and enjoying the activity, whereas introjected and external regulation are reflected by negative correlations between the behavior and self-reports (Deci, Eghrari, Patrick, & Leone, 1994). Second, because the maintenance of behavior is difficult and demands high levels of resources and energy, integrated regulation should be reflected by the maintenance of behavior over time (Pelletier et al., 2001), especially when one faces obstacles that interfere with the regulation of behavior or faces behavior with increasing levels of difficulty (Green-Demers, Pelletier, & Ménard, 1997). Third, the more integrated the regulation of behavior, the more coherent it should be and the less in conflict with the regulation of other behaviors that are valued by a person. Thus, for example, a student-athlete who considers eating healthy food as important as studying and training would be truly self-determined only if he or she does not experience conflicts among the three activities and also regulates the three activities with success. In sum, the issue of measuring integrated regulation is complex and there is, as of yet, no clear resolution. In the future, researchers could examine the extent to which a behavior is integrated by considering whether it has the defining characteristics listed previously and adopting strategies to ensure that measures sufficiently capture these features.

Future Research and Applications

Although this chapter focuses on measurement issues, it seems appropriate to close with a few brief comments on future applications of the SMS and the assessment of regulatory styles in sport more broadly. We have learned a tremendous amount about the different regulatory styles since the publication of Deci and Ryan's (1985) original theorizing on self-determination and motivation. However, future work is needed to determine how best to use the different forms of motivation. The use of the SDI versus the various regulatory styles requires more research. Continued research is needed on the different forms of motivation proposed by self-determination theory with people from varied cultures, backgrounds, and sports. In addition, the mechanisms through which the different regulatory styles in sport affect different outcomes need to be identified.

Also, as suggested by Vallerand (1997, this volume), the various types of motivation exist at multiple levels of abstraction (i.e., general, contextual, and situational). There is some reason to believe that motivations at these different levels of abstraction are somewhat related to each other, and this has been supported by recent empirical research (Guay, Mageau, & Vallerand, 2003; Hagger, Chatzisarantis, & Harris, 2006). An important methodological and theoretical question is how these various levels of abstraction function in the achievement of relevant outcomes. Does the best prediction come from taking into account a combination of motivation at the general level, the contextual level (e.g., sport), and the situational level? Does the best prediction come from a level of abstraction that is close to that of the outcome? Finally, another assessment concern is how to gain access to individuals' views of their own motivation. Attempting to access both the affective and cognitive features of the functional and experiential differences between the perceived forces that move an individual to act, as suggested in this chapter, may be an effective way to progress in the measurement of motivation; such an effort may also represent an important move toward a delicate balance between the affective, cognitive, and behavioral components underlying goal pursuits.

From a practical perspective, researchers, sport psychologists, and coaches could use the SMS to facilitate knowledge about, and interventions to enhance, the motivational development of athletes over time. In addition, researchers should be encouraged to use measures like the SMS when evaluating interventions designed to enhance athletes' persistence, coping with stress, mental preparation for important events, performance, and well-being. Given that the SMS originated from a theory that posits the influence of person and contextual factors on the satisfaction of the basic needs for autonomy, competence, and relatedness, it seems important to examine in more detail how parents' and coaches' interpersonal behaviors relate to the satisfaction of these basic needs, the different forms of motivation in sports, and variability in various outcomes. More specifically, repeated measures of contextual factors in longitudinal or daily diary studies may be especially useful to further illuminate the nature of within-person variation in the different forms of motivation. In turn, within-person variations in motivation could systematically be related to levels of outcomes like mental preparation, performance, and well-being within specific relationships or within specific contexts, over and above between-person differences.

Practical Recommendations for Researchers Involved in Assessing Motivation in Sport

- It is recommended that researchers adapt the Sport Motivation Scale according to their research purpose. Combining the SMS subscales to yield an overall relative autonomy index—by assigning specific weights to the SMS subscales according to their place on the self-determination continuum—is useful in complex designs employing many measures and when the researcher is interested in global effects of motivational orientation.

(continued)

(continued)

• The intrinsic, integrated regulation, and identified regulation subscales from the SMS could be grouped to form a global score of autonomous forms of motivation; and the introjected regulation, external regulation, and amotivation subscales could be grouped to form a global score of controlling forms of motivation. Such grouping is useful for research in which a clear distinction between these two forms of regulation is required, but parsimony remains important.

• Another approach would be to use each subscale independently in validation studies or in cases in which subtle differences among the constructs from the self-determination continuum are required. This would be useful for researchers aiming to establish the concurrent validity of measures (e.g., Hagger, Chatzisarantis, & Harris, 2006) or examining the relative positions of related psychological constructs on the continuum.

• An alternative approach would be to conduct a factor or cluster analysis to identify homogeneous groups of athletes that share the same motivational characteristics. This would be useful for researchers interested in distinguishing particular groups and for practitioners wishing to identify the sources of motivation within their teams or groups of athletes.

• Researchers are encouraged to use the SMS and to pursue studies that assess the different forms of motivation with athletes from different cultures, backgrounds, and sports.

• Further, researchers are encouraged to adopt the SMS as a means to facilitate knowledge about, and interventions to enhance, the motivational development of athletes over time. Researchers need to adopt the SMS to examine motivational orientations among sport participants to further our understanding of the factors that affect between-person as well as within-person variations in motivation.

Motivation in Elite-Level Sport

A Self-Determination Perspective

Darren C. Treasure, PhD
Competitive Advantage International Performance Systems

Pierre-Nicolas Lemyre, PhD
Norwegian University of Sport and Physical Education

Kendy K. Kuczka, PhD
AIA Academy

Martyn Standage, PhD
University of Bath

It is believed by many that motivation is the foundation of sport performance and achievement (e.g., Duda & Treasure, 2001). Without motivation, even the most gifted performer is unlikely to reach his or her athletic potential. Interest in self-determination theory in the context of sport, exercise, and physical education has increased dramatically in recent years (see Ryan & Deci, this volume). The majority of research examining motivation from a self-determination perspective in sport has, however, been conducted with recreational or nonelite athletes (e.g., youth and university sport participants). Consequently, a gap in the literature exists, particularly for practitioners searching for insight into the motivation process at the elite level. If one is interested in elite-level performers, it is important that research be conducted with this segment of the athletic population. However, this is not always possible or perhaps necessary, depending on the specific research question under scrutiny. From the perspective of a performance sport psychologist, though, the research questions of most interest require a very selective sample of high-level sport performers if the results are to be useful from an applied perspective. By definition, elite-level performers represent a very small segment of the general athletic population. This segment can quickly shrink depending on how

Correspondence concerning this article should be addressed to Darren C. Treasure, Competitive Advantage International Performance Systems, 5518 East Saint John Rd., Scottsdale, AZ 85254-5880. E-mail: darren@caiperformancesystems.com limiting, strict, or literal a definition of "elite" one chooses to invoke. This chapter draws on recent empirical research from a self-determination theory perspective, both quantitative and qualitative, to facilitate our understanding of the motivation process in elite-level sport. Subsequently, drawing from these extant findings, we offer evidence-based applied strategies that may facilitate athletic well-being, development, and performance.

Motivation Types

Many people unfamiliar with the context of elite-level sport would be shocked at the myriad challenges and the level of adversity athletes face on an almost daily basis. Extreme training loads, injuries, solitude, competition schedules, and travel demands are but a few of the conditions that make the lifestyle extremely arduous and define the social conditions of the context. Those from the outside looking in at the challenges presented in this context would simply ask the question, "Why do this?" They may then leap to the conclusion that the reasons must be external—such as money and the societal status that come with high-level athletic performance. The question highlights a tendency to assume that many human behaviors are not intrinsically motivated and that much of what people do is for outcomes separate from the actual behavior. In addition, it may be that the general population has an implicit acceptance that elite-level sport is externally reinforced or motivated. Accordingly, in an attempt to explain the development and multifaceted nature of extrinsic motivation, Deci and Ryan (1985) formulated the organismic integration theory (see Ryan & Deci, this volume). As a well-articulated mini-theory embraced by the larger self-determination theory framework, organismic integration theory describes different types of motivation that vary in the degree to which a behavior has been internalized and integrated into an individual's sense of self. Previous research that has examined the motivation of elite-level sport performers has suggested that their behavior is not solely intrinsically motivated, that multiple motives are likely to exist, and that the social conditions defining one's participation are likely to have a significant effect on the motivation process.

For example, Chantal, Guay, Dobreva-Martinova, and Vallerand (1996) examined the motivational profiles of 98 elite Bulgarian athletes from a variety of sports (e.g., canoeing, biathlon, figure skating, boxing, tennis, and skiing). All participants completed the Bulgarian version of the Sport Motivation Scale (SMS; Brière, Vallerand, Blais, & Pelletier, 1995), with performance quantified as titles and medals won over two years at national, world, and Olympic championships. Analyses revealed that less self-determined types of motivation (i.e., introjected regulation and external regulation) promoted better performances within the controlling culture of post-Communist Bulgaria. Indeed, when compared to less successful athletes, the best-performing athletes displayed higher levels of non-self-determined extrinsic motivation (as indexed by a composite score of introjected regulation and external regulation). Specifically, title holders and medal winners reported with more frequency that external rewards, feelings of obligation, and pressure were their primary sources of motivation.

Commensurate with self-determination theory, Chantal and colleagues' findings suggest that the social context has a powerful effect upon the forms of motivation adopted by the athlete. The authors suggest that the highly competitive sport structure that prevailed in Bulgaria at the time may have influenced the athletes' motivation in that the sport structure strongly emphasized winning, regardless of the costs. Within this society, the best-performing athletes would receive material benefits such as travel opportunities, cars, apartments, and financial incentives. Therefore, the best-performing athletes might have been more strongly influenced by the social context emphasizing external incentives and pressures to compete, which led to higher levels of non-self-determined motivation. Similarly, the pressures associated with competition, combined with a fear of losing valuable privileges or incentives, may have fostered a state of amotivation among the top athletes. Departing from the propositions of self-determination theory, the results of Chantal and colleagues' research suggest that in highly competitive and controlling structures it may be less self-determined forms of motivation, as opposed to more autonomous motivational orientations, that facilitate performance.

Results of a recent qualitative study by Mallett and Hanrahan (2004) offer partial support for the findings of Chantal and colleagues (1996) but also provide a richer insight into the motivation of elite-level athletes, particularly in less controlling social conditions. Interpreting the results of semistructured interviews with elite male and female Australian track and field athletes (five males, five females) who had finished in the top 10 at a major championship in track and field in the last six years (i.e., 1996, 2000 Olympic Games; 1995, 1997, 1999 World Championships), Mallett and Hanrahan (2004) suggested that elite athletes have multiple motives for participating that encompass the regulations embraced by the continuum of relative autonomy or perceived locus of causality. Although the interview data revealed excitement, enjoyment, a love for competing at the highest level, and a sense of relatedness with fellow athletes as important motives, less self-determined motives also emerged. Specifically, some athletes identified money and social recognition as motives while others spoke of the job aspect of the sport. Within the context of elite sport, these findings reinforce Deci and Ryan's (1985) multidimensional conceptualization of extrinsic motivation.

Although individuals initially "play" sport during childhood and report intrinsic reasons for participation, the social conditions that define the elite-level sport context are likely to make this nonsustainable. The results of the Mallett and Hanrahan (2004) study, however, suggest that elite-level athletes find a way to internalize and integrate more self-determined forms of extrinsic motivation. This process of internalization and integration of regulations and values is central to self-determination theory and relevant for the regulation of behavior across the life span (Ryan & Deci, 2000). Although little research has specifically addressed this question in the context of elite sport, differences between athletes who train or perform for more or less self-determined reasons are likely to be great. For example, differences in the behavior and performance of athletes motivated to avoid guilt or anxiety (introjected regulation) and those who consciously value and judge the behavior as important and therefore perform it out of choice (identified regulation) are likely to be clearly evident over the course of a season or career.

Although the SMS, the most commonly used scale in the sport domain to assess contextual motivation, does not include a subscale on integrated motivation (Pelletier et al., 1995), the gold standard in elite-level sport may very well be the most autonomous form of extrinsic motivation, namely integrated regulation. Specifically, elite-level athletes may have evaluated and brought into congruence the behaviors and demands of the task with their other values and needs. As Ryan and Deci (2000) contend, actions characterized by integrated motivation share many qualities with intrinsic motivation, although they are still considered extrinsic because they are done to attain separable outcomes rather than for their inherent enjoyment. To identify the most adaptive motivation type at the elite level, future researchers in elite-level sport should look to examine the association between greater internalization and integration of regulations and training or performance markers such as behavioral effectiveness, volitional persistence, interest, enjoyment, positive coping styles, psychological well-being, and performance.

Self-Determination and Training

A fundamental tenet of self-determination theory is that individuals engaged in an activity by choice will experience better consequences than those whose participation is less autonomous. Indeed, research has shown a positive relationship between autonomous motivation and higher levels of task perseverance and psychological well-being, and has shown autonomous motivation to be negatively related to feelings of stress anxiety and self-criticism in sport (e.g., Gagné, Ryan, & Bargmann, 2003; Krane, Greenleaf, & Snow, 1997). In the case of elite sport, however, much of training is not very interesting and, although essential to improving performance, extremely repetitive and monotonous. Research has demonstrated, though, that even the most tedious aspects of training can be transcended through the use of interest-enhancing strategies that assist an individual's internalization of self-determined motivation regulations (Green-Demers, Pelletier, Stewart, & Gushue, 1998). But what about those athletes who do not, or cannot, internalize an autonomous motivation regulation? What about the athlete who becomes more external in his or her motivation for continuing to train and compete? This process is of considerable interest, particularly with regard to the relationship between motivation and maladaptive training responses such as susceptibility to burnout.

Bur... ..t has become a significant area of study for researchers and practitioners interested in elite-level sport as the increase in training loads of elite athletes during the last decade is believed to have led to a growing occurrence of maladaptive training responses (e.g., Gould, 1996; Raglin & Wilson, 2000). Although a plethora of physiological studies adopting a medical model have been conducted to examine various aspects of maladaptive training responses including burnout (see Steinacker & Lehmann, 2002), little psychological research has addressed the antecedents and consequences of this debilitating condition. Emanating from unmet needs and unfulfilled expectations (Gold & Roth, 1993), burnout is a syndrome characterized by progressive disillusionment, with related psychological and physical symptoms, leading to a diminished sense of self-worth (Freudenberger, 1980). Athletes may develop burnout when they experience enduring physiological or psychological exertion in the quest for a desired goal without significant recovery (e.g., Gould & Dieffenbach, 2002; Silva, 1990). When athletes suffer from burnout, they typically experience chronic fatigue, poor sleep patterns, episodes of depression, and a sense of helplessness (Silva, 1990; Smith, 1986). Not surprisingly, their performance is also considerably impaired. Full recovery from burnout represents a complex process that may necessitate many months or even years of rest and removal from sport (e.g., Kellmann, 2002). Recent research has suggested that motivation may be a key variable in explaining this debilitating condition (e.g., Cresswell & Eklund, 2005; Gould, 1996; Hall, Cawthraw, & Kerr, 1997; Lemyre, Treasure, & Roberts, 2006; Raedeke, 1997).

In competitive sport, maladaptive training outcomes such as overtraining and burnout have been hypothesized to follow shifts on the motivation continuum toward more extrinsic sources (Lemyre, Treasure, & Roberts, 2006). Self-determination theory, therefore, appears potentially relevant to investigation of the role of motivation in the development of burnout in elite-level athletes. In a study of young elite American tennis players, Gould, Udry, Tuffey, and Loehr (1996) compared burned-out athletes with a group of tennis players who demonstrated adaptive performance outcomes and reported a healthy motivation toward tennis. The authors stated that players reporting maladaptive performance outcomes manifested higher levels of amotivation because they were less convinced about the purpose of their participation in competitive tennis than their striving counterparts. In a follow-up qualitative study (Gould, Tuffey, Udry, & Loehr, 1996), three nonthriving athletes were closely investigated. These young burned-out players reported being motivated to play tennis by extrinsic sources; they generally felt pressured by their parents and coaches and did not always feel that their results were linked to the amount of effort they put into training and competition. Consistent with the findings of Gould and colleagues and aligned with the fundamental tenets of self-determination theory, results from a recent study by Cresswell and Eklund (2005) on burnout among top amateur rugby union players showed intrinsic motivation to be negatively associated, amotivation positively associated, and extrinsic regulation not related to burnout.

Although athletes in all sports are susceptible to overtraining and burnout, those involved in sports with especially high training demands are likely to be most at risk. At the elite level, swimming is one of the most physically and mentally demanding of all sports. In a recent study that we conducted with 44 athletes from two top 10–ranked American NCAA Division 1A collegiate swimming programs, one male and one female (Lemyre, Treasure, & Roberts, 2006), swimmers swam an average of more than 38,000 yards (34,750 meters) a week in addition to completing a rigorous out-of-water training program. The training program was year-round, and many of the athletes had been training at this level for over 10 years. In this particular study we examined how shifts along the self-determined motivation continuum during the course of a competitive season, as well as swings in negative and positive affect, predicted athlete burnout susceptibility at season's end.

Although participants reported relatively high levels of self-determined motivation throughout the season, it was interesting to note that shifts in the quality of situational motivation from more to less self-determined affective responses, and increases in negative affect accentuated athletes' susceptibility to experiencing burnout at season's end. The results of this study clearly show that maladaptive training responses are more likely to occur when an athlete's reason for participating shifts to a more extrinsic motivation regulation representing a loss of autonomy. As has been suggested by Klinger (1975), it may be that when facing loss of autonomy, individuals are biologically predetermined to enter an incentive–disengagement cycle corresponding to the developmental stages of the burnout process.

Continuing this line of research, we followed up our initial study with a qualitative investigation designed to examine the motivation process of five thriving and five burned-out athletes from the original sample of 44 athletes (Lemyre, Kuczka, Treasure, & Roberts, 2005). The thriving athletes all reported that their swimming involvement was motivated by self-determined reasons and that they experienced great joy in training and competing in swimming during the season. These athletes felt that swimming added an important dimension to their life and that they had control over their involvement in the sport. Alternatively, the burned-out athletes reported less autonomous forms of motivation for being involved in swimming. The reasons mentioned included feeling a responsibility to perform to keep their athletic scholarship, feeling pressured to follow in the footsteps of successful family members, and desiring to finish their swimming career on a high note and recreate best-ever performances, as well as feeling that they had to meet parents' and coaches' expectations. These athletes showed clear signs of amotivation, mentioning that they did not feel their results reflected the amount of commitment they were giving to the sport. From a practical perspective, the findings support our claim that the systematic monitoring of changes in an athlete's quality of motivation may represent an important tool in the prevention of maladaptive performance outcomes within elite sport (Lemyre, Treasure, & Roberts, 2006).

Self-Determination and Performance

Although there are many consequences that one can examine from a self-determination theory perspective, at the elite level of sport, sport performance is the outcome variable of central interest. This fact may explain some of the findings discussed in the previous section that may seem contradictory to certain fundamental tenets of the theory because many outcomes in sport are externally referenced (e.g., winning or outperforming others). It is important to note however, that the determinants of athletic performance are numerous and can be conceptualized in many different ways. For the purpose of this chapter we have conceptualized the determinants of performance in terms of proximity to the execution of the skill. This means that we focus on the psychological antecedents that lead to behaviors that are central to performance rather than performance itself. Although many view motivation as the foundation of sport performance, as "the fire that burns from within," our approach considers the behaviors that are most proximal to athletic performance. Research using the self-determination theory approach has provided insight into the motivation–performance relationship central to elite-level sport.

Pelletier and colleagues (2001) examined the associations between perceived autonomy support, the forms of motivational regulation (intrinsic motivation, identified regulation, introjected regulation, external regulation, and amotivation), and persistence in a prospective study of 174 male and 195 female competitive swimmers (see Sarrazin, Boiché, & Pelletier, this volume). At the beginning of the competitive season, the athletes completed questionnaires that included a measure of perceived autonomy support provided by their coach and the SMS. At 10 and 22 months later, the researchers contacted the teams to determine which athletes were still participating in swimming and which had dropped out. Forty-seven percent of the swimmers had ended their swimming participation, and the dropout rates were equally distributed among the swimmers of different competitive levels.

Among the swimmers studied, perceiving the coach–athlete relationship as controlling fostered less self-determined forms of regulation (external regulation and amotivation), while perceptions that the relationship was autonomy supportive fostered greater levels of self-determined motivation. Swimmers who showed self-determined types of motivation at the first time point showed more persistence at both the second (10 months later) and final (22 months later) time points. In addition, swimmers who exhibited amotivation at the first time point had the highest attrition rate at the two subsequent time points. Introjected regulation was a significant predictor of persistence at the second time point but not at the final time point; external regulation was associated with persistence only at the final time point. The results from this study support self-determination theory in showing that the regulation of behavior can be distinguished along a continuum of self-determination. The findings also show that self-regulation predicts persistence and specifically that how an individual self-regulates (i.e., intrinsic or introjected regulation) has important implications for behavioral persistence.

Sarrazin and colleagues (2002) examined a motivational model of sport dropout that integrates the four-stage causal sequence proposed by Deci and Ryan (1985) and elements of achievement goal theory (Nicholls, 1989). A total of 335 regional-level adolescent female handball players from 53 teams, who trained an average of 4 hours per week, were studied for 21 months (see Sarrazin, Boiché, & Pelletier, this volume). Results indicated that a motivational climate that promoted mastery of the task facilitated athletes' perceptions of competence, autonomy, and relatedness, while a climate that focused on normative comparisons and "winning at all costs" undermined the athletes' perceptions of satisfaction of these three basic psychological needs. Thus, feeling incompetent, nonautonomous, and unrelated to others undermines athletes' self-determined motivation and leads to intentions of ending participation and eventually dropping out of the activity. While these subjects were hardly an elite sample of athletes, this 21-month prospective study supports the four-stage causal sequence suggested by Vallerand (1997, this volume) and indicates that a lack of self-determined motivation may lead to sport dropout. It also supports the concept that the effect of the social context on motivation is mediated by the individual's perceptions of competence, autonomy, and relatedness. The three basic needs explained 78% of the variance in the athletes' self-determined motivation toward playing handball. Therefore, coaches' behavior influences athletes' motivation through athletes' perceptions of autonomy, competence, and relatedness.

Csikszentmihalyi's (1975, 1990) work on flow, which is influential but not directly related to sport performance, has recently been examined within the context of self-determination theory (see Fortier & Kowal, this volume). Specifically, Kowal and Fortier (1999) examined the relationships between situational motivation and flow in 203 masters-level swimmers (105 males, 98 females) from eight swim clubs. Immediately following a swim practice, participants completed questionnaires assessing situational motivation and flow. Results showed that swimming for intrinsic reasons (the most self-determined form of motivation) was positively associated with the highest levels of flow during practice; identified regulation was also positively associated with flow. External regulation and amotivation were negatively associated with flow. That is, swimmers who were motivated in a self-determined manner (i.e., they practiced for the pleasure and satisfaction of engaging in the activity) reported the highest levels of flow compared to swimmers who had less self-determined motivational profiles (i.e., they practiced because of internal pressures or were extrinsically motivated). Although there were no significant differences in perceived autonomy between swimmers who experienced high and low levels of flow, swimmers who experienced the highest levels of flow reported significantly higher levels of perceived competence and relatedness than those swimmers who experienced low levels of flow. These findings suggest that cultivating self-determined forms of motivation and enhancing satisfaction of the three basic psychological needs may facilitate an athlete's attainment of the flow state, which in turn may enhance an athlete's performance.

Basic Needs

According to self-determination theory, satisfaction of the needs for autonomy, competence, and relatedness is essential to sustain a healthy motivational orientation (Ryan & Deci, 2000). These innate psychological needs are most likely to be fulfilled in social contexts where the individual feels that his or her need for autonomy is supported by important others. The basic needs hypothesis advanced by self-determination theory (Ryan & Deci, 2000) has been examined recently in the context of sport. With a sample of 33 female subelite gymnasts between the ages of 7 and 18 years, Gagné and colleagues (2003) used a combination of questionnaires and diaries to investigate the effects of young athletes' perceptions of support from coaches and parents on their need satisfaction, motivation, and well-being (see Gagné & Blanchard, this volume).

The findings revealed that perceptions of parents' and coaches' autonomy support and involvement influenced the quality of the gymnasts' motivation. Specifically, the more the gymnasts perceived their parents or coaches to be autonomy supportive and involved, the more autonomously motivated they were. Results also indicated that daily motivation predicted prepractice well-being and that changes in well-being from pre- to postpractice systematically varied with the athletes' need satisfaction during practices. Analyses at the individual level showed that gymnasts who perceived that their coaches were highly involved in their training had more stable self-esteem than those who perceived their coaches to be uninvolved. The gymnasts' perceptions of parents' and coaches' autonomy support influenced their adoption of more autonomous forms of motivation; parent involvement also increased the likelihood of the athletes' adopting more controlled forms of motivation, but the coaches' involvement did not have this effect. However, these results could not be replicated at the daily level. Not surprisingly, parental involvement, parental autonomy support, and autonomous motivation had effects upon the athletes' practice attendance, supporting the assertion that autonomous forms of motivation influence not only the quality of motivation the athlete experiences, but also his or her behavior. This study supports the importance of parental and coach support to the enhancement of autonomous motivation and the satisfaction of the three basic needs among adolescent athletes, which would lead to increased well-being.

We have obtained a pattern of findings similar to that reported by Gagné and colleagues (2003) in a longitudinal study conducted with elite-level swimmers

(Treasure, Standage, Lemyre, & Ntoumanis, 2004). Responses to questionnaires administered at three time points (corresponding to the objectively easy, very hard, and peaking times of a competitive season) were analyzed to examine whether the perception of an autonomy-supportive climate created by the coaching staff (time 2) mediated levels of intrinsic motivation from time 1 to time 3. We also examined whether need satisfaction at time 2 predicted indices of subjective well-being at time 3. With respect to our first question, results of a mediation analysis (Baron & Kenny, 1986) revealed that perceptions of an autonomy-supportive climate at time 2 partially mediated reported levels of intrinsic motivation from time 1 to time 3. A theoretically consistent pattern of findings emerged with regard to our second question, with basic needs predicting affective responses and vitality at the end of the season. The results therefore provide further support for the basic needs hypothesis advanced by Ryan and Deci (2000) and speak to the need for research focused on identifying strategies that will help practitioners design autonomy-supportive conditions in the context of elite sport to ensure the well-being of the athletes.

Practical Applications

Irrespective of achievement domain, a consistent finding in self-determination theory research—and a fundamental tenet—is the central role that social conditions play in the motivation process. Although not great in quantity, findings from research on the conditions that facilitate (versus undermine) human functioning in elite-level sport do offer insight into the design of social environments that will optimize development and well-being. Training environments that support the autonomy of athletes appear to enhance the self-determined motivation that, we would contend, is vital in optimizing positive outcomes such as basic need satisfaction, persistence, and task perseverance. These positive outcomes serve as a prophylactic measure against maladaptive training or performance consequences such as overtraining or burnout (e.g., Gagné, Ryan, & Bargmann, 2003; Lemyre, Treasure, & Roberts, 2006; Raedeke, 1997; Treasure et al., 2004). Analogous to researchers in education contexts, who have shown that teachers can be taught to be autonomy supportive (Reeve, 1998, 2002), researchers interested in the elite sport experience need to explore ways in which coaches, parents, and other significant social agents can engage in the creation of an autonomy-supportive climate (see "Practical Recommendations for Sport Psychologists Working With Elite-Level Athletes"). This task is particularly salient for individuals invested in talent development programs, where persistence and task perseverance are fundamental for young athletes if they are to reach their athletic potential.

Although social development, health, and well-being are important outcomes in sport, particularly at the recreation and nonelite levels, these are not the critical outcome variables in the context of elite-level sport, where performance matters. Coaches and athletes often want to know only what will enhance people's performance, not what will help them experience psychological well-being or health. The research reviewed in this chapter, however, clearly shows that self-determination theory is relevant to all aspects of elite-level sport, including performance. Athletes who internalize a self-determined motivation regulation and train in an autonomy-supportive environment are likely to experience adaptive outcomes such as persistence, task perseverance, and coping strategies that have been shown to be determinants of athletic development and performance. Perhaps most significant, given the myriad challenges and the level of adversity that elite athletes face, self-determination theory and the research reviewed clearly show that the promotion of autonomous motivation may serve a vital role in protecting athletes from maladaptive training outcomes such as overtraining and burnout.

Practical Recommendations for Sport Psychologists Working With Elite-Level Athletes

- It is of utmost importance that coaches commit time and energy to developing an understanding of motivation and the motivation process. As the research reviewed in this chapter demonstrates, coaches who take the time to understand the motivation process will not only have a competitive advantage over their peers but also enhance the psychological well-being, development, and performance of their athletes. For example, coaches are encouraged to ask questions of their performers to identify their exact reasons for participating in the sport. They are advised not to accept answers like "to win races" as satisfactory and are encouraged to delve deeper into what really motivates performers. For example, a coach might ask a performer, "We can't always win races, matches, or competitions, so what keeps you motivated if you don't win?"

- The training demands athletes must meet in order to achieve and maintain elite performance are considerable. Many of the training methods that are crucial to high-level performance are not inherently interesting. In order for the athlete to "buy into" these behaviors, it is important that the coach (1) provide a meaningful rationale, (2) be seen as acknowledging the athletes' feelings regarding the requested behavior, and (3) be autonomy supportive in interactions with the athlete. This does not mean simply prescribing a training practice and saying to athletes "This is good for you"! Instead, coaches are encouraged to be more comprehensive and to link practices to autonomous goals. A coach might say, "I have designed this practice to help improve your hand–eye coordination. It may be very boring from the outset, but just think how much it will help you to intercept your opponents' balls in a match situation, which may make the difference in performance."

(continued)

(continued)

- Given that differences in performance levels of athletes who train and compete for more versus less self-determined reasons are likely to be great, coaches and sport psychologists are encouraged to guide athletes to internalize and integrate more self-determined forms of motivation. Encouraging athletes to become self-aware with respect to their motivation and offering support and guidance during times of adversity and monotony will assist in this process. For example, coaches may remind their athletes before each practice, "This training session is an essential part of our overall training program to achieve your personal best time this season. It is difficult and will be challenging, but if you apply yourself to the practice, it will mean you will obtain your own personal goals in the future." Here the coach refers to a personal goal (achieving a personal best time); makes it clear that this program is one that has been agreed upon, which enhances autonomy and relatedness ("our overall training program"); acknowledges conflict ("difficult and challenging"); and appeals to effort as a means to demonstrate competence ("if you apply yourself"). These are all hallmarks of autonomy-supportive instructions.

- As shifts in the quality of motivation from more to less self-determined types over the course of a competitive season have been shown to be related to maladaptive training responses, it is recommended that coaches and sport psychologists implement a monitoring system that assesses motivation and affective states on a regular basis. The coach can therefore be active in reminding players where their chosen and agreed-upon goals lie and what role their practices have in advancing these goals. One means of doing this is to use visual aids like diaries and wall charts to plot progress and visually describe goals.

- Coaches are encouraged to establish a training and competition environment that supports the basic psychological needs of athletes. To this end, it is recommended that practitioners develop strategies that will assist athletes in feeling competent, autonomous, and related to teammates and support and coaching staff. These needs and accompanying strategies are as follows:

  1. *Autonomy.* Increase opportunities for athletes' involvement in decision making and provide opportunities for choice in all aspects of their training and performance. The coach might ask athletes to work together to discuss or identify their future goals. This is equally effective in team and individual sports, as it provides a forum for self-reflection about personally relevant goals. The same strategy can then be used in one-to-one discussions with the athletes to establish goals that are agreed upon by them and personally relevant to them.

2. *Competence.* To meet the need for competence, a coach may provide appropriate informational and positive feedback (see Hein & Koka, this volume) and expose athletes to optimal task and skill challenges (Deci & Moller, 2005). Although evaluation in sport is inherently socially comparative, one can implement performance plans that use self-referenced standards and indicators of advancement. The coach can use the previously mentioned visual aids and team talks prior to practices to remind athletes of their goals and of how each practice session fits in with these goals.

3. *Relatedness.* Coaches are encouraged to take the time to get to know their athletes well. This will provide athletes with a sense that they are understood, valued, and respected by the coach, both as a person and as an athlete. One-to-one meetings in which coaches explore the goals and motives of the athlete are useful in this regard, and such meetings may adapt some of the techniques of motivational interviewing (see Markland & Vansteenkiste, this volume). Team talks are also an excellent means of conveying the importance of athletes' personal goals.

Intrinsic Versus Extrinsic Goal Promotion in Exercise and Sport

Understanding the Differential Impacts on Performance and Persistence

Maarten Vansteenkiste, PhD, Bart Soenens, MSc, and Willy Lens, PhD
University of Leuven

The types of goals people have on their minds when doing exercise and sport can differ substantially: Whereas some exercisers and sport participants are concerned with their physical appeal and attractiveness to others, others are more likely to exercise because of health and physical fitness benefits or because exercise helps them to improve their skills and talents. The goal of physical attractiveness is widely publicized in the media and advertising industry (Shaw & Waller, 1995; Stice & Shaw, 1994); and various socializing agents such as fitness instructors, physical education teachers, health practitioners, and dieticians often refer to this goal in an attempt to motivate their participants, pupils, and patients to increase their exercise efforts. A question that needs to be raised, however, is whether referring to the goal of physical appearance really yields the benefits that socializing agents aim to achieve. That is, when individuals adopt the goal of physical attractiveness versus the goal of health and physical fitness, are they more likely to excel at an exercise or sporting activity and freely persist at it over an extended period of time?

The present chapter reviews recent work, based on self-determination theory's (Deci & Ryan, 1985) distinction between intrinsic and extrinsic goals (Deci & Ryan, 2000; Kasser & Ryan, 1993, 1996), that has dealt with these issues in exercise and sport. We first discuss the distinction between intrinsic

Correspondence concerning this article should be addressed to Maarten Vansteenkiste, Department of Psychology, Tiensestraat 102, 3000 Leuven, Belgium. E-mail: Maarten.Vansteenkiste@psy.kuleuven.be and extrinsic goal and review research on the effects of promoting these two types of goals. Then we discuss macro- and micro-mediational mechanisms underlying these effects and conclude by providing directions for future research and practical guidelines.

Individual Intrinsic Versus Extrinsic Goal Pursuit

Self-determination theory (Kasser & Ryan, 1996) distinguishes the intrinsic goals of community contribution, self-development and self-acceptance, affiliation, and physical health from the extrinsic goals of social recognition, image and attractiveness, financial success, and power. Intrinsic goals are said to reflect people's natural growth tendencies to develop satisfying relationships, to strengthen their talents and potential, to connect with the larger world, and to maintain a sense of physical fitness and health. Intrinsic goals are characterized by an "*in*ward" orientation, because they orient people's energy and efforts toward realizing their natural growth trajectories. Intrinsic goal pursuit is said to be positively associated with well-being because such goal pursuit is gratifying in its own right and is likely to be conducive to satisfying individuals' basic needs for autonomy, competence, and relatedness (Ryan, Sheldon, Kasser, & Deci, 1996; Vansteenkiste, Lens, & Deci, 2006).

By contrast, when people focus on attaining extrinsic goals, such as financial success, physical attractiveness, and social recognition, their attention becomes oriented toward acquiring external signs of worth. When people adopt an extrinsic mind-set, they tend to hold an "*out*ward" orientation (Williams, Cox, Hedberg, & Deci, 2000) because they become preoccupied with making a good impression on others instead of developing their inner potential (Kasser, Ryan, Couchman, & Sheldon, 2004). Although people often pursue extrinsic goals because they hope to "buy" their happiness by doing so, self-determination theory maintains, rather paradoxically, that extrinsic goal pursuit will be associated with poorer well-being and adjustment compared to intrinsic goal pursuit. This is so because extrinsic goal pursuit, on average, tends to be contrary to the satisfaction of individuals' basic needs for autonomy, competence, and relatedness.

Various studies have confirmed the hypothesis that intrinsic and extrinsic goals relate differentially to well-being and adjustment. For instance, Kasser and Ryan (1993, 1996) found that the more people attach importance to extrinsic, relative to intrinsic, goals, the lower their life satisfaction and self-actualization and the higher their level of anxiety and depression. Other research has indicated that these relationships hold in both individualistic and collectivistic cultures (e.g., Chirkov & Ryan, 2001; Hagger, Chatzisarantis, Barkoukis, Wang, & Baranowski, 2005; Kim, Kasser, & Lee, 2003; Ryan, Chirkov, Little, Sheldon, Timoshira, & Deci, 1999) and even in settings where extrinsic goals are heavily promoted, such as business schools (e.g., Kasser & Ahuvia, 2002; Vansteenkiste, Duriez, Simons, & Soenens, in press). A few studies (e.g., Frederick & Ryan, 1993; Ryan, Frederick, Lepes, Rubio, & Sheldon, 1997) have examined exercisers' motive for physical attractiveness and their motives for health and physical fitness in relation to exercise adherence. These studies showed that exercising to increase one's physical appeal was either negatively related or unrelated to hours per week of participation, length of workout, and exercise attendance. In contrast, exercising to improve physical fitness correlated positively with exercise attendance and the challenge experienced during workout sessions (Ryan et al., 1997).

It is important to note that people can focus on these different goal contents for very different reasons. For instance, some pursue physical attractiveness because they personally value being attractive and good-looking, whereas others experience an inner urge to live up to the physical appearance ideals in society. As outlined elsewhere (see Ryan & Deci, this volume), self-determination theory argues that people's dynamic reasons for performing an activity can vary in their degree of autonomy. Further, self-determination theory maintains that one's intrinsic versus extrinsic goal pursuits should be distinguished from one's underlying autonomous versus controlled regulations (Deci & Ryan, 2000; Vansteenkiste, Lens, & Deci, 2006), although these are related. The pursuit of intrinsic goals is often based on autonomous reasons, whereas the pursuit of extrinsic goals is often guided by controlled reasons. However, people's intrinsic versus extrinsic goal contents and their autonomous versus controlled reasons predict independent variance in well-being and adjustment (Sheldon, Ryan, Deci, & Kasser, 2004).

Intrinsic Versus Extrinsic Goal Promotion

Most recently, Vansteenkiste and colleagues (see Vansteenkiste, Lens, & Deci, 2006) extended this line of research in a number of ways. Rather than considering the impact of the individual pursuit of intrinsic relative to extrinsic goals on one's adjustment and well-being, the researchers experimentally manipulated these goals. The aim was to examine whether the promotion of an intrinsic instead of an extrinsic goal content in a social context would result in different implications for individuals' learning and persistence, just as intrinsic and extrinsic goal pursuit differentially predict well-being. In a number of experimental studies in the educational context, Vansteenkiste, Simons, Lens, Sheldon, and Deci (2004a) found that portraying a learning activity as serving an intrinsic, relative to an extrinsic, goal increased individuals' performance and voluntary persistence. Such findings were obtained in both adolescents and younger children, although the negative effects of extrinsic goal framing were limited to conceptual learning and did not emerge for rote learning (Vansteenkiste, Simons, Lens, Soenens, & Matos, 2005c). Apparently, extrinsic goal framing prompts some motivated learning; however, the learning activity is approached in a more rigid and narrow-minded fashion because the learning is primarily oriented toward attaining the extrinsic goals. Such a rigid, superficial approach is sufficient to promote memorization of material, but interferes with an in-depth processing of the contents.

Intrinsic Versus Extrinsic Goal Promotion in Exercising

A number of studies in the exercise domain have addressed whether the promotion of different goal contents would similarly affect exercisers' performance and persistence. In a first study by Vansteenkiste and colleagues (2004a; Experiment 3), fourth to sixth grade secondary school students were randomly assigned to either an intrinsic or an extrinsic goal condition before being taught a new Asian sport, tai bo, during their physical education classes. Participants in the intrinsic goal condition were told that doing the exercises was important "to remain in *good shape* and stay *healthy* at a later age" and "to avoid becoming *ill and unhealthy.*" In contrast, participants in the extrinsic goal condition were told that doing the exercise was important "to remain *attractive* and *appealing for others* and to *hide the signs of aging.*" Subsequently, participants were taught a few tai bo exercises during a physical education class, and their physical education teachers graded them during the next physical education class. Participants were invited to voluntarily demonstrate the tai bo exercises to other students one week later, which served as a behavioral indicator of persistence at the exercise activity.

Vansteenkiste and colleagues (2004a) reasoned that portraying the exercise as serving the attainment of physical health and fitness should result in more optimal learning and more persistence because of the closer link this goal has to people's basic psychological needs. On the other hand, portraying the exercises as serving the extrinsic goal of physical attractiveness should be linked to suboptimal learning and persistence, because this goal would distract people from the activity at hand and should result in a poorer commitment toward the exercises. The results indicated that intrinsic goal framing promoted graded performance and persistence compared to extrinsic goal framing.

The observation that extrinsic goal promotion undermines optimal learning compared to intrinsic goal promotion does not answer the question whether extrinsic goal promotion might result in better learning compared to that in a no-goal control group. In fact, the media and many socializing agents refer to physical attractiveness in an attempt to motivate individuals to do sports and exercise—does this truly have a positive impact on motivation compared to situations in which no goal has been provided?

Anecdotal evidence suggests that the pursuit of physical attractiveness may, at least for some people, be highly motivating. For instance, to consider the most extreme example, anorexic patients' concern with being thin strongly motivates them to exercise frequently (Vitousek, Watson, & Wilson, 1998). Further, expectancy-value models (e.g., Eccles & Wigfield, 2002; Feather, 1992) provide a theoretical account for the prediction that extrinsic goal framing should yield better outcomes than not referring to any goal at all. According to expectancy-value models, people will be more motivated to persist at an activity and will be more likely to excel at it if the activity contains a high utility value (Miller & Brickman, 2004). Clearly, if the exercise activity is framed as serving an extrinsic goal, the exercise is likely to be perceived as more useful or instrumental (Lens, Simons, & Dewitte, 2001, 2002; Simons, Vansteenkiste, Lens, & Lacante, 2004) compared to when such a goal rationale is absent. Further to these predictions, Vansteenkiste, Simons, Soenens, and Lens (2004c) hypothesized on the basis of self-determination theory that an extrinsic goal would distract participants' attention from the exercise activity and hamper full absorption, resulting in poorer performance. Intrinsic goal framing would result in a stronger exercise commitment and better performance because such goals are more closely connected to basic need satisfaction.

To examine this issue, we performed a second study in the exercise context among fourth to sixth grade secondary school students, including intrinsic and extrinsic goal framing conditions as well as a no-goal control condition (Vansteenkiste et al., 2004c). We also assessed individuals' longer-term voluntary persistence at the activities at one week, one month, and four months after the experiment. The results provided support for self-determination theory. Extrinsic goal framing resulted in decreased autonomous motivation and poorer performance compared to both the intrinsic goal framing condition and the no-goal control condition, whereas intrinsic goal framing promoted these outcomes compared to the no-goal control condition. Hence, in spite of increasing the perceived utility value of the activity, extrinsic goal framing undermined optimal exercise performance. Concerning participants' persistence, intrinsic goal framing enhanced persistence at all three measurement time points compared to that in the control group. The results for participants' persistence in the extrinsic goal group compared to the no-goal control group were more mixed, with participants in the former group persisting less over the short term (i.e., one week) but more over the moderately long term (i.e., one month) compared to the latter group; no differences were found at four-month follow-up. These results suggest that extrinsic goals can indeed be somewhat motivating, but only in the medium term.

However, the persistence that individuals display under extrinsic goal conditions, compared to intrinsic and no-goal conditions, might be of a qualitatively different sort. Specifically, whereas participants' persistence in the intrinsic goal condition might be in accord with their personal valuation and enjoyment of the exercises, participants' persistence in the extrinsic goal condition might lack such concordance and instead be oriented toward the attainment of external indicators of worth. To examine this hypothesis, Vansteenkiste and colleagues (2004c) performed within-condition correlational analyses of participants' persistence behavior and self-reported autonomous exercise motivation, which reflects their enjoyment and personal commitment toward the exercise. Whereas participants' persistence and self-reported autonomous exercise motivation were positively correlated at all three time points in the intrinsic goal group and the no-goal group, they were uncorrelated in the extrinsic goal group. Thus, intrinsic goal framing had not only prompted a higher level of exercise engagement (i.e., quantity of persistence), but also led to more authentic exercise engagement (i.e., quality of persistence) because individuals' behavior was in accordance with their underlying basic needs, emotions, and preferences (Kuhl & Beckman, 1994). In contrast, although extrinsic goal framing led to some persistence, the exercise persistence was of a rather alienated sort, presumably because extrinsic goals do not have the same need-satisfying characteristics as intrinsic goals. Importantly, these results suggest that considering only the amount of exercisers' persistence obscures information regarding the felt emotional quality of persistence.

Obesity, Healthy Lifestyle Change, and Weight Loss

Further evidence for the reasoning that extrinsic goals might be confined to short-term motivational changes comes from a third study by Vansteenkiste, Simons, Braet, Bachman, and Deci (2005b) among severely obese fifth and sixth grade children. Instead of being taught physical exercises, these children read a nutrition-related text about the four-leafed clover, a simplified version of the Food Pyramid (National Agriculture Library, 2005). These children were instructed that learning more about these issues and trying to adopt the guidelines of the four-leafed clover might be important to the intrinsic goal of health and physical fitness or the extrinsic goal of physical attractiveness to others. All children provided self-reports of their fruit- and candy-eating behavior as well as their soft drink consumption in the week prior to the experiment and in the first and third weeks following the experiment. The collection of baseline and one-week follow-up measures allowed us to examine whether children's eating and drinking patterns would positively change in both goal framing conditions; the additional collection of the three-week follow-up measures allowed us to address whether initial positive changes would be maintained in the long run.

In addition to these eating and drinking outcomes, all the children were invited to voluntarily attend a 10-week diet program that started about one month after the experiment. They were also invited to attend six consecutive weekly physical exercise sessions, which started about six weeks after the experiment. Children's weight was assessed at six weeks, 14 weeks, one year, and two years after the experiment. We expected that both intrinsic and extrinsic goal framing would elicit some positive changes in behaviors, but that these changes would be weaker in the extrinsic goal framing condition and would not be maintained in the long term. Results were in line with our predictions: Both intrinsic and extrinsic goal framing resulted in more healthy lifestyle behavior (i.e., more fruit, less candy, less sodas reported consumed), but these changes were maintained only in the intrinsic goal condition. Similarly, both goal conditions prompted some initial attendance in the diet and exercise programs, but the children involved in the extrinsic goal condition tended to discontinue their positive diet and exercise behaviors while those involved in the intrinsic goal condition maintained these behaviors over time. Finally, both goal framing conditions resulted in weight loss, but intrinsic goal framing had a stronger effect on weight loss, even up to two years after the experiment.

Macro-Mediational and Micro-Mediational Mechanisms

As mentioned previously, self-determination theory suggests that the pursuit and promotion of intrinsic goals predict well-being, performance, and persistence because intrinsic, relative to extrinsic, goals better allow people to satisfy their *basic psychological needs* for autonomy, competence, and relatedness (Deci & Ryan, 2000; Kasser, 2002; Ryan et al., 1996). Kasser (2002) reviewed a diverse sample of studies that provided direct and indirect evidence for this hypothesis. As a whole, these studies indicated that individuals who adopt extrinsic, instead of intrinsic, life goals are less likely to build close and authentic relationships (Kasser & Ryan, 2001; Richins & Dawson, 1992), are more likely to feel pressured and controlled in their lives (Sheldon & Kasser, 1995), and are less likely to experience a sense of competence in their goal pursuit because they tend to overidealize wealth and possessions (Kasser, 2002). In a recent attempt to directly examine these proposed mechanisms in the domain of work and organizational psychology, Vansteenkiste, Neyrinck, Niemic, Soenens, and De Witte (2005a) showed that extrinsically, relative to intrinsically, oriented employees display lower job well-being and more job ill-being because they are less able to get their basic needs met on the job.

We suggest that the proposed mechanism of basic need satisfaction represents a rather global or *macro-mediational process*. Further, we propose that, from both a theoretical and an applied viewpoint, it is important to enrich and complement the study of such macro-mediational mechanisms with the identification of more specific or *micro-mediational mechanisms*. Specifically, such micro-mediational mechanisms, which are more cognitive and attentional, might help explain how extrinsic (relative to intrinsic) goal pursuits and social contexts that promote extrinsic (relative to intrinsic) goals result in thwarted need satisfaction. We speculate that at least three micro-mediational processes—attentional shift, interpersonal comparison, and rigid approach—help to provide insight into the more general and abstract macro-mediational process of thwarted need satisfaction.

To make these theoretical developments more concrete, we start with the example of a woman who is attending an aerobic session with the goal of becoming more attractive because she values beauty and physical attractiveness. Specifically, she is very concerned with slimming and strengthening her abdominal muscles. Alternatively, she might be focused on attractiveness because her fitness instructor told her before the class that today's exercises would help her have a nicer and more muscled abdomen so she would be more appealing to others. Thus, in the first case the woman is focused on attractiveness while doing the exercises because she is in general (i.e., dispositionally) oriented toward extrinsic goals, whereas in the second case the statement by the fitness instructor has activated a temporary extrinsic goal frame for doing the exercises. In the following sections we discuss in greater detail each of the three proposed micro-mediational mechanisms and their role in thwarted need satisfaction.

Attentional Shift

In line with self-determination theory, we argue that individuals with either a dispositional or a temporarily activated extrinsic, rather than intrinsic, goal frame are more likely to orient their attention toward attaining external indicators of worth (Vansteenkiste, Lens, & Deci, 2006). Such a concern with attaining external indicators of worth (i.e., an "outward orientation") is likely to cause an attentional shift away from the activity at hand. Thus, the external signs of worth will play a distracting role and will hinder basic need satisfaction for two reasons.

First, extrinsically oriented individuals are more likely to pressure themselves in their pursuit of an activity like exercise because the attainment of extrinsic goals serves to promote external signs of self-worth. The pursuit of extrinsic goals is likely to be associated with a sense of contingent self-esteem, so that extrinsically oriented individuals will experience a sense of self-aggrandizement if they do well at the exercises and attain the external signs of worth and will approach themselves in a self-derogative and self-critical fashion if they do not excel at the exercises and fail to attain the external indicators of worth (Crocker & Park, 2004; Deci & Ryan, 1995; Kernis, 2003). However, because extrinsically oriented individuals' ego and self-worth are fully implied in the activity, they are more likely to experience their exercise engagement as stressful and autonomy thwarting (Kasser, 2002). Consistent with this reasoning, previous experimental work showed that extrinsic goal framing results in a less autonomous and more controlled regulation than intrinsic goal framing (Vansteenkiste et al., 2004a) and a no-goal control condition (Vansteenkiste et al., 2004c), and also that it prompts an ego-involved approach toward the activity (Vansteenkiste et al., 2004b).

Second, by turning toward these external indicators of worth, extrinsically oriented individuals will engage in the ongoing activity in a less committed and less task-oriented way than intrinsically oriented individuals. Consistent with these hypotheses, experimental studies have shown that extrinsic goal framing hindered a task-oriented approach to the activity relative to an intrinsic goal frame, resulting in poorer performance (e.g., Vansteenkiste et al., 2005c, 2004b). If individuals obtain lower performance scores, they are less likely to feel mastery of the activities, which frustrates their need for competence.

Interpersonal Comparison

When people's attention is oriented toward external indicators of worth, they are likely to engage in *interpersonal comparisons*, thereby evaluating their own extrinsic goal realizations relative to those of others (Sirgy, 1998). With reference to the example of the woman who has been told that doing fitness exercises will help her obtain a slimmer abdomen and become more attractive, it is very likely that after becoming concerned about her figure (attentional shift), she will turn toward comparing herself to her friends in the exercise session (interpersonal comparison). Such interpersonal comparisons are likely to yield three consequences for need satisfaction.

First, by engaging in interpersonal comparisons, people are more likely to experience their behavior as stressful and controlling and hence autonomy thwarting. Consistent with these suggestions, extrinsic goal framing was found to result in a more stressful learning experience and to prompt a more controlled regulation relative to an intrinsic goal frame (Vansteenkiste et al., 2004a, 2004c). A second probable consequence of engaging in interpersonal comparisons is that people are likely to end up feeling inferior and less worthy and competent than others, because they will engage in upward (instead of downward) comparisons (Wood & Wilson, 2003). Such upward interpersonal comparisons are likely to further thwart individuals' need for competence. Third, interpersonal comparisons can be experienced as socially alienating and can interfere with people's relating deeply to others. By devoting attention and energy to interpersonal comparisons, the woman in the fitness class will fail to share her exercise enjoyment with her friends and thus be less likely to feel connected to them.

Rigid Approach

Extrinsically oriented individuals, compared to intrinsically oriented individuals, might put extra effort into the activities that help them attain the desired external indicators of worth, but they are likely to approach the activity in a nonoptimal way. Specifically, with the stronger focus on acquiring the external indicators of worth, the activity is more likely to be carried out in a rigid, narrowly focused way. Such a *rigid approach* is likely to yield two negative consequences for people's need satisfaction.

First, concerning learning and achievement, participants under extrinsic goal framing circumstances are likely to become engaged in the learning activity, but the material is processed in a relatively superficial fashion (Vansteenkiste et al., 2004a, 2005c). Such superficial processing is likely to preclude deep feelings of competence. Further, although such a rigid approach promoted initial persistence at the activity, as mentioned earlier, such gains are not maintained in the long run (e.g., Vansteenkiste et al., 2005b, 2004c), leaving individuals with a sense of ineffectiveness and incompetence for failing to persist at the requested behaviors. Notably, even when extrinsically oriented individuals are able to successfully engage in the behaviors that lead them to attain their extrinsic goals, the benefits associated with extrinsic goal attainment are likely to be short-lived. Kasser (2002) argued that extrinsically oriented individuals quickly set new material standards because they overidealize wealth and possessions. As a result, they are likely to experience a continual discrepancy between their romanticized extrinsic values and their present state, which further fuels their feelings of incompetence.

Second, when individuals are oriented toward obtaining external indicators of worth, they approach not only their activities differently, but also other people. Specifically, individuals may approach others in a self-centered and objectifying fashion (Kasser, 2002), that is, in the most efficient fashion to attain their own extrinsic goal ambitions. Such an approach is likely to thwart the development of satisfying relationships. In fact, a number of studies showed that extrinsically oriented persons were less likely to connect with others in a close, authentic, and interpersonally trusting way and were more likely to have relationships characterized by conflict (Duriez, Vansteenkiste, Soenens, & De Witte, 2005; Kasser & Ryan, 2001; McHoskey, 1999; Richins & Dawson, 1992).

To summarize, extrinsic goals and contexts seem to induce debilitating attentional and cognitive processes relative to intrinsic goals and contexts. It is proposed that extrinsic goals, compared to intrinsic goals, may promote an attentional shift away from the activity at hand toward external indicators. When people become concerned with living up to these external indicators of worth, they are more likely to compare their own extrinsic goal realizations with those of others. Such interpersonal comparisons will, on average, hinder basic need satisfaction and will leave people with a sense of insecurity and intraindividual threat. Such insecurity and threat can evoke defensive behavior or a more active tendency to garner external indicators of worth. As a result, rather paradoxically, individuals' attention shifts back to the activity at hand. However, extrinsic goal-oriented people approach these activities and other people around them in a rigid and self-centered fashion because the activity is undertaken to suppress the intraindividual insecurity that has arisen from their thwarted need satisfaction.

Although speculative, the identification of such micro-mediational processes sheds preliminary light on how extrinsically oriented individuals and extrinsic goal framing contexts interfere with the satisfaction of basic psychological needs in comparison to intrinsic orientations and goal framing. Moreover, the identification of such processes helps us understand how extrinsic goal-oriented individuals get caught in a self-sustaining, negative cycle compared with intrinsic goal-oriented people. Because these various micro-mediational processes result in thwarted need satisfaction, people's feelings of insecurity and intraindividual threat are likely to be heightened. This intraindividual insecurity is likely to be buttressed by a stronger tendency toward attaining extrinsic goals (Arndt, Solomon, Kasser, & Sheldon, 2004; Kasser et al., 2004), which distracts people's attention from the activity at hand and further activates the cycle.

Future Research

Although the results of the studies on intrinsic and extrinsic goals were highly consistent, they were limited to the domains of physical exercise and obesity. Hence, future research might address whether similar findings would be obtained in the domains of sport and eating disorders. Anorexic patients, for instance, are concerned with living up to the media's thin ideal (Vitousek, Watson, & Wilson, 1998), which, from the self-determination theory perspective, represents an extrinsic goal focus. Such a continuous extrinsic goal focus, which is associated with repeated thwarted need satisfaction, might, in conjunction with other psychological and genetic factors, explain why people develop an eating disorder pathology over time and display poor social and psychological functioning (Vansteenkiste, Soenens, & Vandereycken, 2005).

In addition, exercisers and elite sport performers might have in mind intrinsic and extrinsic goals other than those investigated to date. For instance, the extrinsic goals of financial success and social recognition might drive elite sport performers to do their best. Alternatively, exercise and sport could be considered a means for developing skills or a way to forge close connections with others (see also Wankel, 1993), which represent intrinsic goals. Thus, future research might examine to what extent the full range of intrinsic and extrinsic goals is personally adopted or contextually promoted by exercisers and novice and elite sport performers. It would also be interesting to examine whether particular goals are more salient among some sports than among others, and whether these goals differ between individual and team sports. For instance, the extrinsic goal of physical attractiveness might be a more strongly endorsed goal among ballet dancers compared to soccer players, and the intrinsic goal of affiliation might be more strongly pursued and promoted in team compared to individual sports (see also Frederick & Ryan, 1993; Ryan et al., 1997). Regardless of mean-level differences between sport and exercise disciplines, we would predict that the individual pursuit and contextual promotion of extrinsic relative to intrinsic goal contents would harm participants' experiences of flow and full absorption in the activity, and would result in poorer performance and less persistence over time.

Finally, Vallerand and colleagues (Guay, Mageau, & Vallerand, 2003; Vallerand, 1997; Vallerand & Rattelle, 2002) have developed a hierarchical model of motivation with regard to people's autonomous versus controlled reasons for doing exercise and sport. We suggest that a similar model could be developed with regard to participants' intrinsic versus extrinsic goals. Specifically, intrinsic and extrinsic goals can be personally adopted and be promoted by the social environment and can be studied at different levels of generality. To date, the work on intrinsic versus extrinsic goals has primarily focused on the global level, examining the well-being and adjustment implications of people's intrinsic versus extrinsic life goals (see Kasser, 2002), and on the situational level, addressing the impact of experimentally manipulated goal contents on individuals' performance and persistence (see Vansteenkiste, Lens, & Deci, in press). Thus, future research at the domain level is needed. Such research could, for instance, examine whether coaches' or dieticians' promotion of intrinsic, relative to extrinsic, goals affects exercisers', sport performers', and obese individuals' affective experiences during exercise and sport, the quality of their performance, and their persistence.

Practical Implications and Conclusion

Socializing agents, including coaches, physical education teachers, clinicians, and dieticians, often encounter individuals who lack spontaneous interest in exercise. In order to increase such an individual's motivation, they often provide a rationale with the idea that the person will perceive the exercise as more useful (Deci, Eghrari, Patrick, & Leone, 1994). The present research suggests that not all goal rationales yield the same beneficial effect. Whereas the promotion of intrinsic goals increases exercise enjoyment, effort expenditure, performance, and long-term persistence, the promotion of extrinsic goals negatively affects intrinsic enjoyment and performance. Of course, for the intrinsic goals to be truly motivating, they need to be promoted in a realistic and believable manner. The current research further shows that extrinsic goals yield some positive effects in that they are associated with short-term gains in persistence. However, these short-term advantages are associated with considerable costs because (a) people's persistence under extrinsic goal circumstances is not associated with their intrinsic enjoyment and personal valuation of the activity, and so reflects alienated persistence with the behavior, and (b) these short-term gains are not well maintained in the long run.

Thus, in order to evaluate the effectiveness of their motivational strategies, socializing agents need to move beyond short-term indicators of change. If they rely solely on short-term indicators, they may incorrectly conclude that the use of extrinsic goal strategies will produce the same desired long-term effects as the use of intrinsic goal strategies. However, current results suggest that (a) quantitative indicators of change and persistence need to be complemented with qualitative indicators of change, reflecting people's affective experiences, and (b) short-term indicators of change require follow-up assessments over longer periods of time. Overall, these results suggest that being in the action phase (i.e., persisting at exercise behavior), which is considered one of the higher-order phases in the transtheoretical model of change (Prochaska & DiClemente, 1982; Prochaska, DiClemente, & Norcross, 1992), is only half of the story. It is of crucial importance to evaluate the motivational basis of people's acting because persistence with behavior can be aimed at achieving an intrinsic or an extrinsic goal, but these differential goal contents have different impacts on individuals' quality of motivation and long-term persistence.

Another critical issue pertains to the way these different goal contents are communicated to individuals. Previous research (e.g., Vansteenkiste et al., 2004a) shows that it is essential for socializing agents to adopt an autonomy-supportive rather than a controlling style when trying to convey to people the intrinsic goal importance of a particular activity. This is a very difficult and subtle endeavor; that is, if a socializing agent believes in a particular goal content, it may be difficult not to pressure others to value and to pursue that goal as well. For instance, a fitness instructor who truly believes that changing one's lifestyle is important for health reasons may be working with an obese child who wants to lose weight for appearance reasons. The fitness instructor may be perceived as controlling because he or she promotes a set of goals different from those that are valued by the child. If the fitness instructor is not flexible, the two parties may be in conflict over what is important, and this could be frustrating for the child. In other words, socializing agents need to be aware of the way they promote a particular goal content so that they can empathically approach others who hold different goals. In trying to promote a particular goal content, socializing agents need to be empathic and to understand why people value the goals they do, rather than wanting to change the goal focus completely. Motivational interviewing (Miller & Rollnick, 1991, 2002) offers a number of worthwhile motivational conversation "techniques" that are aimed at avoiding interpersonal conflict (see also Markland, Ryan, Tobin, & Rollnick, in press; Markland & Vansteenkiste, this volume; Vansteenkiste & Sheldon, in press).

Self-determination theorists have primarily focused on applying the conceptual distinction between autonomous and controlled motives to the domains of sport and exercise. The studies reviewed here suggest that not only the motives of exercisers and sport performers, but also the types of goals they adopt, can vary considerably in terms of their motivational orientation. Intrinsic versus extrinsic goal contents yield different impacts on well-being, performance, and persistence. We hope that other researchers will tackle some of our research directions in greater detail, as consideration of exercisers' goal contents will allow for a fuller understanding of motivational dynamics in sport and exercise settings.

Practical Recommendations for Sport and Exercise Practitioners

- If coaches, fitness instructors, physical education teachers, dieticians, and clinicians want to point out the relevance of exercise and sport activities, they can highlight how the activities can help individuals attain intrinsic goals such as health, self-development, and social affiliation. For example, a sport coach might ask athletes their reasons for engaging in sport. Answers to such questions as "Aside from winning, what do you get out of your sport?" may help elicit more autonomous or intrinsic goals for participation. Practitioners are also encouraged to avoid making reference to extrinsic goals such as physical attractiveness, fame, or financial success. For example, a personal trainer might emphasize to a client the importance of personal goals in an information-giving manner: "Some people find

(continued)

(continued)

that exercise on a regular basis gives them more energy to do the things they enjoy in their life or makes them feel good about themselves."

- In pointing out the intrinsic goal relevance of an activity, practitioners need to be careful to refer to the intrinsic goals in a believable and realistic fashion and also to adopt an autonomy-supportive and empathic rather than a controlling and alienating style. Therefore practitioners are advised not to present autonomous goals in a controlling manner (e.g., "You should exercise on a regular basis so you will feel good"). Instead, intrinsic goals can be presented using a person-centered approach. For example, an exercise specialist prescribing exercise to a client in a primary care context might get the client to list his or her goals and highlight those that are most personally meaningful.

- In order to evaluate whether a particular motivational strategy to enhance exercise and sport engagement was effective, practitioners could try to take into account both short- and long-term indicators of change and consider whether behavioral change was associated with (a) positive emotions such as enjoyment and (b) an increase in the individual's personal valuation of the changes. For example, coaches might ask athletes to evaluate their enjoyment of their sport using questionnaires before, during, and after a season. At regular intervals during the season, they might have athletes rate the importance of the personal goals agreed on at the beginning of the season. They might also use performance benchmarks as part of one-on-one meetings to discuss how athletes' performances and goal evaluations have changed over the course of the season.

Competence Motivation in Sport and Exercise

The Hierarchical Model of Achievement Motivation
and Self-Determination Theory

David E. Conroy, PhD
Pennsylvania State University

Andrew J. Elliot, PhD
University of Rochester

J. Douglas Coatsworth, PhD
Pennsylvania State University

Competence is a theme that pervades our daily lives from the cradle to the grave. Although we often restrict our conceptions of competence to salient domains such as school, sport, or work, competence is reflected in almost all aspects of life if we conceptualize it as a desire to feel effective in our interactions with the environment on developmentally appropriate tasks (Masten & Coatsworth, 1998; White, 1959). Examples of developmental competence pursuits at different life stages include infants' efforts to locomote, children learning to play well with peers, adolescents exploring new ways of interacting with the opposite sex, adults negotiating marital dynamics, athletes rehabilitating from an injury, exercisers challenging themselves physically, and older adults' struggles to maintain their independence by taking care of themselves on a daily basis.

Many psychological theories of personality and motivation feature competence in some form. *Self* theorists often study competence through a developmental lens in terms of the perceived competence construct (Harter, 1999). This construct refers to how individuals describe their ability in various domains. As

Preparation of this chapter was supported in part by a grant from the National Institute of Child Health and Human Development (HD42535).

Correspondence concerning this article should be addressed to David E. Conroy, Department of Kinesiology, 268 Rec Hall, The Pennsylvania State University, University Park, PA 16802. E-mail: David-Conroy@psu.edu children age, they differentiate their competence across domains and also begin to integrate multiple sources of information about their competence (Horn, 2004). These lower-order perceptions of competence also provide the basis for global self-evaluations (e.g., self-esteem; Harter, 1999). *Personality* theorists use the conscientiousness trait to describe characteristics such as industriousness in the Big Five model of personality (Roberts, Bogg, Walton, Chernyshenko, & Stark, 2004). Excessive attention to competence concerns also has been addressed in a literature on perfectionism (Flett & Hewitt, 2001). *Social cognitive* theorists developed the self-efficacy construct to describe individuals' beliefs in their ability to produce successful outcomes on specific tasks (Bandura, 1997). Self-efficacy has been linked to many important affective, behavioral, and cognitive outcomes in exercise and sport (for reviews see Feltz & Lirgg, 2001; McAuley, Peña, & Jerome, 2001).

In this chapter, we focus on competence from a *motivational* perspective that includes some social cognitive elements. We begin by introducing constructs that feature prominently in the hierarchical model of achievement motivation and then briefly review the key concepts from self-determination theory. Conceptual links between constructs in these two theoretical approaches are presented, and emerging empirical support for these links is reviewed. The chapter concludes with a consideration of future research directions and some implications for practice based on the emerging literature on competence motivation in sport and exercise.

Three Eras of Achievement Motivation

Motivation refers to the process of initiating, directing, and sustaining behavior. In this chapter we treat competence as a basic psychological need for humans that initiates or energizes behavior (Elliot, McGregor, & Thrash, 2002). Both *needs* and *motives* represent "affectively-based motivational dispositions that energize the individual and orient him or her toward valenced possibilities" (Elliot et al., 2002 p. 372). Satisfaction of the basic psychological need for competence supports or enhances an individual's well-being whereas deficits in competence need satisfaction suppress or detract from well-being. Although the need for competence is, by definition, innate, the cumulative effects of socialization processes associated with competence pursuits shape affective structures that initiate achievement behavior. Thus for our purposes, achievement motives are, in essence, the phenotypic expressions of the genotypic need for competence (McClelland, Atkinson, Clark, & Lowell, 1953; Thrash & Elliot, 2002).

Achievement motives represent socialized links between achievement outcomes and self-conscious affective responses (McClelland et al., 1953). Need for achievement (nAch) represents an individual's tendency to experience pride upon succeeding (McClelland et al., 1953) whereas fear of failure (FF) represents an individual's tendency to experience shame and humiliation upon failing (Atkinson, 1957). These motives are thought to develop in childhood and maintain a reasonable level of stability over the life span (McClelland, 1958). Early achievement motivation research focused on these motives as explanatory variables for various achievement processes and outcomes (e.g., level of aspiration), but the literature demonstrates that they are not well suited to capturing the intraindividual variability in specific achievement processes and outcomes (Elliot, 1997). Consequently, achievement motivation researchers shifted their focus to the achievement goal construct in the 1980s.

Achievement goals are dynamic entities that represent an individual's aim or purpose for her or his competence pursuits (Elliot, 2005). Before we elaborate on the specific aims that direct achievement behavior, it is important to note that achievement goals have been conceptualized at varying levels of temporal resolution in the extant sport and exercise psychology literature. Some scholars have focused on goal *orientations* that represent a relatively stable tendency to adopt particular foci in competence pursuits (e.g., Duda, 1989). Others have conceived of goals as highly dynamic states of *involvement* that may vary from moment to moment (e.g., Gernigon, d'Arippe-Longueville, Delignières, & Ninot, 2004; Harwood, 2002). Ironically, the dispositional goal orientation construct returns to the individual difference approach of motive psychologists that the goal-based approach initially sought to remediate (Elliot, 2005). From a conceptual standpoint, we believe it is best to view goals as dynamic entities that are both temporally and contextually bound. To the extent that goals are detached from a context or a particular situation, the goal construct is violated. Contemporary assessment technology does not permit online tracking of variability in goal involvement states at extremely high temporal resolutions in ecologically valid sport and exercise settings, so "perfect" goal assessments are not currently possible. Nevertheless, contextual specificity and temporal proximity to a competence pursuit are desirable qualities of achievement goal assessments.

Definitions of Competence

The aim of achievement behavior can be described in terms of the standards used to evaluate an individual's competence. Competence can be evaluated with task-referenced standards (e.g., "Did I complete the task perfectly?"), self-referenced standards (e.g., "Did I perform this task as well as or better than I did previously?"), or normatively referenced standards (e.g., "Did I perform this task better than others?"). Typically the task- and self-referenced standards are collapsed into a single mastery (or task) goal, whereas the normatively referenced standard is referred to as a performance (or ego) goal (Elliot, 1999). In sport and exercise environments, one can pursue competence in these senses by striving to improve one's skill in producing a new movement (mastery goal), by striving to increase one's speed or endurance in an activity such as running (mastery goal), by striving to outperform a fellow competitor in a competition (performance goal), or by striving to lose more weight than a peer in a weight loss program (performance goal).

Goal Valence

Despite some early consideration of the possibility that goals may focus on avoiding incompetence (e.g., Dweck & Bempechat, 1983; Nicholls, 1984), the vast majority of research has focused exclusively on appetitive goals oriented toward the possibility of competence (see Nicholls, Patashnick, Cheung, Thorkildsen, & Lauer, 1989). Elliot and colleagues (for reviews see Elliot, 1999, 2005) have argued and offered substantial evidence in the past decade that distinguishing appetitive and aversive achievement goals (a) clarifies the nature of the goal construct, (b) strengthens conceptual links between the achievement goal literature and the broader motivation literature, and (c) enhances the predictive power of the goal construct. This work culminated in the 2 × 2 model of achievement goals shown in figure 12.1. This model incorporates both an individual's definition of competence (i.e., mastery vs. performance) and the valence of her or his aim (i.e., approaching competence vs. avoiding incompetence) to identify four salient achievement goals.

Mastery-approach (MAp) goals involve a focus on performing a task as well as possible or on learning and improving relative to one's previous performances. MAp goals are considered especially prominent in sport and exercise due to the salience of skill acquisition and personal improvement as performance metrics in these contexts. *Performance-approach (PAp) goals* involve a focus on outperforming others. Given the prominent role of social comparison in competitive environments, PAp goals are expected to be quite common for athletes as well. *Performance-avoidance (PAv) goals* involve a focus on not being outperformed by others. These goals are thought to be especially likely when individuals are

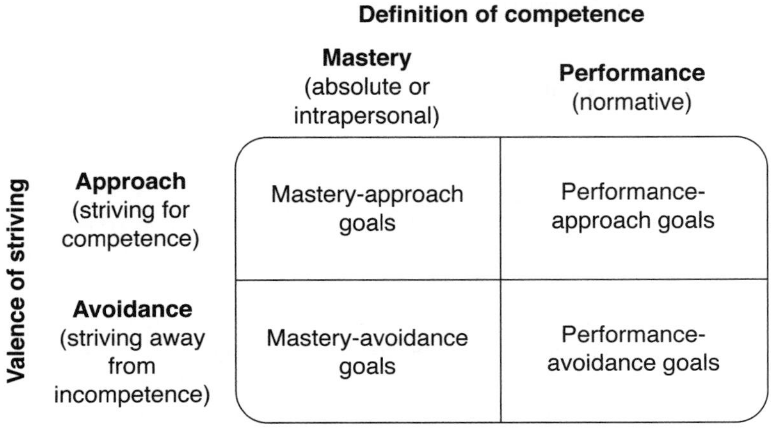

Definition of competence

	Mastery (absolute or intrapersonal)	**Performance** (normative)
Approach (striving for competence)	Mastery-approach goals	Performance- approach goals
Avoidance (striving away from incompetence)	Mastery-avoidance goals	Performance- avoidance goals

Valence of striving (vertical axis label)

Figure 12.1   The 2 × 2 achievement goal framework.

Adapted from A.J. Elliot and H.A. McGregor, 2001, "A 2 × 2 achievement goal framework," *Journal of Personality and Social Psychology,* 80: 502. By permission of the American Psychological Association.

in competitive environments but have oriented their behavior around the possibility of failure instead of success (e.g., with novel or difficult tasks). Finally, *mastery-avoidance (MAv) goals* involve a focus on not making mistakes and on not performing an activity less well than one previously performed it. MAv goals may be especially likely among perfectionists, individuals recovering from injury, aging athletes seeking to maintain their skill level, and athletes seeking to "play it safe" and not make mistakes to protect a competitive advantage. Empirical studies attesting to the value of distinguishing between the valence of mastery and performance goals in sport and exercise environments are emerging (Cury, Da Fonséca, Rufo, & Sarrazin, 2002a; Cury, Da Fonséca, Rufo, Peres, & Sarrazin, 2003; Cury, Elliot, Sarrazin, Da Fonséca, & Rufo, 2002b; for reviews see Elliot, 1999, 2005; Elliot & Conroy, 2005).

Linking Motive- and Goal-Based Approaches

The apparent differences between the motive- and goal-based approaches to studying achievement motivation do not indicate that these approaches are antithetical. Rather, their respective strengths and limitations are quite complementary. The motive-based approach captures stable individual differences in achievement motivation and explains what initiates competence pursuits (Elliot, 1997). It does not explain the specific aim of those pursuits, nor does it account for intraindividual variability in specific achievement processes and outcomes (Elliot, 1997). The goal-based approach utilizes a dynamic construct to account for intraindividual variability in achievement processes and outcomes, and describes the specific aim of achievement behavior in greater detail; however, it fails to account for factors that initiate achievement behavior or for intraindividual stability in achievement processes and outcomes. Accordingly, Elliot (1997) integrated these two perspectives into a unified, hierarchical model of achievement motivation.

The hierarchical model conceptualizes achievement motives (among other variables) as antecedents of achievement goal involvement states, which function as the proximal determinants of achievement processes and outcomes. Specifically, the nAch predisposes individuals to adopting MAp and PAp goals, whereas the FF predisposes individuals to adopt MAv, PAv, and PAp goals. A great deal of cross-sectional research supports the hypothesized pattern of motive–goal associations (Conroy, 2001, 2004; Conroy & Elliot, 2004; Conroy, Elliot, & Hofer, 2003; Elliot & Harackiewicz, 1996; Elliot & McGregor, 1999, 2001; Thrash & Elliot, 2002).

Additionally, FF has been shown to predict residualized changes in avoidance-goal states (Conroy & Elliot, 2004), but no research to date has examined the temporal precedence of the approach motive in relation to approach goals. It also is worth noting that FF predicts concurrent PAp goals. Although one would not expect an avoidance motive to positively predict approach-goal involvement, this finding is well documented (Conroy & Elliot, 2004; Conroy, Elliot, & Hofer, 2003; Elliot & Harackiewicz, 1996; Elliot & McGregor, 1999,

2001; Thrash & Elliot, 2002) and not easily dismissed. Arguments have been made that FF promotes PAp goals (a) for self-presentational reasons (Conroy, 2001) and (b) because PAp goals can serve as an approach-based strategy for avoiding incompetence (Elliot & Church, 1997). Future research may clarify why and how FF leads to PAp goal involvement.

In this hierarchical model, achievement goals also may be preceded by a number of other factors, such as self-based individual differences, relationally based individual differences, demographic characteristics, and neurophysiological predispositions (Elliot, 1999). A number of specific consequences of the 2 × 2 conceptualization of achievement goals in sport have been documented (e.g., Cury et al., 2002a, 2002b, 2003), although they are less well established in sport and exercise than in other domains (e.g., academics). Anticipated consequences that merit investigation in future sport and exercise psychology research range from achievement processes, such as intrinsic motivation, enjoyment, absorption, challenge–threat construals, effort, and affective experiences, to more objective outcomes such as absolute levels of performance and adherence. For our purposes in this chapter, attention will be devoted to examining links between constructs from the hierarchical model of achievement motivation and key motivational outcomes in self-determination theory (i.e., basic psychological need satisfaction, internalization of behavioral regulations).

Key Concepts in Self-Determination Theory

A detailed description of self-determination theory is provided by Ryan and Deci at the beginning of this volume. The focus of this chapter is therefore limited to a review of two key concepts that provide a basis for linking hierarchical model of achievement motivation constructs with self-determination theory: the continuum of behavioral regulations and the role of basic psychological needs.

Behavioral Regulations

Self-determination theory conceptualizes three general classes of behavioral regulations (i.e., reasons for acting): intrinsic motivation, extrinsic motivation, and amotivation (Deci & Ryan, 1985). *Intrinsic motivation* refers to behavior that is enacted for rewards inherent in the activity. Such rewards might include feelings of accomplishment, learning, or stimulation (Pelletier et al., 1995; Vallerand, 2001). For example, an athlete who runs because she enjoys the sensation in her muscles at the end of a long run would be described as intrinsically motivated.

Extrinsic motivation refers to behavior that is enacted for some reason outside of the activity itself. The classic form of extrinsic motivation involves *external regulation*, in which an individual acts to obtain an external reward or avoid an external punishment. Athletes who attend daily practices only because their coaches insist that they do so could be described as motivated by external behavioral regulations. Deci and Ryan (1985) posited that this extreme example of extrinsic motivation does not encompass all extrinsically motivated behaviors. For example, individuals may act to attain pleasant internal psychological states, such as pride, relief, or happiness, or to avoid unpleasant internal psychological states, such as shame, guilt, or anxiety; these reasons represent *introjected regulations*. These regulations describe situations such as those in which people decide to go outside for a run instead of watching television because they anticipate feeling guilty if they were to waste the day in front of the television. Individuals also may act because they value and freely choose an activity even though it does not provide immediate rewards to them (i.e., *identified regulations*). For example, a tennis player whose behavior is governed primarily by identified regulations may spend extra time working on his serve on a hot day when he is tired if he knows that the extra practice will be valuable in preparation for an upcoming tournament. People also could act because they value and choose an activity that is congruent with how they view themselves even though the activity does not provide immediate rewards for them (i.e., *integrated regulations*). An individual with integrated regulations for physical activity may exercise and eat well because she views herself as a "healthy person," and those behaviors are consistent with that self-image. These four behavioral regulations vary with respect to their level of self-determination. Identified and integrated regulations are very similar to intrinsic motivation. The critical difference is that the activity itself is not the reason for action; rather a consequence of the activity is the reason for action.

Amotivation pertains to relatively aimless or purposeless behavior (Deci & Ryan, 1985). According to Pelletier, Dion, Tuson, and Green-Demers (1999), four major beliefs underpin amotivated behavior: (a) The person lacks ability to be successful; (b) the strategy being employed is unlikely to lead to success; (c) success will require too much effort; and (d) the person cannot effect desirable outcomes regardless of his or her efforts (i.e., learned helplessness). Exercisers who join a gym but rarely work out because they believe it would be too difficult for them to get in shape could be described as amotivated. There are some questions as to whether amotivation represents a unique motivational state or simply the absence of intrinsic and extrinsic motivation; however, we include it here for the sake of completeness in describing the range of reasons for action (or inaction).

The aforementioned behavioral regulations can be arranged along a continuum from low levels of self-determination (e.g., amotivation) to the highest levels of self-determination (e.g., intrinsic motivation). As individuals become more self-determined in their behavior, they are said to internalize the behavior (Ryan & Deci, 2002). The primary determinant of internalization is the degree to which an individual's basic psychological needs are satisfied in the course of an activity (Ryan & Deci, 2002).

Basic Psychological Needs

Self-determination theory posits that three basic psychological needs exist: autonomy, competence, and relatedness (Ryan & Deci, 2002). The need for *autonomy* pertains to the feeling on the part of individuals that they are the origin or cause of their behavior (deCharms, 1968). The need for *competence* reflects a desire to feel effective and to feel that one has opportunities to exhibit one's competencies (Elliot, McGregor, & Thrash, 2002; Harter, 1983; White, 1959). The need for *relatedness* involves feeling a sense of connection or belonging with others (Baumeister & Leary, 1995). To the extent that these needs are satisfied during an activity, people will internalize their regulations for that behavior. Additionally, satisfaction of these basic psychological needs has been linked to enhanced psychological well-being, whereas a failure to satisfy these three needs has been linked to deficits in well-being (for a review, see Ryan & Deci, 2002 this volume).

Linking the Hierarchical Model of Achievement Motivation and Self-Determination Theory

Self-determination theory is an ambitious attempt to explain the most fundamental aspects of motivated human behavior. The hierarchical model of achievement motivation can be viewed as a complementary theory that elaborates on specific aspects of competence motivation within self-determination theory. Surprisingly little research has been aimed at integrating these theoretical perspectives in the sport and exercise domain. Thus, we will attempt to strengthen the links between these theoretical approaches by connecting the major constructs from the hierarchical model of achievement motivation (i.e., motives and goals) with the major constructs in self-determination theory.

Links With Achievement Motives

The nAch has roots in early parental demands for mastery and self-reliance (Winterbottom, 1958), high performance expectations, and more autonomy during children's competence pursuits (Rosen & D'Andrade, 1959). Individuals high in nAch also tend to be more securely attached than those low in nAch, suggesting that their need for relatedness was satisfied during infancy (Elliot & Reis, 2003). Accordingly, we speculate that the nAch will be linked to greater satisfaction of individuals' needs for autonomy, competence, and relatedness (at a global level rather than in a specific context or relationship).

In contrast, FF has its roots in affectional deprivation (Greenfeld & Teevan, 1986; Singh, 1992), attachment insecurity (Elliot & Reis, 2003), high performance expectations (Schmalt, 1982; Teevan & McGhee, 1972), love withdrawal or punishment following failure (Elliot & Thrash, 2004; Hermans, ter Laak, & Maes, 1972; Teevan, 1983; Teevan & McGhee, 1972), and perceptions of more critical and less affirming parents (Conroy, 2003; Krohne, 1992;

Teevan & McGhee, 1972). On the basis of this profile and a focus on avoiding incompetence, we expect that FF will be linked to deficits in competence and relatedness need satisfaction (at a global level rather than in a specific context or relationship).

Given that the nAch orients individuals toward competence (whereas FF orients individuals away from incompetence) and that competence is a basic psychological need that supports self-determination, it seems likely that nAch will be linked with more self-determined forms of motivation than FF. In sport and exercise, behavior that is energized by the possibility of being successful instead of a desire to avoid failure should lead individuals to derive greater satisfaction and pleasure from the activity. In general, nAch has been positively associated with intrinsic motivation, and FF has not been associated with intrinsic motivation (Puca & Schmalt, 1999). Most research has examined links between achievement motives and intrinsic motivation without distinguishing the various behavioral regulations.

If the various behavioral regulations are distinguished, we would expect FF to be most closely associated with introjected regulations because the primary satisfaction from FF involves avoiding shame. From a slightly different perspective, individuals who pursue competence in certain personally valued domains to regulate their state self-esteem (i.e., contingent self-esteem) are vulnerable to the vicissitudes of self-conscious emotions such as shame when they fail in those pursuits (Crocker & Park, 2004). At the contextual level of analysis (i.e., motivation over time in a particular domain), track athletes' fears of experiencing shame and embarrassment (core beliefs associated with FF) when they fail were positively associated with introjected regulations for their sport (Conroy, 2004). Interestingly, other reasons athletes endorse for fearing failure were linked with other behavior regulations (e.g., fears of devaluing one's self-estimate were positively associated with amotivation, and fears of having an uncertain future were positively associated with intrinsic motivation). At a global level of analysis (i.e., across contexts and time), self-determination has been negatively associated with self-attributed FF but not significantly associated with implicit FF, self-attributed nAch, or implicit nAch (Thrash & Elliot, 2002).

Links With Achievement Goals

Conceptually, the hierarchical model of achievement motivation conceptualizes perceptions of competence (i.e., competence need satisfaction in a specific domain) as antecedents of achievement goal involvement (Elliot, 1999). Perceptions of competence orient individuals toward the possibility of success and approach achievement goals; perceptions of incompetence orient individuals toward the possibility of failure and avoidance achievement goals. Attachment security, an indicator of early relatedness need satisfaction, has been positively linked to MAp goals and negatively linked to the two avoidance goals (i.e., MAv, PAv; Elliot & Reis, 2003). We are not aware of any evidence linking (a) PAp goal involvement to attachment security or (b) autonomy need satisfaction to achievement goal involvement.

Most research on links between achievement goals and behavioral regulations has focused on intrinsic motivation to the neglect of other behavioral regulations. In experimental research with cognitive and motor tasks, MAp and PAp goals have been shown to facilitate intrinsic motivation relative to PAv goals (Cury et al., 2002a, 2002b, 2003; Elliot & Harackiewicz, 1996). (It should be noted that MAv goals are the latest addition to the 2 × 2 goal framework and thus were not included in any of these studies linking goals to intrinsic motivation.) These studies have been notable for their experimental manipulation of achievement goals in a single experimental session (via task instructions). It appears that both defining competence in mastery (vs. performance) terms and orienting oneself toward competence (vs. incompetence) enhance intrinsic motivation. A basketball player who struggles to make his free throws can increase intrinsic motivation for that task by (a) focusing on using the proper form for the shot or (b) striving to increase his percentage from its current level (as opposed to focusing on not making a common error such as failing to follow through or focusing on having the highest free-throw percentage on the team).

Future Research Directions

Several research priorities are readily apparent when one considers the state of the literature on the hierarchical model of achievement motivation and self-determination theory. First, it will be important to examine the developmental processes by which early effectance motivation is transformed into the differentiated need for competence expressed by achievement motives. From a conceptual standpoint, the hierarchical model of achievement motivation places great importance on distinguishing approach from avoidance goals, whereas self-determination theory does not distinguish approach and avoidance regulations for extrinsically motivated behaviors (e.g., external and introjected regulations). It may be worth considering how approach-oriented external regulations (e.g., striving for an external reward) and avoidance-oriented external regulations (e.g., striving to avoid an external punishment) might differ in their antecedents and consequences. Empirically, the matrix of data linking 2 × 2 goals with the six behavioral regulations (i.e., intrinsic motivation, four forms of extrinsic motivation, amotivation) is largely incomplete. In addition to considering main effects of goals on behavioral regulations, it will be important to consider possible interactions between goals in predicting behavioral regulations (e.g., does simultaneously high MAp and PAp goal involvement lead to more self-determined behavior than states of involvement characterized by high levels of a single approach goal?). As researchers move to complete that matrix of links between goals and behavioral regulations, it would be valuable to complement the cross-sectional designs that are so common in sport psychology research with longitudinal, quasi-experimental, and experimental designs that will strengthen conclusions about the effects of goals on behavioral regulations. The need for longitudinal designs is underscored by the dynamic nature of both the goal and behavioral regulation constructs.

A final question that we believe may lead to valuable insight into functional relations between achievement motivation and self-determination involves the possibility of cross-level interactions between constructs in the hierarchical model of achievement motivation. Specifically, PAp goals have been associated with relatively high levels of intrinsic motivation and appear to be preceded by both nAch and FF. This pattern of relations raises the question whether PAp goals that are energized by nAch have different effects on behavioral regulations than do PAp goals that are energized by FF.

Implications for Practice

Despite the limited research linking the hierarchical model of achievement motivation with self-determination theory, it is possible to provide some guidance for practitioners based on the nascent literature that does link these theoretical perspectives. Self-determination can be enhanced through satisfying an individual's need for competence. The hierarchical model of achievement motivation provides clear directions on how to enhance achievement processes and outcomes in ways that should enhance competence need satisfaction (see "Practical Recommendations for Exercise and Sport Practitioners"). In applying that theory, practitioners should distinguish between more and less malleable constructs in their motivational interventions. For example, achievement motives are deeply engrained affective associations and may be difficult to change with acute environmental manipulations (e.g., Conroy & Coatsworth, 2004). Developmentally oriented practitioners may work on interpersonal and affective training for parents and others who interact extensively with children during the critical childhood years for socializing achievement motives (Heckhausen, 1984; McClelland et al., 1953).

On the other hand, achievement goals are very dynamic entities and should be quite responsive to changes in the motivational climate (caveat: some antecedents of goals will be quite stable and serve to create an appearance of stability in goals). Developing effective guidelines for manipulating motivational climates in sport and exercise would be a valuable step toward enhancing states of mastery and approach-goal involvement. Epstein (1989) identified six social-ecological structures that influence achievement motivation in an activity setting (i.e., task, authority, recognition, grouping, evaluation, time); and, although relatively little is known about the effectiveness of manipulating these structures for enhancing achievement motivation and self-determination among athletes and exercisers, they provide a starting point for practitioners' consideration in sport and exercise contexts.

Practical Recommendations
for Exercise and Sport Practitioners

• Developing perceptions of competence will support or enhance self-determination and intrinsic motivation. For example, sport coaches and managers need to provide varied practices that offer opportunities to gain a sense of competence. This involves grouping athletes and sport performers who have similar ability; giving them cooperative tasks with a clearly defined goal related to skill development and a problem-solving, approach orientation; and stressing the importance of effort and personal as opposed to other-referenced skill development.

• Practitioners should pay attention to how athletes or exercisers evaluate their competence and focus their competence pursuits. Two suggestions are offered for maximizing competence. First, practitioners are encouraged to focus on attaining competence instead of avoiding incompetence. For example, a team coach might ask players to "put in considerable effort to find position and achieve your goal of 10 passing movements before shooting on goal, rather than avoiding receiving the ball in fear of having to make a counterproductive pass." Second, one should evaluate athletes' or exercisers' competence using primarily task- or self-referenced standards (e.g., asking performers, "How well did you do in relation to how well the task can be completed?"; "How did you do compared to your previous attempts?") instead of normatively referenced standards (e.g., asking, "How well did you do compared to others?").

• Sport practitioners are advised to consider how the sport or exercise setting is structured to optimize achievement motivation and its consequences. For optimal benefits, rewards (e.g., praise, prizes) should be structured around evaluative systems that emphasize mastery definitions of competence and a focus on putting in effort to achieve personal success rather than avoiding failure. Sport coaches might tell athletes "Your aim is to win, but win because of effort and personal application, rather than because you have to win." Also, athletes and exercisers should be placed into groups of similar ability so that individual differences in ability are less obvious in environments that naturally invite social comparisons.

Understanding Young People's Motivation Toward Exercise

An Integration of Sport Ability Beliefs, Achievement Goal Theory, and Self-Determination Theory

Chee Keng John Wang, PhD
Nanyang Technological University

Stuart J.H. Biddle, PhD
Loughborough University

What energizes and directs human behavior? This has been a fundamental question at the center of psychological research into human motivation. Numerous motivational theories have been proposed in an attempt to answer this question, each with assumptions about the factors that motivate behavior. As a result, the explanations of human behavior are diverse, and no single theory has yet to claim the ability to explain motivated behavior in its entirety (Roberts, 1992). Modern approaches are beginning to integrate different aspects of motivational theory and research in order to understand motivated behavior. This new trend is in stark contrast with the situation in the past, when different perspectives were often studied in isolation (Weiner, 1992).

Over the last few decades, the study of human motivation has shifted from utilization of a mechanistic perspective, such as drive theory or gestalt theories of motivation, to more complex social cognitive approaches such as those offered by self-efficacy theory, self-determination theory, and achievement goal theory (Biddle, 1997). In the social cognitive approach, human beings are assumed to think about and evaluate their actions in a rational manner (Bandura, 1986). It is argued that these self-based theories of achievement motivation are useful in explaining human action (Biddle, 1997).

The purpose of this chapter is to draw together our studies of motivation in young people in a physical activity context using social cognitive approaches.

Correspondence concerning this article should be addressed to C.K. John Wang, Physical Education & Sports Science, National Institute of Education, Nanyang Technological University, 1 Nanyang Walk, Blk 5 #03-20, Singapore 637616. E-mail: ckjwang@nie.edu.sg

Specifically, most of our work has adopted self-determination theory (Deci & Ryan, 1985), achievement goal theory (Dweck & Leggett, 1988; Nicholls, 1984, 1989), and self theories of ability (Dweck, 1999; Dweck & Leggett, 1988); and we have attempted to examine the congruencies in these theories, the overlap among the constructs, and whether they can be combined into an integrated model to provide an explanation of young people's physical activity behavior. First, we provide an overview of the physical activity context and briefly outline the three theoretical frameworks. Next we present research findings from investigations of the relationships among the conceptions of sport ability, achievement goals, and intrinsic motivation in physical activity settings. The chapter concludes with practical implications and suggestions for future research directions in the domain of physical activity.

The Context of Physical Activity

Physical activity in youth is a popular and important area of research in both health and exercise psychology. There is now a substantial body of evidence concerning regular physical activity and health in young people. Although it is sometimes difficult to detect definitive health benefits of physical activity in youth, due to lack of sensitivity in the measurement of physical activity (Welk, Corbin, & Dale, 2000) and health risk markers, high levels of physical activity can benefit cardiovascular disease risk factors, adiposity, and bone health and are associated with better mental health (Biddle, Gorely, & Stensel, 2004).

Recent studies have yielded evidence that early signs of chronic disease and risk factors for chronic disease such as elevated cholesterol and hypertension can be found in children (Freedman, Srinivasan, Valdez, Williamson, & Berenson, 1997; Twisk, Kemper, van Mechelen, & Post, 1997). In addition, physical activity measured with pedometers has been found to have a negative relationship with overweight (Rowlands, Eston, & Ingledew, 1997). In many countries, levels of children's obesity appear to be increasing, and a concern is expressed about the attractiveness and availability of many sedentary activities. For all these reasons, there is a need to gain further insight into the determinants of physical activity among young people. Understanding the motivation of young people in physical activity is important to practitioners including physical educators, health promoters, and sport development officers in their efforts to help their clients sustain motivation and engagement in physical activity for longer periods of time. Some researchers have suggested that theories based on achievement motivation and perceived competence are a useful way to account for the motivational determinants of physical activity behavior in youth (Sallis, Prochaska, & Taylor, 2000). This chapter focuses on three such theories: achievement goal theory, self theories of ability, and self-determination theory.

Achievement Goal Theory

The achievement goal approach has received widespread attention in the study of motivation in young people and children (Nicholls, 1989) and has been successful in explaining and predicting beliefs, affect, responses, and behavior in achievement settings (Biddle, 1999). However, most research has been conducted in competitive sport settings rather than wider physical activity contexts (e.g., Duda, 1989; Duda, Chi, Newton, Walling, & Catley, 1995; Duda & Nicholls, 1992).

The major theoretical tenet of achievement goal theory is that individuals strive to demonstrate ability and avoid showing incompetence in achievement contexts. Thus, individuals are assumed to differentially endorse two different and subjective ways of defining success and failure and of judging their competence (Nicholls, 1989). These two conceptions result in at least two states of goal involvement. A task-involved person tends to define success or judge his or her competence in a self-referenced manner, based on self-improvement or investment of effort on task mastery. On the other hand, an ego-involved person defines success in a normative fashion, aiming to outperform others or to win with less effort.

It has been suggested that task or ego involvement may be determined by dispositional orientations (Nicholls, 1989). Consequently, the constructs of task and ego orientation have been used to reflect the tendency of an individual to be task or ego involved (or both). It has been found that task-oriented individuals, regardless of levels of perceived competence, tend to exhibit "positive," or adaptive, patterns of motivated behavior. Ego-involved individuals with high perceived competence should also have adaptive motivational patterns (Dweck, 1986; Nicholls, 1984, 1989). However, ego-oriented people with low perceived competence are likely to be motivationally fragile and exhibit maladaptive motivational responses. Nicholls (1989) maintains that the two goal orientations are unrelated (i.e., orthogonal) and thus that individuals can have different combinations of levels of these orientations (i.e., high task/high ego, high task/low ego, low task/high ego, and low task/low ego; Fox, Goudas, Biddle, Duda, & Armstrong, 1994). Therefore, one should take an interactive goal approach together with perceptions of competence in order to gain a better understanding of achievement motivation. However, a comprehensive systematic review on the correlates of achievement goal orientation, conducted by Biddle and colleagues (Biddle, Wang, Kavussanu, & Spray, 2003), showed that more than 80% of the reviewed studies dealt with the effects of the goals independently rather than interactively. Nevertheless, the review did show numerous positive associations with a task orientation, such as positive affect, belief that effort produces success, and the seeking of adaptive achievement strategies.

Self Theories of Ability

Self theories of ability provide another interpretation of the perception of achievement goals. According to Dweck and her colleagues (Dweck, 1999; Dweck & Leggett, 1988; Hong, Chiu, & Dweck, 1995), two clusters of beliefs underpin the adoption of achievement goals. These center on the way people view the malleability of attributes such as intelligence. With an entity belief, a particular attribute is viewed as fixed and relatively stable; with an incremental belief, the attribute is viewed as changeable and open to development. The main concerns of "entity theorists" are how intelligent they are compared to others and how, at all costs, to look "smart" and not "dumb" (Dweck, 1999). To entity theorists, looking smart means achieving easy, low-effort success and outperforming others. Looking smart has a different meaning to the "incremental theorists." Focusing on effort to increase their intelligence, as well as learning and mastering challenging new tasks, makes them feel smart. Classroom research has shown that individuals holding entity beliefs are more likely to have negative reactions, such as helplessness, when faced with setbacks (Dweck & Leggett, 1988), as compared to the incremental theorists. Entity theorists are also more likely to endorse performance (ego) goals, while incremental theorists tend to endorse mastery (task) goals.

In the domain of physical activity, Sarrazin and colleagues (1996) examined the relationship between conceptions of sport ability and the adoption of different goals in children aged 11 to 12 years. They found some support for the relationships between entity beliefs and ego goals and between incremental beliefs and learning goals; however, the relationships were quite weak. Part of the reason for the weak links was the use of dichotomous goals, with children being asked to choose one goal over another. Sarrazin and colleagues then developed a multidimensional assessment of sport ability beliefs that allowed for the assessment of both sets of beliefs. Their Conceptions of the Nature of Athletic Ability Questionnaire (CNAAQ) contained 21 items assessing the six subdomains of *learning* (belief that sport ability is the product of learning), *incremental/improvement* (belief that sport ability can change), *specific* (belief that sport ability is specific to certain sports or groups of sports), *general* (belief that sport ability generalizes across many sports), *stable* (belief that sport ability is stable over time), and *gift* (belief that sport ability is a gift, i.e., "God given"). This questionnaire was administered to over 300 French adolescents. Beliefs that sport ability is incremental and is determined by learning were shown to be related to choosing a learning (task) goal. Beliefs that sport ability is general and is a gift were related to choosing a performance (ego) goal.

In two studies, Biddle and colleagues (Biddle, Soós, & Chatzisarantis, 1999; Lintunen, Valkonen, Leskinen, & Biddle, 1999) tested a motivational model predicting intentions to be physically active from perceived competence, achievement goals, and conceptions of sport ability. Both studies involved large samples of 12- to 16-year-old adolescents. In general, the results supported the contention that beliefs in sport ability as general and as a gift predicted an ego orientation. Beliefs in sport ability as a product of learning or as changeable predicted a task orientation. However, the sizes of the effects were relatively small.

Our review of the literature revealed that some of the subscales used in the CNAAQ showed unsatisfactory internal consistency (for example, α = .40 for specific; α = .41 for stable; Biddle, Soós, & Chatzisarantis, 1999). This indicated a need for further psychometric assessment to confirm the validity and reliability of the scales. Biddle and coworkers (Biddle, Wang, Chatzisarantis, & Spray, 2003) then examined the psychometric properties of the CNAAQ using 3478 children and youth between 11 and 19 years old. The original CNAAQ was reduced to 12 items with two higher-order factors (incremental and entity) and four first-order factors (learning, improvement, gift, and stable). Overall, the results showed strong psychometric support for the multidimensional hierarchical structure. The study also provided support for the invariance of the CNAAQ-2 measurement model across gender and age. Moreover, findings indicated that incremental beliefs predicted self-reported amotivation toward physical education and sport indirectly, through a task goal orientation, but predicted entity beliefs directly. On the other hand, enjoyment of physical activity in youth was directly predicted by task orientation and incremental beliefs. Findings support the important role that sport ability beliefs, goal orientations, and perceptions of competence can have in our understanding of motivated behavior in physical activity.

Self-Determination Theory

Looking at individuals' goal orientation and self-conception of ability is useful for understanding human motivation, but such understanding may be incomplete because the individual's psychological needs have not been considered. According to self-determination theory, people are active organisms seeking to master their internal and external environment (Deci & Ryan, 1985, 1987; Ryan & Deci, 2000a, 2000b). Three psychological needs have been hypothesized to foster this self-motivated process: the needs for competence, relatedness, and autonomy.

In general, conditions that allow satisfaction of the three psychological needs enhance intrinsic motivation, whereas conditions that frustrate these needs undermine intrinsic motivation (see Ryan & Deci, this volume). In other words, motivation and persistence in sport behavior vary according to the degree of self-determination (Deci & Ryan, 1985).

Organismic integration theory was developed to delineate subtle variations in the degree of personal agency involved in motivated tasks. This subtheory of self-determination theory deals with the processes through which behaviors that are regulated externally can be acquired or "taken in" by the individual and perceived as more self-determined (intrinsic) regulation. This process, referred to as *internalization*, involves a shift from an external to an internal locus of causality (Deci & Ryan, 1991) as individuals try to rationalize the behavioral outcomes relevant to their need satisfaction. That is, the more internalized a behavioral regulation, the more it will be experienced as autonomous (Ryan & Connell, 1989). This is believed to be both more motivating in the "internal" sense (see Vansteenkiste, Soenens, & Lens, this volume) and conducive to adaptive mental health.

Deci and Ryan (1985) proposed four main types of behavioral regulation located on the self-determination continuum, known as the perceived locus of causality, each one reflecting a qualitatively different "reason" for acting out the behavior in question. These are external, introjected, identified, and intrinsic forms of regulation (see Pelletier & Sarrazin, this volume; Ryan & Deci, this volume). Deci and Ryan also included integrated regulation as the most self-determined form of extrinsic motivation on the continuum. However, this form of regulation is mostly relevant to an adult population, and since this chapter deals with young people, it will not be elaborated upon further. The four forms of behavioral regulation considered here can be placed on a continuum ranging from highly internal to highly external in the following order: intrinsic, identified, introjected, and external. A state of amotivation exists when the person's behavior has no personal causation and involves no intention to act.

An Intraindividual Approach to Motivation

As stated in the beginning of this chapter, the study of human motivation is complex, as are the motivational processes involved in the domain of physical activity. People may participate in physical activity or sport for different reasons at different times of their lives; different people may participate in the same activity for different reasons. The known reasons include having fun, improving skills, making friends, losing weight, and outperforming others. These dispositional goal orientations may be linked to intrinsic and extrinsic motivation in given contexts and situations, and many researchers have speculated about the nature of such links (Duda et al., 1995; Nicholls, 1989; Ntoumanis, 2001; Rawsthorne & Elliot, 1999). For example, Nicholls (1989) argues that a task (mastery) goal orientation will promote intrinsic motivation because intrinsic motivation is evident when people engage in an activity for its own sake and experience it as an end in itself. With their emphasis on developing competence, these goals are likely to lead to processes such as working hard, seeking challenge, persistence, and task involvement (Butler, 1987; Dweck, 1986; Nicholls, 1989), thereby increasing the intrinsic motivation toward the task. Ego (performance) goals, on the other hand, are expected to have a negative relationship with intrinsic motivation because the experience of engagement in the tasks is taken as a means to an end. In this case, the focus is on demonstrating competence rather than enjoying the task as an end in itself (Nicholls, 1989).

The three major theories outlined earlier have been shown to explain a substantial amount of variance in human behavior and experience in the classroom and in sport and physical activity domains. However, most studies have dealt with a given theory in isolation and have focused on individual differences. Hence little can be gleaned about intraindividual differences in patterns of key motivational indicators from a comprehensive profile of scores on constructs from these three theories. The extent to which these motivational constructs are interrelated in one person, therefore, is not well understood; and some have called for greater consideration of conceptual convergence and elimination of redundancy (Biddle, 1999). The identification of subgroups of young people who represent different combinations or patterns based on these motivational determinants might prove instructive for identifying classes of constructs that exhibit conceptual overlap and congruency. This may make it possible to locate homogeneous groups and develop segmentation strategies to increase the effectiveness of interventions to promote physical activity in young people (Sallis & Owen, 1999).

One approach to examining intraindividual differences is the use of cluster analysis. We assume that there are variations in individuals in terms of achievement goal orientations (task and ego orientations), conceptions of the nature of sport ability (incremental and entity beliefs), self-determination or perceived autonomy, amotivation, and perceived competence, and that homogeneous groupings could be obtained based on these characteristics.

Cluster analysis is different from many of the more commonly applied multivariate statistical techniques, such as discriminant analysis, in that the researcher has no knowledge of the number and characteristics of the groups before applying the analysis (Hair, Anderson, Tatham, & Black, 1998). Cluster analysis has not been used a great deal in sport and exercise science research, although examples are available in the literature on physical activity and health behaviors (De Bourdeaudhuij & Van Oost, 1999) and sources of sport competence information (Weiss, Ebbeck, & Horn, 1997). The next section deals with the results of our investigations of achievement goals, sport ability beliefs, and perceptions of autonomy using this approach.

Research Findings

In a first study (Wang & Biddle, 2001), we examined the relationships between goal orientations, sport ability beliefs, perceived autonomy, amotivation, and perceived competence in a large national sample of British children (n = 2510), aged between 12 and 15 years, using cluster analysis. On the basis of the profiles determined, we examined variations in physical activity participation and perceived physical self-worth in the subgroups identified in the analysis.

Results showed that five distinct clusters could be identified on the basis of their shared characteristics (see figure 13.1). Children in the "highly motivated" cluster (figure 13.1, Cluster 2) had high scores on task orientation, ego orientation, incremental beliefs, entity beliefs, and perceived competence and had significantly higher physical activity and physical self-worth compared to students in the other four clusters. This cluster was made up of predominantly competitive sport participants (83.8%), with more males (66.8%) than females (33.2%). However there was no variation across the three school year groups (Grade 7, 12-13 year olds; Grade 8, 13-14 year olds; Grade 9, 14-15 year olds). On the other hand, a third of the sample was classified as belonging to a cluster designated as "self-determined" (figure 13.1, Cluster 1), which was characterized by high task orientation, low entity beliefs, moderately high perceptions of competence, highest relative autonomy, and low amotivation; these children were also found to be actively involved in physical activity (63% played competitive sport and 34.1% recreational sport) and to have high perception of physical self-worth. In contrast, those clusters with lower task orientation, lower incremental beliefs, lower perceived competence, lower relative autonomy, and higher amotivation tended to report lower levels of physical activity participation and lower physical self-worth.

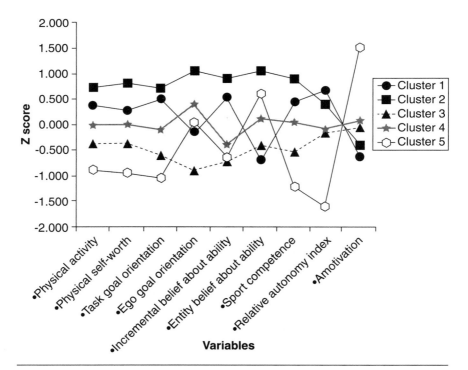

Figure 13.1   Cluster profiles from Wang and Biddle's (2001) study. Cluster 1 = self-determined; Cluster 2 = highly motivated; Cluster 3 = low motivation; Cluster 4 = ego/entity oriented; and Cluster 5 = amotivated.

Reprinted, by permission, from C.K.L. Wang and S.J.H. Biddle, 2001, "Young people's motivational profiles in physical activity: A cluster analysis," *Journal of Sport and Exercise Psychology* 23: 1-22.

The results of this study showed that there are groups of young people with distinct motivational profiles based on constructs derived from the three leading theories of motivation, leading to differences in the physical activity levels and physical self-worth outcome variables. The results also showed that motivation could not be characterized in simplistic terms, such as "high" versus "low" levels on isolated psychological constructs. It may be worthwhile to study motivational constructs from these theories in combination to gain a deeper understanding of motivated behavior in young people. Indeed, it may be that these theories can offer complementary explanations of the processes that underlie engagement in physical activity behavior as illustrated by other researchers (e.g., Hagger, Chatzisarantis, & Biddle, 2002; Hagger, Chatzisarantis, & Harris, 2006).

In our second study (Wang, Chatzisarantis, Spray, & Biddle, 2002), a separate sample of 11- to 14-year-old British children (N = 427) was investigated. We were interested in examining further the interrelationships between achievement goals, sport ability beliefs, autonomy, and amotivation. We conducted a cluster analysis based on dispositional goals and perceived competence while using other main constructs as criterion variables. Self-reported physical activity level was used to validate the differences among the clusters.

The results showed three clusters of youths with unique goal profiles (see figure 13.2). The first cluster was characterized as low task/low ego/low competence; the second cluster exhibited moderate task/low ego/moderate-to-low competence; the third cluster had a high task/high ego/high competence profile. We found that nearly 40% of the sample were represented in the "high motivation" cluster (figure 13.2, Cluster 3) and only 15.1% were in the "low motivation" cluster (figure 13.2, Cluster 1). Consistent with findings from our first study, participants with lower task orientation and lower perceived competence tended to have lower incremental beliefs, higher amotivation, and, importantly for the present discussion, lower relative autonomy. They also reported the lowest levels of physical activity participation. In addition, those high in the three clustering variables tended to have higher autonomy, lower amotivation, and the highest levels of physical activity participation. Another finding was that high levels of introjected regulation were evident among those participants in the cluster characterized by high task/high ego/high competence (Cluster 3). This could be explained by the fact that participation within school physical education may be partly motivated by internal pressure.

In both studies, we found that girls were overrepresented in the clusters that had lower perceived competence and higher amotivation, and this is consistent with participation trends reported widely in the literature (Sallis, Prochaska, & Taylor, 2000). On the other hand, more boys were classified in the clusters representing adaptive motivational profiles (i.e., the highly motivated cluster in Study 1 and the high task/high ego/high perceived competence cluster in Study 2). Higher autonomy was associated with more adaptive motivational profiles, supporting the notion that achievement goals might be important

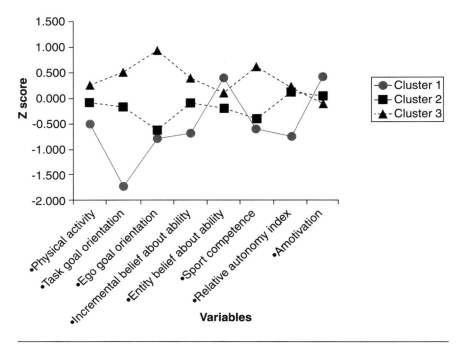

Figure 13.2   Cluster profiles from Wang and colleagues' (2002) study. Cluster 1 = low task/low ego/low competence; Cluster 2 = moderate task/low ego/moderate-to-low competence; Cluster 3 = high task/high ego/high competence.

correlates of self-determined motivation. However, given the less favorable motivational profiles of girls in our first two studies, we conducted a third study (Biddle & Wang, 2003) to gain further insight into the motivational patterns and self-perceptions of female secondary school students.

We investigated 516 girls between 11 and 16 years of age. The clustering variables were goal orientations (task and ego), implicit beliefs (incremental and entity), relative autonomy, amotivation, and key variables from the physical self-perception profile (Fox & Corbin, 1989). A two-stage clustering procedure was used (Hair et al., 1998), and a five-cluster solution was found to be most suitable (see figure 13.3).

The cluster of girls who had the highest physical self-perceptions in terms of sport competence, physical condition, strength, and perceived body attractiveness and rated the importance of these four self-perception domains highly had the highest scores on task orientation, incremental beliefs, and relative autonomy and the lowest scores in amotivation (figure 13.3, Cluster 4). These girls also had the highest physical self-worth, global self-esteem, and physical activity in comparison to other clusters. In contrast, the cluster of girls who

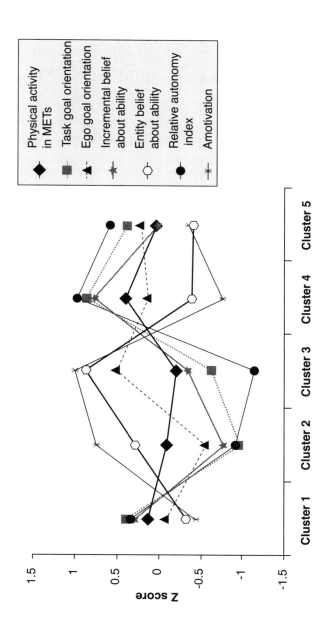

Figure 13.3 Cluster profiles from Biddle and Wang's (2003) study. Cluster 1 = task/incremental oriented; Cluster 2 = ego/entity oriented; Cluster 3 = amotivated; Cluster 4 = highly motivated; Cluster 5 = self-determined.

were characterized as amotivated comprised those who had low task orientation and incremental beliefs, high ego orientation, entity beliefs, and very low self-determination/relative autonomy (figure 13.3, Cluster 3). These girls had moderately high perceptions of their body attractiveness, and this dimension of self was important to them. They were the least physically active among the five clusters. These results show consistency in the patterns of intrinsic and self-determined motivation with conceptually sound variables from other motivational theories. The direction of differences for both goal orientations and ability beliefs is consistent with more self-determined forms of motivation. Given its wider scope, self-determination theory may provide the overarching theory within which more focused theories of goal orientations and ability beliefs can be studied.

In a follow-up study (Wang, Liu, Sun, & Biddle, 2003) in a sample of 345 female students from schools in Singapore, we confirmed the finding that girls with high incremental beliefs, high relative autonomy, and high perceived competence tended to report the highest levels of enjoyment and exerted effort and the lowest levels of boredom in physical activity participation. Girls with low incremental beliefs and high entity beliefs had the lowest relative autonomy, perceived competence, enjoyment, and exerted effort and the highest levels of amotivation and boredom in physical activity, again showing the congruence between ability beliefs and perceptions of autonomy. Those with incremental beliefs about ability are more likely to feel that they can initiate behaviors and strategies for improvement, which is consistent with meeting the needs for autonomy and competence.

In summary, results from our studies have shown that self-determination theory constructs are congruent with profiles of constructs from other conceptually related motivational theories. Specifically, when investigating constructs related to self-determination, achievement goals, and ability beliefs, we find that all three in combination have an association with individuals' motivational patterns, physical activity participation, perceptions of self-esteem, and physical self-worth. High scores on task orientation, incremental beliefs, and relative autonomy are associated with more adaptive motivational patterns, regardless of levels of ego orientation. High scores on entity beliefs are constantly associated with low perceived competence, low relative autonomy, and high amotivation, as well as low physical activity participation. One reason could be that ego-oriented goals involve an external perception, including reference to external criteria of success, and are thus more aligned with lower levels of self-determination. Moreover, task goals are conceptually coherent and are associated with an intrinsic motivational orientation. However, one needs to be careful in assuming that achievement goals map perfectly onto intrinsic and extrinsic motivation. While a task goal orientation is closely allied to an intrinsic motivational orientation, the same cannot be said for extrinsic motivation when one is considering ego goals. With use of the self-determination theory approach, there are qualitatively different types of extrinsic motivation. Ego goals, therefore, could operate in line with extrinsic, introjected, or identified motivation, suggesting that self-determination adds an extra dimension of analysis beyond that offered by achievement goals. As Deci and Ryan (2000) have said, "[W]e believe it is necessary not only to consider what goals people pursue but also why they pursue them" (p. 260).

Another reason for our results could be that entity beliefs do not allow feelings of confidence and control over future outcomes (are aligned with less self-determined and more controlling motivation), especially when perceived competence is low, thus resulting in less adaptive responses. Incremental beliefs, through the pursuit of task goals, allow the feeling that success is under one's personal control (Duda & Nicholls, 1992; Nicholls, 1989), resulting in more adaptive patterns among the motivational constructs from these theories.

Practical Implications of Research Findings

The findings of the studies reviewed in this chapter have important practical implications. First, these studies showed that homogeneous groups of students with similar motivational patterns could be clustered together. This is helpful for studying the unique characteristics of the main subgroups; consequently intervention programs could be designed to better target such groups. Second, our studies show that limiting interventions to one or two psychological constructs may not be advisable. A holistic focus on individuals' behavioral regulations, alongside achievement goals, conceptions of sport ability, and perceived competence, may increase the chance of success of physical activity intervention programs. Third, our findings suggest that if appropriate social and environmental structures are in place (e.g., accessible sport facilities, positive encouragement from teachers and parents), many young people could be motivated toward physical activity. Self-reports of motivation suggest that the majority of young people are quite positively disposed toward physical activity (Wang & Biddle, 2001).

With respect to self-determination theory, the adoption of autonomy-supportive behaviors may result in reduced emphasis on winning, hence avoiding or decreasing tendencies toward ego involvement. Similarly, autonomy-supportive behaviors will reduce the likelihood of externally referenced conceptions of ability. Adults should therefore not label children as "talented" or "gifted" in terms of their sport ability. This kind of labeling may cause children to become overly concerned with justifying the label attached to them and less concerned with meeting challenges that could enhance their skills (Dweck, 1999). In addition, these children may react in a maladaptive way when faced with setbacks because they worry about making mistakes, as this would indicate that they have low ability and do not deserve to be labeled as talented or gifted. Furthermore, fostering an entity belief may lead to amotivation and ego orientation and should be avoided.

On the other hand, encouraging mastery goals through incremental beliefs may result in greater levels of self-determination and more positive motivational patterns. However, our studies and other previous research have shown that performance goals are not necessarily negative as long as they are coupled with high mastery goals (Dorobantu & Biddle, 1997; Fox et al., 1994; Ommundsen & Roberts, 1999). It is also useful to remind ourselves, as stated earlier, that some ego goals may be more associated with self-determined motivational orientations than others. Therefore, an intervention should focus on enhancing the adoption of mastery goals, and not necessarily on avoiding the adoption of performance goals. For example, physical education lessons do not have to exclude or minimize competition or social comparison (grading) if teachers emphasize the importance of personal improvement at the same time and the self-enhancing function of aspects of competition and assessment.

In order to promote mastery goals, the six TARGET areas provide excellent guidelines for emphasizing the importance of personal improvement (see Ames, 1992a, 1992b; Treasure & Roberts, 1995). These areas, put forward by Epstein (1989), lead to the suggestion that the practices of coaches and physical education teachers should provide a motivational climate that encourages a mastery approach. The acronym reflects the practices that engender the optimal motivational climate: tasks/activities/practice sessions (these need to be varied and challenging), authority (the teaching style should allow individuals some say in the decision-making process), recognition (rewards and recognition should be contingent on effort and improvement rather than performance), grouping (individuals should be placed in an environment that encourages cooperative learning in which they can work toward their individual goals), evaluation (individual progress should be evaluated on improvement and mastery), and timing (leaders should vary the difficulty of task and pace of learning to suit abilities of individuals).

In addition to perceived autonomy, as well as sport ability beliefs and achievement goals, teachers' communication style is a key area for intervention. The results of our studies show that when children possess high perceived autonomy in their physical activity participation, they are more likely to have adaptive motivation outcomes such as high perceived competence and high levels of physical activity participation outside of school. If physical activity participation is to be supported and enhanced, physical education teachers should encourage students to make their own decisions (support autonomy) rather than force them into doing physical activity (control). Deci and Flaste (1995) suggest that the role of teachers, parents, or coaches should be to create conditions such that children are able to make their own decisions so that they act as the "origins" of their behavior rather than as "pawns." To succeed in creating an autonomy-supportive context, exercise leaders need to provide a rationale for doing the activities, acknowledge potential conflict, and offer choice to facilitate the process of internalization. These proposals can be misunderstood as a recipe for chaos. This is not the case. Rather, allowing for elements for choice, sometimes within contexts set by the teacher or coach, will be beneficial. Similarly, it can be helpful to provide a rationale for the importance of involvement.

Providing participants with a rationale that is meaningful to them will help them to understand the usefulness and benefits of doing activities. This may help them to value the activities and to adopt a more self-determined motivational orientation. However, even when a meaningful rationale is provided, some children may still feel under pressure to engage in activities because such pressure creates internal conflict (i.e., they don't really want to do the activity). Thus, acknowledging such internal conflict may convey relatedness through empathy and respect for children as individuals. Furthermore, any possible internal or external pressure can be minimized through the provision of real choice. Providing choice allows children to feel a sense of autonomy, control, and empowerment over their own behavior.

Future Directions

The studies reviewed in this chapter provide support for the integration of self-determination theory with achievement goal theory and ability beliefs in understanding individuals' cognition, affect, and behavior in physical activity settings. In closing, we offer recommendations for future research to advance our knowledge of motivation in the physical activity domain.

A first research avenue would be to measure autonomy, as well as goal involvement and sport ability beliefs, at a more situation-specific level. The results of our studies support the general predictions of self-determination theory, achievement goal theory, and sport ability beliefs. However, these variables are contextual measures rather than situation-specific measures (Vallerand & Ratelle, 2002). Targeting situation-specific measures might provide better predictors of cognitive, affective, and behavioral responses and make it possible to design interventions by identifying the important environmental cues or structure (Harwood, Hardy, & Swain, 2000). There is also evidence to suggest that researchers should focus on the pattern of influence on motivational constructs from different levels of generality, for example from the contextual level to the situational level (Hagger, Chatzisarantis, & Harris, 2006; Vallerand, 1997).

A second research area would involve establishing the causal links between perceptions of autonomy and goals and beliefs. Experimental studies need to be conducted to tease out the mechanisms operating among these psychological constructs. This will help to determine the boundary conditions of findings from the correlational studies. Finally, future studies might need to use qualitative approaches, such as in-depth interviews and observations, to provide further insight into participants' motivation. These methods can also serve to triangulate research findings obtained with other approaches.

Practical Recommendations for Sport Coaches and Physical Education Teachers

- Practitioners such as teachers, parents, and coaches are encouraged to recognize the commonalities in the various motivational perspectives when providing instruction and practices. Most important is the recognition that motivational styles like a task-oriented goal involvement or intrinsic motivation are likely to be fostered by similar practices. For example, when a physical education teacher tells a child who is doing archery, "You can improve your success rate on the target if you try hard to keep your feet parallel to your shooting axis and shoulder width," the teacher is providing personal, task-related information but is also providing competence information about effort and contingency with success.

- Practitioners are encouraged to provide appropriate social support and environmental structures for the facilitation of the needs for autonomy, competence, and relatedness. For example, a coach can create an environment that is need satisfying by presenting athletes with varied practices, informing them of the purpose and context of the practice, reminding them of the skills required to be successful in the practice, and asking them to work cooperatively. The coach can instruct athletes on a specific drill using autonomy-supporting language, get the athletes to work together on the drill, then draw the athletes back to a group situation and ask them what constituted successful completion of the drill, why they were doing the drill, and how the drill fits into their overall performance.

- It is recommended that practitioners seek to move young people away from extrinsic and toward more self-determined forms of motivation, while recognizing that "pure" forms of intrinsic motivation are rare. Coaches may acknowledge that some practices are monotonous and boring and unlikely to be enjoyed for their own sake but emphasize the importance of the drill in attaining personal goals within the sport. For example, a physical education teacher may tell students, "I know that repeated shuttle runs are hard work and quite boring, but they will make you so much fitter when it comes to lasting the distance in your matches."

- A useful guideline relating to young people's motivation toward physical activity is to work on an autonomy-supportive communication style that enhances choice, competence, and good interpersonal relations alongside a mastery motivational climate. An authoritarian approach is rarely compatible with children's motives and undermines personal agency and sense of ownership over actions. Autonomy-supportive communication styles need to focus on content (e.g., task-related information) and style (e.g., using questions, suggestions, and language such as "may" and "could" rather than "should" and "must").

Coaching Effectiveness

Exploring the Relationship Between Coaching Behavior and Self-Determined Motivation

Anthony J. Amorose, PhD
Illinois State University

The coach has been identified as a powerful socializing agent in the physical domain (Horn, 2002; Smoll & Smith, 2002). At all competitive levels, from youth to professional sport, the way in which coaches structure practice and game situations, the processes they use to make decisions, the quality and quantity of feedback they provide in response to athletes' performances, the relationships they establish with athletes, the techniques they use to motivate their players, and so on, can all have an impact on athletes' behaviors, cognitions, and affective responses. For instance, coaches can influence whether athletes learn and achieve at a high level, enjoy their experience, demonstrate effort and persistence, and develop a sense of competence and a self-determined motivational orientation (Chelladurai, 1993; Horn, 1987, 2002; Mageau & Vallerand, 2003; Murray & Mann, 2001; Smoll & Smith, 2002). Of course, certain coaching behaviors can also lead to negative achievement-related and psychological outcomes (e.g., poor performance, low self-esteem, high levels of competitive anxiety, burnout). Thus understanding which behaviors translate into positive experiences and functioning on the part of the athletes is critical for researchers and practitioners alike. In other words, what do coaches do that make them more or less effective in promoting high levels of performance and achievement and facilitating athletes' psychological and emotional well-being?

With this general question in mind, the goal of this chapter is to explore the research linking coaching behaviors and athletes' motivation. The chapter begins with a brief discussion of the aspects of motivation relevant to coaches' behavior according to Deci and Ryan's (1985; Ryan & Deci, 2000, 2002)

Correspondence concerning this article should be addressed to Anthony J. Amorose, College of Applied Science and Technology, School of Kinesiology and Recreation, Campus Box 5000, Turner Hall, Illinois State University, Normal, Illinois 61790-5000. E-mail: ajamoro@ilstu.edu self-determination theory. The next section presents a sample of specific research studies on the relationship between various coaching behaviors and the motivation of athletes in organized sport. While there is some evidence to support the influence of the coach on athletes' motivation, many questions and issues remain to be resolved. Thus, the third section presents recommendations for future research. Finally, the research and theory are translated into practical strategies that coaches or others working with athletes might be able to use to facilitate self-determined motivation.

The Nature and Determinants of Self-Determined Motivation

Ryan and Deci (this volume) propose that the reasons why individuals choose to participate, exert effort, and persist in an activity can be classified along a continuum of self-determined behavior. The authors highlight intrinsic motivation as the prototypical form of self-determined motivation, four types of extrinsic motivation ranging from higher to lower levels of self-determination, and amotivation as the most extrinsic form of motivation. Forms of extrinsic motivation include *integrated regulation, identified regulation, introjected regulation,* and *external regulation* (Ryan & Deci, this volume). Of course, people may participate in sport for multiple reasons, including a combination of intrinsic and extrinsic motives (Weiss & Ferrer-Caja, 2002). Nevertheless, a growing body of research has provided strong evidence of the benefits of engaging in activities for more self-determined reasons. For example, people who are intrinsically motivated toward an activity are more likely to choose to participate and work hard when extrinsic rewards and reinforcements are not available, to experience lower levels of performance-related anxiety, and to exhibit greater levels of skill learning relative to people with a more extrinsic motivational orientation (see Vallerand & Losier, 1999; Weiss & Ferrer-Caja, 2002).

Intrinsic motivation for sport participation generally tends to be quite high, yet there are still certain elements of sport that will not necessarily be intrinsically rewarding to many athletes (e.g., conditioning, repetitive training). For these activities, the primary rationale for engagement is more likely to be extrinsic. Nevertheless, participating for more *self-determined extrinsic* reasons, such as participating in an activity because it is of personal value (identified regulation), has also been associated with more positive psychological outcomes relative to doing the activity to avoid feelings of guilt or to enhance one's ego (introjected regulation) or because of some external demand or reward contingency (external regulation) (Ryan & Deci, 2002; Vallerand & Ratelle, 2002). Given the benefits of engaging in activities for more self-determined reasons, identifying factors related to the promotion and development of these forms of behavioral regulation has been an important element of self-determination theory and the extant research in the field (Ryan & Deci, 2002).

One of the central tenets of self-determination theory is that fulfillment of the fundamental human needs for competence, autonomy, and relatedness is essential for facilitating self-motivation, social development, and personal well-being (Ryan & Deci, 2000). The *need for competence* reflects the need to perceive our behavior as effective. The *need for autonomy* represents the need to perceive that we are the origin of our own actions. The need for *relatedness* represents the need to feel a secure sense of belongingness. According to self-determination theory, individuals will seek out activities and experiences to satisfy these three fundamental needs. Furthermore, activities that provide support for these needs will be engaged in for more self-determined reasons. Ultimately, self-determination theory suggests that anything that influences the needs of competence, autonomy, and relatedness can ultimately affect the type of motivation one develops in a given context (Vallerand & Ratelle, 2002).

The events that can act on one's need satisfaction and subsequent motivation are manifold in their extent and diversity. For instance, the extent to which people become ego versus task involved in an activity has been shown to affect perceptions of competence, autonomy, and consequently intrinsic motivation (see Duda & Hall, 2001; Ryan, Koestner, & Deci, 1991). The effects of numerous social-contextual events have received support as well, for example rewards, feedback, imposed deadlines, competition, surveillance, and interpersonal styles (Deci, Koestner, & Ryan, 2001; Henderlong & Lepper, 2002; Mageau & Vallerand, 2003; Ryan & Deci, 2002; Vallerand & Losier, 1999). Importantly, many of the events shown to affect need satisfaction and motivation are either directly or indirectly under the control of a coach. For example, coaches are in a position to distribute rewards, to provide performance-related feedback, to structure the environment to emphasize ego-involved or task-involved goals, and so on. According to Mageau and Vallerand (2003), an athlete's relationship with his or her coach is ultimately one of the most important determinants of that athlete's motivation.

Scholars have attempted to determine how these various coaching behaviors are associated with athletes' motivational orientations. Consistent with the coaching effectiveness perspective, one of the underlying goals in this research has been to determine which behaviors are positively or negatively related to motivation, as this information has important consequences for developing interventions to help athletes. The research has utilized self-determination theory, as well as Vallerand's hierarchical model of motivation (Vallerand, this volume; Vallerand & Ratelle, 2002), as a framework for testing and interpreting the relationships. These theoretical approaches argue that any actions on the part of the coach that positively affect an athlete's perceptions of competence, autonomy, or relatedness will ultimately help to facilitate or promote more self-determined forms of motivation in the athlete, whereas those behaviors that thwart or inhibit the satisfaction of these needs will have the opposite effect.

Prior to the presentation of some examples of specific research studies, it seems worthwhile to acknowledge that the existing coaching effectiveness research typically focuses on the athletes' perceptions of their coaches' behaviors rather than on the actual behaviors of a coach. Consistent with the assumptions of self-determination theory and other social cognitive approaches to motivation (Pintrich, 2003; Roberts, 2001), the actions of a coach in and of themselves are relatively less important than how an athlete perceives, interprets, and evaluates a coach's behaviors (Horn, 2002). For example, a coach might provide two different athletes with the following feedback in response to their performance: "Great job, you are really making me proud." While this seemingly positive statement would generally be expected to facilitate motivation, that might not always be the result given that two different athletes might interpret the statement in different ways. One athlete, for instance, might focus on the positive competence information inherent in the statement. According to cognitive evaluation theory, a mini-theory embedded within self-determination theory, the coach's action would likely be perceived by this athlete as informational, leading to enhanced feelings of competence and increased intrinsic motivation. A second athlete, however, might interpret this exact same statement as controlling, specifically by focusing on the fact that the coach is proud and not wanting to let the coach down in the future. Thus, the *functional significance* of the interaction with the coach involves increased feelings of pressure and decreased feelings of autonomy, which in turn would undermine intrinsic motivation. While any number of factors may influence how athletes perceive, interpret, and evaluate the behaviors exhibited by their coaches (see Horn, 2002), the key point is that we must consider the athletes' perspective on the behavior. Thus much of the research reviewed in this chapter has assessed coaching behaviors using measures that tap the athletes' perceptions of their coaches' actions.

Research on Coaching Behavior and Motivation

The following sections provide a brief review of the published field-based research illustrating the link between various coaching behaviors and the motivation of athletes participating in organized competitive sport. The review is by no means exhaustive, but rather highlights some of the coaching effectiveness studies that provide support for self-determination theory. As a way to organize the information, the studies are grouped according to the primary type of coaching behavior being investigated. Specifically, they are examples of research exploring (a) feedback patterns, (b) general leadership styles, (c) the motivational climate, and (d) autonomy-supportive versus controlling behaviors. While I have presented these as distinct areas, it is important to acknowledge that in reality there is considerable overlap among these dimensions of coaching behavior. It is therefore assumed that democratic coaching styles, autonomy-supportive coaching styles, and mastery motivational climates contain characteristics that are very similar, and it is expected that such commonalities will be reflected in the patterns of influence among the constructs on motivation, salient outcomes, and actual behavior.

Feedback Patterns

Much of the field-based research linking coaches' feedback patterns and athletes' motivation was informed by early experimental studies looking at the effects of positive and negative feedback on intrinsic motivation (e.g., Vallerand & Reid, 1984; Whitehead & Corbin, 1991). Results of these studies consistently revealed an association between positive performance feedback and high perceptions of competence and intrinsic motivation, whereas negative feedback had the opposite effect (see Hein & Koka, this volume).

While these studies provide valuable information in support of self-determination theory, the feedback given by coaches in an actual sport setting is more complex than is implied by the distinction between positive and negative. Consequently, much of the field-based research has employed more elaborate measures such as the Coaching Behavior Assessment System (CBAS) developed by Smoll and Smith (2002). Based on extensive observations of youth sport coaches, the CBAS includes 12 categories of coaching behavior broadly classified as either reactive or spontaneous. Reactive behaviors, those that a coach exhibits in direct response to a player's behavior, include two coaching responses to a player's desirable or successful performances (reinforcement and nonreinforcement), five coaching responses to a player's performance errors or mistakes (mistake-contingent encouragement, mistake-contingent technical instruction, punishment, punitive technical instruction, and ignoring mistakes), and one response to player misbehaviors (keeping-control behaviors). The CBAS identifies four types of spontaneous coaching behavior as well, including general technical instruction, spontaneous general encouragement, team organizational behaviors, and game-irrelevant general communication.

On the basis of their research using the CBAS, particularly with male youth baseball programs, Smoll and Smith (2002) developed what they termed the "positive approach" to coaching. Effective coaching behaviors, from this approach, include providing high frequencies of reinforcement for effort and good performances, encouragement following errors, and lots of general and mistake-contingent instruction while at the same time minimizing punitive behaviors and nonresponses. In support of this approach, the researchers have found that coaches who are trained to engage in these behaviors and actually do so have players who report a number of positive outcomes such as higher self-esteem, greater levels of enjoyment, lower anxiety, and lower attrition rates (e.g., Barnett, Smoll, & Smith, 1992; Smoll, Smith, Barnett, & Everett, 1993).

Although Smoll and Smith's research has not specifically addressed the effects of coaches' feedback patterns on athletes' motivational orientations, other researchers using the CBAS, or slight variations of the measures, have found that coaches who are perceived to adopt the general feedback pattern recommended as part of the positive approach have athletes who report higher levels of intrinsic motivation. For instance, Black and Weiss (1992) used a questionnaire version of the CBAS to determine the relationship between the types of feedback age-group swimmers (aged 10-18 years) perceived that their coaches gave in response to their performances and the athletes' perceptions of ability, success, and intrinsic motivation. Results indicated no relationship between coaching behaviors and the psychological responses among the 10- to 11-year-old swimmers; however, significant associations were found for the 12- to 14- and the 15- to 18-year-old athletes. Generally, higher levels of perceived swimming competence, success, and intrinsic motivation were associated with higher frequencies of perceived praise and praise combined with information following successful swims, as well as with greater encouragement and encouragement combined with information following poor swims. Further, for the oldest group, more frequent criticism following poor performances was associated with less positive psychological responses.

Thelma Horn and I obtained similar results in a study we conducted with male and female NCAA Division I athletes (Amorose & Horn, 2000). In addition to assessing indices of intrinsic motivation, we assessed a number of perceived coaching behaviors, including those on a questionnaire version of the CBAS. While our results revealed slight gender differences in the pattern of relationships, in general the feedback dimensions that were related to high levels of intrinsic motivation (i.e., higher interest-enjoyment, perceived competence, effort, importance, choice, and lower tension-pressure) included high frequencies of positive and informationally based feedback; they also included low frequencies of punishment-oriented feedback and ignoring players' mistakes as well as nonreinforcement of players' successful performances. We explained these results using cognitive evaluation theory, suggesting that high frequencies of positive and informational feedback and low frequencies of punishment-oriented feedback and ignoring behaviors would lead to more positive perceptions of competence on the part of the athletes, which in turn would facilitate intrinsic motivation.

Clearly the feedback provided by coaches can have a significant impact on athletes' motivation. Numerous studies, both in and out of sport, have demonstrated this relationship (Henderlong & Lepper, 2002; Horn, 2002). In general, the research indicates that providing frequent praise and information should translate into increased perceived competence and more self-determined motivation, whereas criticizing athletes or ignoring their performances altogether should have the opposite effect. Despite the intuitive appeal of these findings and their implications (e.g., that coaches should provide lots of praise and reinforcement), it is important to acknowledge that providing feedback effectively is considerably more complex. For instance, providing seemingly effective feedback such as praise and technical instruction may actually lead to negative motivational outcomes if the feedback is given noncontingently and inappropriately, if it contains controlling locutions, or if it is insincere. Similarly, negative motivational effects are likely when feedback provided to athletes suggests unrealistic performance expectations and promotes ego involvement (Henderlong & Lepper, 2002; Horn, 1987, 2002; Mageau & Vallerand, 2003).

General Leadership Styles

Studies have also provided support for the influence of coaching behavior on athletes' motivation based on the general leadership styles that coaches exhibit. This research has relied primarily on the Leadership Scale for Sport (LSS; Chelladurai & Saleh, 1980) as a way to classify and assess key coaching behaviors. The LSS is made up of five subscales, two of which assess the coach's decision-making style (democratic and autocratic), two of which assess the coach's motivational tendencies (social support and positive feedback), and one that assesses the coach's instructional tendencies (training and instruction). A high score on the autocratic subscale indicates a coach who displays a rigid decision-making style and demands stringent obedience from the athletes with regard to those decisions. On the other hand, a high score on the democratic subscale reflects a coach whose leadership style includes and encourages athletes' opinions with regard to goals, decisions, and tactics. The social support dimension taps the extent to which coaches establish positive interpersonal relationships with their players and demonstrate care and concern for the athletes' well-being. The positive feedback subscale reflects how frequently coaches praise and reinforce athletes' performances. Finally, coaches who score high on training and instruction exhibit high frequencies of behaviors oriented toward improving their athletes' performance.

Numerous studies have used the LSS to test various elements of Chelladurai's multidimensional model of leadership (see Chelladurai, 1993). Recently, we have conducted a series of studies specifically looking at how college athletes' perceptions of their coaches' leadership styles are related to their intrinsic motivation. For instance, we included the LSS in the previously mentioned Amorose and Horn (2000) study. In general, high levels of intrinsic motivation were associated with athletes who perceived their coaches to exhibit a leadership style that emphasized training and instruction and exhibited democratic behaviors rather than autocratic behavior.

In a subsequent study (Amorose & Horn, 2001), we attempted to extend our findings by examining how first-year college athletes' perceptions of their coaches' general leadership styles related to *changes* in the athletes' intrinsic motivation from pre- to postseason. Results indicated that changes in intrinsic motivation were associated with the degree to which the coaches were perceived to engage in training and instruction, autocratic behavior, and social support. Consistent with cognitive evaluation theory and our previous research (Amorose & Horn, 2000), we suggested that high frequencies of training and instruction were associated with an increase in the athletes' intrinsic motivation through enhancement of the athletes' perceptions of competence. The relationship between high frequencies of autocratic behavior and decreases in intrinsic motivation was assumed to occur because an autocratic leadership style lowered the athletes' sense of autonomy. Somewhat unexpectedly, however, we found that a high frequency of social support was linked with a decrease in intrinsic motivation. While it seems reasonable to assume that social support would facilitate intrinsic motivation, presumably by fulfilling the need for relatedness (see Deci & Ryan, 1985; Ryan & Powelson, 1991), we suggested that an athlete with a coach who displays socially supportive behavior may feel pressure to not let the coach down. Thus, it may have been that social support was perceived as controlling and consequently lowered autonomy and intrinsic motivation. Ultimately, the question may not be the amount of social support that has motivational consequences, but rather the quality of the support provided by coaches.

In our most recent study (Hollembeak & Amorose, 2005), we attempted to address some notable limitations of our previous research. First, rather than simply speculating that perceived competence and autonomy can explain the relationship between the various dimensions of coaching behavior and athletes' intrinsic motivation, we specifically tested whether these needs mediated the relationships. Second, we included the need for relatedness as a possible mediator, as this potential determinant of intrinsic motivation has generally been ignored in the literature, despite the fact that a coach might have a significant influence on the satisfaction of this need.

Athletes from a variety of sports who were competing in U.S. collegiate NCAA Division I competitions completed self-report measures assessing perceptions of their coaches' leadership style using the LSS, as well as their perceptions of competence, autonomy, and sense of relatedness and intrinsic motivation. Using structural equation modeling, we tested a series of models to determine which pattern of relationships best fit the data. While a few unexpected relationships emerged, by and large the study provided support for our hypotheses and for self-determination theory in general. For instance, all three of the needs—perceived competence, autonomy, and relatedness—positively predicted intrinsic motivation. Further, our results clearly demonstrated that the relationships between the coaching behaviors and intrinsic motivation were mediated by the three needs. Each of the perceived coaching behaviors, with the exception of social support, was related to at least one of the three psychological needs; however, only autocratic and democratic behaviors were found to have a significant indirect effect on intrinsic motivation. Athletes who perceived their coaches as autocratic felt lower levels of autonomy and relatedness and subsequently reported less intrinsic motivation. Athletes perceiving their coaches as democratic, on the other hand, reported high levels of autonomy and intrinsic motivation. Interestingly, multigroup analyses provided evidence that the pattern of relationships between the coaching behaviors, the athletes' needs, and their intrinsic motivation were invariant for males and females, for scholarship and nonscholarship athletes, and across individual and team sport participants.

In summary, the research reviewed indicates that perceived leadership styles exhibited by coaches are linked with athletes' motivational orientation. The most consistent finding involves the coaches' decision-making styles. While there are clearly occasions in sport when a more autocratic style will be appropriate and effective (see Chelladurai & Trail, 2001; Hagger & Chatzisarantis, 2005), from a motivational perspective coaches would do well to allow athletes to be involved in decisions relevant to their participation and behavior in sport.

Motivational Climate

The way coaches structure practices and learning experiences, the way they provide feedback and give recognition, their strategies for grouping athletes, and so on, can help to establish what has been referred to as the "motivational climate" (Ames, 1992). The climate is generally defined by the meaning of success and failure as emphasized in the social environment (McArdle & Duda, 2002; Treasure, 2001). For instance, a mastery (task involved) motivational climate focuses on learning, improvement, and effort as the keys to success. Coaches who create this type of climate will provide optimally challenging and personally meaningful learning activities, reward and encourage progress toward athletes' self-set goals, evaluate athletes based on their effort and skill learning, and promote cooperation among team members. Conversely, a performance (ego involved) motivational climate is an environment where the focus is on winning, outperforming others, and the use of norm-reference criteria of success and failure. In this climate, encouragement and rewards from coaches will typically be given only to the better players on the team and for the demonstration of superior performance. Further, coaches will often punish athletes who make mistakes and promote and encourage intrateam rivalries.

Based primarily on an achievement goal theory perspective of motivation (see Conroy, Elliot, & Coatsworth, this volume; Roberts, 2001; Wang & Biddle, this volume), considerable research has demonstrated that the climate initiated by teachers and coaches in classrooms and on athletic fields can have major implications for participants. For instance, those who perceive that they participate under a mastery motivational climate report positive achievement-related outcomes such as high perceptions of competence, greater enjoyment and lower anxiety, enhanced learning, and better sporting behavior, whereas participating under a performance climate generally results in less positive achievement-related outcomes (Duda, 1996; McArdle & Duda, 2002; Treasure, 2001; Weiss & Ferrer-Caja, 2002).

Importantly, theory and research also support the link between the motivational climate and athletes' motivational orientation. Conceptually, a task-involved focus should lead to high levels of intrinsic motivation, as athletes in these settings are investing in the activity more for its own sake than as some means to an end. In an ego-involved climate, however, sport participation would be expected to be based on less self-determined forms of motivation, given that the participation becomes a means to an end (i.e., a way to demonstrate superior ability) and that considerable pressure is placed on the athlete in this situation.

A number of studies have provided support for these predictions in a variety of sport and physical activity settings (McArdle & Duda, 2002; Standage,

Gillison, & Treasure, this volume; Treasure, 2001). For instance, correlational studies in sport have consistently shown a positive relationship between athletes' intrinsic motivation and their perceptions of a mastery motivational climate, while the opposite pattern emerges with a performance motivational climate (Newton, Duda, & Yin, 2000; Seifriz, Duda, & Chi, 1992). Theeboom, DeKnop, and Weiss (1995) also provided support in an intervention study. Two groups of children (aged 8 to 12 years) were taught *wushu*, a Chinese martial arts activity, with use of either a mastery- or a performance-oriented teaching style. Following the three-week intervention, results showed that the children in the mastery climate group exhibited greater enjoyment and demonstrated better motor skills than did those in the performance climate group. Postprogram interviews with the children strongly suggested that those in the mastery group exhibited higher perceptions of competence and higher levels of intrinsic motivation as well, although these differences were not significant based on the statistical analyses.

Additional support for a mastery-oriented climate was provided in a prospective study on female adolescent handball players (Sarrazin, Vallerand, Guillet, Pelletier, & Cury, 2002). The study was essentially a test of Vallerand and Ratelle's (2002) hierarchical model of motivation, which, consistent with the basic tenets of self-determination theory, suggests a sequence of events whereby social factors influence an individual's needs for competence, autonomy, and relatedness, which in turn affect the individual's motivational orientation and subsequently various cognitive, behavioral, and affective consequences. In this study the social factors were represented by the athletes' perceptions of the motivational climate, and the motivational consequences included the athletes' intention to continue to participate and actual long-term engagement (i.e., participation in the following season). While there were a number of interesting findings, the most important results came from the structural equation modeling analyses. As expected, a mastery motivational climate was a positive predictor of the athletes' perceived competence, autonomy, and sense of relatedness, which in turn were positively associated with the athletes' level of self-determined motivation. A performance motivational climate, on the other hand, was negatively related to the athletes' motivation through the effect on autonomy. Interestingly, the model revealed that athletes who reported higher levels of self-determined motivation had less intention to discontinue participation and were less likely to drop out the following season, suggesting that ultimately the climate has an influence on actual motivated behavior (see Sarrazin, Boiché, & Pelletier, this volume).

Considerable attention has been devoted to understanding motivation in physical activity settings from an achievement goal theory perspective (see Wang & Biddle, this volume; Weiss & Ferrer-Caja, 2002). The combination of this theory and self-determination theory, as well as the extant research, provides strong support for the link between the motivational climate that exists within a team and athletes' motivational orientation (Hagger & Chatzisarantis, 2005;

Ryan & Deci, 1989; Weiss & Ferrer-Caja, 2002). Although there is considerable debate about whether practitioners should *always* promote task involvement instead of ego involvement in athletes (Hardy, 1997; Harwood, Hardy, & Swain, 2000; Roberts, 2001), in general it appears that positive motivational outcomes are likely to occur for most athletes when the climate created by their coaches focuses more on learning, improving, and effort.

Autonomy-Supportive Behaviors

In the context of self-determination theory, one of the more frequently studied social-contextual determinants of motivation involves the degree to which a parent, teacher, supervisor, coach, or anyone in a position of authority is autonomy supportive versus controlling in his or her interactions. An individual who is autonomy supportive engages in behaviors that acknowledge another person's thoughts and feelings; encourages choice, self-initiation, and self-regulation of the person's behavior; and minimizes the use of pressure and demands to control others (Deci & Ryan, 1985, 1987). Conversely, a controlling interpersonal style is characterized by pressuring another person to think, feel, and act in a way consistent with the needs and wants of the authority figure. Basically, authority figures who engage in autonomy-supportive behaviors help to satisfy the needs of those whom they work with, whereas controlling behaviors serve to diminish need satisfaction and subsequent self-determined motivation.

In a recent conceptual paper, Mageau and Vallerand (2003) expanded on the behaviors that, in combination, represent an autonomy-supportive interpersonal style. Specifically, they argued that autonomy-supportive coaches (a) provide choice to their athletes within specific limits and rules; (b) provide athletes with a meaningful rationale for the activities, limits, and rules; (c) ask about and acknowledge the athletes' feelings; (d) provide opportunities for athletes to take initiative and act independently; (e), provide noncontrolling performance feedback; (f) avoid overt control, guilt-induced criticism, and controlling statements and limit the use of tangible rewards; and (g) minimize behaviors that promote ego involvement.

Mageau and Vallerand (2003) elaborate on the specifics of these dimensions and provide considerable evidence that authority figures who exhibit these autonomy-supportive behaviors facilitate positive motivational outcomes. Rather than reiterating their review here, I have provided a few examples of recent research that offer additional support for their conclusions and self-determination theory in general. Interestingly, these examples focus not only on the motivation outcomes associated with an autonomy-supportive interpersonal style, but also on implications for the psychological well-being of athletes.

Reinboth, Duda, and Ntoumanis (2004) examined the relationship between coaching behavior and adolescent soccer and cricket players' need satisfaction and psychological and physical well-being. Specifically, these researchers tested a model in which the extent to which the athletes perceived that their coaches (a) were autonomy supportive (i.e., provided athletes with choices and options),

(b) promoted a mastery motivational climate, and (c) provided social support influenced the athletes' perceptions of competence, autonomy, and relatedness, which in turn influenced their subjective vitality, intrinsic interest in sport, and physical well-being. Although the authors did not test how each of the coaching behaviors dimensions was related to all three of the needs, structural equation modeling analyses indicated that autonomy support, the motivational climate, and social support were positive predictors of the athletes' needs for autonomy, competence, and relatedness, respectively. In turn, perceived competence and autonomy, but not relatedness, were positively related to the psychological and physical well-being of the athletes.

In an interesting and novel approach, Gagné, Ryan, and Bargmann (2003) examined the links between autonomy support and involvement of coaches and parents and need satisfaction, motivation, and well-being of young female gymnasts using a diary study. The details of this research design and the methods used in the study are described more fully by Gagné and Blanchard (this volume). Importantly, the results provided evidence of the relationship between social influences, need satisfaction, and psychological well-being. For example, aggregated data showed that athletes who perceived their coaches and parents to be autonomy supportive and involved generally reported more self-determined motivation for gymnastics. Further, hierarchical linear modeling analyses revealed that when athletes' needs were satisfied during practice, which would at least partly be a function of their coaches' behaviors, the athletes experienced increases in indices of psychological well-being (i.e., positive affective, self-esteem, subjective vitality).

When findings in sport are combined with evidence outside of the sport setting (e.g., Baard, 2002; Reeve, 2002), it is clear that an autonomy-supportive interpersonal style is an extremely effective motivational technique. Unfortunately, many authority figures such as teachers and coaches tend to rely on a more controlling interpersonal style (Mageau & Vallerand, 2003). Further, there is the general perception that individuals who engage in controlling behaviors are actually more effective (see Boggiano, Flink, Shields, Seelbach, & Barrett, 1993). While these claims need to be tested specifically with coaches, there is plenty of anecdotal and empirical evidence that coaches can be very controlling (d'Arripe-Longueville, Fournier, & Dubois, 1998; Hagger & Chatzisarantis, 2005), which from a motivational standpoint is less effective than being autonomy supportive.

Summary

Research has provided researchers and practitioners with some important and valuable information regarding the link between various coaching behaviors and athletes' motivation. In almost all cases, the research presents strong support for self-determination theory. In other words, various dimensions of the interpersonal context have significant implications for need satisfaction and motivation in athletes. Nevertheless, there is considerable work to be done.

The following section elaborates on some future directions for research on sport motivation and coaching effectiveness.

Future Research Directions

Despite the importance generally attributed to coaches, coaching effectiveness research is relatively limited in scope. A number of recent papers have presented some excellent suggestions for future research on links between coaching behavior and motivational outcomes (see Horn, 2002; Mageau & Vallerand, 2003; Weiss & Ferrer-Caja, 2002). Rather than repeat all of these recommendations, I would like to highlight a few that I believe will significantly enhance our knowledge.

First, much of the research has focused exclusively on intrinsic motivation. One of the great contributions of self-determination theory, though, is the distinctions between intrinsic motivation, the various forms of extrinsic motivation, and amotivation. Clearly not all aspects of sport will be inherently interesting, and thus we need to consider how coaches affect these other forms of motivated behavior. In particular, how is it that coaches can facilitate internalization and integration of nonintrinsically motivating behaviors in an attempt to promote long-term engagement?

One idea comes from research by Vansteenkiste and colleagues (e.g., Vansteenkiste, Simons, Sheldon, Lens, & Deci, 2004; Vansteenkiste, Soenens, & Lens, this volume), who have found that the way in which instructions are provided for an activity has important motivational implications. Specifically, framing an activity to emphasize the intrinsic goals of the activity (e.g., emphasizing the personal value and relevance, presenting clear and meaningful rationale for engagement), especially within an autonomy-supportive context, leads to high achievement and self-determined motivation. Exploring the effectiveness of this type of strategy for promoting internalization by coaches might be extremely valuable.

This example also highlights the need to continue to explore additional dimensions of coaching behavior. The existing research has focused on a limited number of coaching behavior dimensions, yet there are clearly many other aspects of coaching that are likely to have motivational implications. Notwithstanding the difficulty of identifying which behaviors to target given the complexity of coaching and interpersonal interactions in general, we need to expand the types of behaviors we explore. Obviously, this will require considerable attention to measurement issues, which have constituted a significant limitation of the coaching effectiveness research (see Horn, 2002).

In addition to expanding the types of coaching behaviors examined, we need to look at the interactive effects of these behaviors. For instance, Mageau and Vallerand (2003), in their recent motivational model of the coach–athlete relationship, suggest that autonomy-supportive behaviors should have positive effects on one's motivation only when accompanied by adequate structure and support on the part of the coach. Thus, it is the combination of these dimensions of the coaches' behavior that will provide the most accurate and complete understanding of athletes' motivation.

The call for increased attention to potential interaction effects is not limited to coaching behaviors (see Pintrich, 2003; Vallerand, 2002). For instance, future studies should explore how the needs for competence, autonomy, and relatedness function together to affect athletes' motivational orientations. In the original formulation of cognitive evaluation theory, Deci and Ryan (1985) argued that increased perceptions of competence will facilitate intrinsic motivation only when an individual feels a sense of autonomy. Interestingly, Markland (1999) found, contrary to theoretical predictions, that variations in perceived competence positively influenced intrinsic motivation for exercise only under conditions of low autonomy. Attempting to clarify how the needs for competence and autonomy work together, along with feelings of relatedness, should provide important theoretical information regarding the determinants of athletes' motivational orientation. This is especially true given recent evidence that empirically supports the complementarity of the psychological needs and their effects on motivation (Hagger, Chatzisarantis, & Harris, 2006).

As mentioned previously, one of the main underlying goals of the research reviewed in this chapter has been to uncover the coaching behaviors that are effective in facilitating self-determined motivation in athletes. While there is still a long way to go in terms of fully understanding the motivational processes underlying coaching behaviors in sport, some general conclusions regarding effective behaviors can be promoted based on previous research; these include being autonomy supportive, involving athletes in the decision-making process, demonstrating care and consideration for athletes, and providing positive and informational feedback. Nevertheless, anyone who has ever coached knows that one style does not work for all athletes or in all situations. Instead, the behaviors that are optimally effective will depend on the characteristics of the situation and the individual athletes. Thus there is a need for research on the important moderating factors that affect the relationships between coaches' behaviors and positive or negative motivational outcomes. For instance, there is some evidence that age influences how feedback is interpreted as a cue of positive or negative ability (Amorose & Weiss, 1998; Graham, 1990). Further, certain psychological characteristics might make an athlete more attuned to specific elements in the situation, thus affecting its motivational implications (Vallerand, 2002). Potentially an unlimited number of factors might function as moderating variables in the coach–athlete relationship (see Chelladurai, 1993; Horn, 2002; Smoll & Smith, 2002). Uncovering the key factors, however, should allow researchers to make more specific recommendations to coaches about how to most effectively motivate different athletes depending on the circumstances.

Motivational processes are not static but rather are continuous, constantly changing as a function of interpersonal and social-contextual variations (Weiss

& Ferrer-Caja, 2002). With few exceptions, however, the field-based research in sport has almost exclusively employed cross-sectional designs. Consequently, our information is limited to inferences about relationships among the variables at a particular time; we do not have important information about patterns of change in antecedents, motivational orientations, and behavioral consequences. Thus, we need studies assessing key variables over extended periods of time.

In addition to exploring changes over time, the continued support for the basic relationships described by self-determination theory should signal that we are ready to develop and test coaching effectiveness interventions. There are clearly good examples of interventions that have manipulated key coaching behaviors such as feedback pattern (Smoll & Smith, 2002), the motivational climate (Treasure, 2001), and autonomy-supportive behaviors (Mageau & Vallerand, 2003). Scholars should expand on these programs, as well as attempt to (a) understand which aspects of the interventions are more or less effective for influencing distinct motivational outcomes, (b) determine the optimal length of time required to yield meaningful changes in motivation, and (c) examine the most effective way to train coaches to adopt these behaviors.

The final suggestion for future research involves increased attention to the antecedents of coaches' behaviors. All of the major models of coaching behavior have indicated that characteristics of the coach, the situation, and the athletes they work with will likely influence the behaviors that coaches exhibit (Chelladurai, 1993; Horn, 2002; Smoll & Smith, 2002). More specific to self-determination theory, Mageau and Vallerand's (2003) model of the coach–athlete relationship argues that the coach's personal orientation, the coaching context, and the coach's perceptions of the athletes' behavior and motivation will affect the degree to which a coach engages in autonomy-supportive versus controlling behaviors. As indicated by Horn (2002), there has been very little research-based information on reasons why coaches exhibit the leadership styles, behaviors, and feedback patterns that they do, which makes this an area wide open for research.

Evidence from areas outside sport and physical activity has shed some light on potential factors that sport researchers might want to explore. For instance, research in the academic domain indicates that teachers who perceive greater pressure and responsibility with regard to their students' achievement are likely to adopt a more controlling interpersonal style (e.g., Pelletier, Séguin-Lévesque, & Legault, 2002). Research on parental behaviors has also indicated that factors such as feeling pressure, being in a stressful environment, and being more ego involved in their children's performance often lead parents to adopt a more controlling parenting style (see Grolnick & Apostoleris, 2002). While there are likely real differences between the teacher–student, parent–child, and coach–athlete relationships, it is not unreasonable to expect that coaches who become tied up in the achievement of their athletes, feel pressure to win (either from within or from external sources), and generally believe that a controlling interpersonal style is more effective may tend to use more controlling rather than autonomy-supportive motivational strategies.

Another potential determinant of coaches' behaviors that is ripe for research involves their perceptions of the athletes they work with (Horn, 2002; Mageau & Vallerand, 2003). Coaches treat athletes differently based on a variety of perceived characteristics and behaviors (Horn, Lox, & Labrador, 2001). Recently, Pelletier and Vallerand (1996) provided evidence in a mock teaching situation that supervisors were more autonomy supportive in their interactions when they believed the individual they were working with was intrinsically motivated; they were more controlling when working with those they believed to be extrinsically motivated. Similar support for this behavioral confirmation effect has recently been provided in actual classroom settings (Pelletier, Séguin-Lévesque, & Legault, 2002). Given the benefits of more self-determined forms of motivation, it would seem imprudent for coaches to engage in behaviors that undermine the facilitation of self-determined motivation. Yet, as these studies show, coaches who initially believe their athletes are more extrinsically motivated end up treating the athletes in a more controlling fashion, which in turn decreases the very type of motivation they may want to facilitate. This behavioral confirmation effect is an interesting phenomenon and should be the focus of attention in the sport domain.

Research exploring the antecedents of coaches' behaviors not only should provide researchers and coaches with important theoretical information, but also should be useful with regard to designing coaching education programs. As noted by Horn (2002), it will clearly be easier to develop interventions to help change or modify coaches' behavior once we know why coaches exhibit the behaviors that they do in the first place. Consequently, understanding of the antecedents of coaches' behavior will be beneficial for both theoretical and practical reasons.

Practical Implications

While we still have considerable work to do in order to fully understand how coaching behaviors affect athletes, both self-determination theory and the supporting research provide some general information about how to promote motivation among athletes. As Kurt Lewin (1951) once said, "There is nothing so practical as a good theory" (p. 169); and the amount of support for self-determination theory across multiple achievement contexts suggests that we can use the basic tenets of this theory in a very practical way to help promote self-determined motivation as well as positive development and well-being of athletes. Specifically, anything coaches can do to satisfy their athletes' needs for competence, autonomy, and relatedness should be effective.

A number of scholars have provided general suggestions for facilitating one or more of the needs identified by self-determination theory or motivation in general (e.g., Baard, 2002; Duda, 1996; Horn & Harris, 2002; Pintrich, 2003; Weiss & Williams, 2004). Given that the most effective behaviors are likely to vary across athletes and situations, providing very specific recommendations is somewhat difficult. Instead, "Recommendations for Practitioners for Enhancing Perceived Competence," "Strategies for Enhancing Autonomy," and "Strategies for Enhancing a Sense of Relatedness" outline some strategies and guidelines consistent with theory and research. Given the general nature of the practical strategies, it will be up to coaches, or anyone working with athletes, to apply them to the specific circumstances they encounter. This is where the "art" of coaching takes over.

Recommendations for Practitioners for Enhancing Perceived Competence

- Practitioners like coaches and trainers are encouraged to design activities that optimally challenge athletes' skills and abilities. These challenging activities should be agreed through a "contract" between the coach and the performer and evaluations of the contractual activities should be scheduled throughout a competitive season to monitor progress.

- Coaches and trainers should encourage skill-building activities that are clearly meaningful and interesting to athletes. These include practices and drills that mesh well with athletes' personal goals. For example, a coach may provide a netball team with a series of optimal and suboptimal attacking set plays and challenge the performers to work cooperatively to score from the optimal plays and try to gain an advantage from the suboptimal plays.

- Sport coaches should encourage athletes to try new things within assigned practices and should support creativity while simultaneously giving athletes multiple opportunities to experience success. Thus a field hockey coach might provide a clear practice task such as shooting the ball into the net from 10 yards but give players a number of options for how they could do that.

- Coaches and trainers are encouraged to help athletes make connections among the amount of effort they apply over time, successful mastery of the skills, and resultant affective experiences. They might do this by calling athletes together after practices or arranging one-to-one meetings and asking athletes to make links between trying hard and optimal performance. This raises an athlete's awareness of the connections between personally relevant outcomes and the level of personal competency required to achieve them.

- It is recommended that coaches also provide contingent, appropriate, and specific feedback in a timely fashion and supply positive reinforcement for improvement, progress, and mastery, not just successful outcomes.

(continued)

(continued)

- It is important for coaches to acknowledge that it is acceptable for athletes to make mistakes, as mistakes are part of the learning process, and to encourage athletes to try new skills and techniques within practice sessions. It is therefore useful not to be too prescriptive when providing practices so that there is an element of trial and error. If drills or practice sessions are followed by questioning (e.g., "What did you find worked best when doing this drill?"), then athletes will be able to learn the process of developing a new skill.

Strategies for Enhancing Autonomy

- When appropriate, coaches are advised to allow athletes to have a say in how practices are structured. Ways to do this include involving athletes in the decision-making and goal-setting process and incorporating their ideas, interests, and needs into activities that are relevant to their participation. This process provides a sense of ownership over an athlete's goals and will foster self-determined motives.

- Coaches are also encouraged to provide opportunities for athletes to serve as leaders, display responsibility, and experience autonomy, allowing them to feel empowered to take action and exercise control over their actions and behaviors. For example, soccer coaches might arrange players in threes to run at the goal with a single player assigned as the captain. The captain would decide when the final pass was made before there was a shot on goal. The captain's role might be rotated among the players.

- One important role of the coach or trainer is to help athletes set realistic goals. Once set, the coach or trainer should highlight effort and perseverance as the means by which to accomplish these goals. Again, this can be done in one-to-one or team meetings in which the needs of the athletes are discussed and the goals agreed upon between the coach and the athletes in a "contract."

- It is also important that in situations involving external rewards, athletes are helped to interpret such rewards as informational (i.e., resulting from personal mastery and learning) as opposed to controlling and manipulative. Therefore the coach may highlight the importance of effort and skill when trophies are "won" and suggest to athletes who "lose" trophies that they performed according to their own effort and skill, or highlight when they should feel good about their efforts and attribute loss to external, uncontrollable factors.

- Coaches should also be mindful about the use of excessive pressure and guilt-inducing criticism. They are encouraged to communicate in coaching sessions in a way that is questioning and oriented toward athlete or team skills and development rather than focused on external outcomes.

Strategies for Enhancing a Sense of Relatedness

• The onus is on the coach to help athletes develop and maintain positive relationships via their participation in sport practices. Coaches are in a position to provide opportunities for their athletes to hang out, socialize, and network around practices as well as encouraging discussion and cooperation within practices.

• A strong, positive coach–athlete relationship based on caring, trust, and respect is important for the development of a sense of relatedness. Therefore it is important to involve athletes in the decision-making process (e.g., "Let's talk about your goals and aims over the next few practice sessions"), talk to athletes as equals (e.g., "OK, people, let's all put in as much effort as we can in the next practice"), and invoke standards that are optimally challenging (e.g., "I know you can do this task if you put all your effort into it").

• It is important that coaches actively listen to athletes and acknowledge athletes' thoughts and feelings when making decisions. One way they can do this is to use a questioning approach in which they ask athletes to evaluate their own performances.

• Coaches also have a role in involving significant others (e.g., parent, friends) relevant to an athlete and to help them recognize, reinforce, and validate the athlete's participation in sport.

• Again, allowing athletes to have a say in making decisions will enhance athletes' collective sense of ownership in the practices and activities they do and empower them to make decisions about team goals with their peers. A means of doing this is to adopt frequent breakouts in practice to discuss purposes and strategies.

A Self-Determination Theory Approach to Dropout in Athletes

Philippe Sarrazin, PhD, and Julie C.S. Boiché, PhD
Université Joseph Fourier

Luc G. Pelletier, PhD
University of Ottawa

In most Western countries, sport has become an important social phenomenon, and a large number of people today regularly engage in competitive and recreational sport programs. This mass involvement, however, masks a high rate of dropout in the majority of activities. A large number of athletes, and more particularly key groups such as adolescents and girls, cease their sport participation each year. In general, national sport organizations note that the greatest rates of dropout occur between the ages of 12 and 15, leading to a rather low percentage of practice in populations at the beginning of adulthood. Preventing sport dropout is not only of interest to sport organizations and governing bodies but is also a matter of public health, given the multiple benefits of sport on psychological, social, and physical well-being. Several studies show the existence of a positive link between regular physical activity and physical self-perceptions, self-esteem, and social acceptance among youth (see Brustad, Babkes, & Smith, 2001). Apart from these benefits, physical activity also helps to prevent anxiety or depression.

In addition, it is now clearly established that physical activity has a positive impact on several biological functions, and it is a key variable in the prevention of overweight and obesity (e.g., Clark & Blair, 1988). In France, for example, a recent epidemiological study has shown that the proportion of overweight or obese people among adults is increasing, leading to a current incidence rate over 40% (ObÉpi, 2003). On the other hand, recent data reveal that only 30% of French people aged between 15 and 75 years are sufficiently physically

Correspondence concerning this article should be addressed to Philippe Sarrazin, Laboratoire Sport et Environnement Social (SENS), Université Joseph Fourier, Grenoble 1, France. E-mail: philippe.sarrazin@ujf-grenoble.fr active (Ministry for Youth and Sport, 2006). Adults are more likely to be physically active if they practiced sport during their childhood or adolescence (e.g., Perkins, Jacobs, Barber, & Eccles, 2004). Thus, there are many reasons to investigate the causes and process of sport dropout among teenagers and young adults. By distinguishing between several types of reasons to practice sport and the antecedents and consequences of these reasons, self-determination theory offers a particularly fruitful framework for understanding this phenomenon. The purpose of this chapter is to provide a review of studies based on the tenets of self-determination theory that have focused on sport dropout.

A Four-Stage Causal Sequence

Proponents of self-determination theory (e.g., Deci & Ryan, 1985, 2000) propose a four-stage causal sequence behind the motivational processes leading to psychological and behavioral outcomes, which has been formally stated in the hierarchical model of intrinsic and extrinsic motivation (Vallerand, 1997): Social factors → psychological mediators → types of motivations → consequences. As the motivational sequence is discussed in detail elsewhere in this volume (e.g., Hagger & Chatzisarantis; Vallerand; Standage, Gillison, & Treasure), we describe it only briefly here.

Different Types of Sport Motivation According to the Self-Determination Continuum

Self-determination theory considers motivation in terms of the extent to which it is autonomous or emanates from the self. In the domain of sport, seven constructs are distinguished and assessed by the Sport Motivation Scale (SMS; Pelletier et al., 1995; see also Pelletier & Sarrazin, this volume) or its French version (Brière, Vallerand, Blais, & Pelletier, 1995). The highest level of self-determined motivation is represented by the intrinsic motivation construct, which is present when the activity is pursued for its own sake void of external reinforcement. Vallerand and his colleagues (e.g., Pelletier et al., 1995; Vallerand et al., 1992) have proposed a distinction between three types of intrinsic motivation: intrinsic motivation to know (i.e., when one practices sport to learn or to try new things), intrinsic motivation for accomplishment (i.e., when one practices sport to achieve personal goals), and intrinsic motivation to experience stimulation (i.e., when one practices sport to attain pleasant physical sensations).

On the other hand, extrinsic motivation refers to situations in which participation in sport is considered a means to an end. From lower to higher levels of self-determination, three major types of extrinsic motivation have been proposed: *external*, *introjected*, and *identified* regulation. When individuals experience external regulation, they seek to attain desirable consequences for their behavior or avoid negative ones. For example, athletes who participate in their sport in order to gain material or symbolic rewards like trophies, or to avoid criticism from their parents or a coach, can be characterized as externally regulated. With introjected regulation, contingent consequences of sport participation no longer come from the environment, but instead are imposed directly by the individual on him- or herself. Athletes characterized by such a motivation often declare that they practice sport because they would feel bad if they did not. Finally, people who freely choose to engage in a behavior not because they see it as pleasant in itself, but rather to attain personally valued goals, are characterized by identified regulation. An example is an athlete who participates in his or her sport because it is an effective way to meet people or to achieve good physical conditioning. Finally, at the non-self-determined extreme of the continuum of motivation is the construct of amotivation, which refers to the individual's perception of an absence of contingency between actions and outcomes in the environment. Athletes who say they do not really know why they participate in sport are said to be amotivated.

Relationship Between Motivation and Dropout

One postulate of self-determination theory and the hierarchical model of motivation is that the more self-determined a person is, the more likely he or she is to experience positive affective, cognitive, and behavioral consequences. Dropout might be considered a negative behavioral consequence or outcome that is derived from non-self-determined forms of motivation (i.e., external and introjected regulations, as well as amotivation), whereas self-determined forms of motivation (i.e., intrinsic motivation and identified regulation) are supposed to lead to more persistence in behavior. In educational settings, two studies, grounded in the same model, have supported this hypothesized link between motivation and persistence (Vallerand & Bisonnette, 1992; Vallerand, Fortier, & Guay, 1997).

Social Factors as Determinants of Sport Motivation

In sport, as in other contexts, social factors are expected to influence motivation (Deci & Ryan, 1985, 2000; Vallerand, 1997). Coaches' behavior in the sport context seems to be a particularly important influential factor (e.g., Mageau & Vallerand, 2003; Amorose, this volume). Coaches shape the sport setting by designing practice sessions, grouping athletes, giving recognition, evaluating performance, and providing leadership and authority. Coaches establish a "motivational climate" (Ames, 1992), which can have an important impact on athletes' self-determined motivation by nourishing or impeding the satisfaction of basic psychological needs. Indeed, self-determination theory suggests that individuals' social environment is likely to affect the level of self-determined forms of motivation toward an activity through the satisfaction of needs for autonomy, competence, and relatedness.

Review of the Studies

To our knowledge, two studies have adopted the self-determination theory framework to study sport dropout (for a review, see Chatzisarantis, Hagger, Biddle, Smith, & Wang, 2003). In these studies, the previously mentioned four-stage causal sequence was tested, either in part or in full. In particular, three main hypotheses were examined: (1) the impact of the perceived motivational climate engendered by the coach on the athletes' need satisfaction, (2) the influence of need satisfaction on the development of more or less self-determined forms of motivation toward the athlete's sporting activities, which would influence (3) behavioral outcomes such as persistence or dropout of the athlete.

The first study was conducted in Canada (Pelletier, Fortier, Vallerand, Tuson, & Brière, 2001) with 369 competitive swimmers. At the beginning of a season, swimmers filled out a questionnaire about perceived interpersonal behaviors on the part of the coach and motivational orientation toward swimming. Dropout behavior was assessed during the next two seasons. The second study was carried out in France (Sarrazin, Vallerand, Guillet, Pelletier, & Cury, 2002) with 335 adolescent female handballers. At the beginning of a season, the athletes completed a questionnaire assessing handball experience, motivational orientation toward the activity, perceived motivational climate provided by the coach, degree of satisfaction of psychological needs, and future intentions to participate in sport. Twenty-one months later, cases of dropout were identified.

Apart from the type of sport, there were several differences between these two studies. First, the assessments of sport dropout were not identical. In their study, Pelletier and colleagues (2001) considered dropout as a quantitative variable, as they were able to identify dropout at several periods during two seasons and could characterize persistence using a five-point scale. This procedure permitted a precise assessment of persistence and dropout over time. On the other hand, Sarrazin and colleagues (2002) considered dropout as a dichotomous variable; that is, athletes were identified as either having dropped out or continuing their participation at the beginning of the next season. The reasoning behind this dichotomy was that teenagers do not always have the opportunity to cease an activity during the course of a season even if their needs are not being satisfied. Young athletes may consider discontinuing their participation during the season but can be pressured by their parents or the coach to "end what they began," even if they do not continue the following season.

Secondly, a mediating variable between motivation and behavior was added in the study by Sarrazin and colleagues (2002). Indeed, according to the theory of planned behavior (Ajzen & Fishbein, 1980) or the sport commitment model (Scanlan, Simons, Carpenter, Schmidt, & Keeler, 1993), the most proximal predictor of the adoption of a particular behavior is an individual's intention to adopt it. Consequently, motivational orientations were expected to influence the athletes' intentions to drop out from the activity, which in turn were expected to predict dropout behavior (see Chatzisarantis, Biddle, and Meek, 1997, for a review of intentions from a self-determination theory perspective).

A third difference between the two studies was the operationalization of athletes' motivational orientation in the statistical analysis used to test the hypothesized model (for a comprehensive discussion on this topic, see Pelletier & Sarrazin, this volume). In Sarrazin and colleagues' (2002) study, the different motivational constructs were aggregated into a single score, the index of self-determination or relative autonomy index (Vallerand, 1997). Depending on its position on the theoretical continuum of self-determination, the athlete's score for each kind of regulation received a particular weight, leading to a single score for the degree of self-determined motivation experienced by the athlete. Therefore, positive scores on this index indicated high levels of self-determined motivation while negative scores reflected low levels of self-determined motivation, and scores close to zero reflected "undifferentiated" levels of motivation. This index was used as a direct, independent predictor of motivational outcomes. In the study by Pelletier and colleagues (2001), the score obtained by athletes for each kind of motivational orientation was treated separately in order to test for its specific impact on sport dropout or persistence.

A final difference arises from the type of motivational climate engendered by athletes' coaches, which was assessed in both studies. In line with earlier research adopting the self-determination theory framework, Pelletier and colleagues' (2001) study focused on the effects of two interactive styles: a controlling versus an autonomy-supportive style. In essence, autonomy-supportive coaches are responsive (e.g., spend time listening, acknowledge athletes' feelings and perspectives), are supportive (e.g., praise the quality of performances), offer explanations (e.g., provide a rationale for tasks and limits), and provide choice and opportunities for initiative and independent thought. In contrast, controlling coaches essentially take charge (e.g., maintain control over instructional materials, use directives and commands) and motivate through pressure (e.g., threats, criticisms, and compulsion) (Amorose, this volume; Hein & Koka, this volume; Mageau & Vallerand, 2003).

The study by Sarrazin and colleagues (2002), on the other hand, focused on the effects of a task-involving versus ego-involving motivational climate fostered by coaches, based on achievement goal theory (Ames, 1992; Duda & Hall, 2001; Nicholls, 1989). An emphasis on the learning process, investment, progress, and the promotion of cooperation among team members characterizes a task-involving motivational climate. In contrast, an emphasis on competition whereby "winning is everything," mistakes are punished, reinforcement and attention are differentially provided as a function of ability level, and rivalry is promoted among players on the same team exemplifies an ego-involving climate. We should note that there may be considerable overlap between autonomy-supportive environments and task-involving motivational climates, and the behaviors exhibited by coaches using the two approaches may be congruent (as acknowledged by Wang & Biddle, this volume). However, there may be different emphases. For example, an autonomy-supportive environment is most likely to focus on choice and interest, while a task-involving motivational climate more likely focuses on personal improvement of individual skills. This is not to say that either approach would not be relevant to the other setting.

The longitudinal studies on athlete dropout (Pelletier et al., 2001; Sarrazin et al., 2002) are important as they contribute both to theoretical knowledge regarding the processes that underpin sport dropout or persistence and to the design of practical interventions to change motivational styles and the antecedents of dropout in order to maximize persistence and ameliorate dropout. Two important sets of effects are evident from these studies: the pattern of relations between motivational orientations and athlete dropout and persistence and the role of psychosocial antecedents of dropout and persistence such as the motivational climate engendered by the coach and specific autonomy-supportive behaviors demonstrated by the coach.

- *On the interplay between motivation and persistence or dropout.* In both studies, preliminary analyses showed several differences in motivational orientations between athletes who dropped out and those who exhibited persistence. Athletes who dropped out were significantly less intrinsically motivated (both studies), had lower levels of identified regulation (Pelletier et al.'s study), and were more externally regulated and more amotivated (both studies) than athletes who exhibited persistence. Additional analyses using structural equation modeling to test the hypotheses revealed consistency in the results from the two studies. In the study by Sarrazin and colleagues, lower levels of self-determined motivation in athletes significantly predicted their intentions to drop out of the activity, which in turn led to higher rates of actual dropout behaviors (see figure 15.1). In other words, the more self-determined the athletes were, the stronger their intention to pursue their activity and the more likely they were to continue participating. This positive impact of athletes' self-determined motivation was replicated in Pelletier and colleagues' study, which also highlighted the role of each motivational orientation (see figure 15.2). Research adopting self-determination theory to explain dropout in educational contexts has shown that the more self-determined individuals are, the greater their levels of adaptive motivational outcomes (Vallerand & Bisonnette, 1992; Vallerand, Fortier, & Guay, 1997). Indeed, Pelletier and colleagues found that intrinsic motivation and identified regulation significantly predicted persistence at time points 2 and 3. On the other hand, amotivation negatively predicted persistence at both time points. Introjected regulation was a significant positive predictor of persistence only at time point 2, and external regulation a negative predictor of persistence only at time point 3. The positive relationship between introjected regulation and persistence at time point 2 was surprising insofar as it is a non-self-determined type of motivation. Nevertheless, some empirical studies have shown that this particular form of motivation exerts short-term effects on behavior (e.g., Vallerand et al., 1997).

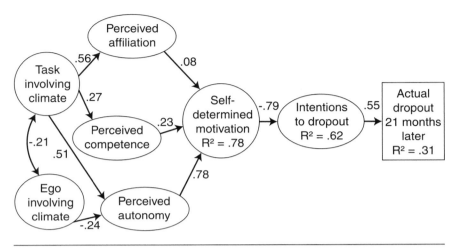

Figure 15.1   Summary of results from Sarrazin and colleagues' (2002) study.

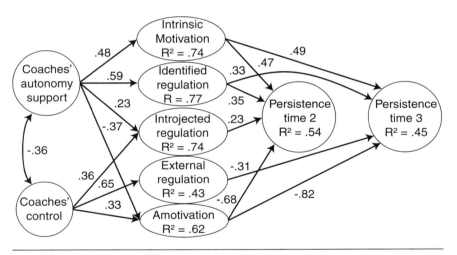

Figure 15.2   Summary of results from Pelletier and colleagues' (2001) study.

• *On the psychosocial antecedents of motivation.* In both studies, athletes' perception of the motivational climate provided by the coach was expected to influence their motivational orientations in keeping with self-determination theory. Indeed, according to cognitive evaluation theory (Deci & Ryan, 1985), individuals' perception of their social environment is presumed to have a more pervasive influence on self-determined forms of motivation than the objective social environment. Both studies used a self-report measure assessing the task-involving versus ego-involving (Sarrazin et al.) or autonomy-supportive versus controlling (Pelletier et al.) nature of the motivational climate fostered by the coach. The two studies showed differences in the perceived motivational climate between athletes who exhibited dropout and those who persevered. Athletes who exhibited dropout perceived their coach to be less autonomy supportive and more controlling (Pelletier et al.) or less task involving and more ego involving (Sarrazin et al.).

Moreover, results of Pelletier and colleagues' study showed that perception of coaches' behavior was related to the different types of motivation (see figure 15.2). More specifically, the relationship between swimmers' perceptions of coaches' autonomy support and a perceived controlling motivational climate was significant but moderately negative. This suggests that perceptions of autonomy support and a perceived controlling climate may not be exact opposites. Perception of autonomy support and the absence of a perceived controlling climate are associated positively with the self-determined types of motivation (i.e., intrinsic motivation and identified regulation), whereas the perception of a controlling climate and the absence of autonomy support are associated with external regulation. These observations support Ryan and Deci's (2000) proposition that the experience of autonomy facilitates internalization and the experience of a controlling climate yields less overall internalization. However, it is also interesting to note that perceptions of autonomy support and a controlling climate are both positively associated with introjected regulation, which suggests that coaches sometimes use components of both types of interpersonal behaviors. The perception of both types of interpersonal behaviors (i.e., autonomy supportive and controlling) seems to capture the essence of introjected regulation, which is "taking in a regulation but not fully accepting it as one's own" (Deci & Ryan, 2000, p. 72). Finally, amotivation, which is defined as a state in which people do not act, or act without intent, or lack the intention to act, is positively associated with perceptions of control and negatively associated with the perception of autonomy support.

Sarrazin and colleagues (2002) extended these results in testing the mediational role played by need satisfaction. Structural equation modeling analyses showed that the impact of the motivational climate on self-determined forms of motivation was mediated by the individual's perceptions of competence, autonomy, and relatedness (see figure 15.1). These three perceptions explained 78% of the variance in self-determined motivation toward handball. In other words, coaches' behavior seemed to influence athletes' motivation through its effects on athletes' perceptions of competence, autonomy, and relatedness. This result was recently corroborated in other studies using varied dimensions of the motivational climate provided by coaches (Gagné, Ryan, & Bargmann, 2003; Hollembeak & Amorose, 2005; Reinboth, Duda, & Ntoumanis, 2004).

In accordance with previous studies (e.g., Vallerand et al., 1997), Sarrazin et al. (2002) found that the most important predictor of self-determined motivation was autonomy, followed by competence and to a lesser extent relatedness. Although Ryan and Deci (2000) state that the satisfaction of all three psychological needs is required to reach optimal adjustment, this result indicates that people assign greater priority to the need for self-determination in the context of sport, while competence and relatedness play more distal roles in the maintenance of self-determined forms of motivation.

Finally, this study (Sarrazin et al., 2002) addressed how task-involving versus ego-involving dimensions of the climate fostered by coaches related to the three psychological needs. The results revealed that the more the handballers perceived the motivational climate as task involving, the more competent they felt. This was the case presumably because this type of motivational climate highlights athletes' progress and effort and thus maximizes opportunities to feel competent. In addition, the more the handballers perceived the motivational climate as task involving, the more related they felt, probably because an important aspect of this type of climate is to emphasize cooperation and to foster an appreciation of team members (Duda & Hall, 2001). Lastly, handballers' perception that a high task-involving and low ego-involving climate pervaded their sessions predicted perceived autonomy. The reason is probably that a task-involving motivational climate facilitates self-determined regulation (Duda & Hall, 2001) and prompts a shift toward a more internal locus of causality. In contrast, when ego involvement is encouraged, perceived autonomy is expected to decrease because the evaluation of one's performance is contingent on external normative criteria (Nicholls, 1989). Therefore, successful outcomes are less perceived as under a person's volitional control (Duda & Hall, 2001), and a shift toward a more external locus of causality is likely. Moreover, in an ego-involving climate, people experience a feeling of pressure to maintain self-esteem, which can undermine perceived autonomy (Deci & Ryan, 2000).

As players' perceptions of the motivational climate engendered by coaches were measured at the same time their need satisfaction was assessed, there was a possibility that (1) handballers' feelings of competence, autonomy, and relatedness were influenced by their perception of their coach; (2) the perceived motivational climate fostered by coaches was influenced by players' needs; or (3) both were influenced by an unmeasured third variable. The role of a coach-established task- or ego-involving climate on *changes* in the satisfaction of the three psychological needs was analyzed elsewhere in another study (Sarrazin, Guillet, & Cury, 2001). The three perceptions were measured by a questionnaire at the beginning and the end of a season in 236 adolescent female handballers. In the middle of the season, perceptions of coaches' motivational climate were also evaluated. Results were in agreement with the study by Sarrazin and colleagues (2002), showing that feelings of competence, autonomy, and relatedness at the end of the season were both predicted by a task-involving motivational climate and negatively predicted by an ego-involving motivational climate after controlling for the level of each variable at the beginning of the season.

Research Perspectives and Future Directions

The results presented in this chapter provide evidence that self-determination theory is a relevant theoretical framework for the study of sport dropout. Nevertheless, research should be carried out in several directions in order to improve understanding of the phenomenon. First, although coaches are obviously highly important in the motivational process, influences from other significant figures should be investigated. For example, studies examining the influence of parents and peers on the satisfaction of basic psychological needs and motivational orientations would improve this line of research.

Second, the dropout literature could be enriched by studies focusing on exploration of the different motivational profiles that exist in the sport context (e.g., Hodge & Petlichkoff, 2000; Wang & Biddle, this volume). Analyses using the self-determination index allow for tests of the impact of a graduated level of self-determined motivation on persistence and dropout. On the other hand, analyses using the individual motivational orientation scales allow one to test the possible additive effects of the various types of regulation on persistence and dropout. Nevertheless, it would be interesting to use cluster analysis to study how the different forms of regulation contribute to the formulation of particular motivational profiles in sport and to assess the relationship of these regulation styles with persistence and dropout. This might permit the identification of groups of athletes "at risk" of dropping out.

Third, the empirical studies presented in this chapter suggest that task-oriented or autonomy-supportive motivational climates are more beneficial than other types of climates for sport persistence because of their positive impact on athletes' self-determined motivation. Nevertheless, it is possible to consider the coach-established climate and athletes' motivation as interactive rather than viewing the former as an antecedent of the latter. Recent experimental research (e.g., Vansteenkiste, Simons, Lens, Sheldon, & Deci, 2004; Vansteenkiste, Soenens, & Lens, this volume) has shown that framing a task in terms of an intrinsic goal and introducing it in an autonomy-supportive way results in the most optimal behavioral outcomes relative to any other combination of goal and context. These experiments have been carried out at the situational level and can be extrapolated to interventions to change autonomous motivational styles at the contextual level (Vallerand, 1997). For example, the diathesis-stress model of achievement processes (Boggiano, 1998) proposes a causal system different from that advanced by self-determination theory and a more complex picture of the role of intrinsic motivation processes. According to this model, coaches' support of autonomy is helpful for all athletes in terms of persistence, while a controlling climate established by a coach should have negative consequences on persistence, but only for players who are extrinsically motivated—not for those who are intrinsically motivated. The self-regulation process could buffer the adverse effects of controlling climates used by coaches because intrinsically motivated individuals rely more on self-initiated and regulated effort whereas extrinsically motivated individuals rely more on external evaluations when faced with difficult conditions (Boggiano, 1998). Therefore, an intrinsic motivational orientation offers a protective effect from controlling motivational climates.

Finally, the model tested in the two studies reviewed here failed to take into account the existence of other relevant contexts in the life of athletes. From an empirical and theoretical point of view, however, it is highly probable that the degree of conflict between sport and other interests in the athlete's life is likely to have an impact on his or her decision to pursue or discontinue sport participation. This "conflict of interest" hypothesis was found to be an important reason for sport dropout among teenagers in some descriptive studies (e.g., Lindner, Johns, & Butcher, 1991). However, since the authors used a retrospective design, conflict between sport and other activities was not established as a predictor of dropout over time. Moreover, this assumption was not formulated on the basis of any theoretical framework. Recent developments in self-determination theory suggest a possible role for the concept of conflict. Indeed, the concept of internalization of a behavior refers to an evolution of the individual's regulation that leads to its integration into his or her life and that is in harmony with his or her goals and values (Ryan & Deci, 2002). Similarly, Vallerand (1997) proposed that, depending on the level of self-determined motivational orientation reported by an individual, the relationship between sport and other interests can take the form of conflict or compensation.

These arguments lead us directly to the formulation of a hypothesis linking athlete's self-determination toward different life domains, including sport, with salient behavioral outcomes such as sport participation. On the basis of a recent study in an academic context (Sénécal, Julien, & Guay, 2003), it is proposed that conflict between sport and other life areas from which the athletes cannot necessarily disengage may lead them to cease their sport participation. These other life domains may differ depending on the person's age and life stage; the older an athlete, the more differentiated his or her life areas become, as has been shown in previous research (Hagger, Biddle, and Wang, 2005). Teenagers are a group that is more "at risk" for sport dropout in this respect, and therefore efforts should be focused on preempting and preventing dropout from sport among adolescents in order to promote future generations of physically active adults. For this age group, areas to take into consideration should be school and peer relationships, given that school, sport, and friendship have been shown to be three relevant domains through which teenagers perceive and define themselves (Harter, 1985).

Conclusion and Practical Implications

The results presented in this chapter have at least two important practical implications for the issue of dropout in athletes. First, self-determined motivation is a key variable to consider in any attempt to predict, prevent, or reverse sport dropout. The results discussed here show that low levels of self-determined forms of motivation (intrinsic motivation, identified regulation, or both), as well as a high amount of external regulation or amotivation, predicted dropout in athletes. Consequently, self-determined motivation should be nurtured in order to facilitate athletes' persistence in sport.

A second implication is that the social context—more precisely, the motivational climate fostered by coaches—plays a fundamental role in the process. Results of these studies have shown that a motivational climate that supports satisfaction of the needs for autonomy, competence, and relatedness will foster self-determined motivation and, in turn, promote perseverance in sport. By contrast, when any of these psychological needs is frustrated or blocked, non-self-determined forms of motivation and diminished sport involvement are the outcomes. The studies presented here focused on two types of motivational climate engendered by coaches. Compared to a controlling context, an autonomy-supportive context represents an important determinant that can affect the level of athletes' self-determined motivation. Pelletier and colleagues (2001) showed that when coaches are autonomy supportive and less controlling, players are more likely to report high levels of self-determined forms of motivation.

On the other hand, Sarrazin and colleagues (2002) showed that when the motivational climate instilled by the coach was ego involving, perceptions of autonomous and self-determined forms of motivation decreased. When the climate was task involving, perceptions of autonomy, competence, and relatedness and in turn self-determined motivation were enhanced. A task-involving climate maximizes opportunities for athletes to feel competent, autonomous, and connected with one another. By contrast, because an ego-involving climate focuses individuals on normative criteria (e.g., current ability level, overconcern about mistakes, within-team rivalries), it undermines perceptions of competence, autonomy, and relatedness.

Practical Considerations to Minimize Dropout From Sport

- Given the links between athletes' intrinsic motivation and identified regulation and perceived autonomy support, coaches are encouraged to avoid controlling practices and to foster a task-involving climate. Coaches should therefore be instructed to provide practices and tasks that highlight the value of sport outcomes. They can do this, for example, by providing a varied practice routine with many different components to maintain interest (e.g., different warm-up exercises, varied drills, core fitness work, skill development training, scaled-down practice games, altered scoring practices such as awarding points for the number of passes completed

(continued)

[hockey, soccer] or the number of steals [basketball]). They can also do this by using noncontrolling language (avoiding "shoulds" and "musts"), providing performers with a say in decision making (e.g., "What would be the best practice to do to improve your agility?"), adopting a questioning approach with respect to why athletes do certain practices (e.g., "Why was I suggesting that you fall back when the opponents were attacking in that drill?").

• Autonomy support also occurs when a coach takes the athlete's perspective, provides choice, reflects the athlete's feelings, and encourages the athlete's initiative. It is suggested that coaches provide an environment in which athletes can chart their personal progress (e.g., "How did you do compared to your previous effort?"), acknowledge sustained efforts (e.g., "Excellent effort! Did it feel good to try so hard to improve your best?"), and highlight to athletes that all team members have an important role (e.g., "Each one of you has a job to do in this team, and if you all try hard to stick to your job then you are likely to improve your best team performance").

• A controlling motivational climate occurs when a coach pressures athletes to perform up to external standards or uses rewards and constraints to manipulate athletes' behavior. Coaches are therefore encouraged to avoid focusing on ability level, criticizing mistakes and errors, and setting up rivalries as opposed to cooperation among team members. These behaviors are more likely to undermine self-determined forms of motivation in athletes. Thus coaches are advised to avoid the use of such external contingencies when presenting practices and plays to athletes.

Self-Determination Theory and Well-Being in Athletes

It's the Situation That Counts

Marylène Gagné, PhD
Concordia University

Céline Blanchard, PhD
Department of Psychology, University of Ottawa

In this chapter, we review research supporting the assertion of self-determination theory that feeling competent, autonomous, and related positively influences well-being in the context of practicing sport. We first review the definition and operationalization of well-being according to self-determination theory and compare this with the most frequently used operationalizations of well-being in sport psychology. We then review research on the antecedents of well-being in sport and evaluate it according to self-determination theory. This section includes discussion of factors such as goal orientations, interest and enjoyment, good sporting behavior, coping styles, coach behavior, team cohesion and support, and mastery. We then examine a new trend in sport psychology research: the use of diary studies. We outline the advantages of such methodology for addressing some unanswered issues in the sport domain, present a contemporary diary study, and discuss how it has helped uncover the dynamic interplay between personal and contextual influences on athletes' motivation and well-being according to self-determination theory. Finally, we offer some practical implications emerging from the work reviewed for the practice of sports and the coaching of athletes.

Correspondence concerning this article should be addressed to Marylène Gagné, Department of Management, John Molson School of Business, Concordia University, 1455 de Maisonneuve Blvd. Ouest, Montreal, Quebec H3G 1M8, Canada. E-mail: mgagne@jmsb.concordia.ca

Well-Being According to Self-Determination Theory

Ryan and Deci (2001) distinguish between hedonic and eudaemonic well-being. Hedonic well-being refers to happiness, pleasure, and positive affect, whereas eudaemonic well-being refers to the actualization of human potential, or the realization of one's true nature. The central difference between these views of well-being is that the former is based simply on the satisfaction of any type of desire, whereas the latter is based on the satisfaction of needs that are essential for human functioning and growth. Self-determination theory therefore defines well-being as "optimal functioning and experience" (Ryan & Deci, 2001, p. 142).

Self-determination theory argues that psychological well-being is derived from need satisfaction. Needs are defined as "innate psychological nutriments that are essential for ongoing psychological growth, integrity, and well-being" (Deci & Ryan, 2000, p. 229). Self-determination theory identifies three fundamental needs: autonomy, competence, and relatedness. Thus, the very definition of a need involves its influence on well-being. A need is considered basic and necessary since the thwarting or neglect of the need leads to maladaptive consequences such as the halting of development and decreases in psychological or physical well-being (or both).

The advantage of such theorizing is that knowing what to satisfy allows for the prediction of environmental factors that will affect well-being in specific contexts. Factors that influence the satisfaction of these needs, such as coaching behavior, will, in effect, increase or decrease well-being. Why does need satisfaction lead to changes in well-being? The reason is that the satisfaction of these needs influences organismic processes such as intrinsic motivation and the internalization of extrinsic motivation. These processes are strong influences on psychological development. Intrinsic motivation not only requires that needs be satisfied, but also requires an element of novelty or optimal challenge and is often indicated by an increase in interest or involvement in tasks and activities (Deci & Ryan, 2000). It is thus important to foster intrinsic motivation in order to foster well-being and growth. What better domain than sport for illustrating and fostering intrinsic motivation!

Ryff and her colleagues (Ryff & Singer, 1998, 2000; Ryff & Keyes, 1995) propose a definition of well-being that is worth noting and is somewhat in line with the one proposed by Deci and Ryan (2000). They present a multidimensional approach to the measurement of well-being. Specifically, this definition includes the dimensions of autonomy, personal growth, self-acceptance, life purpose, mastery, and positive relatedness. According to Ryff and colleagues, individuals are bound to report subjective well-being if they score high on these dimensions. We will limit our review to the definition and measurement of well-being in the sport and athletic domain.

Well-Being in Sport

In sport psychology, well-being has been assessed most often through the following operationalizations: self-esteem (level, stability, and contingency), feelings of guilt and shame, mood, anxiety (trait and state), happiness, satisfaction with the sport (based on the measure of life satisfaction in Diener, Emmons, Lausen, & Griffin, 1985), subjective vitality, and physical symptoms. Some measures of well-being have been designed specifically for use with athletes. These include (a) the Subjective Exercise Experience Scale (McAuley & Courneya, 1994), which measures positive well-being, psychological distress, and fatigue; (b) the Athlete Stress Inventory, which includes negative mood, team compatibility, physical well-being, and academic self-efficacy dimensions (Seggar, Pedersen, Hawkes, & McGown, 1997); (c) the Intrinsic Satisfaction with Sport Scale (Duda & Nicholls, 1992); (d) the Athlete Burnout Measure (Raedeke & Smith, 2001); (e) and the Exercise-Induced Feelings Inventory (Gauvin & Rejeski, 1993), which includes dimensions of positive engagement, revitalization, tranquility, and physical exhaustion. A closer look at the research conducted within sport psychology reveals much overlap in the definitions and operationalizations of well-being used within this domain, and operationalizations include components of both hedonic and eudaemonic well-being.

There is also considerable overlap in the well-being measures used in the sport domain and in self-determination research in other domains. The most frequent operationalizations of well-being in self-determination research in other domains have been positive and negative affect, subjective vitality, anxiety, depressive symptoms, self-actualization, and psychosomatic symptoms (see Ryan & Deci, 2001, for a review). The operationalizations of well-being used in self-determination theory research are in keeping with the definition of eudaemonia, as most of them represent manifestations of well-being based on growth and development.

Self-Determination and Well-Being in Sport

Several authors posit that self-determined motivation plays a crucial role in the well-being of individuals (Deci & Ryan, 2002; Ryan & Deci, 2001; Vallerand, 1997; Vallerand & Losier, 1999). Results from studies conducted in domains such as health, work, and therapy provide support for this hypothesis. In addition, some interesting research findings provide evidence for such a relationship in the sport domain. What follows is a review of the self-determination literature and research pertaining to the link between self-determined motivation and well-being. The studies are in line with both hedonic and eudaemonic definitions of well-being. The first series of studies provided evidence for the link between self-determined motivation and indices of well-being. Most of the studies discussed in this first section were cross-sectional, and most involved bivariate correlations between self-determined motivation and well-being. A second series of studies presented findings linking motivational antecedents (social and intrapersonal factors), mediating variables, motivation, and well-being. Models tested using correlational designs or longitudinal designs have been reported in this literature.

At this juncture, a few studies have shown that participating in sport for more autonomous reasons leads to more adaptive outcomes like psychological well-being. At least two studies have shown that self-determined motivation leads to higher levels of well-being. For instance, Frederick and Ryan (1993) showed that participants who reported participation in sport for reasons of interest and enjoyment exhibited significant associations with perceived satisfaction and competence, whereas self-reported reasons related to appearance and body image were positively associated with anxiety and depression. The positive relationship between self-determined motivation and well-being was further supported in a study by Brière and colleagues (Brière, Vallerand, Blais, & Pelletier, 1995). In the validation studies for the French version of the Sport Motivation Scale, it was found that the three types of intrinsic motivation (stimulation, accomplishment, and knowledge; Vallerand, 1997) and identified regulation correlated with positive affect, enjoyment, and satisfaction. In contrast, external regulation and amotivation were positively related to anxiety, often associated with lower levels of psychological well-being.

Researchers have also attempted to link self-determination to sporting behavior orientations that may have knock-on effects for psychological well-being. Good sporting behavior refers to "concern and respect for the rules and officials, social conventions, the opponent, as well as one's full commitment to one's sport and the relative absence of a negative approach to sport" (Vallerand, Brière, Blanchard, & Provencher, 1997, p. 198). Good sporting behavior is a dimension of sport participation that taps into some of the aspects of positive relatedness, one of the six dimensions of well-being proposed by Ryff and Keyes (1995). Positive relatedness refers globally to satisfying relationships, concern about the welfare of others, and strong empathy. This is interesting because good sporting behavior could be viewed as a measure of interpersonal adjustment, which, according to Ryff, is an essential component of subjective well-being. Results from a few studies provide support for the link between self-determined motivation and athletes' interpersonal orientation in sport. For instance, a study by Vallerand and Losier (1994) showed that self-determined motivation was positively linked to good sporting behavior. Recently, Chantal and Bernache-Assollant (2003), using a powerful cross-lagged panel design, tested this relationship further and showed that self-determined motivation leads to good sporting behavior with no reciprocal relationship. This sets this indicator of psychological well-being aside as an outcome rather than an antecedent of self-determined motivation.

Another area of inquiry that appears to be gaining some ground pertains to coping strategies, and these coping strategies have clear links with outcome variables such as psychological well-being. Traditionally, coping strategies were categorized according to two dimensions: problem-focused strategies (or task oriented) and emotion-focused strategies. *Problem-focused strategies* aim at doing something concrete in altering or changing the source of a stress. The *emotion-focused* dimension implies that strategies are used to reinterpret the meaning of a stressful situation and regulate negative emotions arising from that situation (Lazarus & Folkman, 1984). These two dimensions of coping are often combined under a higher-order coping dimension that promotes psychological adjustment, since both may be helpful when one is faced with a stressful situation. According to Skinner, Edge, Altman, and Sherwood (2003), constructive engagement with stressors yields coping styles that are organized, flexible, and constructive and likely to have a positive influence on psychological well-being. Yet another coping dimension, *disengagement-oriented coping* (Endler & Parker, 1994), refers to strategies that are employed in order to disengage oneself from the task and to focus on task-irrelevant cues.

Two recent studies have addressed the impact of motivational styles from self-determination theory on coping and, in turn, the impact of coping on goal attainment, affect, and well-being before and after a competition. Specifically, Amiot and her collaborators (Amiot, Gaudreau, & Blanchard, 2004) showed that self-determined motivation was positively associated with the use of task-oriented coping strategies during a competition, whereas non-self-determined motivation positively predicted the use of disengagement-oriented coping. Coping was also found to be associated with goal attainment, with task-oriented coping positively predicting goal attainment during the competition and disengagement-oriented coping negatively predicting goal attainment. Finally, goal attainment positively predicted an increase in positive emotions, a conceptually related component of well-being, from precompetition to post-competition and negatively predicted an increase in negative emotions from pre- to postcompetition (see also Gaudreau, 2005, for similar results). These findings are important because they provide valuable tools to help athletes improve their performance and also become emotionally mature via the use of efficacious coping strategies.

Another relevant line of research has emerged from the hierarchical model of intrinsic and extrinsic motivation (Vallerand, 1997). Here, researchers have attempted to better grasp the link between self-determination and well-being by testing the role of relevant social antecedents. As cognitive evaluation theory suggests, environmental factors may foster, and in some contexts hinder, psychological need satisfaction and in turn well-being. Therefore, the investigation of such factors is necessary to provide a better understanding of the effects of motivation on well-being in sport contexts. A review of the literature reveals two factors that seem to have been the focus of research in this area, notably motivational climate and interpersonal approaches. Again, the research attempting to link social factors and self-determination is vast, but research that actually includes the impact of these factors and self-determination theory variables on well-being in a sport context is relatively limited.

Kowal and Fortier (2000) examined the link between the three basic psychological needs of competence, relatedness, and autonomy, and situational motivation in swimmers on the experience of a "flow state" (see Fortier & Kowal, this volume). According to Csikszentmihalyi (1990), flow is a positive psychological state akin to subjective psychological well-being. Globally, Kowal and Fortier's findings revealed that the three basic psychological needs were good predictors of situational motivation and, in turn, that situational motivation predicted flow. In addition, some studies have been conducted in order to link motivational climate to self-determination, as well as linking self-determination to well-being. In a recent meta-analysis, Ntoumanis and Biddle (1999) examined the effects of task involvement and ego involvement in sport on affective responses, finding that being task oriented when practicing a sport was related to experiencing higher positive affect following exercise. The authors argued that this is the case because task-oriented people are likely to be more intrinsically motivated and have a heightened sense of control, which may lead them to experience greater well-being. In a second meta-analysis, Ntoumanis and Biddle (1998) examined whether climates that foster task orientation versus ego orientation also influenced well-being. They found that a task-oriented climate was positively related to positive affect and intrinsic motivation and negatively related to feelings of worry, whereas an ego-oriented climate was negatively related to positive affect and intrinsic motivation and positively related to feelings of worry.

Other researchers have attempted to link the coaching approach to the three basic psychological needs, motivation, and well-being consequences. According to self-determination theory, social climates are best represented by controlling and informational aspects. One recent study provides some support for the role of the interpersonal approach of the coach, its influence on the three basic psychological needs, self-determination, and, in turn, positive emotions and satisfaction with the sport (Blanchard, Amiot, Vallerand, & Provencher, 2005). Globally, results from this study show that a controlling interpersonal style, in which the coach makes the majority of the decisions and offers very few opportunities for athletes to participate in the planning related to their sport participation, tends to thwart the basic need for autonomy. Results further show that the three basic needs are important predictors of self-determined motivation in sport, ensuring greater levels of well-being. Interestingly, this study provides support for another antecedent of self-determined motivation, notably team cohesion. Team cohesion is viewed as a process whereby a group "sticks together" in order to attain their instrumental or emotional objectives (Carron, Brawley, & Widmeyer, 1990). Findings show that team cohesion is a strong predictor of all three needs, most importantly the basic need for relatedness. Finally, Reinboth, Duda, and Ntoumanis (2004) reported some very interesting results in their study showing that perceived autonomy support from the coach was linked to the need for autonomy, that the perceived focus of the coach on mastery and improvement was associated with the need for competence, and that the athletes' perceptions of social support were linked to the need for relatedness. In turn, the need for competence predicted intrinsic motivation, subjective vitality (another component of well-being), and fewer physical symptoms. The need for autonomy predicted intrinsic motivation and subjective vitality.

To sum up, the research presented illustrates that the tenets of self-determination theory have helped us to better understand the antecedents of and processes that lead to psychological well-being in sport contexts, including variables that are considered components of well-being (e.g., vitality, positive affect). This research shows that higher levels of self-determined motivation are linked to well-being in sport. In addition, the research shows that environmental factors such as motivational climate and interpersonal approaches, as well as mediators like psychological needs and coping, are useful for tapping into the processes underlying the relationship between self-determination and well-being. Finally, the theory provides indispensable guidelines for testing models, especially mediational models that examine the processes or mechanisms by which self-determined forms of motivation influence well-being. Such models are extremely helpful for applied and intervention efforts. It should be noted, however, that most of the research just discussed is cross-sectional in design. Research in this field would benefit from designs that require the assessment of motivation and well-being at multiple time points. A recent study conducted by Gagné, Ryan, and Bargmann (2003) that adopted a diary method represents a step in that direction.

Diary Studies

What psychological processes are most important for the maintenance of an athlete's day-to-day well-being when he or she practices a sport? Traditional designs, such as cross-sectional correlational studies that use surveys or experimental studies that measure well-being once or twice, can only partially address this question. Analyses are mostly at the level of the person, such that one simply compares people who are exposed to different environments or conditions. At best, some repeated measurements can give some information about changes over time, but these are usually limited to two or, at best, three assessments. Moreover, these methods require that participants recall how they felt during many practice sessions and "average" these feelings over a period of time (e.g., in the past month).

Diary studies allow for the collection of daily information from individuals who practice a particular sport. Diary studies involve asking respondents, in this case athletes, to report on their experiences each time they practice their sport during a given period (often about four weeks). It is also possible to use "experiential" sampling procedures whereby athletes are paged at random times during the day to report on how they are feeling at that moment (see Gauvin & Szabo, 1992). These methods allow researchers to immediately capture what the person is experiencing and how the person is reacting to these experiences each time the person engages in a sport activity. They also permit the examination of development of certain attitudes or the prediction of future behaviors from previous specific events. Data are often analyzed using hierarchical linear modeling (Bryk & Raudenbush, 1992), which allows for the simultaneous testing of both within- and between-person variations in a dependent variable as a function of an independent variable. Daily experiences potentially have a huge effect on the motivation for practicing a sport and on the effects that this practice can have on well-being.

Gagné, Ryan, and Bargmann (2003) conducted a diary study with 33 gymnasts, aged 7 to 18 years. The gymnasts completed a diary before and after each practice for four weeks, for a total of 15 practice sessions. The diary completed before each practice contained a measure of the gymnasts' reasons for coming to practice that day as an indicator of their motivation, as well as baseline measures of well-being comprising indices of self-esteem, positive and negative affect, and vitality. After each practice, the gymnasts completed a second diary that contained measures of need satisfaction and the same measures of well-being. Need satisfaction was measured as autonomy support from the coaches, relatedness to teammates, and feelings of competence and mastery during the practice of gymnastics that day. The authors conducted person-level analyses by aggregating the data across the 15 practice sessions for each gymnast, as well as practice-level analyses using hierarchical level modeling. At the person level, autonomous motivation for coming to practice and need satisfaction during practice were both positively related to well-being both before and after practice. However, very few significant correlations were found between motivation and need satisfaction on the one hand and change in well-being from pre- to postpractice on the other. The disadvantage of this method of analysis is that by aggregating across practices, one loses the variation of motivation and need satisfaction that could affect variations in well-being; in other words, we do not know if daily well-being fluctuates with daily variations in motivation and need satisfaction. Using hierarchical-level modeling, the authors found that incoming well-being was influenced by the gymnasts' motivation for coming to practice, but that changes in well-being from pre- to postpractice were not. Instead, they found that need satisfaction was the sole predictor of changes in well-being during practice. Thus, it was not why the gymnasts came to practice that affected their postpractice well-being, but what happened during practice, in terms of their interactions with coaches and teammates and also in terms of how well they performed during practice.

It is important to note that these effects would not have been found with traditional research designs. Few studies acknowledge the influence of within-person variations in the independent predictors in models predicting independent outcome variables based on self-determination theory. Much of the research confines itself to between-person analyses, which examine linear changes in dependent variables based on means. Between-person analyses tell the researcher nothing about whether these levels fluctuated together during practices. In Gagné and colleagues' study, levels of affect, vitality, and esteem were averaged across days of the diary study and found to be related to average levels of motivation coming into practice. However, such traditional multiple regression approaches are not appropriate because such analyses miss valuable within-participant variations, there are too few cases, and conducting linear regression using daily observations is inappropriate because the observations are not independent of each other. The appropriate analysis was therefore hierarchical linear modeling. This has the advantage of treating within-person variations in a given construct as a random effect in a regression model with between-participant effects. This meant that the effects of predictors at different levels of the independent variables such as practice (pre- and post-) could be tested on the dependent variable (well-being). It also meant that the effect of incoming well-being was influenced by the gymnasts' motivation for coming to practice but that changes in well-being from pre- to postpractice were not. This finding was not apparent from analyses that aggregated the variables across practice level.

Future Directions

Overall, studies that have addressed the link between self-determination theory and psychological well-being in athletes have shown that higher levels of self-determination do lead to more positive affect, satisfaction, vitality, and good sporting behavior. Lower levels of self-determination lead to anxiety and depression. It does appear, however, that more research is needed to better capture the links between self-determined motivation and broader definitions of well-being, more specifically eudaemonia.

The present review of the literature reveals that research in self-determination and well-being would benefit from the measurement of both the hedonic and eudaemonic dimensions of well-being. As suggested by Ryan and Deci (2001), "[T]he most interesting results may be those that highlight the factors leading to divergence rather than just convergences in the hedonic and eudaemonic indicators of well-being" (p. 148). Research pertaining to the role of self-determination in sport and athletes' identity, self-actualization, and growth is recommended. The multidimensional assessment of well-being proposed by Ryff and Keyes (1995) could certainly provide some valuable insights into the well-being of athletes.

As well, we identified only one study indicating a link between self-determination and physical symptoms, notably the study by Reinboth and colleagues (2004). The physical health of young athletes and the link between self-determination and injuries in the sport domain could represent an interesting line of research. Furthermore, the use of new methodologies, such as diary studies and "experiential" sampling procedures, combined with powerful new statistical techniques, will allow us to better understand the proximal factors that influence the development of motivation and the maintenance of well-being in athletes.

Implications for Coaching

Our review revealed that the way athletes approach their sport significantly influences their well-being. Being motivated in a self-determined manner promotes an orientation toward good sporting behavior, which implies a concern and respect for rules and for others; positive coping strategies; a task orientation that focuses the athlete on mastery; and the experience of flow. Interpersonal interactions with coaches and teammates play a crucial role in fostering self-determination. Gagné and colleagues' (2003) diary study suggests that daily experiences during the practice of a sport are very important. In particular, the satisfaction of basic psychological needs for competence, autonomy, and relatedness is crucial to maintain or increase athletes' well-being. The way to satisfy psychological needs is through the provision of choice (fostering autonomy), through the promotion of interactions between athletes and their coaches and teammates (supporting relatedness), and through the mastery of one's sport (intensifying the sense of competence). So it is important to pay attention to the way training sessions are presented and conducted, as well as the interactions that take place. Coaches must pay attention to how they interact with their athletes, must be autonomy supportive, and must provide constructive feedback on performance (see Hein & Koka, this volume). In the case of young athletes, parents are also likely to have an impact on their child's psychological need satisfaction with respect to a sport through their involvement and support. Finally, fostering a supportive and stimulating team climate also has an impact on need satisfaction and ultimately on well-being. The diary study shows that need satisfaction is a proximal factor influencing well-being. Initial motivation for practicing a sport seems to be a more distal factor influencing well-being relative to what actually happens during practice. Based on these conclusions, "Recommendations for Practitioners to Enhance Well-Being Through Self-Determined Motivation" outlines a series of recommendations for practitioners involved in motivating athletes and sport performers.

What happens during sport practice and training can also have implications for persistence and performance. Evidence suggests that the immediate environment or motivational climate that prevails during sport practice and training is what counts the most in terms of promoting well-being, and we believe that it can also have long-term effects on the development of motivation and persistence at the sport.

As Krane, Greenleaf, and Snow (1997) stated in their case study of an elite gymnast, "[W]hen the athletic environments stress public evaluation, normative feedback, outcome-focused goals, and interpersonal competence, athletes are likely to develop an ego-involved orientation" (p. 58). We would add that such an environment is likely to foster a controlling, nonautonomous motivational style as opposed to an autonomous one, leading to a reduction in well-being.

Recommendations for Practitioners to Enhance Well-Being Through Self-Determined Motivation

- Practitioners such as sport coaches, trainers, and managers are encouraged to use a participative approach. By offering choice and involving athletes in decision-making, coaches will foster a sense of competence and satisfaction, which is linked to positive affect. For example, a coach can provide practices in which athletes work cooperatively on a skill and then evaluate within their groups which aspects were successful. This approach requires skillful setup but once under way necessitates little intervention from the coach other than some directive questioning. The coach can observe the proceedings and judge, from the level of enthusiasm, discussion, and laughter over trial-and-error approaches, the link between a participative approach and positive affect.

- It is also important to use strategies that enhance team cohesion and cooperation. Practitioners should encourage teammates to interact in a constructive manner and offer encouragement and feedback to each other. One way of doing this is to provide practices in which athletes take turns acting as an observer and then provide feedback to their partner after swapping roles.

- A focus on fostering athletes' mastery of sport-related skills, as opposed to demonstrating competence through performance, is recommended. Coaches are encouraged to help their athletes view success in terms of personal goals like mastering relevant skills. For example, it is suggested that coaches highlight the skills necessary for a successful performance and explicitly make the link between the effort and application needed and success in skill completion, with performance as an adjunct outcome.

(continued)

(continued)

- Coaches are advised to view sports as an athlete's opportunity for growth and development, which implies setting long-term goals that are personally relevant, are agreed upon between the coach and the athlete, and have measurable outcomes in terms of effort and application. In doing so, the coach is likely to provide a forum in which athletes identify sport as a means to demonstrate competence and maintain their sense of well-being.

A Hierarchical Model of Intrinsic and Extrinsic Motivation for Sport and Physical Activity

Robert J. Vallerand, PhD
Université du Québec à Montréal

An athlete is much more than a sport participant. He or she is a person with a distinct personality, involved in a variety of contexts including sport, education, and relationships, who may act differently depending on the situation and context. Therefore, he or she may experience different types of outcomes, some of which may eventually become enduring. It is believed that motivation is in a prime position to help us understand such behaviors and outcomes. Indeed, much research in intrinsic and extrinsic motivation has shown that motivation can vary as a function of social and personal factors and that it can influence several types of outcomes (see Deci & Ryan, 2000; Vallerand, 1997, 2001).

Vallerand and coworkers (1997, Vallerand, 2001; Vallerand & Perreault, 1999; Vallerand & Ratelle, 2002) proposed the hierarchical model of intrinsic and extrinsic motivation (HMIEM) with the aim of integrating past intrinsic and extrinsic motivation research as well as leading to novel and testable hypotheses to orient future research on intrinsic and extrinsic motivation. This model addresses the multiple ways to represent motivation in individuals, the structure and functions of these different representations, and their determinants and consequences. As we shall see, the model embraces several of the elements of self-determination theory (Deci & Ryan, 2000).

The purpose of this chapter is to briefly present the HMIEM and a selection of recent studies derived from the model that were conducted mainly in sport and physical activity settings. The first section is devoted to this task. A second section deals with integrative studies that have focused on an integrated

Correspondence concerning this article should be addressed to Robert J. Vallerand, Laboratoire de recherche sur le comportement social, Université du Québec à Montréal, Box 8888, Succursale Centre-Ville, Montréal (Québec), Canada, H3C 3P8. E-mail: vallerand.robert_j@uqam.ca motivational sequence as well as on motivation at more than one level of generality. This is followed by a section on future research. The chapter ends with some practical implications and concluding comments.

The Hierarchical Model of Intrinsic and Extrinsic Motivation

The HMIEM (Vallerand, 1997, 2001, in press; Vallerand & Ratelle, 2002) posits five postulates dealing with the structure, determinants, and consequences of intrinsic and extrinsic motivation and of amotivation (see figure 17.1 and table 17.1 for each postulate and related corollaries). The following sections present these postulates with the associated empirical evidence.

Postulate 1

A complete analysis of motivation must include intrinsic motivation, extrinsic motivation, and amotivation.

In line with self-determination theory (Deci & Ryan, 1985, 1991, 2000; Ryan & Deci, this volume) and much research on motivation (see Vallerand, 1997, 2001, in press), the first postulate posits that in order to provide a complete analysis of motivational processes, three important constructs must be considered: intrinsic motivation, extrinsic motivation, and amotivation. The importance of clearly distinguishing all three concepts is supported by (1) their ability to explain a considerable range of human behaviors, (2) their capacity to represent essential aspects of human experience, and (3) the variety of important consequences they engender.

Intrinsic Motivation

Intrinsic motivation (IM) implies engaging in an activity for the pleasure and satisfaction inherent in the activity (e.g., Deci, 1975; Deci & Ryan, 1985). A basketball player who practices a new move because he or she enjoys it is said to be intrinsically motivated. Although the majority of researchers advocate a unitary IM construct, Vallerand and his colleagues (1989, 1992, 1993) have suggested a tripartite taxonomy of IM. First, *IM to know* implies engaging in activities because of the pleasure and satisfaction derived from learning, exploring, and understanding new things. Second, *IM to accomplish things* refers to engaging in activities because of the pleasure and satisfaction derived from *trying* to surpass oneself, to create, or to accomplish something. Third, *IM to experience stimulation* operates when one is engaged in an activity because of the stimulating sensations associated with it. Research in education (e.g., Fairchild, Horst, Finney, & Barron, 2005; Vallerand et al., 1989, 1992, 1993) and sport and exercise (e.g., Hein, Müür, & Koka, 2004) provides support for the tripartite conceptualization of IM.

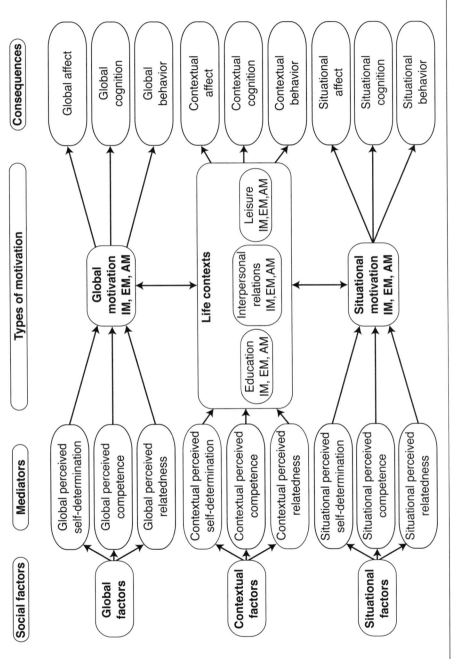

Figure 17.1 Reprinted, by permission, from R.J. Vallerand, 2001, A hierarchical model of intrinsic and extrinsic motivation in sport and exercise. In *Advances in motivation in sport and exercise*, edited by G.C. Roberts (Champaign, IL: Human Kinetics), 263-319.

Table 17.1　Postulates and Corollaries of the Hierarchical Model of Intrinsic and Extrinsic Motivation

Postulate 1	A complete analysis of motivation must include intrinsic motivation, extrinsic motivation, and amotivation.
Postulate 2	Intrinsic and extrinsic motivation exist at three levels of generality: the global, contextual, and situational levels.
Postulate 3	Motivation is determined by social factors and top-down effects from motivation at the proximal level higher up in the hierarchy.
Corollary 3.1	Motivation can result from social factors that are either global, contextual, or situational depending on the level of generality.
Corollary 3.2	The impact of social factors on motivation is mediated by perceptions of competence, autonomy, and relatedness.
Corollary 3.3	Motivation results from top-down effects from motivation at the proximal level higher up in the hierarchy.
Postulate 4	There is a recursive bottom-up relationship between motivation at a given level and motivation at the next-higher level in the hierarchy.
Postulate 5	Motivation leads to important consequences.
Corollary 5.1	Consequences are decreasingly positive from intrinsic motivation to amotivation.
Corollary 5.2	Motivational consequences exist at the three levels of the hierarchy, and the degree of generality of the consequences depends on the level of the motivation that has produced them.

Extrinsic Motivation

Extrinsic motivation (EM) refers to engaging in an activity as a means to an end and not for its own sake. There are at least four different types of EM, some of which are more self-determined than others (Deci & Ryan, 1985, 1991, 2000; Ryan, Connell, & Grolnick, 1992). In other words, individuals may *choose* to perform an activity even though they do not do it for pleasure. External regulation refers to behavior that is regulated through external means, such as rewards and constraints. For instance, an athlete might say, "I'm going to today's practice because I want the coach to let me play tomorrow." With introjected regulation, individuals begin to internalize the reasons for their actions. However, this type of EM is not self-determined because individuals still experience pressure, although this time the pressure is self-imposed (e.g., through guilt and anxiety). An example of someone with introjected regulation is the athlete who goes to a practice because he or she would feel guilty about missing it. It is only with identified regulation that behavior is conducted out of choice. When athletes display identified regulation, they highly value an activity, judge it to be important, and engage in it out of choice. The activity is then performed freely even if it is not pleasant in itself. An example of someone with identified regulation is the basketball player who does not like to run "suicides" but who nevertheless chooses to do so because she knows that building her stamina will allow her to become a better player. Finally, integrated regulation also involves engaging in an activity out of choice; however, in this case the choice fits in with other constituents of the person's self. In other words, the choices are made as a function of their coherence with other aspects of the self. An example of someone with integrated regulation is the ice hockey player who chooses to postpone a Friday night out with his friends to stay home in order to be in top shape for the big game on Saturday afternoon.

Amotivation

Finally, amotivation (AM) refers to the lack of intentionality (Deci & Ryan, 1985) and thus the relative absence of motivation (Vallerand, O'Connor, & Hamel, 1995). When amotivated, individuals experience feelings of incompetence and expectancies of uncontrollability (Abramson, Seligman, & Teasdale, 1978). They are relatively without purpose with respect to the activity and therefore have little motivation (intrinsic or extrinsic) to perform it. Recent research has underscored the role of AM in dropping out of sport (Pelletier, Fortier, Vallerand, & Brière, 2001) and physical activity (Ntoumanis, Pensgaard, Martin, & Pipe, 2004).

Over the years, numerous studies have provided empirical support for the first postulate of the model. Results from confirmatory factor analyses on the different motivation scales that have been validated using the present perspective have consistently provided support for the existence of IM, EM, and AM (see Vallerand, 1997, in press; Vallerand & Fortier, 1998). In addition, we will see later how predictions that motivational types relate to determinants and consequences in specific ways yield further support for their construct validity.

Of importance for the model is the proposition from self-determination theory (Deci & Ryan, 1985) that the different motivational orientations represent different levels of self-determination, which can be ordered along a self-determination continuum or perceived locus of causality. Thus, IM is the most self-determined motivational type, followed by integrated regulation, identified regulation, introjected regulation, external regulation, and finally AM, which involves the least amount of self-determination. Research in sport and physical activity provides support for the self-determination continuum (e.g., Chatzisarantis, Hagger, Biddle, Smith, & Wang, 2003; Li & Harmer, 1996). As we will see in Postulate 5, this continuum is very useful as it allows us to predict the impact of the different types of motivation on important consequences.

Postulate 2

Intrinsic motivation, extrinsic motivation, and amotivation exist at three different levels of generality: the global, contextual, and situational levels.Central to the hierarchical model is that motivation exists at different levels of generality. In the HMIEM these levels of generality are termed the *global, contextual,* and *situational* levels. The subsequent sections outline the theoretical bases for making these generality distinctions and the implications for this distinction in terms of the prediction of self-determined forms of motivation and action.

A Multidimensional View of Motivation at Three Levels of Generality

Based on 35 years of research on intrinsic and extrinsic motivation, Postulate 2 of the hierarchical model states that IM, EM, and AM exist at three levels of generality: global, contextual, and situational. Motivation at the global level refers to a general motivational orientation to interact with the environment in an intrinsic, extrinsic, or amotivated way. It is similar to a personality trait according to which one is predominantly intrinsically or extrinsically motivated, or even amotivated. Thus, an athlete with an intrinsic global orientation has a type of personality that predisposes him or her to be intrinsically motivated in interacting with the environment. Motivation at the contextual level refers to an individual's usual motivational orientation toward a specific context, or a "distinct sphere of human activity" (Emmons, 1995). Research on intrinsic and extrinsic contextual motivation has typically focused on three contexts: education or work, interpersonal relationships, and leisure. While for most people, sport is a part of the leisure context, for many athletes it represents a full-fledged life context in and of itself. An athlete with an intrinsic contextual orientation toward sport is predisposed to be intrinsically motivated in sport, but not necessarily in other life contexts. Finally, motivation at the situational level refers to the motivation individuals experience when engaging in a specific activity at a given moment in time. Situational motivation refers to a motivational state. An athlete who stays after practice to learn a new move on a Friday evening would be perceived to be intrinsically motivated at that point in time.

It is important to distinguish among these three different levels, as such a conceptualization provides a more refined understanding of motivational processes involved in human behavior and may guide action in a more adaptive fashion. For example, an athlete who displays AM during a basketball practice (at the situational level) may do so because he or she has an amotivated contextual motivation toward basketball or because the practice is dull. These two possibilities lead to two very different courses of action for the coach, namely making practice more interesting or having a talk with the athlete to determine the nature of the problem. Recent research (Vallerand, Guay, Mageau, Blanchard, & Cadorette, 2005b) has provided support for the three-level hierarchical structure proposed by the HMIEM.

A Multidimensional Assessment of Motivation

Over the years, scales have been developed to assess these different forms of motivation at the global, contextual, and situational levels. At the global level, the Global Motivation Scale (GMS; Guay, Blais, Vallerand, & Pelletier, 1999) has been developed. It assesses the three different types of IM, three types of EM (identified, introjected, and external), and AM toward life in general. More recently, Pelletier and his colleagues have added an integrated regulation subscale to this instrument (Pelletier, Dion, & Lévesque, 2004; Pelletier, Dion, Slovinec-D'Angelo, & Reid, 2004). Results with the GMS indicate that the scale is both reliable and valid. For instance, Guay, Mageau, and Vallerand (2003) have shown that the GMS (without the integrated regulation subscale) has an adequate factorial structure, internal consistency, and temporal stability (a correlation of .68 was obtained for the overall self-determined motivation index over a one-year interval). Furthermore, the different subscales of the GMS were found to be unrelated to social desirability (Guay et al., 1999).

On a methodological note, it is important to highlight that researchers have, on occasion, integrated the different types of motivation (at one specific level) into a single motivation index, called the self-determination index (the self-determination index has also been called the relative autonomy index by the Rochester group). For example, the GMS can be aggregated into a single index in this way. The advantage of using such an index is the significant reduction of variables needed to represent the different types of motivation at a given level. One calculates the self-determination index (e.g., Fortier, Vallerand, & Guay, 1995; Grolnick & Ryan, 1987; Vallerand & Bissonnette, 1992; Vallerand, Fortier, & Guay, 1997) by specifically weighting and adding the scores of the subscales so as to derive a single score. Because the various types of motivation are theoretically posited to lie on a continuum of self-determination from IM to integrated, identified, introjected, and external regulation and to AM (Deci & Ryan, 1985, 2000, 2002), weights are given to the motivational items according to their placement on this continuum. Obviously, the higher the scores on the self-determined forms of motivation (i.e., IM and integrated and identified regulation) and the lower the scores on the non-self-determined forms of motivation (i.e., AM and external and introjected regulation), the more self-determined the overall index.

Specifically, the self-determination index is calculated as follows. IM and integrated and identified regulation items are assigned the weights of +3, +2, and +1, respectively, because they represent self-determined forms of motivation (Deci & Ryan, 1985). Amotivation and external and introjected regulation items, because they are conceptualized as less self-determined forms of motivation, are assigned the weights of –3, –2, and –1, respectively. All three types of IM are given the same weight (+3). The total for the three types of IM is divided by 3 to make it comparable to scores for the other scales. If integrated regulation is not used in the index, IM and identified regulation are given the weights of

+2 and +1, respectively, while AM is given the weight of –2. Introjected and external regulation are then added up, divided by 2, and given the weight of –1. In both self-determination indices, the total score reflects the person's relative level of self-determined motivation. A positive score indicates that the person's motivational profile is relatively self-determined, whereas a negative score reflects the presence of a relatively non-self-determined motivational profile. Research reveals that this index, which has been used in some of the studies reviewed in this chapter, displays high levels of reliability and validity (e.g., Fortier, Vallerand, & Guay, 1995; Ryan & Connell, 1989; Vallerand & Bissonnette, 1992; Vallerand, Fortier, & Guay, 1997).

Scales assessing motivation at the contextual level have also been developed. Because our main interest was in college students and because that research revealed education, leisure, and interpersonal relationships to be their three main life contexts (Blais, Vallerand, Gagnon, Briére, & Pelletier, 1990), scales were developed to measure motivation in these contexts. For instance, the Academic Motivation Scale (AMS; Vallerand et al., 1989, 1992, 1993; see also Fairchild et al., 2005, for additional support for the validity of the AMS) assesses contextual motivation toward education; the Interpersonal Motivation Inventory (IMI; Blais, Vallerand, Pelletier, & Brière, 1994) assesses contextual motivation in interpersonal relationships; and the Leisure Motivation Scale (LMS; Pelletier, Vallerand, Green-Demers, & Blais, Brière, 1996) measures contextual motivation toward leisure activities. Because sport represents an important type of leisure activity for most people and a full-fledged life context for athletes, we have also developed a scale to assess sport motivation both in French (the Echelle de Motivation dans les Sports [EMS]; Brière, Vallerand, Blais, & Pelletier, 1995) and in English (Sport Motivation Scale [SMS]; Pelletier et al., 1995). The SMS has been validated in several other languages as well (see Pelletier & Sarrazin, this volume). Scales have also been developed to assess these motivational constructs with respect to physical activity and exercise. Specifically, the Behavioural Regulation in Exercise Questionnaire (BREQ; Mullan, Markland, & Ingledew, 1997), the Exercise Motivation Scale (EMS; Li, 1999), and the Perceived Locus of Causality Scale (Goudas, Biddle, & Fox, 1994) have been developed to assess contextual motivation toward exercise and physical activity.

All these scales assess the seven motivational constructs described earlier (the three types of IM; identified, introjected, and external regulation; and AM). Typically, integrated regulation has not been assessed because it does not seem to be present in young adults, although Pelletier and Kabush (2005) have recently added an integrated regulation subscale to the SMS. Indices of reliability and validity for all the scales have been found to be more than adequate (Li & Harmer, 1996; Vallerand, 1997, 2001, in press; Vallerand & Fortier, 1998).

At the situational level, two main techniques are used to measure motivation. The first approach is to measure situational motivation by way of the free-choice period (Deci, 1971) in which individuals can spend their free time on any activity, including the one used during the experiment. The assumption underlying this measure is that individuals intrinsically motivated toward an activity will return to the activity. However, the free-choice measure can be problematic under certain conditions, as research has shown that at times it can reflect IM (Deci, 1971), introjection (Ryan, Koestner, & Deci, 1991), or identified regulation (Deci, Eghrari, Patrick, & Leone, 1994) (for more information, see Vallerand, 1997; Vallerand & Fortier, 1998). In addition, the free-choice measure does not allow assessment of the variety of self-determined types of motivation we are discussing. Finally, it is not easy to use, especially in field settings. It would thus appear that the free-choice measure is limited in scope as a motivational measure.

Another way to measure situational motivation is with a self-report measure. Use of such a technique makes it possible to consider the multidimensional aspects of motivation. We thus developed the Situational Motivation Scale (SIMS; Guay, Vallerand, & Blanchard, 2000), which measures IM (without distinguishing types of IM), identified and external types of EM, and AM. The choice to measure only four motivational types was dictated by the need to keep the scale as brief as possible in order to capture situational motivation in many lab or field situations without overloading participants with a long questionnaire. Indices of reliability and validity have been found to be very satisfactory (see Guay, Vallerand, & Blanchard, 2000). The SIMS has attracted a lot of attention since its publication (e.g., Edwards, Portman, & Bethea, 2002; Lévesque & Pelletier, 2003; Standage & Treasure, 2002; Standage, Duda, & Ntoumanis, 2003). Research conducted in sport and in physical education has shown support for the internal consistency of the subscales, an appropriate factor structure, the presence of a simplex structure, and clear predictions with respect to various effects and outcomes as predicted by self-determination theory or the HMIEM.

Postulate 3

Motivation at a given level results from two potential sources: (1) social factors and (2) top-down effects from motivation at the proximal level.

The third postulate of the model tackles the role of motivational determinants at the three levels of generality. It is subdivided into three corollaries.

Corollary 3.1

Motivation at a given level can result from social factors that can be global, contextual, or situational depending on the level in the hierarchy.

The term "social factors" is used to refer to both human (people) and nonhuman (signs) factors encountered in one's social environment. These factors can also be distinguished according to their level of generality. *Situational factors* concern transient variables encountered in a specific activity, at a specific time, that may not remain constant. Receiving a pat on the back from a teammate after a nice play is an example of a situational factor. *Contextual factors* refer to recurrent variables that are systematically encountered in a specific life context but not in others. For example, a controlling coach represents a contextual factor restricted to the sport context and not relevant to the education context (see Amorose, this volume; Hagger & Chatzisarantis, 2005; Mageau & Vallerand, 2003, on the motivational impact of a controlling coach). *Global factors* are social factors whose impact extends to several life contexts. Parents represent such a factor during our upbringing. Because they are initially involved in most of the activities of children, parents can have a profound effect on children's global motivation (see Assor, Roth, & Deci, 2004; Grolnick & Apostoleris, 2002). It is crucial to take social factors into account because, as seen later, they have been found to have a deep impact on motivation (see Deci & Ryan, 2000; Vallerand, 1997, in press).

Corollary 3.2

The impact of social factors on motivation is mediated by perceptions of competence, autonomy, and relatedness.

According to cognitive evaluation theory, a subtheory of self-determination theory (Deci, 1975; Deci & Ryan, 1980, 1985, 1991, 2000), the impact of situational factors on motivation is mediated by perceptions of autonomy, competence, and relatedness. These perceptions relate to basic psychological human needs. The *need for competence* pertains to the human desire to efficiently interact with one's environment so as to feel competent in producing desired outcomes and preventing undesired outcomes (Connell & Wellborn, 1991; Deci, 1975; Deci & Ryan, 1985; Harter, 1978; White, 1959). The *need for autonomy* refers to the human desire to be the origin of one's behaviors (deCharms, 1968; Deci, 1975, 1980; Deci & Ryan, 1985). Finally, the *need for relatedness* implies a desire to feel connected to significant individuals (for recent reviews on belongingness, relatedness, or both, see Baumeister & Leary, 1995; Deci & Ryan, 2000; Richer & Vallerand, 1998; Ryan, 1993).

Cognitive evaluation theory proposes that, to the extent that social factors foster perceptions of competence, autonomy, and relatedness in individuals, self-determined types of motivation (IM as well as integrated and identified regulation) will be enhanced whereas non-self-determined types of motivation (introjected and external regulations and AM) will be undermined (see Deci, Vallerand, Pelletier, & Ryan, 1991). Thus, an activity that promotes perceptions of autonomy, competence, and relatedness is performed volitionally since it nurtures these three basic psychological needs. The hierarchical model further posits that such mediating effects take place at each of the three levels in the hierarchy.

Much research has brought forth empirical support for the mediational role of need satisfaction at the situational level in several activities, including sport and physical activity (see Vallerand, 1997, 2001, in press, for reviews). For instance, Kowal and Fortier (2000) showed that situational perceptions of competence, autonomy, and relatedness mediated the effects of perceived success and motivational climate on situational motivation in swimming. Other studies have shown that need satisfaction mediated the *changes* in situational motivation both in laboratory (Vallerand & Reid, 1984) and in sport settings (basketball; Guay, Vallerand, & Blanchard, 2000, Study 4).

Several studies have now shown support for the mediational role of need satisfaction between social factors and motivation at the contextual level, both in sport and in physical activity settings (Hollembeak & Amorose, 2005; Ntoumanis, 2001, 2005; Reinboth, Duda, & Ntoumanis, 2004; Sarrazin, Vallerand, Guillet, Pelletier, & Cury, 2002). For instance, Ntoumanis (2001) found that a classroom in which emphasis was placed on improvement led to perceptions of competence, while a classroom where the focus was on cooperative learning and perceived choice led, respectively, to perceptions of relatedness and autonomy in British adolescent physical education students. In addition, while all three mediators were related as hypothesized to the different types of motivation, the most important predictor was perceived competence. This is notable, as typically, perceived autonomy is more prevalent in sport (e.g., Sarrazin et al., 2002). It is possible that in a learning environment (such as physical activity classes), one needs to experience some sense of competence and mastery in order to display IM and identified regulation. On the other hand, in sport one is typically already competent and may be expecting some sense of autonomy while acting competently. Thus, perceptions of autonomy may represent a more important mediator in sport and perceptions of competence may be more important in physical activity, at least during the learning phase. Finally, no research to date provides support for the mediating role of perceptions of competence, autonomy, and relatedness at the global level of the hierarchy. Future research is thus needed in order to further establish the generalizability of these results at the global level of the model.

Corollary 3.3

In addition to the influence of psychological mediators, motivation at a given level also results from top-down effects from motivation at the proximal level higher up in the hierarchy.

One important novel contribution of the model is that it acknowledges the possibility that motivation at one level of the hierarchy can affect motivation at lower levels. That is, motivation at a given level is hypothesized to have top-down effects on motivation at the next-lower level. Thus, global motivation should have a stronger impact on contextual motivation than on situational motivation. Similarly, the relevant contextual motivation should influence situational more than global motivation does. This corollary allows us to consider motivation as an intrapersonal phenomenon. To illustrate such effects, we can take the example of someone who is globally motivated in an intrinsic way. We can expect this individual to be intrinsically motivated in several life contexts as well, because the top-down effect of motivation is assumed to go from the global to the contextual level. Similarly, we can expect the person who is intrinsically motivated at the contextual level in exercise to also be intrinsically motivated at the situational level on exercise-related tasks. Life contexts are also important because they represent schemas in which the motivational representation and information related to given contexts are stored. Thus, when one is about to engage in one's sport, the task and other cues associated with this context can trigger one's usual (contextual) motivation toward that sport. If one's predominant contextual motivation toward that sport is intrinsic, then, all other factors being equal, one should have a tendency to display IM toward the sport at that point in time at the situational level.

Researchers have now examined the top-down effects in sport and physical activity contexts. For instance, Gagné, Ryan, and Bargmann (2003) conducted a study with gymnasts in which they measured athletes' contextual motivation toward gymnastics at Time 1 and their situational motivation (with a scale similar to the SIMS) each day for 15 days. The researchers reported that the correlations between contextual motivation and situational motivation were always positive and varied from .22 to .50. In line with the HMIEM, these findings reveal that higher levels of self-determined motivation at the contextual level lead to self-determined motivation at the situational level. In addition, the findings indicate that while the top-down effect was present each day for 15 consecutive days, its impact varied daily, presumably due to the presence of situational factors that varied in importance depending on the day.

Of further interest is a study by Ntoumanis and Blaymires (2003), who tested the specificity hypothesis of Corollary 3.3 in physical education settings. Participants completed contextual measures of motivation toward physical activity (Perceived Locus of Causality Scale; Goudas, Biddle, and Fox, 1994) and education (AMS; Vallerand et al., 1992, 1993). One month later the students engaged in a typical science class in the classroom and a typical physical education class in the gymnasium. Following each class, students completed the SIMS for assessment of the motivation they had experienced in class that day. In line with the top-down specificity hypothesis, Ntoumanis and Blaymires predicted that students' situational motivation during the science class would be positively predicted by their contextual motivation toward education and not from contextual motivation toward physical education. Conversely, it was predicted that students' situational motivation toward physical activity in the gymnasium should be predicted by their contextual motivation toward physical activity and not by contextual motivation toward education. Results from regression analyses confirmed these hypotheses. These findings provide support for the HMIEM's position that it is not simply any motivation at the contextual level that will influence one's situational motivation, but rather the contextual motivation pertinent to the activity being performed. Other studies, including some conducted in sport, have provided support for the specificity hypothesis (Vallerand, Chantal, Guay, & Brunel, 2005a).

As mentioned earlier, life contexts can be seen as schemas that serve to store contextual cues as well as the relevant contextual motivation. If this is so, then presenting relevant contextual cues should be sufficient to trigger the appropriate contextual motivation, even outside of awareness, thereby influencing situational motivation. Much research in social cognition has shown that this is the case (see Bargh & Ferguson, 2000; Fitzsimons & Bargh, 2004). A recent study by Ratelle, Baldwin, and Vallerand (2005) showed the applicability of this process with respect to IM. In two studies, Ratelle and colleagues demonstrated that simply hearing a sound initially paired with a controlling message on a first task was sufficient to produce a decrease in situational motivation on a second task. Why? Because, according to the HMIEM, working on a new type of task (the first one) created a new context in which cues related to that new context, such as the task properties and the sound paired with the task, were stored with the contextual motivation related to such types of tasks. So, when a task relevant to that context came along (the second task), the mere sound triggered the relevant contextual motivation stored in the schema along with the cue, and the top-down effect took place. Furthermore, it appears that the effect took place without participants being aware of it, as they indicated not remembering hearing any sounds. These findings underscore the fact that situational motivation can be influenced by contextual motivation through processes that are triggered nonconsciously.

Some studies in areas other than sport have shown that global motivation predicts contextual motivation. For example, Guay, Mageau, and Vallerand (2003) looked at the top-down effect in two longitudinal investigations adopting a cross-lagged panel design in education (Study 1, spanning five years, and Study 2, one year). The design was a very powerful one, adopting measures of global-level and contextual-level motivation on two occasions across considerable time periods, and permitted the testing of hypotheses relating to reciprocal effects in the model. Importantly, it addressed whether there were top-down effects of global motivation on contextual motivation but no bottom-up effect from context to global levels. Results revealed the presence of a top-down effect in both studies. The more self-determined the global motivation, the more self-determined the contextual motivation toward education even years later. In another study, Vallerand, Guay, Mageau, Blanchard, and Cadorette (2005b, Study 1) showed that the more self-determined the global motivation, the more college students displayed self-determined contextual motivations toward education, interpersonal relationships, and leisure. These findings have been replicated in a three-month prospective study involving contextual motivation toward the leisure (Vallerand et al., 2005b, Study 2) and health contexts (Williams, Grow, Freeman, Ryan, & Deci, 1996). Finally, another study determined the role of global motivation in contextual motivation toward exercise (Vallerand et al., 2005b, Study 3). The researchers first assessed adults' global motivation. Four weeks later they assessed adults' contextual motivation toward exercise. Results showed that global motivation influenced contextual motivation toward exercise over time. As in past studies, the more self-determined the global motivation, the more self-determined the motivation toward exercising at the contextual level.

It thus appears that Postulate 3 and its corollaries have been empirically supported by several studies. Specifically, the role of social factors, as well as that of need satisfaction as a psychological mediator of the impact of social factors on motivation, was found at the situational and contextual levels. Finally, the top-down effect of motivation at higher levels on motivation at the proximal lower level was supported.

Postulate 4

There is a recursive bottom-up relationship between motivation at the proximal level and motivation at the next level up in the hierarchy.

The fourth postulate concerns the recursive relationship among motivations at different levels of the hierarchy. According to this postulate, we need to consider these recursive effects in order to explain the motivational changes that take place over time. The specific goal of this postulate is to specify how the dynamics between motivation at the various levels of generality can account for these motivational changes. Postulate 4 would be exemplified by the basketball player who has a contextual sport motivation characterized by external regulation such as fame and recognition. The player typically comes to practices and games predisposed to experience external regulation at the situational level. However, with the arrival of a new coach who is autonomy supportive and who encourages players to focus on the game and not the end results, the player experiences IM more and more during games and practices, to the point that at the end of the season his contextual motivation toward basketball has become predominantly intrinsic (on this issue, see Amorose, this volume; Amorose & Horn, 2001; Wilson & Rodgers, this volume). It is believed that there is an interplay between situational and contextual motivation such that increases in the situational IM fed back into contextual IM in an ongoing fashion, eventually producing enduring increases in contextual IM toward basketball by the end of the season.

Blanchard, Amiot, Saint-Laurent, Vallerand, and Provencher (2005a) conducted a study to test this interplay between the contextual and situational levels, leading to the change in contextual motivation of basketball players participating in a tournament. Measures of contextual motivation (using the French form of the SMS; Brière et al., 1995) were obtained before the first and second game of the tournament and 10 days after the tournament. Moreover, measures of situational motivation (using the SIMS) were obtained immediately after the two games of the tournament. Finally, players' assessments of personal and team performance, as well as objective results of the games, were collected in order to test the role of situational factors in the prediction of situational motivation. Results from a path analysis showed that contextual motivation for basketball predicted situational motivation during each of the two basketball games during the tournament. Moreover, situational motivation for both basketball games was also predicted by the situational factors (team and personal performance). In turn, situational motivation influenced contextual motivation subsequent to each game, as well as 10 days after the tournament.

The results from Blanchard and colleagues (2005a) are important because they demonstrate that there is an interplay of influences between motivation at two adjacent levels (e.g., the contextual and situational). These results also provide strong support for the hierarchical model, especially with respect to Corollary 3.1 (the motivational effect of social factors—personal and team performance), Corollary 3.3 (the top-down effect of contextual motivation on situational motivation), and Postulate 4 (the recursive effect of situational motivation on contextual motivation). Guay, Mageau, and Vallerand (2003, Study 1) also found support for the bottom-up effects from contextual motivation in education to changes in global motivation over a five-year period. It appears that the interplay among motivations at different levels of the hierarchy is responsible for the occurrence of motivational changes over time.

Postulate 5

Motivation leads to important consequences.

A final point of interest with respect to motivation is that it leads to important consequences of three types: affective, cognitive, and behavioral. Indeed, much experimental research in psychology reveals that motivation does cause consequences and is not simply related to them (see Amabile, 1985; Lepper & Cordova, 1992). Similar experimental research in sport has recently demonstrated that inducing IM leads to more positive outcomes than inducing external regulation (Parfitt & Gledhill, 2004; Simons, Dewitte, & Lens, 2003).

Corollary 5.1

Consequences are decreasingly positive from intrinsic motivation to amotivation.

This first corollary relates motivational consequences to types of motivation and is in line with Deci and Ryan's hypothesized self-determination continuum. Because we know the location of the different types of motivation on the self-determination continuum and know that self-determination is associated with enhanced psychological functioning (Deci, 1980; Ryan, Deci, & Grolnick, 1995), we can predict the impact of the different types of motivation on consequences. More specifically, IM is expected to lead to the most positive consequences, followed by integration and identification. External regulation should be associated with negative consequences, and AM with the most negative ones. Introjection is hypothesized to lead to consequences that lie between those generated by external regulation and identification. As shown later, much correlational research supports Corollary 5.1.

Corollary 5.2

Motivational consequences exist at three levels of the hierarchy, and the level of generality of the consequences depends on the level of the motivation that has produced them.

This second corollary pertains to the level of generality of motivational consequences. According to the hierarchical model, the level of generality of a particular consequence is a function of the level of generality of the motivation that produced that particular consequence. Thus, situational consequences such as feelings of satisfaction, concentration, and behavioral persistence with respect to a particular task at a specific point in time are expected to be mainly determined by situational motivation. Likewise, contextual consequences, resulting from contextual motivation, will be specific to the context at hand and will be of moderate generality. Lastly, consequences at the global level of generality, resulting from global motivation, will be the most general ones. This is not to say that motivation at one level of generality cannot predict outcomes at other levels. For instance, contextual and global motivation would be expected to be related to situational outcomes. However, it is predicted that the relationships between motivation at these two higher levels of generality and situational outcomes are mediated by situational motivation. It is this latter motivation that produces situational outcomes. The same reasoning applies to global outcomes. They may be related to situational and contextual motivation. However, it is expected that the more enduring outcomes are derived from global motivation.

Over the past decade or so, a considerable amount of research has addressed the relationship between the different types of motivation and a variety of outcomes in sport and physical activity, especially at the situational and contextual levels. It is beyond the scope of this chapter to review all of these studies. The interested reader will find more comprehensive reviews of such research in Vallerand (in press) and in several chapters of this book. Research at the global level has shown that self-determined global motivation predicted increases in global adjustment in individuals from the general population over a one-year period (Ratelle et al., 2004). For illustrative purposes, we can say that research in sport and physical activity settings at the situational level has provided support for Postulate 5 with outcomes as diversified as flow (Kowal & Fortier, 1999; see Fortier & Kowal, this volume); enjoyment (Simons, Dewitte, & Lens, 2003); fatigue, distress, and perceived exertion (Parfitt & Gledhill, 2004); concentration (Kowal & Fortier, 1999; Vallerand et al., 2005, Study 3); persistence (Gagné, Ryan, & Bargmann, 2003); and effort and performance (Simons, Dewitte, & Lens, 2003).

Research on outcomes at the contextual level in sport and physical activity has exploded over the past 10 years. Support for Postulate 5 has been obtained with outcomes such as satisfaction in sport (Brière et al., 1995; Li, 1999), flow (Jackson et al., 1998), burnout (Cresswell & Ecklund, 2005; Raedeke, 1997; see Treasure, Lemyre, Kuczka, & Standage, this volume), boredom (Ntoumanis,

2001), concentration (Brière et al., 1995; Pelletier et al., 1995; Ntoumanis, 2001), effort (Ferrer-Caja & Weiss, 2000; Pelletier et al., 1995), and intentions to persist and actual persistence at the activity (Chatzisarantis, Biddle, & Meek, 1997; Fortier & Grenier, 1999; Hagger & Chatzisarantis, this volume; Pelletier et al., 1995, 2001; Ryan, Frederick, Lepes, Rubio, & Sheldon, 1997; Sarrazin et al., 2002; Sarrazin, Boiché, & Pelletier, this volume; Thøgersen-Ntoumani & Ntoumanis, in press; Wilson & Rodgers, 2004, this volume; Wilson, Rodgers, Fraser, Murray, & McIntyre, 2004). Finally, research has also explored the contribution of sport motivation at the contextual level to outcomes related to good sporting behavior orientation or the tendency to show respect and concern for the rules and sport participants (Vallerand et al., 1996; Vallerand, Brière, Blanchard, & Provencher, 1997). For instance, Vallerand and Losier (1994) showed that self-determined motivation positively predicted increases in good sporting behavior over time in hockey players. These findings were replicated with physical education students (Chantal & Bernache-Assolant, 2003). Chantal, Robin, Vernat, and Bernache-Assolant (2005) also showed that self-determined motivation positively predicted good sporting behavior, which positively predicted instrumental aggression (being aggressive in order to reach a goal within the game) but negatively predicted reactive aggression (wanting to hurt someone). Finally, Donahue and colleagues (2005) showed that IM toward sport positively predicted good sporting behavior while external regulation negatively predicted it. In turn, good sporting behavior negatively predicted steroid use in over 1200 national-level Quebec athletes.

Typically, the more self-determined the level of situational motivation, the more one intends to continue engagement in the activity. One caveat applies, however. A major difference seems to emerge between the physical activity (i.e., exercise) and the sport studies. Specifically, while all studies reveal the presence of the hypothesized continuum, there is a difference with the main positive predictor of intentions. The results of a meta-analysis conducted mainly with sport studies (Chatzisarantis et al., 2003) revealed IM as the main predictor. On the other hand, in physical activity studies, identified regulation appears to be the main predictor (e.g., see Wilson & Rodgers, 2004). One possible explanation proposed by Vallerand (1997; Vallerand & Rousseau, 2001; see also Gagné & Deci, 2005) deals with the nature of the activity. When the task to be performed is perceived as interesting, IM should lead to the most positive outcomes. However, when the task is uninteresting, identified regulation may become a more important determinant of positive consequences than IM. What is needed is a motivational force leading the person to choose to engage in the activity despite the fact that it is not interesting. Identified regulation can provide such a force. In the context of sport, tasks are typically interesting and thus IM is likely to be the main predictor, as was found in the meta-analysis of Chatzisarantis and colleagues (2003). Conversely, in physical activity settings, at least initially, tasks are likely to be much less interesting. Thus, in order for these activities to be engaged in, identified regulation has to be involved, as was found in the exercise studies. While this suggestion makes sense and is in line with the available data, additional research is needed to provide firmer empirical support for this hypothesis within the confines of the same study.

Integrative Studies

The studies reviewed next provide a more comprehensive perspective on IM and EM processes in sport and physical activity in that they tested the validity of a causal sequence involving the environment, motivation, and outcomes, as well as assessing the interplay of motivation at more than one level of generality.

An Integrated Motivational Sequence

One of the key hypotheses of the HMIEM is that the impact of the environment on individuals takes place through a causal chain of processes that can be presented as follows: Social factors → psychological mediators (need satisfaction) → self-determined motivation → consequences (see Vallerand, 1997; Vallerand & Losier, 1999). This sequence can occur at all three levels of the hierarchy. Following the lead of the study by Vallerand and colleagues (1997) on high school dropouts, several studies have tested this causal sequence in sports at the contextual level (Blanchard et al., 2005a; Pelletier et al., 2001; Sarrazin et al., 2002). All used structural equation modeling and showed support for the hypothesized sequence. While the social factors assessed vary from team climate (Sarrazin et al., 2002) to the coach's behavior (Blanchard Amiot, Vallerand, & Provencher, 2005b; Pelletier et al., 2001) to team cohesion (Blanchard et al., 2005b), their impact on self-determined motivation goes through perceptions of competence, autonomy, and relatedness, which lead to motivation. In turn, motivation leads to various affective and behavioral consequences. For instance, in the study by Sarrazin and colleagues (2002), task- and ego-involving climates were found, respectively, to positively and negatively predict perceptions of competence, autonomy, and relatedness, and perceptions of competence, autonomy, and relatedness positively predicted self-determined motivation. In turn, self-determined motivation predicted intention to persist in handball, which led to persistence 21 months later. Pelletier and colleagues (2001) found support for a similar sequence from autonomy support to motivation and to persistence in swimming over 22 months.

Research on the integrated causal sequence has also been tested in exercise settings at the contextual level (Ferrer-Caja & Weiss, 2000; Ntoumanis, 2001, 2005; Standage, Duda, & Ntoumanis, 2003; Wilson & Rodgers, 2004). Different learning structures (Ntoumanis, 2001), motivational climates (Ferrer-Caja & Weiss, 2000; Standage, Duda, & Ntoumanis, 2003), autonomy support from friends (Wilson & Rodgers, 2004), and the physical education teacher (Ntoumanis, 2005) positively influenced self-determined motivation through their impact on perceptions of competence, autonomy, and relatedness. Finally, self-determined motivation positively predicted a variety of contextual cognitive, affective, and behavioral outcomes. Noteworthy are the studies of Ntoumanis (2005) and Ferrer-Caja and Weiss (2000), which showed support for the motivational sequence using teacher-rated assessments of behavior.

It appears that only one study has provided support for the proposed sequence at the situational level in sport. This study with masters swimmers (Kowal & Fortier, 2000) showed that motivational climates predicted perceptions of competence, autonomy, and relatedness, which led to self-determined situational motivation, which in turn predicted the experience of flow. Clearly, future research is needed on this issue at the situational level.

The results just discussed are important in that they provide strong support for the proposed sequence in a variety of settings and with different activities. However, typically such research has used only a cross-sectional design, with all measures being obtained at the same point in time. Future research using more refined designs is needed, such as the adoption of prospective or longitudinal designs at the contextual level and experimental designs at the situational level, in order to provide more definite support for the proposed direction of causality. For instance, Grouzet, Vallerand, Thill, and Provencher (2005) manipulated success and failure feedback on a leisure task and then assessed perceptions of competence and autonomy, situational motivation, and cognitive and affective outcomes. Support was obtained for the proposed sequence. Because the success/failure variable was manipulated and participants were randomly assigned to these conditions, the alternative hypothesis, which stated that having a self-determined motivation leads one to perceive the social factor more positively, was eliminated. Thus, there is experimental support for some aspects of the causal sequence. We need additional evidence on the motivational sequence at the global level and the contextual level in sport and physical activity with respect to other outcomes such as performance, creativity, and learning, as well as friendships (on this see Weiss & Smith, 2002).

Motivation at Two or Three Levels of Generality

A key aspect of the HMIEM is that motivation results from both social and intrapersonal forces that may exist at the various levels of generality. For instance, we have seen that there was support for the top-down effect from contextual to situational motivation (e.g., Ntoumanis, 2001). We have also seen that situational factors influenced situational motivation (see Vallerand, in press, for a complete review on this issue). Brunel and Vallerand (2005) tested the relative importance of the top-down effect and the impact of situational factors on situational motivation over time. These authors reasoned that in a new situation, participants' contextual motivation should influence situational motivation the most because such participants are not used to the surroundings or the meanings that the social factors convey. However, months later, when the meanings conveyed by situational factors become clearer, these factors should have a more potent influence on situational motivation. Results of a study with French athletes provided support for the hypotheses.

Researchers have also started to look at how contextual motivation sets psychological processes in motion at the situational level so that affective outcomes can be experienced at that level. For instance, Amiot, Gaudreau, and Blanchard (2004) showed that self-determined contextual motivation toward sport as assessed before a game led to the use of situational adaptive cognitive skills, which in turn facilitated the reaching of goals during the game. Finally, reaching one's goals led to an increase in positive affect after the game. On the other hand, non-self-determined contextual motivation led to the use of poor situational coping skills and failing to reach one's goals, which led to the experience of less positive affect after the game. Future research is needed to determine if the impact of contextual motivation on situational-level coping skills takes place through the top-down effect from contextual to situational motivation.

Finally, it appears that only one study has integrated motivation at the three levels of the hierarchy in the context of sport and physical activity. In this study, Vallerand and colleagues (2005b, Study 3) tested the interplay among motivations at the three levels of the hierarchy with participants in a fitness program. On the basis of Corollary 3.3 (the top-down effect), the researchers hypothesized that global motivation, measured with the global motivation scale at the beginning of the fitness program, would influence contextual motivation toward exercise (as assessed by a measure adapted from the SMS) four weeks later. In turn, contextual motivation toward exercise would influence situational motivation, which in turn would determine the situational consequences of concentration and enjoyment during exercising. Results from structural equation modeling supported the model. These findings have also been obtained in the context of education (see Vallerand, Chantal, Guay, & Brunel, 2005a, Study 1).

In sum, the research reviewed in this section reveals that we have started to uncover the dynamic relationships between social and intrapersonal motivational factors, leading to a better understanding of aspects of the processes through which motivation and outcomes are experienced at different levels of generality.

Future Directions

Over the 10 years or so since its first publication (Vallerand, 1997), much research has been conducted on the HMIEM in sport and physical activity settings. Such research has led to a better understanding of the processes through which motivational changes and outcomes take place. Further, it is believed that the model can lead to additional novel and testable research hypotheses in the area of sport and physical activity. The following are a few research directions based on the model.

One broad avenue of research pertains to global motivation. Research in sport and physical activity has neglected the study of global motivation perhaps because the study of contextual motivation in sport and physical activity yields results that are more readily applicable. However, research in other realms of activity has revealed that global motivation plays a more important role than initially anticipated. Three functions can be noted. First, global motivation can influence global outcomes such as psychological adjustment. Because global self-determined motivation reflects a positive way of interacting with one's environment, it would be predicted that a self-determined motivation orientation should lead to more adaptive functioning and psychological adjustment. In a longitudinal study with adults from the general population, Ratelle and colleagues (2004) showed that self-determined global motivation positively predicted increases in psychological adjustment that took place over a one-year period. Because experiencing a positive psychological adjustment may provide additional strength to face difficult situations and failure experiences, this first function of global motivation deserves attention in sport and physical activity.

A second way in which global motivation has been found to affect functioning is through the protective role it may play. A recent study by Pelletier, Dion, and Lévesque (2004) has shown this with respect to bulimic symptoms. Research reveals that a substantial percentage of women engage in pathological eating behavior such as bingeing, vomiting, fasting, and purging (Heatherton, Nichols, Mahamedi, & Keel, 1995). Stice (2001) has provided a model aimed at understanding this process. According to this model, society puts pressure on women to be thin, leading women to internalize society's stereotypes. Because the ideal body weight conveyed in the media by supermodels is very low, accepting such a stereotype leads women to be dissatisfied with their body. Body dissatisfaction, in turn, leads to maladaptive forms of weight control, which lead to bulimic symptomatology. In their study, Pelletier and colleagues found that a global self-determined motivation led women to perceive less pressure from society to have a thin body and to much less internalization of society's stereotypes regarding thinness. Finally, global self-determined motivation had a direct negative effect on bulimic symptomatology. These important results show that self-determined global motivation serves a protective function with respect to problems at the global level. Because problems such as bulimic symptomatology do occur in sport, research along these lines would appear fruitful.

Finally, it seems clear that global motivation serves an integrative function regarding development that takes place among life contexts. Research with adults (Koestner, Bernieri, & Zuckerman, 1992) and children (Joussemet, Koestner, Lekes, & Houlfort, 2004) has shown that people with a predominantly autonomous causality orientation (the equivalent of a self-determined global motivation) display behavior that is in line with their attitudes and inner values. On the other hand, individuals with a control (or non-self-determined) orientation show a lack of coherence. It thus appears that people who have a self-determined global motivation are more likely to behave in line with their inner values. Furthermore, they are more likely to internalize experiences in a more coherent fashion and thus to derive a more coherent sense of self (Deci & Ryan, 2000). Thus, athletes with a self-determined global motivation would be expected to have a contextual motivation for sport that is better integrated with other contextual motivations and so experience fewer conflicts among life contexts. Therefore a more focused involvement both in sport and in other life contexts should ensue. These and related issues would seem to warrant the attention of sport and physical activity researchers.

A second research avenue involves the interplay of different contextual motivations and their implications for situational motivation and outcomes. At least three types of influence may exist: conflicting, facilitative, and compensative. Some studies have addressed the conflict that may take place between two contextual motivations and the outcomes that may derive from such a relationship between two motivations. Thus, Sénécal, Vallerand, and Guay (2001) showed that the conflict that resulted from work and family contextual motivational orientations was predictive of feelings of burnout and poor psychological adjustment in members of the general population. Similarly, Ratelle, Sénécal, Vallerand, and Provencher (2005) showed that conflict between leisure and education contextual motivations was predictive of lower levels of psychological adjustment in college students. On the other hand, Hagger and Chatzisarantis and their colleagues (e.g., Hagger et al., 2003, 2005) have shown that having a self-determined motivation toward physical activity at school facilitates self-determined motivation toward physical activity during one's leisure time. Finally, compensation takes place when losses in self-determined motivation in one context lead a person to compensate in another context by becoming more intrinsically motivated in that second context. Future research is needed to pursue this line of scientific inquiry in order to determine when each type of effect occurs and to identify the nature of the processes governing each effect with athletes and exercise participants.

A final area for future research pertains to the role of unconscious (or implicit) motivational processes. Much research in social cognition has now shown that our behavior can be influenced by factors that are outside of our awareness (see Bargh & Ferguson, 2000; Fitzsimons & Bargh, 2004). As shown in the study by Ratelle, Baldwin, and Vallerand (2005), certain cues that are present in a given context can trigger, by their mere unnoticed presence, certain types of contextual motivation that will influence situational motivation at that point in time. These can be sounds, smells, and messages lingering in the back of the mind. Along these lines, Lévesque and Pelletier (2003) showed that to present out-of-awareness primes dealing with intrinsic or extrinsic motivation is sufficient to induce the situational motivation implied by the primes. In an even more provocative study, Hodgins, Yacko, and Gottlieb (2005, Study 3) showed that priming members of a university rowing team with words denoting autonomy (e.g., "choice," "freedom") led to faster times on a rowing machine than priming members with words conveying control (e.g., "must," "should") and words conveying a lack of personal investment in the task (e.g., "passive," "uncontrollable"). In other words, priming self-determined motivation outside of awareness increases performance! These findings are important in underscoring the fact that at least part of our behavior, and even performance, can be influenced by factors that influence our motivation outside of our consciousness. For obvious theoretical and practical reasons, it is believed that sport psychologists would do well to start exploring the role of such motivational processes.

Practical Implications and Conclusion

Sport and physical activity represent formidable opportunities not only to preserve, but also to enhance, the psychological welfare of participants. The HMIEM lends itself to a number of practical implications (see "Practical Recommendations for the Promotion of Self-Determined Motivation Based on the Hierarchical Model"). Unfortunately, due to space limitations I have restricted this presentation to a few examples of such practical implications. In any case, it would appear paramount to ensure that participants can satisfy their needs for competence, autonomy, and relatedness within sport and physical activity contexts.

The purpose of the present chapter was to review recent research on the hierarchical model of intrinsic and extrinsic motivation (Vallerand, 1997) conducted in the realms of sport and physical activity. We have seen that over the past 10 years or so, much research has provided support for the model in these contexts. It was also seen that based on the model, new and testable hypotheses can be derived, leading to new avenues for future research. Most notably, the study of the functions of global motivation, of the interplay among contextual motivations from different life contexts, and of unconscious forces would appear most promising. I highlighted in the introduction that athletes are more than mere sport participants. The hierarchical model and the research that it generates should lead to a better understanding of the psychological processes underlying the complex motivational phenomena experienced by individuals engaged in sport and physical activities.

Practical Recommendations for the Promotion of Self-Determined Motivation Based on the Hierarchical Model

- Situational factors promoting participants' needs are important as they lead to positive motivational effects at the situational level, as well as to more enduring effects that occur through a recursive process. Practitioners involved in motivating people therefore need to provide daily practices

(continued)

that enhance the needs for autonomy, competence, and relatedness. For example, a sport trainer might ask athletes to warm up using a varied set of drills and practices and present these in a fashion that appeals to their goals, such as preparing themselves for effortful performance in the upcoming practice and avoiding injury.

• Contextual factors promoting the participants' needs should be put in place to ensure stability in the positive motivational impact on participants' motivation and outcomes. This means that practitioners are responsible for providing practices and drills that pervade across various situations within sport. For example, physical education teachers can foster the need to set intrinsic goals based on effort by using a questioning approach to help pupils establish what success means to them (e.g., "Why do you participate in sport?"; "Why do we do a warm-up before sport practice?"; "What do you enjoy the most about sport?"). This useful skill can then be transferred when the pupils approach novel sports in the future.

• The coach is perhaps the most important contextual factor within sport. The coach's interactional style and the structure he or she instills should meet participants' needs. However, beyond autonomy support, the coach (or physical education teacher) should never forget that those participating in sport and physical activity are more than simply athletes. Thus, paying attention to other life contexts (e.g., education, relationships) is important, as such an approach conveys the message that one cares about the whole person and not simply about what the athlete can accomplish in sport. Furthermore, caring about the person in life contexts other than sport may foster positive cross-context motivational effects on participants' motivation and outcomes.

• In addition to coaches, parents have a unique opportunity to promote self-determined global motivation in their children through positive involvement in sport, physical activity, or both. Parents need to realize that their role is to support their children's interest in sport and not to ensure that children behave as others think they should. In addition, by creating a supportive system, parents will help their children develop a strong self-determined contextual motivation toward sport or physical activity, which eventually will have positive recursive effects on their global motivation and personality functioning. For example, parents are encouraged to adopt a supportive and questioning approach to the sport activities that their children pursue. This should manifest as taking an interest in the child's activity but not to the extent of controlling or interfering in the child's decision making. That is, one needs to avoid becoming a "pushy parent," an influence that coaches are all too aware of and sometimes have to skillfully deflect.

- Sport participants themselves also represent a powerful influence on their own motivation and the outcomes they experience (through the top-down effects). Administrators, coaches, and parents need to accept the active role of participants in motivation and outcomes and even promote this adaptive force. They can do this by helping participants understand how best to channel this motivational force in a way that is autonomous but still respectful of other participants. Sport practitioners and those involved in motivating others are encouraged to investigate these potential influences through semistructured questioning forums like team talks or one-to-one discussions with athletes.

Intrinsic Motivation and Self-Determination in Exercise and Sport

Reflecting on the Past and Sketching the Future

Nikos L.D. Chatzisarantis, PhD
University of Plymouth

Martin S. Hagger, PhD
University of Nottingham

Self-determination theory is an increasingly popular theory of human motivation in exercise and sport psychology. Its popularity stems primarily from the fact that it explains a wide variety of phenomena on the basis of very few principles related to the three basic psychological needs of competence, autonomy, and relatedness. The aim of the present volume was to gather together contributions from eminent researchers involved in applying the theory to the domain of exercise and sport. In doing so the book has provided an invaluable compendium of the current state of the research in the area, as well as outlining key theoretical advances and practical recommendations that have paramount importance in the exercise and sport domain but are equally applicable to a wider range of behavioral contexts. Indeed, many of the authors in the present volume are pioneers in the advancement of theory above and beyond the application of the theory to exercise and sport.

Our aim in this final chapter is to summarize evidence in the areas addressed by the contributors to this book and make recommendations for future research. The contributions in the present volume can be encapsulated under five subheadings that summarize key research questions relevant to self-determination theory applied to the domain of exercise and sport: (a) methodological issues; (b) self-determination theory and the antecedents of motivation; (c) self-determination

Correspondence concerning this article should be addressed to Nikos L.D. Chatzisarantis, School of Psychology, University of Plymouth, Drake Circus, Plymouth, Devon, PL48AA. Email: N.Chatzisarantis@Plymouth.ac.uk theory and psychological outcomes; (d) self-determination theory and exercise and sport behavior; and (e) theoretical integration and advancement.

Methodological Issues

One of the key themes omnipresent in this volume is the methodologies used to address hypotheses from self-determination theory. Many of the studies reported herein adopt an empirical, positivist approach to address their proposed research questions and have adopted a variety of research designs, including cross-sectional, prospective, longitudinal panel, time-series, experimental, and intervention paradigms. In this section we outline some of the issues that have arisen from the methodologies used and how researchers have tackled them. Of considerable prominence is the definition of motivation and the use of psychometric instruments to assess the key motivational constructs from self-determination theory, so our discussion will start there. We then move on to research aimed at mapping the processes involved in the predictions set out by self-determination theory, particularly mediational models of behavior change. Finally we discuss the importance of experimental designs in informing understanding of the motivational process and inference of causality.

Definitions and Measurement of Motivation in Sport

One important line of research raised in this volume by Pelletier and Sarrazin, as well as by Markland and Ingledew, concerns measurement of motivation. From a self-determination theory perspective, a fundamental characteristic of motivation is the degree of relative autonomy that underpins the regulation of and participation in exercise and sport behavior. This form of motivation (termed the "why" of human motivation) consists of autonomous (identified and integrated forms of regulation and intrinsic motivation) and controlling motives (external and introjected regulations); and, in the context of exercise and sport, the measurement of these forms of motivation is predominantly achieved using three psychometric instruments: Markland and Tobin's (2004) Behavioural Regulation in Exercise Questionnaire, Li's (1999) Exercise Motivation Scale, and Pelletier and colleagues' (1995) Sport Motivation Scale. As the chapters outlining these instruments attest, their development has been punctuated by rigorous psychometric evaluation to confirm their integrity, including tests of construct, predictive, and concurrent validity and internal reliability using sophisticated means such as confirmatory factor analyses, structural equation modeling, and known group differences.

However, at least three different ways have been promulgated in the literature to represent the continuum of relative autonomy underlying exercise and sport motivation, derived from the continuum known as the perceived locus of causality (Ryan & Connell, 1989). One means of representing the continuum is to use responses to scales measuring autonomous and controlling motivational styles to calculate a self-determination or *relative autonomy* index; this index reflects the degree of relative autonomy underlying motivation in the sport or exercise context for each individual. A second way is to create a two-dimensional or dichotomous model of motivation in which scores from scales measuring autonomous and controlling forms of motivation from these instruments are aggregated to form two global autonomous and controlling motivational constructs. A third approach is to create a four-, five-, or six-dimensional model of motivation in which the scale for each individual form of autonomous and controlling motivation is treated separately: external, introjected, and identified regulations; intrinsic motivation; integrated regulation; and amotivation (these last two depending whether they are included in the scale adopted). Research has advocated the use of all of these methods depending on the research questions involved (Pelletier & Sarrazin, this volume; Sarrazin, Boiché, & Pelletier, this volume; Vallerand, this volume).

One limitation of instruments measuring autonomous and controlling motives has to do with measurement of integrated regulation, the fourth type of extrinsic motivation proposed by organismic integration theory. Although some instruments such as the Exercise Motivation Scale assess integration (Li, 1999), more research is needed to examine construct validity of this construct in exercise and sport. This is so because integrated regulation is a complex type of motivation that describes both the *vertical* coherence between the different goals and roles that people enact in life and the *horizontal* congruence between goals and roles on the one hand and psychological needs on the other (Sheldon & Kasser, 1995). Researchers would do well to apply the methods adopted by Sheldon and Kasser in future research on motivation in exercise and sport with a view to understanding the role that integrated regulation has in this context.

Definitions and Measurement of Motivation in Exercise

Instruments measuring individuals' relative autonomy in the domain of exercise and sport are aimed at identifying the "why" of human motivation (Deci & Ryan, 2000). As Markland and Ingledew (this volume) point out, at least four different instruments measuring reasons for participating in exercise distinguish between intrinsic and extrinsic motivational styles. These instruments are the Reasons for Exercise Inventory (REI; Silberstein, Striegel-Moore, Timko, & Rodin, 1988); the revised version of Motivation for Physical Activities Measure (MPAM-R; Ryan, Frederick, Lepes, Rubio, & Sheldon, 1997); the Personal Incentives for Exercise Questionnaire (PIEQ; Duda & Tappe, 1989), derived from personal investment theory (Maehr & Braskamp, 1986); and the revised version of Markland and Hardy's (1993) Exercise Motivations Inventory (EMI; Markland & Ingledew, 1997).

Generally speaking, the intrinsic motives that these instruments measure reflect self-determined reasons for engaging in tasks such as exercising for interest/enjoyment, competence, fitness, challenge, revitalization (i.e., feeling good after exercising), positive health (i.e., promotion of well-being), mood, strength/endurance, nimbleness, and social interaction. Conversely, extrinsic motives from these instruments reflect reasons for engaging in exercise such as appearance improvement, stress management, health pressures (i.e., pressures arising from some specific medical advice or medical condition), ill-health avoidance, social recognition, body tone, and weight management (Markland & Ingledew, 1997; Ryan et al., 1997). These instruments have been subjected to varying levels of psychometric assessment, the most rigorous being the EMI developed by Markland and coworkers (e.g., Markland & Ingledew, 1997).

Process Models in Exercise and Sport

Mediational Models

Another theme evident in research applications of self-determination theory concerns investigation of the processes by which interpersonal context and motives influence participation in physical activities and sport. This has led to the development of mediational models aimed at outlining the mechanisms that underlie the effects of motivational variables on psychological and behavioral outcomes in accordance with the hypotheses from self-determination theory. In the context of sport, Amorose (this volume) and Sarrazin, Boiché, and Pelletier (this volume) cite models indicating that psychological needs mediate effects of social factors (e.g., coaching behaviors) on autonomous forms of motivation (Amorose & Horn, 2000, 2001) and that autonomous motivation mediates the effects of interpersonal context and psychological needs on sport participation (Pelletier, Fortier, Vallerand, & Brière, 2001; Sarrazin, Vallerand, Guillet, Pelletier, & Cury, 2002). In the context of exercise, numerous authors (Edmunds, Ntoumanis, & Duda, this volume; Hagger & Chatzisarantis, this volume; Standage, Gillison, & Treasure, this volume; Wilson & Rodgers, this volume) have highlighted that autonomous motivational styles mediate effects of interpersonal context on physical activity participation. Therefore there appears to be converging evidence that both psychological needs and autonomous motives mediate the effects of social factors and interpersonal context on exercise and sport behavior.

The Hierarchical Model of Motivation

A number of contributors to the present volume (Edmunds, Ntoumanis, & Duda; Hagger & Chatzisarantis; Pelletier & Sarrazin; Vallerand) have indicated that the differentiated motivational orientations identified in organismic integration theory operate at the three levels of generality outlined in Vallerand's hierarchical model of motivation. The model broadens and deepens self-determination theory by focusing on the importance of context, outcomes, and level of specificity or generality of motivational orientations (Vallerand & Ratelle, 2002). The three levels of generality (global, contextual, and situational), the associated top-down and bottom-up relations between motivational constructs at these levels, and their association with contexts and outcomes have been the subject of an increasing body of research providing some support for the corollaries of the theory (e.g., Edmunds, Ntoumanis, & Duda, 2006; Guay, Mageau, & Vallerand, 2003; Hagger, Chatzisarantis, & Harris, 2006). Interestingly, instruments measuring motivational styles such as Pelletier and colleagues' (1995) Sport Motivation Scale and Markland and Tobin's (2004) Behavioural Regulation in Exercise Questionnaire focus on contextual-level motivation, and much of the research on motivation and its effects on behavior and outcomes in the domain of exercise and sport has been conducted at the contextual level. An important tenet of the model at this level is the proposed interplay in motivational orientations across contexts (Vallerand & Ratelle, 2002). This suggests that autonomous motives, contexts, and outcomes in one context will have "sideways" influences on motives, contexts, and outcomes in other related contexts in addition to the top-down and bottom-up effects proposed between levels of generality. This corollary has been exploited in recent research suggesting that motivation can be transferred across contexts (Hagger & Chatzisarantis, this volume).

In terms of the mechanisms, the hierarchical model proposes that a person's motivational orientation at the contextual level will mediate the influence of that person's global motivational traits on her or his motivation in a given situation in a top-down manner (Guay, Mageau, & Vallerand, 2003). In addition, the recursive nature of the model is such that repeated situational experiences feed information on motivation back to contextual and global levels in a bottom-up process (Vallerand & Ratelle, 2002). While the model extends theory by stipulating interplay between forms of motivation at different levels of generality and effects on outcomes and contexts, the hypothesized links among the model constructs have not been investigated extensively in the exercise and sport domain. Further, there have been precious few holistic tests of the model across any domain, and exercise and sport psychologists would do well to provide a more comprehensive test of corollaries of the model in the future.

The Need for Experimental Designs and Inference of Causality

One of the recurrent themes of this volume has to do with methodological issues and, more specifically, the lack of intervention or experimental studies in the exercise and sport psychology literature. While cross-sectional, prospective, and longitudinal panel designs have provided valuable evidence to support hypotheses from self-determination theory in the context of exercise and sport, these are limited, particularly with regard to the generalizability and the causal inferences that can be made on the basis of such data. It is therefore important to stress that the time is ripe for exercise and sport psychologists to go beyond cross-sectional and prospective designs and begin testing causal links through experimental and intervention studies. Intervention and experimental studies can provide insights into how psychological needs and interpersonal context influence physical activity participation and well-being, as well as providing evidence regarding causal links between variables. The innovative experimental and intervention studies reported by the contributors to this volume (e.g., Conroy, Elliot, & Coatsworth; Vansteenkiste, Soenens, & Lens; Vallerand) are indicative of cutting-edge research involving methods that effectively tap the causal mechanisms underpinning motivation in self-determination theory in exercise and sport. Exercise and sport psychologists should pay heed to the wealth of experimental and intervention studies attesting to tenets of self-determination theory in other areas of applied psychology (Deci, Eghrari, Patrick, & Leone, 1994; Williams, 2002) and use such studies as blueprints for further research in the exercise and sport domain.

Self-Determination Theory and the Antecedents of Motivation

Where do intrinsic or autonomous forms of motivation come from? A specific line of research cited by contributors to this volume is preoccupied with the antecedents of intrinsic motivation. One of the key influences is the interpersonal context that pervades in motivational situations that can either foster or undermine self-determined or autonomous motivation (Ryan & Deci, this volume), and this is a recurrent theme in the present volume. Interpersonal context refers to the overall structure of the environment or practices that exercisers or athletes engage in when performing their task, be it jogging in the park or throwing a discus. This context includes a number of influential factors such as the motivational orientations of the other exercisers or athletes. However, the factor that is most pervasive and that has received the most attention in research in exercise and sport is the behavior of teachers and coaches, which can foster autonomous motivation if they are autonomy supportive or undermine it if they are controlling.

It is by no means surprising that the interpersonal context is the focus of many studies in the present volume, given that self-determination theory views this context as one of the most important antecedents of human motivation (Deci & Ryan, 1985, 2000; Ryan & Deci, this volume; Vallerand, this volume). In general, self-determination theory differentiates between two types of interpersonal context: *autonomy supportive* and *controlling*. The interpersonal context is said to be autonomy supportive when social agents (e.g., coaches, parents, peers, teachers) encourage choice and participation in decision making, provide a meaningful rationale, use neutral language (e.g., use "may" and "could" rather than "should" and "must") during interpersonal communication, and acknowledge people's feelings and perspectives. The interpersonal context is said to be controlling when significant others do not explain why performance of behavior may be important, use pressuring language during interpersonal communication (e.g., "should" and "must"), or do not acknowledge difficulties associated with performance of behavior.

A clear finding to emerge from previous applications of self-determination theory is that the interpersonal context influences motivation for exercise and sport participation. For example, research has consistently indicated that frequent administration of positive feedback enhances self-esteem and increases levels of enjoyment and lowers anxiety and attrition rates in exercise and sport (e.g., Smoll, Smith, Barnett, & Everett, 1993). However, as pointed out by Amorose and Hein and Koka in this volume, athletes' interpretation of feedback and other types of social support is as important a determinant of their motivation as the frequency of feedback (Deci & Ryan, 1985, 2000; Hein & Koka, this volume). Broadly speaking, frequent feedback, instruction, and social support enhance self-determined motivation (Hein & Koka, this volume). However, as Amorose and Horn (2000) have recently documented, overuse of social support may undermine intrinsic motivation as it may be perceived as controlling. Again, much of this research is cross-sectional in design, and intervention studies using procedures such as those employed by Vallerand and Reid (1984) in the sport context, and Deci and colleagues (1994) in other contexts, can test whether the adoption of an autonomous interpersonal style by social agents like coaches, parents, and physical education teachers can facilitate autonomous motivation in exercisers and athletes.

Self-Determination Theory and Psychological Outcomes

One of the prominent tenets of self-determination theory is that motivation will affect salient behavioral and psychological outcomes. Clearly, the effect of self-determined forms of motivation on behavior is a cornerstone of the theory, particularly in terms of maintenance and persistence, and as a consequence we will deal with this in the next section. However, the effects of self-determined forms of motivation on adaptive psychological outcomes that are likely to increase people's quality of life are also important, and these effects have been reported by a number of contributors to this volume (Fortier & Kowal; Gagné & Blanchard; Wilson & Rodgers). Moreover, these outcomes are not only likely to contribute to an enhanced sense of self and fulfillment, but also may be mediators of behavioral outcomes. For example, outcomes such as satisfaction as a result of engaging in a behavior are likely to contribute to future decisions to engage in a behavior and to affect motivational orientations toward engaging in similar behaviors in the future (Hagger, Chatzisarantis, & Harris, 2006). This section highlights the effects of self-determination theory constructs on adaptive psychological outcomes such as psychological well-being and flow, as well as maladaptive outcomes such as dropout and burnout in sport.

Self-Determination Theory and Psychological Well-Being

In the exercise and sport psychology literature, psychological well-being refers to *hedonic* enjoyment, which, broadly speaking, denotes the experience of pleasure versus displeasure (see Wilson & Rodgers, this volume). Self-determination theory also recognizes another form of psychological well-being, termed *eudaemonia*. Eudaemonia is derived from personally expressive activities that facilitate self-realization through the fulfillment of personal potentials and through the advancement of one's purposes in living (Waterman, 1993). According to self-determination theory, only needs and goals that are rooted in human nature (i.e., autonomy, competence, and relatedness) produce eudaemonia and an enhanced sense of purpose in life (Deci & Ryan, 2000; Sheldon & Elliot, 1999). Therefore the experience of eudaemonia is important with respect to long-term well-being and optimal fulfillment.

Wilson and Rodgers (this volume) and Gagné and Blanchard (this volume) report findings indicating that autonomous motives and the satisfaction of psychological needs are associated with both hedonic and eudaemonic indicators of psychological well-being, in accordance with self-determination theory. In particular, the three types of intrinsic motivation from the Sport Motivation Scale (stimulation, accomplishment, and knowledge; Vallerand, 1997) and identified regulation are positively associated with positive affect, enjoyment, satisfaction, and good sporting behavior (Gagné & Blanchard, this volume). In contrast, external regulation and amotivation are related to anxiety (Brière, Vallerand, Blais, & Pelletier, 1995; Vallerand & Losier, 1994).

In addition, a diary study conducted by Gagné, Ryan, and Bargmann (2003) showed that daily variations in autonomous motivation were a function of daily variation in need satisfaction, and that daily autonomous motivation predicted daily well-being. Moreover, research has shown that motivational styles pertaining to the autonomous and controlling forms of motivation help explain the process by which interpersonal context influences well-being. As Gagné and Blanchard (this volume) have argued, the fact that daily variation in psychological well-being is a function of daily variation in need satisfaction and motivation suggests that the situation is an important but largely ignored source of influence on daily levels of psychological well-being. It seems therefore that self-determination theory helps explain the influences on well-being constructs that are directly related to optimal situational experience in exercise and sport.

However, Wilson and Rodgers (this volume) have argued that certain issues with respect to psychological well-being warrant further investigation. In particular, more experimental and intervention studies are needed to establish causal relationships between psychological needs, motives, and psychological well-being. Further, more research addressing the interplay between different needs and well-being is called for. The satisfaction of psychological needs and enhancement of psychological well-being are not mutually exclusive but complementary processes (Wilson & Rodgers, this volume). Consequently, it can be expected that optimal experience will be derived in contexts where inputs generated by psychological needs are perceived to work synergistically. However, when inputs generated by psychological needs are antagonistic or in conflict, then psychopathology and lower levels of well-being may result. Researchers should also commit resources to studying whether certain types of psychopathology prevalent in exercise and sport (e.g., burnout and anorexia) are characterized by different types of need frustration.

Elite Athletes, Well-Being, and Psychopathology in Sport

Another important line of research recently embraced by scholars adopting self-determination theory concerns the motivation and psychological well-being of elite athletes. Treasure, Lemyre, Kuczka, and Standage (this volume) note that elite-level performers represent a very small but interesting special population because they face myriad challenges on an almost daily basis. Extreme training loads, injuries, and competition schedules are but a few of the circumstances that make the lifestyle extremely demanding and unique from a motivational point of view. Not surprisingly, researchers dealing with elite athletes have consistently pointed out that the motivational profile of elite athletes is different from the motivational profiles of the general public and recreational athletes.

In particular, research applications of self-determination theory have shown that elite athletes display very high levels of both extrinsic and intrinsic forms of motivation (Chantal, Guay, Dobreva-Martinova, & Vallerand, 1996). This profile can be easily explained on the basis of the nature of competitive sport structures. Specifically, elite athletes have the tendency to endorse extrinsic forms of motivation because monetary rewards have long been part of the currency of competitive sport. However, elite athletes are likely to display high levels of intrinsic motivation as well, because elite sport also provides plenty of opportunities for developing and honing new skills. It therefore seems that different types of motivation may coexist in elite athletes, creating a profile distinctly different from that shown by research in other competitive competence-related areas such as educational attainment (Deci, Vallerand, Pelletier, & Ryan, 1991).

However, the high levels of extrinsic motivation that characterize elite athletes may not necessarily be beneficial for psychological well-being and long-term adherence to sport. Indeed, extrinsic motivation has been shown to facilitate sport dropout as well undermining psychological well-being (Gagné & Blanchard, this volume; Sarrazin, Boiché, & Pelletier, this volume). Further, Treasure and colleagues (this volume) suggest that burnout in athletes is associated with high levels of extrinsic motivation and amotivation. It seems therefore that maladaptive training responses are more likely to occur when an athlete's reason for participating, or locus of causality, shifts to a more extrinsic motivational regulation representing decreased levels of relative autonomy.

One reason elite athletes cite high levels of extrinsic motivation is that the social environment in which they operate, or the motivational climate, may endorse such motivational outcomes. This is typically the case in elite-level sport, as performance is often contingent on rewards such as praise or even extrinsic rewards like money. In addition to investigating the effects of motivational climate and environment on motivation and psychological well-being in sport, researchers focusing on elite athletes need to examine the mediating effects that these variables have on psychopathology and maladaptive psychological outcomes. For example, phenomena related to anorexia and burnout are relevant outcomes in athletes and therefore warrant further investigation.

Self-Determination Theory and the Flow State

The "flow" state (Csikszentmihalyi, 1990) is a subjective human experience that shares some characteristics with intrinsic motivation and has been the subject of recent investigations using a self-determination theory approach. Flow represents a highly involved state of optimal functioning in which a person experiences high levels of commitment, enjoyment, positive emotion, and interest. In a sport context, the experience of flow is considered a highly desirable state because it represents a sense of optimal functioning at performing a skill or a task and is accompanied by adaptive outcomes such as effort, concentration, skill execution, and commitment (Fortier & Kowal, this volume). Ryan and Deci (this volume) suggest that such experiences arise out of a combination of appropriate resource availability (i.e., an athlete's skills) and opportunities for action (i.e., an optimally challenging task). Fortier and Kowal have presented a series of studies showing that athletes are more likely to report being in a state of "flow" if they have high levels of autonomous motivation. The authors suggest that future researchers should examine the effects on the flow state of autonomous forms of motivation at different levels in Vallerand's (this volume) hierarchy. This is particularly relevant in terms of interventions to foster flow, as flow is a situational, changeable, state-like construct that may respond best to interventions focused on enhancing intrinsic motivation at the same level of generality.

Self-Determination Theory and Exercise and Sport Behavior

Self-determination theory is primarily about behavior. It focuses on the motivational antecedents of behavioral engagement and provides an account of the underlying reasons for such engagement. In particular, it focuses on the persistence or maintenance of behavior. Interestingly, the outcome of behavioral engagement is unlikely to differ whether one is intrinsically or extrinsically motivated (Ryan & Deci, this volume). Instead, the difference lies in the subjective experience of the behavioral engagement by the individual and, most importantly, in the degree to which the individual is likely to persist with the behavior and invest effort or form plans or intentions to participate in the behavior in the future (Hagger & Chatzisarantis, this volume; Ryan & Deci, this volume; Standage, Gillison, & Treasure, this volume). Most importantly, persistence, maintenance, and change in behavior over time should be the focal outcome variables on the basis that more self-determined forms of motivation will be related to behavioral commitment (Fortier & Kowal, this volume). Conversely, more controlling forms of motivation are related to behavioral desistence, especially once the forms of external reinforcement are removed. This section summarizes the research in the present volume pertaining to the behavioral effects of self-determined motivation on behavioral outcomes in exercise and sport.

Effects of Motivation on Participation in Exercise

An interesting line of research dealing with participation motives concerns the processes by which intrinsic and extrinsic motives influence exercise participation. Markland and Ingledew (this volume) suggest that extrinsic motives have deleterious effects on physical activity participation because, on average, these motives are experienced as controlling. In contrast, intrinsic motives have beneficial effects on physical activity participation because they are more directly associated with satisfaction of psychological needs and therefore are experienced as autonomous. However, Markland and Ingledew argue that extrinsic motives can be experienced as self-determined autonomous in cases in which an individual identifies with and values the outcomes of the physical activity or has integrated exercise participation with his or her other core values and beliefs. Thus, being extrinsically motivated per se may not necessarily result in negative consequences or maladaptive outcomes (Fortier & Kowal, this volume; Ryan et al., 1997).

The beneficial effects of autonomous motivation on physical exercise and sport behavior are not confined to persistence but also extend to the transference of motivation from one context to another. Deci and Ryan (1985, p. 278) originally used the term "generalization of behavioral change" to describe motivational changes that can be flexibly applied or performed in a variety of contexts and conditions. From a self-determination theory perspective, such flexible transference of physical activity or other health behavior is more likely to take place when motivation is autonomous rather than controlling. In the domain of physical activity, we have recently addressed this question of generalization of behavioral change (Hagger, Chatzisarantis, Barkoukis, Wang, & Baranowski, 2005; Hagger, Chatzisarantis, Culverhouse, & Biddle, 2003), suggesting that motivation in an educational context (i.e., physical education) can be transferred to motivation and intentional action in another, related context (i.e., leisure-time physical activity). While we have recently supported this research experimentally (Chatzisarantis & Hagger, 2006), further experimental studies testing hypotheses related to generalization of behavioral change are needed.

Effects of Motivation on Participation in Sport

In accordance with tenets of self-determination theory, research has clearly documented that self-determined or autonomous motives are positively associated with persistence in sport while controlling motives are positively associated with dropout from sport (Pelletier & Sarrazin, this volume; Sarrazin, Boiché, & Pelletier, this volume). It seems therefore that, as Deci and Ryan (1985) originally predicted, engaging in sport for autonomous reasons (e.g., for fun, interest, or personally relevant goals) facilitates persistence whereas engaging for controlling reasons is associated with reduced maintenance. However, as noted earlier, some athletes endorse both intrinsic and extrinsic motives for engaging in their sport (Chantal et al., 1996). This is not surprising, particularly in athletes involved in a very prescriptive, controlling program of sport training. From a motivational perspective, this is not problematic in terms of persistence per se; provided that the athlete also has autonomous motives, he or she will continue to participate in sport once the reinforcing contingencies surrounding the extrinsic motives are removed. It is when the extrinsic contingencies undermine autonomous motivation that the athlete may drop out as a result of a controlling social structure and a lack of autonomy support from social agents like coaches and managers (Sarrazin, Boiché, & Pelletier, this volume).

Interestingly, it may be that athletes internalize and integrate the controlling contexts and behaviors provided for them by their coaches as long as they believe that the practices serve personally valued goals linked with psychological need satisfaction. This idea is supported by recent theorizing (e.g., Hagger & Chatzisarantis, 2005) and empirical evidence (e.g., Iyengar, Ross, & Lepper, 1999; Gagne & Blanchard, this volume) suggesting that if significant others are of appropriate status and operate in a collectivist or cohesive group environment (as exists in a sport team), but adopt a controlling rather than an autonomy-supportive approach, individuals may still report high levels of intrinsic motivation. Using team sport players as an example, Hagger and Chatzisarantis (2005) state, "It is possible that [if] a collectivist group norm operated . . . they [players] were prepared to forego personal choice and volition because the group respected and had internalised the instructions and autocratic style of the coach. In such a context it is possible for intrinsic motivation to flourish in a team where autonomy support is not evident and controlling leadership styles pervade" (p. 124).

Theoretical Integration and Advancement

Recent research has focused on combining self-determination theory with other theories to provide multitheory explanations for behavior in exercise and sport. Such theoretical integration is enacted for two primary reasons. First, self-determination theory and other theories such as theories of social cognition may provide complementary explanations of behavioral phenomena. For example, the integration of self-determination theory and theories of intention by a number of researchers has provided useful explanations for the deliberative, decision-making processes involved in future engagement in exercise behavior and has helped to determine the origins of exercise intentions (see Edmunds, Ntoumanis, & Duda, this volume; Fortier & Kowal, this volume; Hagger & Chatzisarantis, this volume; Standage, Gillison, & Treasure, this volume). Second, self-determination theory may offer an explanatory framework for the effects of strategies and techniques aimed at influencing behavior. An important example is the self-determination theory readings of motivational interviewing put forward by Markland and Vansteenkiste (this volume).

Self-Determination Theory and Theories of Intention

Deci and Ryan (1987) mentioned intentions as a key aspect of volitional or chosen behavior derived from deCharms' theorizing on motivation. Since then, a number of researchers have examined the role of self-determination theory constructs on intentions and the direct antecedents of intention. Theories of intention such as the theory of planned behavior aim to explain variance in volitional behavior and reflect the degree of planning and effort a person is prepared to invest in a behavior. Importantly, intentions are belief based, and the suggestion is that these beliefs are likely to be tied in with psychological needs and motivational orientations. Research has corroborated these proposals, indicating that intentions to engage in exercise are a function of autonomous motivational constructs (see Fortier & Kowal, this volume; Hagger & Chatzisarantis, this volume). Furthermore, it seems that the specific belief-based constructs thought to be the antecedents of intentions mediate the effects of autonomous motivation on intentions as previous research suggests (Hagger & Chatzisarantis, this volume; Wilson, Rodgers, Blanchard, & Gessell, 2003). According to Hagger and colleagues (2006), the reason for this integration is that autonomous motives act as a source of information when one is making decisions to act and their influence is akin to the top-down effects in Vallerand's (this volume) hierarchical model of motivation. Future research should focus on examining multitheory interventions aimed at affecting change in constructs from both self-determination theory and theories of intention in exercise and sport in order to examine the overall effectiveness of integrated theories.

Motivational Interviewing and Self-Determination Theory

Motivational interviewing is one very promising strategy that can be conceptualized and understood in terms of self-determination theory in the physical activity domain. Motivational interviewing and self-determination theory may offer complementary explanations because both approaches are based on the same fundamental assumption, that humans have an innate propensity for personal growth (Markland & Vansteenkiste, this volume). Markland and Vansteenkiste noted that four general and interrelated principles stem from the definition of motivational interviewing and underpin its specific techniques and strategies: (a) the expression of empathy, (b) the development of discrepancy, (c) rolling with resistance, and (d) support for self-efficacy. Together these principles are congruent with supporting the psychological needs for autonomy (particularly the development of discrepancy, if done correctly, and rolling with resistance), competence (particularly the strategy of supporting self-efficacy), and relatedness (particularly expressing empathy). Therefore a self-determination theory reading of motivational interviewing extends the literature on motivational interviewing in providing an explanatory system outlining the mechanisms behind the technique's effectiveness in changing exercise behavior.

One crucial difference between self-determination theory and motivational interviewing is that while self-determination theory explains how interpersonal and intrapersonal factors influence behavior, motivational interviewing is a motivational technique and not a theory. In adopting self-determination theory, a researcher can formulate and test hypotheses related to the process by which motivational techniques influence behavior, while this is not possible with motivational interviewing. However, because self-determination theory and motivational interviewing both acknowledge the importance of intrinsic motivation, several authors have proposed that tenets of self-determination theory can be used to understand when and how motivational interviewing facilitates behavioral change (Markland, Ryan, Tobin, & Rollnick, 2005; Vansteenkiste & Sheldon, 2006).

Of greater importance are the benefits that practitioners can glean from research testing the effects of motivational interviewing with self-determination theory as a guide. According to Markland and Vansteenkiste (this volume), the use of self-determination theory in intervention studies can provide predictions about when motivational interviewing is likely to promote controlling forms of extrinsic motivation and when it promotes autonomous forms of extrinsic motivation. Therefore, intervention studies adopting self-determination theory and motivational interviewing can further improve the efficacy of techniques for promoting physical activity participation. In turn, the clinical insights gained from motivational interviewing can further inform and enhance self-determination theory's conception of the motivationally facilitative environment.

Self-Determination Theory and Achievement Goal Theory

Wang and Biddle (this volume) note that autonomous motives from self-determination theory, in combination with constructs from achievement goal theory (Nicholls, 1989), have a direct association with individuals' motivational patterns, physical activity participation, perceptions of self-esteem, and physical self-worth. The authors found significant and theoretically predictable relationships between autonomous motivation and other conceptually related constructs from theories of achievement motivation, namely task orientation, ego orientation, beliefs about success, and physical activity participation. In particular, their findings indicated that autonomous motivation mediated effects of achievement goals and beliefs about success on physical activity and psychological well-being. These results compare favorably with Sarrazin and colleagues' (this volume) finding that autonomous and controlling motives mediate the effect of a task-involving motivational climate on persistence in sport competitors over a season. This mediating effect of autonomous motivation suggests that goals reflecting improvement can facilitate exercise and sport behavior insofar as the pursuit of task-related goals is perceived to support personal autonomy.

The innovative 2 × 2 conceptualization of achievement goals deepens existing conceptualizations of competence within self-determination theory (Conroy,

Elliot, & Coatsworth, this volume). Conroy and colleagues have argued that substantial evidence exists to corroborate the view that an individual's definition of competence (i.e., mastery vs. performance, task orientation vs. ego orientation) interacts with the valence of her or his aim (i.e., approaching competence vs. avoiding incompetence) and can be delimited by four salient achievement goals: *mastery-approach (MAp)*, *performance-approach (PAp)*, *performance-avoidance (PAv)*, and *mastery-avoidance (MAv)* goals. Although research employing this 2 × 2 model is in its infancy (for reviews see Elliot, 1999; Elliot & Conroy, 2005), interesting results are emerging in the exercise and sport psychology literature. First, there is evidence to suggest that approach goals are associated with satisfaction of psychological needs. MAp goals have been found to be positively associated with satisfaction of the need for relatedness, whereas the two avoidance goals (i.e., MAv and PAv) have been negatively linked to satisfaction of the need for relatedness (Elliot & Reis, 2003). Second, evidence indicates that MAp and PAp goals facilitate self-determined motivation relative to PAv goals (e.g., Cury, Elliot, Sarrazin, Da Fonséca, & Rufo, 2002). It seems, therefore, that defining competence in terms of mastery (vs. performance) and competence (vs. incompetence) enhances self-determined motivation. However, it is important to note that researchers have not yet examined the relationships between the 2 × 2 conceptualization of achievement goals and autonomous and controlling forms of extrinsic motivation (integrated, identified, introjected, and external regulations).

Another issue that future research needs to address relates to understanding approach and avoidance reactions of extrinsically motivated individuals. As Conroy and colleagues (this volume) suggest, the hierarchical model of achievement motivation distinguishes between approach and avoidance reactions, whereas self-determination theory does not consider approach and avoidance reactions in relation to extrinsically motivated behaviors (e.g., external and introjected regulations). Thus it may be worthwhile to investigate whether particular associations between cognitive representations of extrinsic motivation and approach and avoidance reactions form in memory, as well as how these approach-oriented external motivations (e.g., striving for an external reward) and avoidance-oriented external regulations (e.g., striving to avoid an external punishment) influence exercise and sport behavior. Empirically, the cognitive link between extrinsic motivation and approach or avoidance reaction can be investigated through the use of the implicit association test or simple "go–no go" tasks.

Conclusions

In closing, we feel that the present volume has been a resounding success in its aim to provide a comprehensive showcase for the cutting-edge theory and research conducted by leading experts adopting self-determination theory in the exercise and sport domain. We have highlighted some of the key findings obtained by the eminent contributors to this volume with respect to methods; the prediction of outcomes, behavior, and motivation; and theoretical integration. We have also issued calls based on these findings for additional research to advance the extant literature and knowledge with respect to this influential theory in the exercise and sport domain. In particular, we have called for greater commitment to innovative research designs that will tap the mechanisms behind the motivational processes leading to motivated behavior and adaptive psychological outcomes. Prominent among designs that are likely to fulfill this aim are experimental and intervention studies that tap the proposed causal mechanisms implied in cross-sectional research. Research to date has identified the "what" and "why" of human motivation in exercise and sport; future experiments will address the "how" questions to unveil the true nature of the mechanisms involved. This volume stands as a testament to the versatility of self-determination theory in its ability to provide rich and comprehensive explanations for behavioral and psychological phenomena in exercise and sport. The future looks bright for self-determination theory and its application in exercise and sport and, judging by the contributions of the authors of this volume, it is in good hands.

R E F E R E N C E S

PREFACE

deCharms, R. (1968). *Personal causation: The internal affective determinants of behavior.* New York: Academic Press.

White, R.W. (1959). Motivation reconsidered: The concept of competence. *Psychological Review, 66,* 297-333.

INTRODUCTION

Bagoien, T.E., & Halvari, H. (2005). Autonomous motivation: Involvement in physical activity, and perceived sport competence: Structural and mediator models. *Perceptual and Motor Skills, 100,* 3-21.

Bandura, A. (1989). Human agency in social cognitive theory. *American Psychologist, 44,* 1175-1184.

Baumeister, R.F., Bratslavsky, E., Muraven, M., & Tice, D.M. (1998). Ego depletion: Is the active self a limited resource? *Journal of Personality and Social Psychology, 74,* 1252-1265.

Beauchamp, P.H., Halliwell, W.R., Fournier, J.F., & Koestner, R. (1996). Effects of cognitive-behavioral psychological skills training on the motivation, preparation, and putting performance of novice golfers. *Sport Psychologist, 110,* 157-170.

Brown, K.W., & Ryan, R.M. (2003). The benefits of being present: Mindfulness and its role in psychological well-being. *Journal of Personality and Social Psychology, 84,* 822-848.

Brown, K.W., & Ryan, R.M. (2005). Multilevel modeling of motivation: A self-determination theory analysis of basic psychological needs. In A.D. Ong & M. van Dulmen (Eds.), *Handbook of methods in positive psychology.* New York: Oxford University Press.

Chandler, C.L., & Connell, J.P. (1987). Children's intrinsic, extrinsic and internalized motivation: A developmental study of children's reasons for liked and disliked behaviours. *British Journal of Developmental Psychology, 5,* 357-365.

Chirkov, V., & Ryan, R.M. (2001). Parent and teacher autonomy-support in Russian and U.S. adolescents: Common effects on well-being and academic motivation. *Journal of Cross-Cultural Psychology, 32,* 618-635.

Chirkov, V., Ryan, R.M., Kim, Y., & Kaplan, U. (2003). Differentiating autonomy from individualism and independence: A self-determination theory perspective on internalization of cultural orientations and well-being. *Journal of Personality and Social Psychology, 84,* 97-110.

Csikszentmihalyi, M. (1990). *Flow: The psychology of optimal experience.* New York: Harper.

deCharms, R. (1968). *Personal causation.* New York: Academic Press.

Deci, E.L. (1975). *Intrinsic motivation.* New York: Plenum Press.

Deci, E.L., Eghrari, H., Patrick, B.C., & Leone, D. (1994). Facilitating internalization: The self-determination theory perspective. *Journal of Personality, 62,* 119-142.

Deci, E.L., Koestner, R., & Ryan, R.M. (1999). A meta-analytic review of experiments examining the effects of extrinsic rewards on intrinsic motivation. *Psychological Bulletin, 125*, 627-668.

Deci, E.L., & Ryan, R.M. (1980). The empirical exploration of intrinsic motivational processes. In L. Berkowitz (Ed.), *Advances in experimental social psychology* (Vol. 13, pp. 39-80). New York: Academic Press.

Deci, E.L., & Ryan, R.M. (1985a). The general causality orientations scale: Self-determination in personality. *Journal of Research in Personality, 19*, 109-134.

Deci, E.L., & Ryan, R.M. (1985b). *Intrinsic motivation and self-determination in human behavior.* New York: Plenum Press.

Deci, E.L., & Ryan, R.M. (2000). The "what" and "why" of goal pursuits: Human needs and the self-determination of behavior. *Psychological Inquiry, 11*, 227-268.

Doganis, G. (2000). Development of a Greek version of the sport motivation scale. *Perceptual and Motor Skills, 90*, 505-512.

Fortier, M.S., Vallerand, R.J., Brière, N.M., & Provencher, P.J. (1995). Competitive and recreational sport structures and gender: A test of their relationship with sport motivation. *International Journal of Sport Psychology, 26*, 24-39.

Frederick, C.M., & Ryan, R.M. (1993). Differences in motivation for sport and exercise and their relations with participation and mental health. *Journal of Sport Behavior, 16*, 124-146.

Frederick, C.M., & Ryan, R.M. (1995). Self-determination in sport: A review using cognitive evaluation theory. *International Journal of Sport Psychology, 26*, 5-23.

Friedman, M. (2003). *Autonomy, gender, politics.* New York: Oxford University Press.

Gagné, M., Ryan, R.M., & Bargmann, K. (2003). The effects of parent and coach autonomy support on need satisfaction and well-being of gymnasts. *Journal of Applied Sport Psychology, 15*, 372-390.

Gaumond, S. (2000). *Parental influences on adolescents' physical activity motivation and behavior.* Unpublished master's thesis. University of Ottawa, Ottawa, Ontario, Canada.

Goudas, M., Biddle, S., & Fox, K. (1994). Perceived locus of causality, goal orientations, and perceived competence in school physical education classes. *British Journal of Educational Psychology, 64*, 453-463.

Goudas, M., Biddle, S., & Underwood, M. (1995). A prospective study of the relationships between motivational orientations and perceived competence with intrinsic motivation and achievement in a teacher education course. *Educational Psychology, 15*, 89-96.

Green-Demers, I. (2004, May). On the threshold of autonomous behavior regulation: The role of guilt and shame in the development of personal responsibility and self-determined motivation. Paper presented at the Second International Conference on Self-Determination Theory, Ottawa, Ontario.

Grolnick, W.S., & Ryan, R.M. (1989). Parent styles associated with children's self-regulation and competence in school. *Journal of Educational Psychology, 81*, 143-154.

Grouzet, F.M.E., Kasser, T., Ahuvia, A., Fernandez-Dols, J.M., Kim, Y., Lau, S., Ryan, R.M., Saunders, S., Schmuck, P., & Sheldon, K. (in press). The structure of goal contents across 15 cultures. *Journal of Personality and Social Psychology.*

Hagger, M.S., Chatzisarantis, N.L.D., Culverhouse, T., & Biddle, S.J.H. (2003). The process by which perceived autonomy support in physical education promotes leisure-time physical activity intentions and behavior: A trans-contextual model. *Journal of Educational Psychology*, *95*, 784-795.

Harlow, H. (1950). Learning and satiation of response in intrinsically motivated complex puzzle performance by monkeys. *Journal of Comparative Physiology and Psychology*, *43*, 289-294.

Harter, S. (1981). A new self-report scale of intrinsic versus extrinsic orientation in the classroom: Motivational and informational components. *Developmental Psychology*, *17*, 300-312.

Hull, C.L. (1943). *Principles of behavior: An introduction to behavior theory.* New York: Appleton-Century-Crofts.

Jordan, J.V. (1997). Do you believe that the concepts of self and autonomy are useful in understanding women? In J.V. Jordan (Ed.), *Women's growth in diversity: More writings from the Stone Center* (pp. 29-32). New York: Guilford Press.

Kasser, T. (2002). *The high price of materialism.* Cambridge, MA: MIT Press.

Kasser, T., & Ryan, R.M. (1996). Further examining the American dream: Differential correlates of intrinsic and extrinsic goals. *Personality and Social Psychology Bulletin*, *22*, 280-287.

Kowal, J., & Fortier, M.S. (2000). Testing relationships from the hierarchical model of intrinsic and extrinsic motivation using flow as a motivational consequence. *Research Quarterly for Sport and Exercise*, *71*, 171-181.

Krapp, A., & Ryan, R. (2002). Selbstwirksamkeit und Lernmotivation. Eine kritische Betrachtung der Theorie von Bandura aus der Sicht der Selbstbestimmungstheorie und der pädagogisch-psychologischen Interessentheorie. [Self efficacy and motivation for learning. A critical view of the theory of Bandura from the perspective of self-determination theory and the theory of psychological interest in education.] In M. Jerusalem & D. Hopf (Eds.), *Lernwirksame Schulen* (pp. 54-82). Weinheim: Beltz.

Ladygina-Kohts, N.N. (2002). In F.B.M de Waal (Ed.), *Infant chimpanzee and human child: A classic 1935 comparative study of ape emotions and intelligence.* New York: Oxford University Press.

Little, T.D. (1997). Mean and covariance structures (MACS) analysis of cross-cultural data: Practical and theoretical issues. *Multivariate Behavioral Research*, *32*, 53-76.

Mandigo, J.L., & Holt, N.L. (2002). Putting theory into practice: Enhancing motivation through OPTIMAL strategies. *Avante*, *8*, 21-29.

Markus, H.R., Kitayama, S., & Heiman, R.J. (1996). Culture and "basic" psychological principles. In E.T. Higgins & A.W. Kruglanski (Eds.), *Social psychology: Handbook of basic principles.* New York: Guilford Press.

Matsumoto, H., & Takenaka, K. (2004). Motivational profiles and stages of exercise behavior change. *International Journal of Sport and Health Science*, *2*, 89-96.

Matsumoto, H., Takenaka, K., & Tayaka, N. (2003). Development of the exercise motivation scale for exercise adherence based on self-determination theory: Reliability and validity. *Japanese Journal of Health Promotion*, *5*, 120-129.

McAuley, E., & Tammen, V.V. (1989). The effects of subjective and objective competitive outcomes on intrinsic motivation. *Journal of Exercise and Sport Psychology*, *11*, 84-93.

Moller, A.C., Deci, E.L., & Ryan, R.M. (2006). Choice and ego-depletion: The moderating role of autonomy. *Personality and Social Psychology Bulletin, 32*, 1024-1036.

Mullan, E., & Markland, D. (1997). Variations in self-determination across the stages of change for exercise in adults. *Motivation and Emotion, 21*, 349-362.

Mullan, E., Markland, D., & Ingledew, D.K. (1997). A graded conceptualisation of self-determination in the regulation of exercise behaviour: Development of a measure using confirmatory factor analytic procedures. *Personality and Individual Differences, 23*, 745-752.

Newburg, D., & Rotella, B. (1996). Understanding gifted athletes. *Journal of Performance Education, 1*, 145-156.

Nix, G.A., Ryan, R.M., Manly, J.B., & Deci, E.L. (1999). Revitalization through self-regulation: The effects of autonomous versus controlled motivation on happiness and vitality. *Journal of Experimental Social Psychology, 35*, 266-284.

Ntoumanis, N. (2000). Motivational clusters in a sample of British physical education classes. *Psychology of Sport and Exercise, 3*, 177-194.

Orlick, T. (1996). Winning the downhill is an uphill battle: An interview with Kerrin Lee-Gartner, Canadian alpine ski team. *Journal of Performance Education, 1*, 48-55.

Parish, L.E., & Treasure, D.C. (2003). Physical activity and situational motivation in physical education: Influence of the motivational climate and perceived ability. *Research Quarterly for Exercise and Sport, 2*, 173-182.

Pedersen, D.M. (2002). Intrinsic-extrinsic factors in sport motivation. *Perceptual and Motor Skills, 95*, 459-476.

Pelletier, L.G., Dion, S., Tuson, K.M., & Green-Demers, I. (1999). Why do people fail to adopt environmental behaviors? Towards a taxonomy of environmental amotivation. *Journal of Applied Social Psychology, 29*, 2481-2504.

Pelletier, L.G., Fortier, M.S., Vallerand, R.J., & Brière, N.M. (2001). Associations among perceived autonomy support, forms of self-regulation, and persistence: A prospective study. *Motivation and Emotion, 25*, 279-306.

Pelletier, L.G., Fortier, M.S., Vallerand, R.J., Tuson, K., Brière, N.M., & Blais, N.M. (1995). Toward a new measure of intrinsic motivation, extrinsic motivation, and amotivation in sports: The Sport Motivation Scale (SMS). *Journal of Sport and Exercise Psychology, 17*, 35-53.

Reeve, J., & Deci, E.L. (1996). Elements within the competitive situation that affect intrinsic motivation. *Personality and Social Psychology Bulletin, 22*, 24-33.

Reeve, J., Olson, B.C., & Cole, S.G. (1985). Motivation and performance: Two consequences of winning and losing a competition. *Motivation and Emotion, 9*, 291-298.

Reis, H.T., Sheldon, K.M., Gable, S.L., Roscoe, J., & Ryan, R.M. (2000). Daily well-being: The role of autonomy, competence, and relatedness. *Personality and Social Psychology Bulletin, 26*, 419-435.

Rose, E.A., Markland, D., & Parfitt, G. (2001). The development and initial validation of the Exercise Causality Orientations Scale. *Journal of Sports Sciences, 19*, 445-462.

Ryan, R.M. (1982). Control and information in the intrapersonal sphere: An extension of cognitive evaluation theory. *Journal of Personality and Social Psychology, 43*, 450-461.

Ryan, R.M. (1995). Psychological needs and the facilitation of integrative processes. *Journal of Personality, 63*, 397-427.

Ryan, R.M., & Connell, J.P. (1989). Perceived locus of causality and internalization: Examining reasons for acting in two domains. *Journal of Personality and Social Psychology, 57*, 749-761.

Ryan, R.M., & Deci, E.L. (2000a). Intrinsic and extrinsic motivations: Classic definitions and new directions. *Contemporary Educational Psychology, 25*, 54-67.

Ryan, R.M., & Deci, E.L. (2000b). Self-determination theory and the facilitation of intrinsic motivation, social development and well-being. *American Psychologist, 55*, 68-78.

Ryan, R.M., & Frederick, C.M. (1997). On energy, personality and health: Subjective vitality as a dynamic reflection of well-being. *Journal of Personality, 65*, 529-565.

Ryan, R.M., Frederick, C.M., Lepes, D., Rubio, N., & Sheldon, K.M. (1997). Intrinsic motivation and exercise adherence. *International Journal of Sport Psychology, 28*, 335-354.

Ryan, R.M., Koestner, R., & Deci, E.L. (1991). Ego-involved persistence: When free-choice behavior is not intrinsically motivated. *Motivation and Emotion, 15*, 185-205.

Ryan, R.M., & Lynch, J. (1989). Emotional autonomy versus detachment: Revisiting the vicissitudes of adolescence and young adulthood. *Child Development, 60*, 340-356.

Selye, H. (1976). *The stress of life* (rev. ed.). New York: McGraw-Hill.

Skinner, B.F. (1953). *Science and human behavior.* New York: Macmillan.

Tanaka, K., & Yamauchi, H. (2000). Influence of autonomy on perceived control beliefs and self-regulated learning in Japanese undergraduate students. *North American Journal of Psychology, 2*, 255-272.

Vallerand, R.J. (1997). Toward a hierarchical model of intrinsic and extrinsic motivation. In M.P. Zanna (Ed.), *Advances in experimental social psychology* (Vol. 29, pp. 271-360). San Diego: Academic Press.

Vallerand, R.J., & Bissonnette, R. (1992). Intrinsic, extrinsic, and amotivational styles as predictors of behavior: A prospective study. *Journal of Personality, 60*, 599-620.

Vallerand, R.J., & Losier, G.F. (1999). An integrative analysis of intrinsic and extrinsic motivation in sport. *Journal of Applied Sport Psychology, 11*, 142-169.

Vallerand, R.J., & Reid, G. (1984). On the causal effects of perceived competence on intrinsic motivation: A test of cognitive evaluation theory. *Journal of Sport Psychology, 6*, 94-102.

Vansteenkiste, M., & Deci, E.L. (2003). Competitively contingent rewards and intrinsic motivation: Can losers remain motivated? *Motivation and Emotion, 27*, 273-299.

Vansteenkiste, M., Lens, W., Dewitte, S., De Witte, H., & Deci, E.L. (2004). The "why" and "why not" of job search behavior: Their relation to searching, unemployment experience, and well-being. *European Journal of Social Psychology, 34*, 345-363.

Vansteenkiste, M., Simons, J., Braet, C., Bachman, C., & Deci, E.L. (2005). Promoting maintained weight loss through healthy lifestyle changes among severely obese children: An experimental test of self-determination theory. Unpublished manuscript, University of Leuven.

Vansteenkiste, M., Simons, J., Soenens, B., & Lens, W. (2004). How to become a per-severing exerciser: The importance of providing a clear, future goal in an autonomy-supportive way. *Journal of Sport and Exercise Psychology, 26,* 232-249.

Vlachopoulos, S.P., Karageorghis, C.I., & Terry, P.C. (2000). Motivation profiles in sport: A self-determination theory perspective. *Research Quarterly for Exercise and Sport, 71,* 387-397.

Wankel, L.M. (1993). The importance of enjoyment to adherence and psychological benefits from physical activity. *International Journal of Sport Psychology, 24,* 151-169.

White, R.W. (1959). Motivation reconsidered: The concept of competence. *Psychological Review, 66,* 297-333.

Williams, G.C., Grow, V.M., Freedman, Z., Ryan, R.M., & Deci, E.L. (1996). Moti-vational predictors of weight loss and weight-loss maintenance. *Journal of Personality and Social Psychology, 70,* 115-126.

Williams, G.C., Rodin, G.C., Ryan, R.M., Grolnick, W.S., & Deci, E.L. (1998). Autono-mous regulation and adherence to long-term medical regimens in adult outpatients. *Health Psychology, 17,* 269-276.

Wilson, P.M., Rodgers, W.M., Blanchard, C.M., & Gessell, J. (2003). The relation-ship between psychological needs, self-determined motivation, exercise attitudes, and physical fitness. *Journal of Applied Social Psychology, 33,* 2373-2392.

Wilson, P.M., Rodgers, W.M., & Fraser, S.N. (2002). Examining the psychometric properties of the behavioural regulation in exercise questionnaire. *Measurement in Physical Education and Exercise Science, 6,* 1-21.

Wilson, P.M., Rodgers, W.M., Fraser, S.N., & Murray, T.C. (2004). Relationships between exercise regulations and motivational consequences in university students. *Research Quarterly for Exercise and Sport, 75,* 81-91.

CHAPTER 1

Amabile, T.M. (1993). Motivational synergy: Toward new conceptualizations of intrinsic and extrinsic motivation in the workplace. *Human Resources Review, 3,* 185-201.

Biddle, S.J.H., & Mutrie, N. (2001). *Psychology of physical activity: Determinants, well-being and interventions.* London: Routledge.

Cash, T.F., Novy, P.L., & Grant, J.R. (1994). Why do women exercise? Factor analysis and further validation of the Reasons for Exercise Inventory. *Perceptual and Motor Skills, 78,* 539-544.

Crawford, S., & Eklund, R.C. (1994). Social physique anxiety, reasons for exercise, and attitudes toward exercise settings. *Journal of Sport and Exercise Psychology, 16,* 70-82.

Davis, C., Fox, J., Brewer, H., & Ratusny, D. (1995). Motivations to exercise as a func-tion of personality characteristics, age, and gender. *Personality and Individual Differences, 19,* 165-174.

Deci, E.L., & Ryan, R.M. (1985). *Intrinsic motivation and self-determination in human behavior.* New York: Plenum Press.

Deci, E.L., & Ryan, R.M. (2000). The "what" and "why" of goal pursuits: Human needs and the self-determination of behavior. *Psychological Inquiry, 11,* 227-268.

Duda, J.L., & Tappe, M.K. (1987, September). Personal investment in exercise: The development of the Personal Incentives for Exercise Questionnaire. Paper presented at the Association for the Advancement of Applied Sport Psychology, Newport Beach, CA.

Duda, J.L., & Tappe, M.K. (1989a). The personal incentives for exercise questionnaire: Preliminary development. *Perceptual and Motor Skills, 68,* 1122.

Duda, J.L., & Tappe, M.K. (1989b). Personal investment in exercise among adults: The examination of age and gender-related differences in motivational orientation. In A.C. Ostrow (Ed.), *Aging and motor behavior* (pp. 239-256). Indianapolis: Benchmark Press.

Frederick, C.M., & Ryan, R.M. (1993). Differences in motivation for sport and exercise and their relations with participation and mental health. *Journal of Sport Behavior, 16,* 124-146.

Frederick, C.M., & Ryan, R.M. (1995). Self-determination in sport: A review using cognitive evaluation theory. *International Journal of Sport Psychology, 26,* 5-23.

Frederick-Recascino, C.M. (2002). Self-determination theory and participation motivation research in the sport and exercise domain. In E.L. Deci & R.M. Ryan (Eds.), *Handbook of self-determination research* (pp. 277-294). Rochester, NY: University of Rochester Press.

Gill, D.L., Gross, J.B., & Huddleston, S. (1983). Participation motivation in youth sports. *International Journal of Sport Psychology, 14,* 1-14.

Ingledew, D.K., & Ferguson, E. (in press). Personality and riskier sexual behaviour: Motivational mediators. *Psychology and Health.*

Ingledew, D.K., Hardy, L., & de Sousa, K. (1995). Body shape dissatisfaction and exercise motivations. *Journal of Sports Sciences, 13,* 60.

Ingledew, D.K., & Markland, D. (2005, September). *Behavioural regulation of exercise: Effects of personality traits and participation motives.* Paper presented at the annual meeting of the European Health Psychology Society, Galway, Ireland.

Ingledew, D.K., Markland, D., & Medley, A.R. (1998). Exercise motives and stages of change. *Journal of Health Psychology, 3,* 477-489.

Ingledew, D.K., & Sullivan, G. (2002). Effects of body mass and body image on exercise motives in adolescence. *Psychology of Sport and Exercise, 3,* 323-338.

Kasser, T., & Ryan, R.M. (1993). A dark side of the American dream: Correlates of financial success as a central life aspiration. *Journal of Personality and Social Psychology, 65,* 410-422.

Kasser, T., & Ryan, R.M. (1996). Further examining the American dream: Differential correlates of intrinsic and extrinsic goals. *Personality and Social Psychology Bulletin, 22,* 280-287.

Lazarus, R.S., & Folkman, S. (1989). *Manual for the Hassles and Uplifts Scales: Research edition.* Palo Alto, CA: Consulting Psychologists Press.

Maehr, M.L., & Braskamp, L.A. (1986). *The motivation factor: A theory of personal investment.* Lexington, MA: Lexington Press.

Maltby, J., & Day, L. (2001). The relationship between exercise motives and psychological well-being. *Journal of Psychology, 135,* 651-660.

Markland, D. (1999). Internally informational versus internally controlling exercise motives and exercise enjoyment: The mediating role of self-determination. In

P. Parisi, F. Pigozzi, & G. Prinzi (Eds.), *Sport science '99 in Europe. Proceedings of the 4th annual congress of the European College of Sport Science.* Rome: University Institute of Motor Sciences.

Markland, D., & Hardy, L. (1993). The Exercise Motivations Inventory: Preliminary development and validity of a measure of individuals' reasons for participation in regular physical exercise. *Personality and Individual Differences, 15,* 289-296.

Markland, D., & Hardy, L. (1997). On the factorial and construct validity of the Intrinsic Motivation Inventory: Conceptual and operational concerns. *Research Quarterly for Exercise and Sport, 68,* 20-32.

Markland, D., & Ingledew, D.K. (1997). The measurement of exercise motives: Factorial validity and invariance across gender of a revised Exercise Motivations Inventory. *British Journal of Health Psychology, 2,* 361-376.

Markland, D., Ingledew, D.K., Hardy, L., & Grant, L. (1992). A comparison of the exercise motivations of participants in aerobics and weight-watcher exercisers. *Journal of Sports Sciences, 10,* 609-610.

Markland, D., Taylor, A., & Adams, J. (in preparation). Body dissatisfaction and exercise behaviour: The mediating role of exercise motives and relative autonomy.

Markland, D., & Tobin, V. (2004). A modification to the Behavioural Regulation in Exercise Questionnaire to include an assessment of amotivation. *Journal of Sport and Exercise Psychology, 26,* 191-196.

McDonald, K., & Thompson, J.K. (1992). Eating disturbance, body image dissatisfaction, and reasons for exercising: Gender differences and correlational findings. *International Journal of Eating Disorders, 11,* 289-292.

Pelletier, L.G., Fortier, M.S., Vallerand, R.J., & Brière, N.M. (2001). Associations among perceived autonomy support, forms of self-regulation, and persistence: A prospective study. *Motivation and Emotion, 25,* 279-306.

Prochaska, J.O., & Marcus, B.H. (1994). The transtheoretical model: Applications to exercise. In R.K. Dishman (Ed.), *Advances in exercise adherence* (pp. 161-180). Champaign, IL: Human Kinetics.

Rodgers, W.M., & Brawley, L.R. (1991). The role of outcome expectancies in participation motivation. *Journal of Sport and Exercise Psychology, 13,* 411-427.

Rolls, B.J., Federoff, I.C., & Guthrie, J.F. (1991). Gender differences in eating behavior and body weight regulation. *Health Psychology, 10,* 133-142.

Ryan, R.M., Chirkov, V.I., Little, T.D., Sheldon, K.M., Timoshina, E., & Deci, E.L. (1999). The American dream in Russia: Extrinsic aspirations and well-being in two cultures. *Personality and Social Psychology Bulletin, 25,* 1509-1524.

Ryan, R.M., & Connell, J.P. (1989). Perceived locus of causality and internalization: Examining reasons for acting in two domains. *Journal of Personality and Social Psychology, 57,* 749-761.

Ryan, R.M., & Deci, E.L. (2000). Self-determination theory and the facilitation of intrinsic motivation, social development, and well-being. *American Psychologist, 55,* 68-78.

Ryan, R.M., Deci, E.L., & Grolnick, W.S. (1995). Autonomy, relatedness, and the self: Their relation to development and psychopathology. In D. Cicchetti & D.J. Cohen

(Eds.), *Developmental psychopathology, Vol. 1: Theory and methods* (pp. 618-655). Oxford: Wiley.

Ryan, R.M., Frederick, C.M., Lepes, D., Rubio, N., & Sheldon, K. (1997). Intrinsic motivation and exercise adherence. *International Journal of Sport Psychology, 28,* 335-354.

Ryan, R.M., Rigby, S., & King, K. (1993). Two types of religious internalization and their relations to religious orientations and mental health. *Journal of Personality and Social Psychology, 65,* 586-596.

Ryan, R.M., Sheldon, K.M., Kasser, T., & Deci, E.L. (1996). All goals are not created equal: An organismic perspective on the nature of goals and their regulation. In P.M. Gollwitzer & J.A. Bargh (Eds.), *The psychology of action: Linking cognition and motivation to behavior* (pp. 7-26). New York: Guilford Press.

Ryan, R.M., Vallerand, R.J., & Deci, E.L. (1984). Intrinsic motivation in sport: A cognitive evaluation theory interpretation. In W.F. Straub & J.M. Williams (Eds.), *Cognitive sport psychology* (pp. 231-242). New York: Sport Science Associates.

Sheldon, K.M., Ryan, R.M., Deci, E.L., & Kasser, T. (2004). The independent effects of goal contents and motives on well-being: It's both what you pursue and why you pursue it. *Personality and Social Psychology Bulletin, 30,* 475-486.

Silberstein, L.R., Striegel-Moore, R.H., Timko, C., & Rodin, J. (1988). Behavioral and psychological implications of body dissatisfaction: Do men and women differ? *Sex Roles, 19,* 219-232.

Smith, B.L., Handley, P., & Eldredge, D.A. (1998). Sex differences in exercise motivation and body-image satisfaction among college students. *Perceptual and Motor Skills, 86,* 723-732.

Striegel-Moore, R.H., Silberstein, L.R., & Rodin, J. (1986). Toward an understanding of risk factors for bulimia. *American Psychologist, 41,* 246-263.

CHAPTER 2

American Psychiatric Association. (1994). *Diagnostic and statistical manual of mental disorders.* (4th ed.). Washington, DC: American Psychiatric Association.

Biddle, J.H., & Mutrie, N. (2001). *Psychology of physical activity: Determinants, well-being and interventions.* London: Routledge.

Black, A.E., & Deci, E.L. (2000). The effects of instructors' support and students' autonomous motivation on learning organic chemistry: A self-determination theory perspective. *Science Education, 84,* 740-756.

Brewer, M. (1991). The social self: On being the same and different at the same time. *Personality and Social Psychology Bulletin, 17,* 475-482.

Brewer, M. (1993). The role of distinctiveness in social identity and group behavior. In M. Hogg & D. Abrams (Eds.), *Group motivation: Social psychological perspectives* (pp. 1-16). London: Harvester, Wheatsheaf.

Chirkov, V.I., & Ryan, R.M. (2001). Parent and teacher autonomy support in Russian and U.S. adolescents: Common effects on well-being and academic motivation. *Journal of Cross-Cultural Psychology, 32,* 618-635.

Chirkov, V.I., Ryan, R.M., Kim, Y., & Kaplan, U. (2003). Differentiating autonomy from individualism and independence: A self-determination theory perspective on internalization of cultural orientations and well-being. *Journal of Personality and Social Psychology, 8,* 97-110.

Deci, E.L., Eghrari, H., Patrick, B.C., & Leone, D. (1994). Facilitating internalization: The self-determination theory perspective. *Journal of Personality, 62,* 119-142.

Deci, E.L., & Ryan, R.M. (1985). *Intrinsic motivation and self-determination in human behavior.* New York: Plenum Press.

Deci, E.L., & Ryan, R.M. (2000). The "what" and "why" of goal pursuits: Human needs and the self-determination of behavior. *Psychological Inquiry, 11,* 227-268.

Deci, E.L., Ryan, R.M., Gagné, M., Leone, D.R., Usunov, J., & Kornazheva, B.P. (2001). Need satisfaction, motivation, and well-being in the work organizations of a former Eastern bloc country: A cross-cultural study of self-determination. *Personality and Social Psychology Bulletin, 27,* 930-942.

Department of Culture, Media, and Sport. (2004). *Choosing health? Choosing activity: A consultation on how to increase physical activity.* London: The Stationary Office.

Diener, E. (2000). Subjective well-being: The science of happiness and a proposal for a national index. *American Psychologist, 55,* 34-43.

Diener, E., & Diener, M. (1995). Cross cultural correlates of life satisfaction and self-esteem. *Journal of Personality and Social Psychology, 68,* 653-663.

Edmunds, J.K., Duda, J.L., & Ntoumanis, N. (2005). Psychological needs theories as predictors of exercise-related cognitions and affect among an ethnically diverse cohort of female exercise group participants. Manuscript submitted for publication.

Edmunds, J.K., Ntoumanis, N., & Duda, J.L. (2005a). Examining exercise dependence symptomatology from a self-determination perspective. Manuscript submitted for publication.

Edmunds, J.K., Ntoumanis, N., & Duda, J.L. (2005b). Facilitating exercise engagement: An experimental test of self-determination theory. Manuscript in preparation.

Edmunds, J.K., Ntoumanis, N., & Duda, J.L. (2006). A test of self-determination theory in the exercise domain. *Journal of Applied Social Psychology, 36,* 2240-2265.

Ellsworth, P.C., & Gonzalez, R. (2003). Questions and comparisons: Methods of research in social psychology. In M.A. Hogg & J. Cooper (Eds.), *Sage handbook of social psychology.* London: Sage.

Godin, G., & Shephard, R.J. (1985). A simple method to assess exercise behavior in the community. *Canadian Journal of Applied Sport Sciences, 10,* 141-146.

Hagger, M.S., Chatzisarantis, N.L.D., Barkoukis, V., Wang, C.K.J., & Baranowski, J. (2005). Perceived autonomy support in physical education and leisure-time physical activity: A cross-cultural evaluation of the trans-contextual model. *Journal of Educational Psychology, 97,* 287-301.

Hagger, M.S., Chatzisarantis, N., Culverhouse, T., & Biddle, S.J.H. (2003). The processes by which perceived autonomy support in physical education promotes leisure-time physical activity intentions and behavior: A trans-contextual model. *Journal of Educational Psychology, 95,* 784-795.

Hagger, M.S., Chatzisarantis, N.L.D., & Harris, J. (2006). From psychological need satisfaction to intentional behavior: Testing a motivational sequence in two behavioral contexts. *Personality and Social Psychology Bulletin, 32,* 131-138.

Hamer, M., Karageorghis, C.I., & Vlachopoulos, S.P. (2002). Motives of exercise participation as predictors of exercise dependence among endurance athletes. *Journal of Sports Medicine and Physical Fitness, 42,* 233-238.

Hausenblas, H.A., & Symons Downs, D. (2002a). Exercise dependence: A systematic review. *Psychology of Sport and Exercise, 3,* 89-123.

Hausenblas, H.A., & Symons Downs, D. (2002b). How much is too much? The development and validation of the exercise dependence scale. *Psychology and Health, 17,* 387-404.

Iyengar, S.S., & Lepper, M.R. (1999). Rethinking the value of choice: A cultural perspective on intrinsic motivation. *Journal of Personality and Social Psychology, 76,* 349-365.

Koestner, R., & Losier, G.F. (2002). Distinguishing three ways of being internally motivated: A closer look at introjection, identification, and intrinsic motivation. In E.L. Deci & R.M. Ryan (Eds.), *Handbook of self-determination research.* Rochester, NY: University of Rochester Press.

Landry, J.B., & Solomon, M. (2004). African American women's self-determination across the stages of change for exercise. *Journal of Sport and Exercise Psychology, 26,* 457-469.

Li, F. (1999). The Exercise Motivation Scale: Its multifaceted structure and construct validity. *Journal of Applied Sport Psychology, 11,* 97-115.

Loumidis, K.S., & Roxborough, H. (1995). A cognitive-behavioural approach to excessive exercise. In J. Annett, B. Cripps, & H. Steinberg, *Exercise addiction: Motivation for participation in sport and exercise* (pp. 45-53). Leicester, UK: British Psychological Society.

Markland, D., & Tobin, V.J. (2004a). Further evidence for the mediating role of psychological need satisfaction in the relationship between social-contextual supports and intrinsic motivation: A comparison of competing models. Manuscript submitted for publication.

Markland, D., & Tobin, V.J. (2004b). A modification to the Behavioural Regulation in Exercise Questionnaire to include an assessment of amotivation. *Journal of Sport and Exercise Psychology, 26,* 191-196.

Markus, H.R., & Kitayama, S. (1991). Culture and the self: Implications for cognition, emotion and motivation. *Psychological Review, 98,* 224-253.

Mullan, E., & Markland, D. (1997). Variations in self-determination across the stages of change for exercise in adults. *Motivation and Emotion, 21,* 349-362.

Mullan, E., Markland, D., & Ingledew, D.K. (1997). A graded conceptualization of self-determination in the regulation of exercise behavior: Development of a measure using confirmatory factor analytic procedures. *Personality and Individual Differences, 23,* 745-752.

National Audit Office. (2001). *Tackling obesity in England: A report by the controller and auditor general.* London: The Stationary Office.

Ogles, B.M., Masters, K.S., & Richardson, S.A. (1995). Obligatory running and gender: An analysis of participation motives and training habits. *International Journal of Sport Psychology, 26,* 233-248.

Pelletier, L.G., Fortier, M.S., Vallerand, R.J., & Brière, N.M. (2001). Associations among perceived autonomy support, forms of self-regulation, and persistence: A prospective study. *Motivation and Emotion, 25,* 279-306.

Reeve, J. (2002). Self-determination theory applied to educational settings. In E.L. Deci & R.M. Ryan (Eds.), *Handbook of self-determination research* (pp. 183-203). Rochester, NY: University of Rochester Press.

Reeve, J. (2004, May). Two approaches to motivating others: What self-determination theory practitioners can learn from social-cognitive practitioners (and vice versa). Paper presented at the Second International Conference on Self-Determination Theory, Ottawa, Ontario.

Ryan, R.M., Chirkov, V.I., Little, T.D., Sheldon, K.M., Timoshina, E., & Deci, E.L. (1999). The American dream in Russia: Extrinsic aspirations and well-being in two cultures. *Personality and Social Psychology Bulletin, 25,* 1509-1524.

Ryan, R.M., & Deci, E.L. (2000a). The darker and brighter sides of human existence: Basic psychological needs as a unifying concept. *Psychological Inquiry, 11,* 319-338.

Ryan, R.M., & Deci, E.L. (2000b). Self-determination theory and the facilitation of intrinsic motivation, social development, and well-being. *American Psychologist, 55,* 68-78.

Ryan, R., & Frederick, C. (1997). On energy, personality and health: Subjective vitality as a dynamic reflection of well-being. *Journal of Personality, 65,* 529-565.

Scanlan, T.K., Carpenter, P.J., Schmidt, G.W., Simons, J.P., & Keeler, B. (1993). An introduction to the Sport Commitment Model. *Journal of Sport and Exercise Psychology, 15,* 1-15.

Sheldon, M., & Bettencourt, B.A. (2002). Psychological need-satisfaction and subjective well-being within social groups. *British Journal of Social Psychology, 41,* 25-38.

Sheldon, K.M., Williams, G., & Joiner, T. (2003). *Self-determination theory in the clinic: Motivating physical and mental health.* New Haven, CT: Yale University Press.

Skinner, E. (2002). Self-determination, coping, and development. In E.L. Deci & R.M. Ryan (Eds.), *Handbook of self-determination research.* Rochester, NY: University of Rochester Press.

U.S. Department of Health and Human Services. (1996). *Physical activity and health: A report of the Surgeon General.* Atlanta: U.S. Department of Health and Human Services, Centers for Disease Control and Prevention, National Center for Chronic Disease Prevention and Health Promotion.

U.S. Department of Health and Human Services. (2003). *Physical activity and health: A report of the Surgeon General.* Atlanta: U.S. Department of Health and Human Services, Centers for Disease Control and Prevention, National Center for Chronic Disease Prevention and Health Promotion.

Vallerand, R.J. (1997). Toward a hierarchical model of intrinsic and extrinsic motivation. In M.P. Zanna (Ed.), *Advances in experimental social psychology* (pp. 271-360). New York: Academic Press.

Vallerand, R.J., Blanchard, C., Mageau, G.A., Koestner, R., Ratelle, C.F., Léonard, M., Gagné, M., & Marsolais, J. (2003). Les passions de l'âme: On obsessive and harmonious passion. *Journal of Personality and Social Psychology, 85,* 756-767.

Watson, D., Clark, L., & Tellegen, A. (1988). Development and validation of brief measures of positive and negative affect: The PANAS scales. *Journal of Personality and Social Psychology, 54*, 1063-1070.

Williams, G.C., Grow, V.M., Freedman, Z.R., Ryan, R.M., & Deci, E.L. (1996). Motivational predictors of weight loss and weight-loss maintenance. *Journal of Personality and Social Psychology, 30*, 115-126.

Wilson, P.M., & Rodgers, W.M. (2002). The relationship between exercise motives and physical self-esteem in female exercise participants: An application of self-determination theory. *Journal of Applied Biobehavioral Research, 7*, 30-43.

Wilson, P.M., & Rodgers, W.M. (2004). The relationship between perceived autonomy support, exercise regulations and behavioral intentions in women. *Psychology of Sport and Exercise, 5*, 229-242.

Wilson, P.M., Rodgers, W.M., Blanchard, C.M., & Gessell, J. (2003). The relationship between psychological needs, self-determined motivation, exercise attitudes and physical fitness. *Journal of Applied Social Psychology, 33*, 2373-2392.

Wilson, P.M., Rodgers, W.M., & Fraser, S.N. (2002). Examining the psychometric properties of the behavioural regulation in exercise questionnaire. *Measurement in Physical Education and Exercise Science, 6*, 1-21.

CHAPTER 3

Ajzen, I. (1985). From intentions to actions: A theory of planned behavior. In J. Kuhl & J. Beckmann (Eds.), *Action-control: From cognition to behavior* (pp. 11-39). Heidelberg: Springer.

Ajzen, I. (1991). The theory of planned behavior. *Organizational Behavior and Human Decision Processes, 50*, 179-211.

Ajzen, I. (2003). Constructing a TPB questionnaire: Conceptual and methodological considerations. Retrieved April 14, 2003, from University of Massachusetts Department of Psychology Web site: www-unix.oit.umass.edu/~aizen.

Ajzen, I., & Driver, B.E. (1991). Prediction of leisure participation from behavioral, normative, and control beliefs: An application of the theory of planned behavior. *Leisure Sciences, 13*, 185-204.

Armitage, C.J., & Conner, M. (2001). Efficacy of the theory of planned behaviour: A meta-analytic review. *British Journal of Social Psychology, 40*, 471-499.

Bandura, A. (1997). *Self-efficacy: The exercise of control.* New York: Freeman.

Black, A.E., & Deci, E.L. (2000). The effects of instructors' autonomy support and students' autonomous motivation on learning organic chemistry: A self-determination theory perspective. *Science Education, 84*, 740-756.

Chatzisarantis, N.L.D., & Biddle, S.J.H. (1998). Functional significance of psychological variables that are included in the theory of planned behaviour: A self-determination theory approach to the study of attitudes, subjective norms, perceptions of control and intentions. *European Journal of Social Psychology, 28*, 303-322.

Chatzisarantis, N.L.D., Hagger, M.S., Biddle, S.J.H., & Karageorghis, C. (2002). The cognitive processes by which perceived locus of causality predicts participation in physical activity. *Journal of Health Psychology, 7*, 685-699.

Chirkov, V.I., & Ryan, R.M. (2001). Parent and teacher autonomy support in Russian and U.S. adolescents: Common effects on well-being and academic motivation. *Journal of Cross-Cultural Psychology, 32*, 618-635.

Chirkov, V.I., Ryan, R.M., Kim, Y., & Kaplan, U. (2003). Differentiating autonomy from individualism and independence: A self-determination theory perspective on internalization of cultural orientations and well-being. *Journal of Personality and Social Psychology, 8*, 97-110.

Conner, M., & Abraham, C. (2001). Conscientiousness and the theory of planned behavior: Toward a more complete model of the antecedents of intentions and behavior. *Personality and Social Psychology Bulletin, 27*, 1547-1561.

Deci, E.L., Driver, R.E., Hotchkiss, L., Robbins, R.J., & Wilson, I.M. (1993). The relation of mothers' controlling vocalizations to children's intrinsic motivation. *Journal of Experimental Child Psychology, 55*, 151-162.

Deci, E.L., Eghrari, H., Patrick, B.C., & Leone, D.R. (1994). Facilitating internalization: The self-determination theory perspective. *Journal of Personality, 62*, 119-142.

Deci, E.L., & Ryan, R.M. (1985). *Intrinsic motivation and self-determination in human behavior.* New York: Plenum Press.

Deci, E.L., & Ryan, R.M. (1987). The support of autonomy and the control of behavior. *Journal of Personality and Social Psychology, 53*, 1024-1037.

Deci, E.L., & Ryan, R.M. (2000). The "what" and "why" of goal pursuits: Human needs and the self-determination of behavior. *Psychological Inquiry, 11*, 227-268.

Deci, E.L., Ryan, R.M., Gagné, M., Leone, D.R., Usunov, J., & Kornazheva, B.P. (2001). Need satisfaction, motivation, and well-being in the work organizations of a former Eastern bloc country. *Personality and Social Psychology Bulletin, 27*, 930-942.

Deci, E.L., Schwartz, A.J., Sheinman, L., & Ryan, R.M. (1981). An instrument to assess adults' orientations towards control versus autonomy with children: Reflections on intrinsic motivation and perceived competence. *Journal of Educational Psychology, 73*, 642-650.

Deci, E.L., Vallerand, R.J., Pelletier, L.G., & Ryan, R.M. (1991). Motivation in education: The self-determination perspective. *Educational Psychologist, 26*, 325-346.

Efron, B. (1982). *The jackknife, bootstrap and other resampling plans.* Philadelphia: SIAM.

Elliot, A. J., McGregor, H. A., & Thrash, T. M. (2002). The need for competence. In E. L. Deci & R. M. Ryan (Eds.), *Handbook of self-determination research* (pp. 361-387). Rochester, NY: University of Rochester Press.

Field, A.P. (2001). Meta-analysis of correlation coefficients: A Monte Carlo comparison of fixed- and random-effects methods. *Psychological Methods, 6*, 161-180.

Field, A.P. (2003). The problems using fixed-effects models of meta-analysis on real-world data. *Understanding Statistics, 2*, 77-96.

Gagné, M. (2003). The role of autonomy support and autonomy orientation in prosocial behavior engagement. *Motivation and Emotion, 27*, 199-223.

Godin, G., & Shephard, R.J. (1985). A simple method to assess exercise behavior in the community. *Canadian Journal of Applied Sport Sciences, 10*, 141-146.

Gollwitzer, P.M. (1999). Implementation intentions: Strong effects of simple plans. *American Psychologist, 54,* 493-503.

Guay, F., Boggiano, A.K., & Vallerand, R.J. (2001). Autonomy support, motivation, and perceived competence: Conceptual and empirical linkages. *Personality and Social Psychology Bulletin, 27,* 643-650.

Hagger, M.S. (2006). Meta-analysis in sport and exercise research: Review, recent developments, and recommendations. *European Journal of Sport Science, 6,* 103-115.

Hagger, M.S., Chatzisarantis, N., & Biddle, S.J.H. (2001). The influence of self-efficacy and past behaviour on the physical activity intentions of young people. *Journal of Sports Sciences, 19,* 711-725.

Hagger, M.S., Chatzisarantis, N., & Biddle, S.J.H. (2002a). The influence of autonomous and controlling motives on physical activity intentions within the Theory of Planned Behaviour. *British Journal of Health Psychology, 7,* 283-297.

Hagger, M.S., Chatzisarantis, N., & Biddle, S.J.H. (2002b). A meta-analytic review of the theories of reasoned action and planned behavior in physical activity: Predictive validity and the contribution of additional variables. *Journal of Sport and Exercise Psychology, 24,* 3-32.

Hagger, M.S., Chatzisarantis, N.L.D., Barkoukis, V., Wang, C.K.J., & Baranowski, J. (2005). Perceived autonomy support in physical education and leisure-time physical activity: A cross-cultural evaluation of the trans-contextual model. *Journal of Educational Psychology, 97,* 287-301.

Hagger, M.S., Chatzisarantis, N.L.D., Culverhouse, T., & Biddle, S.J.H. (2003). The processes by which perceived autonomy support in physical education promotes leisure-time physical activity intentions and behavior: A trans-contextual model. *Journal of Educational Psychology, 95,* 784-795.

Hagger, M.S., Chatzisarantis, N.L.D., & Harris, J. (2006). From psychological need satisfaction to intentional behavior: Testing a motivational sequence in two behavioral contexts. *Personality and Social Psychology Bulletin, 32,* 131-138.

Hagger, M.S., Chatzisarantis, N.L.D., Hein, V., Pihu, M., Soós, I., & Karsai, I. (2006). Teacher, peer, and parent autonomy support in physical education and leisure-time physical activity: A trans-contextual model of motivation in three cultures. Unpublished manuscript, University of Nottingham, Nottingham, UK.

Hagger, M.S., Chatzisarantis, N.L.D., Hein, V., Pihu, M., Soós, I., & Karsai, I. (in press). The perceived autonomy support scale for exercise settings (PASSES): Development, validity, and cross-cultural invariance in young people. *Psychology of Sport and Exercise.*

Hardeman, W., Johnston, M., Johnston, D.W., Bonetti, D., Wareham, N.J., & Kinmonth, A.L. (2002). Application of the theory of planned behaviour change interventions: A systematic review. *Psychology and Health, 17,* 123-158.

Hayamizu, T. (1997). Between intrinsic and extrinsic motivation: Examination of reasons for academic study based on the theory of internalization. *Japanese Psychological Research, 37,* 98-108.

Hedges, L.V., & Olkin, I. (1985). *Statistical methods for meta-analysis.* Orlando, FL: Academic Press.

Hunter, J.E., & Schmidt, F. (1990). *Methods of meta-analysis: Correcting error and bias in research findings.* Newbury Park, CA: Sage.

Koestner, R., Lekes, N., Powers, T.A., & Chicoine, E. (2002). Attaining personal goals: Self-concordance plus implementation intentions equals success. *Journal of Personality and Social Psychology, 83,* 231-244.

Mullan, E., Markland, D., & Ingledew, D.K. (1997). A graded conceptualisation of self-determination in the regulation of exercise behaviour: Development of a measure using confirmatory factor analysis. *Personality and Individual Differences, 23,* 745-752.

Ntoumanis, N. (2005). A prospective study of participation in optional school physical education based on self-determination theory. *Journal of Educational Psychology, 97,* 444-453.

Prestwich, A., Lawton, R., & Conner, M. (2003). The use of implementation intentions and the decision balance sheet in promoting exercise behaviour. *Psychology and Health, 10,* 707-721.

Reeve, J. (2002). Self-determination theory applied to educational settings. In E.L. Deci & R.M. Ryan (Eds.), *Handbook of self-determination research* (pp. 183-203). Rochester, NY: University of Rochester Press.

Reeve, J., Bolt, E., & Cai, Y. (1999). Autonomy-supportive teachers: How they teach and motivate students. *Journal of Educational Psychology, 91,* 537-548.

Reeve, J., & Jang, H. (2006). What teachers say and do to support students' autonomy during a learning activity. *Journal of Educational Psychology, 98,* 209-218.

Rhodes, R.E., Courneya, K.S., & Jones, L.W. (2002). Personality, the theory of planned behavior, and exercise: A unique role for extroversion's activity facet. *Journal of Applied Social Psychology, 32,* 1721-1736.

Rosenthal, R., & Rubin, D. (1982). Comparing effect sizes of independent studies. *Psychological Bulletin, 92,* 500-504.

Ryan, R.M., & Connell, J.P. (1989). Perceived locus of causality and internalization: Examining reasons for acting in two domains. *Journal of Personality and Social Psychology, 57,* 749-761.

Sheeran, P., & Orbell, S. (1998). Do intentions predict condom use? Meta-analysis and examination of six moderator variables. *British Journal of Social Psychology, 37,* 231-250.

Sheeran, P., & Taylor, S. (1999). Predicting intentions to use condoms: A meta-analysis and comparison of the theories of reasoned action and planned behavior. *Journal of Applied Social Psychology, 29,* 1624-1675.

Standage, M., Duda, J.L., & Ntoumanis, N. (2003). A model of contextual motivation in physical education: Using constructs from self-determination and achievement goal theories to predict physical activity intentions. *Journal of Educational Psychology, 95,* 97-110.

Triandis, H.C. (1989). The self and social behavior in differing cultural contexts. *Psychological Review, 96,* 506-520.

Vallerand, R.J. (1997). Toward a hierarchical model of intrinsic and extrinsic motivation. In M.P. Zanna (Ed.), *Advances in experimental social psychology* (pp. 271-359). New York: Academic Press.

Vansteenkiste, M., Simons, J., Lens, W., & Sheldon, K.M. (2004). Motivating learning, performance, and persistence: The synergistic effects of intrinsic goal contents and autonomy-supportive contexts. *Journal of Personality and Social Psychology, 87,* 246-260.

Williams, G.C. (2002). Improving patients' health through supporting the autonomy of patients and providers. In E.L. Deci & R.M. Ryan (Eds.), *Handbook of self-determination research* (pp. 233-254). Rochester, NY: University of Rochester Press.

Williams, G.C., Frankel, R.M., Campbell, T.L., & Deci, E.L. (2000). Research on relationship-centered care and healthcare outcomes from the Rochester biopsychosocial program: A self-determination theory integration. *Families, Systems and Health, 18,* 79-90.

Williams, G.C., Freedman, Z.R., & Deci, E.L. (1998). Supporting autonomy to motivate glucose control in patients with diabetes. *Diabetes Care, 21,* 1644-1651.

Williams, G.C., Gagné, M., Ryan, R.M., & Deci, E.L. (2002). Facilitating autonomous motivation for smoking cessation. *Health Psychology, 21,* 40-50.

Williams, G.C., Rodin, G.C., Ryan, R.M., Grolnick, W.S., & Deci, E.L. (1998). Autonomous regulation and long-term medication adherence in adult outpatients. *Health Psychology, 17,* 269-276.

Williams, G.C., Saizow, R., Ross, L., & Deci, E.L. (1997). Motivation underlying career choice for internal medicine and surgery. *Social Science and Medicine, 45,* 1705-1713.

Wilson, P.M., & Rodgers, W.M. (2004). The relationship between perceived autonomy support, exercise regulations and behavioral intentions in women. *Psychology of Sport and Exercise, 5,* 229-242.

Yamauchi, H., & Tanaka, K. (1998). Relations of autonomy, self-referenced beliefs, and self-regulated learning among Japanese children. *Psychological Reports, 82,* 803-816.

CHAPTER 4

Ames, C. (1992). Classrooms: Goals, structures and student motivation. *Journal of Educational Psychology, 84,* 261-271.

Anderssen, N., Wold, B., &, Torsheim., T. (2005). Tracking of physical activity in adolescence. *Research Quarterly for Exercise and Sport, 76,* 119-129.

Biddle, S.J.H. (2001). Enhancing motivation in physical education. In G.C. Roberts (Ed.), *Advances in motivation in sport and exercise* (pp. 101-127). Champaign, IL: Human Kinetics.

Biddle, S.J.H., Gorely, T., & Stensel, D.J. (2004). Health-enhancing physical activity and sedentary behaviour in children and adolescents. *Journal of Sports Sciences, 22,* 679-701.

Black, A.E., & Deci, E.L. (2000). The effects of instructors' autonomy support and students' autonomous motivation on learning organic chemistry: A self-determination theory perspective. *Science Education, 84,* 740-756.

Butler, R. (1987). Task-involving and ego-involving properties of evaluation: Effects of different feedback conditions on motivational perceptions, interest, and performance. *Journal of Educational Psychology, 79,* 474-482.

Cury, F., Biddle, S., Famose, J., Goudas, M., Sarrazin, P., & Durand, M. (1996). Personal and situational factors influencing intrinsic interest of adolescent girls in school physical education: A structural equation modelling analysis. *Educational Psychology, 16*, 305-315.

Deci, E.L., Eghrari, H., Patrick, B.C., & Leone, D. (1994). Facilitating internalization: The self-determination theory perspective. *Journal of Personality, 62*, 119-142.

Deci, E. L., Koestner, R., & Ryan, R. M. (2001). Extrinsic rewards and intrinsic motivation in education: Reconsidered once again. *Review of Educational Research, 71*, 1-27.

Deci, E.L., Nezlek, J., & Sheinman, L. (1981). Characteristics of the rewarder and intrinsic motivation of the rewardee. *Journal of Personality and Social Psychology, 40*, 1-10.

Deci, E.L., & Ryan, R.M. (1985). *Intrinsic motivation and self-determination in human behavior.* New York: Plenum Press.

Deci, E.L., & Ryan, R.M. (1991). A motivational approach to self: Integration in personality. In R.A. Dienstbier (Ed.), *Nebraska symposium on motivation: Perspectives on motivation* (Vol. 38, pp. 237-288). Lincoln, NE: University of Nebraska Press.

Deci, E.L., & Ryan, R.M. (2000). The "what" and "why" of goal pursuits: Human needs and the self-determination of behavior. *Psychological Inquiry, 11*, 227-268.

Deci, E.L., & Ryan, R.M. (Eds.). (2002). *Handbook of self-determination research.* Rochester, NY: University of Rochester Press.

Deci, E.L., Vallerand, R.J., Pelletier, L.G., & Ryan, R.M. (1991). Motivation and education: The self-determination perspective. *Educational Psychologist, 26*, 325-346.

Deci, E.L., & Vansteenkiste, M. (2004). Self-determination theory and basic need satisfaction: Understanding human development in positive psychology. *Ricerche di Psicologia, 27*, 17-34.

Department of Health. (2004). *At least five a week: Evidence on the impact of physical activity and its relationship to health. A report from the Chief Medical Officer.* London: Department of Health.

Elliot, A.J., & McGregor, H.A. (2001). A 2 × 2 achievement goal framework. *Journal of Personality and Social Psychology, 80*, 501-519.

Ferrer-Caja, E., & Weiss, M.R. (2000). Predictors of intrinsic motivation among adolescent students in physical education. *Research Quarterly for Exercise and Sport, 71*, 267-279.

Gagné, M., Ryan, R.M., & Bargmann, K. (2003). Autonomy support and need satisfaction in the motivation and well-being of gymnasts. *Journal of Applied Sport Psychology, 15*, 372-390.

Goudas, M., & Biddle, S. (1994). Perceived motivational climate and intrinsic motivation in school physical education classes. *European Journal of Psychology of Education, 2*, 241-250.

Goudas, M., Biddle, S.J.H., & Fox, K.R. (1994). Perceived locus of causality, goal orientations, and perceived competence in school physical education classes. *British Journal of Educational Psychology, 64*, 453-463.

Hagger, M.S., Chatzisarantis, N.L.D., Barkoukis, V., Wang, C.K.J., & Baranowski, J. (2005). Perceived autonomy support in physical education and leisure-time physical activity: A cross-cultural evaluation of the trans-contextual model. *Journal of Educational Psychology, 97*, 287-301.

Hagger, M.S., Chatzisarantis, N., Culverhouse, T., & Biddle, S.J.H. (2003). The processes by which perceived autonomy support in physical education promotes leisure-time physical activity intentions and behavior: A trans-contextual model. *Journal of Educational Psychology, 95,* 784-795.

Hagger, M.S., Chatzisarantis, N.L.D., & Harris, J. (2006). From psychological need satisfaction to intentional behavior: Testing a motivational sequence in two behavioral contexts. *Personality and Social Psychology Bulletin, 32,* 131-138.

Joint Health Surveys Unit. (1998). *Health survey for England: The health of young people 1995-97.* London: The Stationary Office.

Kasser, V., & Ryan, R.M. (1999). The relation of psychological needs for autonomy and relatedness to vitality, well-being, and mortality in a nursing home. *Journal of Applied Social Psychology, 29,* 935-954.

National Audit Office. (2001). *Tackling obesity in England.* London: The Stationary Office.

Nicholls, J.G. (1989). *The competitive ethos and democratic education.* Cambridge, MA: Harvard University Press.

Ntoumanis, N. (2001). A self-determination approach to the understanding of motivation in physical education. *British Journal of Educational Psychology, 71,* 225-242.

Ntoumanis, N. (2005). A prospective study of participation in optional school physical education based on self-determination theory. *Journal of Educational Psychology, 97,* 444-453.

Ntoumanis, N., & Biddle, S.J.H. (1999). A review of motivational climate in physical activity. *Journal of Sports Sciences, 17,* 643-665.

Ntoumanis, N., Pensgaard, A.M., Martin, C., & Pipe, K. (2004). An idiographic analysis of amotivation in compulsory school physical education. *Journal of Sport and Exercise Psychology, 26,* 197-214.

Papaioannou, A. (1994). The development of a questionnaire to measure achievement orientations in physical education. *Research Quarterly for Exercise and Sport, 65,* 11-20.

Parish, L.E., & Treasure, D.C. (2003). Physical activity and situational motivation in physical education: Influence of the motivational climate and perceived ability. *Research Quarterly for Exercise and Sport, 74,* 173-182.

Reeve, J. (1998). Autonomy support as an interpersonal motivating style: Is it teachable? *Contemporary Educational Psychology, 23,* 312-330.

Reeve, J., Deci, E.L., & Ryan, R.M. (2004). Self-determination theory: A dialectical framework for understanding socio-cultural influences on student motivation. In S. Van Etten & M. Pressley (Eds.), *Big theories revisited* (pp. 31-60). Greenwich, CT: Information Age Press.

Reis, H.T., Sheldon, K.M., Gable, S.L., Roscoe, J., & Ryan, R.M. (2000). Daily well-being: The role of autonomy, competence, and relatedness. *Personality and Social Psychology Bulletin, 26,* 419-435.

Ryan, R.M. (1982). Control and information in the intrapersonal sphere: An extension of cognitive evaluation theory. *Journal of Personality and Social Psychology, 43,* 450-461.

Ryan, R. (1995). Psychological needs and the facilitation of integrative processes. *Journal of Personality, 63,* 397-427.

Ryan, R.M., & Deci, E.L. (1989). Bridging the research traditions of task/ego involvement and intrinsic/extrinsic motivation: Comment on Butler. (1987). *Journal of Educational Psychology, 81,* 265-268.

Ryan, R.M., & Deci, E.L. (2000a). Intrinsic and extrinsic motivations: Classic definitions and new directions. *Contemporary Educational Psychology, 25,* 54-67.

Ryan, R.M., & Deci, E.L. (2000b). Self-determination theory and the facilitation of intrinsic motivation, social development, and well-being. *American Psychologist, 55,* 68-78.

Ryan, R.M., & Deci, E.L. (2002). An overview of self-determination theory: An organismic-dialectical perspective. In E.L. Deci & R.M. Ryan (Eds.), *Handbook of self-determination research* (pp. 3-33). Rochester, NY: University of Rochester Press.

Sallis, J.F. (2000). Age-related decline in physical activity: A synthesis of human and animal studies. *Medicine and Science in Sports and Exercise, 32,* 1598-1600.

Sallis, J.F., & Owen, N. (1999). *Physical activity and behavioral medicine.* Thousand Oaks, CA: Sage.

Sheldon, K.M., Elliot, A.J., Kim, Y., & Kasser, T. (2001). What is satisfying about satisfying events? Testing 10 candidate psychological needs. *Journal of Personality and Social Psychology, 80,* 325-339.

Sheldon, K.M., Williams, G.C., & Joiner, T. (2003). *Self-determination theory in the clinic: Motivating physical and mental health.* New Haven, CT: Yale University Press.

Shephard, R.J., & Trudeau, F. (2000). The legacy of physical education: Influences on adult lifestyle. *Pediatric Exercise Science, 12,* 34-50.

Standage, M., Duda, J.L., & Ntoumanis, N. (2003). A model of contextual motivation in physical education: Using constructs from self-determination and achievement goal theories to predict physical activity intentions. *Journal of Educational Psychology, 95,* 97-110.

Standage, M., Duda, J.L., & Ntoumanis, N. (2005). A test of self-determination theory in school physical education. *British Journal of Educational Psychology, 75,* 411-433.

Standage, M., Duda, J.L., & Ntoumanis, N. (2006). Students' motivational processes and their relationship to teacher ratings in school physical education: A self-determination theory approach. *Research Quarterly for Exercise and Sport, 77,* 100-110.

Standage, M., Duda, J.L., & Pensgaard, A.M. (2005). The effect of competitive outcome and task-involving, ego-involving, and co-operative structures on the psychological well-being of individuals engaged in a co-ordination task. *Motivation and Emotion, 29,* 41-68.

Standage, M., & Gillison, F. (2005). Examining the relationship between exercise motivation and habitual "out of school" physical activity: The role of school physical education. *Proceedings of the British Psychological Society, 13,* S97.

U.S. Department of Health and Human Services. (1996). *Physical activity and health: A report of the Surgeon General.* Atlanta: U.S. Department of Health and Human Services, Centers for Disease Control and Prevention, National Center for Chronic Disease Prevention and Health Promotion.

Vallerand, R.J. (1997). Toward a hierarchical model of intrinsic and extrinsic motivation. In M.P. Zanna (Ed.), *Advances in experimental social psychology* (Vol. 29, pp. 271-360). New York: Academic Press.

Vallerand, R.J., Fortier, M.S., & Guay, F. (1997). Self-determination and persistence in a real-life setting: Toward a motivational model of high school dropout. *Journal of Personality and Social Psychology, 72,* 1161-1176.

Vansteenkiste, M., & Deci, E.L. (2003). Competitively contingent rewards and intrinsic motivation: Can losers remain motivated? *Motivation and Emotion, 27,* 273-299.

CHAPTER 5

Assor, A., Roth, G., & Deci, E.L. (2004). The emotional costs of parents' conditional regard: A self-determination theory analysis. *Journal of Personality, 72,* 47-88.

Breckon, J. (2005). Exercise motivation and adherence: The use of motivational interviewing. *Sport and Exercise Scientist, 3,* 8-9.

Burke, B.L., Arkowitz, H., & Dunn, C. (2002). The efficacy of motivational interviewing and its adaptations. In W.R. Miller & S. Rollnick (Eds.), *Motivational interviewing: Preparing people for change* (2nd ed., pp. 217-250). New York: Guilford Press.

Chief Medical Officer. (1999). Ten tips for better health. In *Saving lives: Our healthier nation.* London: DoH.

Connell, J.P., & Wellborn, J.G. (1991). Competence, autonomy, and relatedness: A motivational analysis of self-system processes. In M.R. Gunnar & L.A. Sroufe (Eds.), *The Minnesota symposium on child psychology* (Vol. 23, pp. 43-77). Hillsdale, NJ: Erlbaum.

Deci, E. L., Eghrari, H., Patrick, B. C., & Leone, D. R. (1994). Facilitating internalization: The self-determination theory perspective. *Journal of Personality, 62,* 119-142.

Deci, E.L., Koestner, R., & Ryan, R.M. (1999). A meta-analytic review of experiments examining the effects of extrinsic rewards on intrinsic motivation. *Psychological Bulletin, 25,* 627-668.

Deci, E.L., & Ryan, R.M. (1985). *Intrinsic motivation and self-determination in human behavior.* New York: Plenum Press.

Deci, E.L., & Ryan, R.M. (1991). A motivational approach to self: Integration in personality. In R. Dienstbier (Ed.), *Nebraska symposium on motivation: Perspectives on motivation* (Vol. 38, pp. 237-288). Lincoln, NE: University of Nebraska Press.

Deci, E.L., & Ryan, R.M. (2000). The "what" and "why" of goal pursuits: Human needs and the self-determination of behavior. *Psychological Inquiry, 11,* 227-268.

Department of Culture, Media and Sport. (2002). *Game plan: A strategy for delivering government's sport and physical activity objectives.* London: Strategy Unit Joint Report.

Department of Health. (1996). *Strategy statement on physical activity.* London: DoH.

Department of Health. (2001). *Exercise referral systems: A national quality assurance framework.* London: DoH.

Department of Health. (2004). *The health survey for England (2003).* London: DoH.

Foote, J., DeLuca, A., Magura, S., Warner, A., Grand, A., Rosenblum, A., & Stahl, S. (1999). A group motivational treatment for chemical dependency. *Journal of Substance Abuse, 17,* 181-192.

Ginsberg, J.I.D., Mann, R.E., Rotgers, F., & Weekes, J.R. (2002). Motivational interviewing with criminal justice populations. In W.R. Miller & S. Rollnick (Eds.), *Motivational interviewing: Preparing people for change* (2nd ed., pp. 333-347). New York: Guilford Press.

Grolnick, W.S. (2003). *The psychology of parental control: How well-meant parenting backfires.* Mahwah, NJ: Erlbaum.

Grolnick, W.S., & Ryan, R.M. (1987). Autonomy and support in education: Creating the facilitating environment. In N. Hastings & J. Schweiso (Eds.), *New directions in educational psychology, Vol. 2: Behaviour and motivation* (pp. 213-232). London: Falmer Press.

Hagger, M.S., & Chatzisarantis, N.L.D. (2005). *The social psychology of exercise and sport.* Buckingham, UK: Open University Press.

Hagger, M.S., Chatzisarantis, N.L.D., & Harris, J. (2006). From psychological need satisfaction to intentional behavior: Testing a motivational sequence in two behavioral contexts. *Personality and Social Psychology Bulletin, 32,* 131-138.

Health Education Authority. (1994). *Moving on: International perspectives on promoting physical activity.* London: HEA.

Ingledew, D.K., Markland, D., & Medley, A. (1998). Exercise motives and stages of change. *Journal of Health Psychology, 3,* 477-489.

Markland, D., Ingledew, D.K., Hardy, L., & Grant, L. (1992). A comparison of the exercise motivations of participants in aerobics and weight watcher exercisers. *Journal of Sports Sciences, 10,* 609-610.

Markland, D., Ryan, R.M., Tobin, V.J., & Rollnick, S. (2005). Motivational interviewing and self-determination theory. *Journal of Social and Clinical Psychology, 24,* 785-805.

McAuley, E., Wraith, S., & Duncan, T.E. (1991). Self-efficacy, perceptions of success, and intrinsic motivation for exercise. *Journal of Applied Social Psychology, 21,* 139-155.

Miller, W.R. (1983). Motivational interviewing with problem drinkers. *Behavioural Psychotherapy, 11,* 147-172.

Miller, W.R. (1994). Motivational interviewing: III. On the ethics of motivational intervention. *Behavioural and Cognitive Psychotherapy, 22,* 111-123.

Miller, W.R. (1996). Motivational interviewing: Research, practice, and puzzles. *Addictive Behaviors, 21,* 835-842.

Miller, W.R. (1999). Toward a theory of motivational interviewing. *Motivational Interviewing Newsletter: Updates, Education and Training, 6,* 2-4.

Miller, W.R., Benefield, R.G., & Tonigan, J.S. (1993). Enhancing motivation for change in problem drinking: A controlled comparison of two therapist styles. *Journal of Consulting and Clinical Psychology, 61,* 455-461.

Miller, W.R., & Rollnick, S. (1991). *Motivational interviewing: Preparing people to change addictive behavior.* New York: Guilford Press.

Miller, W.R., & Rollnick, S. (2002). *Motivational interviewing: Preparing people for change* (2nd ed.). New York: Guilford Press.

Mullan, E., & Markland, D. (1997). Variations in self-determination across the stages of change for exercise in adults. *Motivation and Emotion, 21,* 349-362.

Pelletier, L.G., Fortier, M.S., Vallerand, R.J., & Brière, N.M. (2001). Associations among perceived autonomy support, forms of self-regulation, and persistence: A prospective study. *Motivation and Emotion, 25,* 279-306.

Reeve, J. (1998). Autonomy support as an interpersonal motivating style: Is it teachable? *Contemporary Educational Psychology, 23,* 312-330.

Reeve, J. (2002). Self-determination theory applied to educational settings. In E.L. Deci & R.M. Ryan (Eds.), *Handbook of self-determination research* (pp. 193-204). Rochester, NY: University of Rochester Press.

Resnicow, K., DiIorio, C., Soet, J.E., Borrelli, B., Hecht, J., & Ernst, D. (2002). Motivational interviewing in health promotion. It sounds like something is changing. *Health Psychology, 21*, 444-451.

Rogers, C.R. (1957). The necessary and sufficient conditions for therapeutic personality change. *Journal of Consulting Psychology, 21*, 95-103.

Rollnick, S., Kinnersley, P., & Stott, N.C.H. (1993). Methods of helping patients with behaviour change. *British Medical Journal, 307*, 188-190.

Rollnick, S., & Miller, W.R. (1995). What is motivational interviewing? *Behavioural and Cognitive Psychotherapy, 23*, 325-334.

Ryan, R.M., & Connell, J.P. (1989). Perceived locus of causality and internalization: Examining reasons for acting in two domains. *Journal of Personality and Social Psychology, 57*, 749-761.

Ryan, R.M., & Deci, E.L. (2000). Self-determination theory and the facilitation of intrinsic motivation, social development, and well-being. *American Psychologist, 55*, 68-78.

Ryan, R.M., Deci, E.L., & Grolnick, W.S. (1995). Autonomy, relatedness, and the self: Their relation to development and psychopathology. In D. Cicchetti & D.J. Cohen (Eds.), *Developmental psychopathology, Vol. 1: Theory and methods* (pp. 618-655). Oxford: Wiley.

Ryan, R.M., Rigby, S., & King, K. (1993). Two types of religious internalization and their relations to religious orientations and mental health. *Journal of Personality and Social Psychology, 65*, 586-596.

Soenens, B., Vansteenkiste, M., Luyten, P., Duriez, B., & Goossens, L. (2005). Maladaptive perfectionistic self-representations: The mediational link between psychological control and adjustment. *Personality and Individual Differences, 38*, 487-498.

U.S. Department of Health and Human Services. (2000). *Healthy People 2010: Understanding and improving health* (2nd ed.). Washington, DC: U.S. Government Printing Office.

U.S. Department of Health and Human Services. (2004). *Healthy People 2010: Progress review: Physical activity and fitness.* Washington, DC: U.S. Government Printing Office.

Vansteenkiste, M., & Sheldon, K.M. (2006). "There's nothing more practical than a good theory": Integrating motivational interviewing and self-determination theory. *British Journal of Clinical Psychology, 45*, 63-82.

Vansteenkiste, M., Simons, J., Lens, W., Soenens, B., & Matos, L. (2005). Examining the impact of extrinsic versus intrinsic goal framing and internally controlling versus autonomy-supportive communication style upon early adolescents' academic achievement. *Child Development, 76*, 483-501.

Vansteenkiste, M., Simons, J., Soenens, B., & Lens, W. (2004). How to become a persevering exerciser: The importance of providing a clear, future intrinsic goal in an autonomy supportive way. *Journal of Sport and Exercise Psychology, 26*, 232-249.

Vansteenkiste, M., Soenens, B., & Vandereycken, W. (2005). Motivation to change in eating disorder patients: A conceptual clarification on the basis of self-determination theory. *International Journal of Eating Disorders, 37,* 1-13.

CHAPTER 6

Baumeister, R.F., & Leary, M.R. (1995). The need to belong: Desire for interpersonal attachments as a fundamental human motivation. *Psychological Bulletin, 117,* 497-529.

Blair, S.N., & Connelly, J.C. (1996). How much exercise should we do? The case for moderate amounts and intensities of exercise. *Research Quarterly for Exercise and Sport, 67,* 193-205.

Blanchard, C.M., Rodgers, W.M., & Gauvin, L. (2003). The influence of exercise duration and cognitions during running on feeling states in an indoor running track environment. *Psychology of Sport and Exercise, 5,* 119-133.

Craft, L.L., & Landers, D.M. (1998). The effect of exercise on clinical depression and depression resulting from mental illness: A meta-analysis. *Journal of Sport and Exercise Psychology, 20,* 339-357.

Crocker, P.R.E., Sabiston, C., Forrestor, S., Kowalski, N., Kowalski, K., & McDonough, M. (2003). Predicting change in physical activity, dietary restraint, and physique anxiety in adolescent girls: Examining covariance in physical self-perceptions. *Canadian Journal of Public Health, 94,* 332-337.

Cronbach, L.J., & Meehl, P.E. (1955). Construct validity in psychological tests. *Psychological Bulletin, 52,* 281-302.

Daley, A., & Maynard, I.W. (2003). Preferred exercise mode and affective responses in physically active adults. *Psychology of Sport and Exercise, 4,* 347-356.

deCharms, R. (1968). *Personal causation: The internal affective determinants of behavior.* New York: Academic Press.

Deci, E.L., & Ryan, R.M. (1985). *Intrinsic motivation and self-determination in human behavior.* New York: Plenum Press.

Deci, E.L., & Ryan, R.M. (1991). A motivational approach to self: Integration in personality. In R. Dienstbier (Ed.), *Nebraska symposium on motivation: Perspectives on motivation* (Vol. 38, pp. 237-288). Lincoln, NE: University of Nebraska Press.

Deci, E.L., & Ryan, R.M. (2000). The "what" and "why" of goal pursuits: Human needs and the self-determination of behavior. *Psychological Inquiry, 11,* 227-268.

Deci, E.L., & Ryan, R.M. (2002). *Handbook of self-determination research.* Rochester, NY: University of Rochester Press.

Fox, K.R. (1997). *The physical self: From motivation to well-being.* Champaign, IL: Human Kinetics.

Georgiadis, M.M., Biddle, S.J.H., & Chatzisarantis, N. (2001). The mediating role of self-determination in the relationship between goal orientations and physical self-worth in Greek exercisers. *European Journal of Sport Science, 1,* 1-9.

Hagger, M.S., Biddle, S.J.H., & Wang, C.K.J. (2005). Physical self-perceptions in adolescence: Generalizability of a multidimensional, hierarchical model across gender and grade. *Educational and Psychological Measurement, 65,* 297-322.

Hagger, M.S., Chatzisarantis, N.L.D., & Harris, J. (2006). From psychological need satisfaction to intentional behavior: Testing a motivational sequence in two behavioral contexts. *Personality and Social Psychology Bulletin, 32*, 131-138.

Kowalski, K.C., Crocker, P.R.E., Kowalski, N.P., Chad, K.E., & Humbert, M.L. (2003). Examining the physical self in adolescent girls over time: Further evidence against the hierarchical model. *Journal of Sport and Exercise Psychology, 25*, 5-18.

Leary, M.R., & Tangney, J.P. (2003). *Handbook of self and identity*. New York: Guilford Press.

Long, B.C., & van Stavel, R. (1999). Effects of exercise training on anxiety: A meta-analysis: *Journal of Applied Sport Psychology, 7*, 167-189.

Markland, D. (1999). Self-determination moderates the effects of perceived competence on intrinsic motivation in an exercise setting. *Journal of Sport and Exercise Psychology, 21*, 351-361.

Markland, D., & Hardy, L. (1997). On the factorial and construct validity of the intrinsic motivation inventory: Conceptual and operational concerns. *Research Quarterly for Exercise and Sport, 68*, 20-32.

Martens, R. (1978). *Joy and sadness in children's sports*. Champaign, IL: Human Kinetics.

Martin Ginis, K.A., & Leary, M.R. (2004). Self-presentational processes in health damaging behavior. *Journal of Applied Sport Psychology, 16*, 59-74.

Martin Ginis, K.A., Latimer, A.E., & Jung, M.E. (2003). No pain no gain? Examining the generalizability of the exerciser stereotype to moderately active and excessively active targets. *Social Behaviour and Personality, 31*, 283-290.

Messick, S. (1995). Validity of psychological assessment: Validation of inferences from persons' responses and performances as scientific inquiry into score meaning. *American Psychologist, 50*, 741-749.

Mullan, E., & Markland, D. (1997). Variations in self-determination across the stages of change for exercise in adults. *Motivation and Emotion, 21*, 349-362.

Mullan, E., Markland, D., & Ingledew, D.K. (1997). A graded conceptualization of self-determination in the regulation of exercise behavior: Development of a measure using confirmatory factor analysis procedures. *Personality and Individual Differences, 23*, 745-752.

Parfitt, G., & Gledhill, C. (2004). The effect of choice of exercise mode on psychological responses. *Psychology of Sport and Exercise, 5*, 111-117.

Parfitt, G., Rose, E.A., & Markland, D. (2000). The effect of prescribed and preferred intensity exercise on psychological affect and the influence of baseline measures of affect. *Journal of Health Psychology, 5*, 231-240.

Reeve, J., & Sickenius, B. (1994). Development and validation of a brief measure of the three psychological needs underlying intrinsic motivation: The AFS scales. *Educational and Psychological Measurement, 54*, 506-515.

Reis, H.T., Sheldon, K.M., Gable, S.L., Roscoe, J., & Ryan, R.M. (2000). Daily well-being: The role of autonomy, competence and relatedness. *Personality and Social Psychology Bulletin, 26*, 419-435.

Ryan, R.M., & Deci, E.L. (2001). On happiness and human potentials: A review of research on hedonic and eudaimonic well-being. In S. Fiske (Ed.), *Annual review of psychology* (Vol. 52, pp. 141-166). Palo Alto, CA: Annual Reviews.

Shavelson, R.J., Hubner, J.J., & Stanton, G.C. (1976). Self-concept: Validation of construct interpretations. *Review of Educational Research, 46,* 407-411.

Sheldon, K.M., & Elliot, A.J. (1999). Goal striving, need satisfaction, and psychological well-being: The self-concordance model. *Journal of Personality and Social Psychology, 76,* 482-497.

Sheldon, K.M., Elliot, A.J., Kim, Y., & Kasser, T. (2001). What's satisfying about satisfying events? Comparing ten candidate psychological needs. *Journal of Personality and Social Psychology, 80,* 325-339.

Vallerand, R.J. (2001). A hierarchical model of intrinsic and extrinsic motivation in sport and exercise. In G.C. Roberts (Ed.), *Advances in motivation in sport and exercise* (pp. 263-319). Champaign, IL: Human Kinetics.

White, R.W. (1959). Motivation reconsidered: The concept of competence. *Psychological Review, 66,* 297-333.

Wilson, P.M. (2004). Psychological need satisfaction and exercise: An application of self-determination theory. Paper presented at the annual meeting of the Canadian Society for Psychomotor Learning, Saskatoon, Saskatchewan.

Wilson, P.M., Muon, S., Longely, K., & Rodgers, W.M. (2005). Examining the contributions of perceived psychological need satisfaction to affective experiences in exercise contexts. Paper presented at the annual meeting of the Canadian Society for Psychomotor Learning, Niagara Falls, Ontario.

Wilson, P.M., & Rodgers, W.M. (2002). The relationship between exercise motives and physical self-esteem in female exercise participants: An application of self-determination theory. *Journal of Applied Biobehavioural Research, 7,* 30-43.

Wilson, P.M., & Rodgers, W.M. (2003). Psychological need satisfaction in exercise scale: Measurement development and preliminary validation. Paper presented at the annual meeting of the Canadian Society for Psychomotor Learning, Hamilton, Ontario.

Wilson, P.M., Rodgers, W.M., Blanchard, C.M., & Gessell, J.G. (2003). The relationships between psychological needs, self-determined motivation, exercise attitudes, and physical fitness. *Journal of Applied Social Psychology, 33,* 2373-2392.

Wilson, P.M., Rodgers, W.M., & Fraser, S.N. (2002a). Cross-validation of the revised motivation for physical activity measure in active women. *Research Quarterly for Exercise and Sport, 73,* 471-477.

Wilson, P.M., Rodgers, W.M., & Fraser, S.N. (2002b). Examining the psychometric properties of the behavioural regulation in exercise questionnaire. *Measurement in Physical Education and Exercise Science, 6,* 1-21.

Wilson, P.M., Rodgers, W.M., Fraser, S.N., Murray, T.C., & McIntrye, C.A. (2004). The relationship between psychological need satisfaction and self-perceptions in females. *Journal of Sport and Exercise Psychology, 26,* S200.

CHAPTER 7

Abblett, M.R. (2002). Motivation for change in psychotherapy: The relationship between the transtheoretical model and self-determination theory and prediction of clinical services utilization. *Dissertation Abstracts International B, The Sciences and Engineering, 63*, 4-B, 2047.

Ajzen, I. (1985). *Action control: From cognition to behavior.* Berlin and New York: Springer-Verlag.

Ajzen, I. (1991). The theory of planned behavior. *Organizational Behavior and Human Decision Processes, 50*, 179-211.

Armitage, C.J., & Arden, M.A. (2002). Exploring discontinuity patterns in the transtheoretical model: An application of the theory of planned behaviour. *British Journal of Health Psychology, 7*, 89-103.

Biddle, S.J.H., & Nigg, C.R. (2000). Theories of exercise behavior. *International Journal of Sport Psychology, 31*(2), 290.

Caspersen, C.J., Powell, K.E., & Christenson, G.M. (1985). Physical activity, exercise, and physical fitness: Definitions and distinctions for health-related research. *Public Health Reports, 100*(2), 126-131.

Chatzisarantis, N.L.D., & Biddle, S.J.H. (1998). Functional significance of psychological variables that are included in the theory of planned behaviour: A self-determination theory approach to the study of attitudes, subjective norms, perceptions of control and intentions. *European Journal of Social Psychology, 28*, 303-322.

Chatzisarantis, N.L.D., Biddle, S.J.H., & Meek, G.A. (1997). A self-determination theory approach to the study of intentions and the intention-behaviour relationship in children's physical activity. *British Journal of Health Psychology, 2*, 343-360.

Chatzisarantis, N.L.D., Hagger, M.S., Biddle, S.J.H., & Karageorghis, C. (2002). The cognitive processes by which perceived locus of causality predicts participation in physical activity. *Journal of Health Psychology, 7*, 685-699.

Chatzisarantis, N.L.D., Hagger, M.S., Biddle, S.J.H., Smith, B., & Wang, J.C.K. (2003). A meta-analysis of perceived locus of causality in exercise, sport, and physical education contexts. *Journal of Sport and Exercise Psychology, 25*, 284-306.

Conner, M., & Norman, P. (Eds.). (2005). *Predicting health behaviour: Research and practice with social cognition models* (2nd ed.). Maidenhead: Open University Press.

Csikszentmihalyi, M. (1975a). *Beyond boredom and anxiety.* San Francisco: Jossey-Bass.

Csikszentmihalyi, M. (1975b). Play and intrinsic rewards. *Journal of Humanistic Psychology, 15*, 41-63.

Csikszentmihalyi, M. (1990). *Flow: The psychology of optimal experience.* New York: Harper Perennial.

Csikszentmihalyi, M., & LeFevre, J. (1989). Optimal experience in work and leisure. *Journal of Personality and Social Psychology, 56*, 815-822.

Csikszentmihalyi, M., & Nakamura, J. (1989). The dynamics of intrinsic motivation: The study of adolescents. In C. Ames & R. Ames (Eds.), *Research on motivation in education* (Vol. 3, pp. 45-71). San Diego: Academic Press.

Csikszentmihalyi, M., & Rathunde, K. (1993). The measurement of flow in everyday life: Toward a theory of emergent motivation. In J.E. Jacobs (Ed.), *Nebraska symposium on motivation, 1992: Developmental perspectives on motivation. Current theory in research in motivation* (Vol. 40, pp. 57-97). Lincoln, NE: University of Nebraska Press.

Csikszentmihalyi, M., Rathunde, K., & Whelan, S. (1993). *Talented teenagers: The roots of success and failure.* New York: Cambridge University Press.

deCharms, R. (1968). *Personal causation: The internal affective determinants of behavior.* New York: Academic Press.

Deci, E.L. (1971). Effects of extrinsically mediated rewards on intrinsic motivation. *Journal of Personality and Social Psychology, 18,* 105-115.

Deci, E.L., & Ryan, R.M. (1985). *Intrinsic motivation and self-determination in human behavior.* New York: Plenum Press.

Deci, E.L., & Ryan, R.M. (Eds.). (2002). *Handbook of self-determination research.* Rochester, NY: University of Rochester Press.

Deci, E.L., & Vansteenkiste, M. (2004). Self-determination theory and basic need satisfaction: Understanding human development in positive psychology. *Ricerche di Psicologia, 27,* 23-40.

Fortier, M., & Grenier, M. (1999). Déterminants personnels et situationnels de l'adhérence à un programme d'exercice: Une étude prospective. *Revue STAPS, 49,* 25-38.

Fortier, M., Hogg, W., O'Sullivan, T., Blanchard, C., Reid, R., Sigal, R., Doucet, E., Boulay, P., Pipe, A., Angus, D., & Chambers, L. (2006). The PAC Project: Interdisciplinary and innovative study on physical activity counselling to increase the physical activity level of patients. Retrieved November 4, 2006, from University of Ottawa, Faculty of Health Sciences Web site: http://www.health.uottawa.ca/pac/: University of Ottawa.

Fortier, M., Sweet, S., Tulloch, H., Blanchard, C., Sigal, R., & Kenny, G. (2006). Self-determination and exercise stage progression: A longitudinal study. Manuscript submitted for publication.

Frederick, C., Morrison, C., & Manning, T. (1996). Motivation to participate, exercise affect, and outcome behaviors toward physical activity. *Perceptual and Motor Skills, 82,* 691-701.

Frederick-Recascino, C.M. (2002). Self-determination theory and participation motivation research in the sport and exercise domain. *Handbook of self-determination research* (pp. 255-294). Rochester, NY: University of Rochester Press.

Graef, R.M., Csikszentmihalyi, M., & McManama-Gianinno, S. (1983). Measuring intrinsic motivation in everyday life. *Leisure Studies, 2,* 155-168.

Hagger, M.S., & Armitage, C. (2004). The influence of perceived loci of control and causality in the theory of planned behavior in a leisure-time exercise context. *Journal of Applied Biobehavioral Research, 9,* 45-64.

Hagger, M.S., Chatzisarantis, N.L.D., Barkoukis, V., Wang, C.K.J., & Baranowski, J. (2005). Perceived autonomy support in physical education and leisure-time physical activity: A cross-cultural evaluation of the trans-contextual model. *Journal of Educational Psychology, 97,* 287-301.

Hagger, M.S., Chatzisarantis, N.L.D., & Biddle, S.J.H. (2002). The influence of autonomous and controlling motives on physical activity intention within the Theory of Planned Behaviour. *British Journal of Health Psychology, 7,* 283-297.

Hagger, M.S., Chatzisarantis, N., Culverhouse, T., & Biddle, S.J.H. (2003). The processes by which perceived autonomy support in physical education promotes leisure-time physical activity intentions and behavior: A trans-contextual model. *Journal of Educational Psychology, 95,* 784-795.

Hagger, M.S., Chatzisarantis, N.L.D., & Harris, J. (2006). From psychological need satisfaction to intentional behavior: Testing a motivational sequence in two behavioral contexts. *Personality and Social Psychology Bulletin, 32,* 131-138.

Haworth, J.T., & Hill, S. (1992). Work, leisure, and psychological well-being in a sample of young adults. *Journal of Community and Applied Social Psychology, 2,* 147-160.

Humphries, C. (2005). *Exploring physical activity maintenance in middle aged and older women: A qualitative study.* Unpublished master's thesis, University of Ottawa, Ottawa, Ontario, Canada.

Ingledew, D.K., Markland, D., & Medley, A.R. (1998). Exercise motives and stages of change. *Journal of Health Psychology, 3,* 477-489.

Ingledew, D.K., Markland, D., & Sheppard, K.E. (2004). Personality and self-determination of exercise behaviour. *Personality and Individual Differences, 36,* 1921-1932.

Jackson, S.A. (1992). Athletes in flow: A qualitative investigation of flow states in elite figure skaters. *Journal of Applied Sport Psychology, 4,* 161-180.

Jackson, S.A. (1995). Factors influencing the occurrence of flow state in elite athletes. *Journal of Applied Sport Psychology, 7,* 138-166.

Jackson, S.A., & Csikszentmihalyi, M.C. (1999). *Flow in sports: The keys to optimal experiences and performances.* Champaign, IL: Human Kinetics.

Jackson, S.A., & Marsh, H. (1996). Development and validation of a scale to measure optimal experience: The Flow State Scale. *Journal of Sport and Exercise Psychology, 18,* 17-35.

Jackson, S.A., & Roberts, G.C. (1992). Positive performance states of athletes: Toward a conceptual understanding of peak performance. *Sport Psychologist, 6,* 156-171.

Kimiecik, J.C., & Jackson, S.A. (2002). Optimal experience in sport: A flow perspective. In T.S. Horn (Ed.), *Advances in sport psychology* (2nd ed., pp. 501-527). Champaign, IL: Human Kinetics.

Kowal, J., & Fortier, M.S. (1999). Motivational determinants of flow: Contributions from self-determination theory. *Journal of Social Psychology, 139,* 355-368.

Kowal, J., & Fortier, M.S. (2000). Testing relationships from the hierarchical model of intrinsic and extrinsic motivation using flow as a motivational consequence. *Research Quarterly for Exercise and Sport, 71,* 171-181.

Kowal, J., & Fortier, M.S. (2005). Determinants of physical activity behavior change in middle-aged women: Integrating concepts from self-determination theory and theory of planned behavior. Unpublished manuscript, University of Ottawa.

Landry, J.B., & Solomon, M.A. (2002). Self-determination theory as an organizing framework to investigate women's physical activity behaviour. *Quest, 54,* 332-354.

Landry, J.B., & Solomon, M.A. (2004). African American women's self-determination across the stages of change for exercise. *Journal of Sport and Exercise Psychology, 26,* 457-469.

Leblanc, L. (1999). *The influence of motivation and barriers on stages of exercise behavior change.* Unpublished master's thesis. University of Ottawa, Ottawa, Ontario, Canada.

Li, F. (1999). The Exercise Motivation Scale: Its multifaceted structure and construct validity. *Journal of Applied Sport Psychology, 11,* 97-115.

Mannell, R.C., Zuzanek, J., & Larson, R. (1988). Leisure states and "flow" experiences: Testing perceived freedom and intrinsic motivation hypotheses. *Journal of Leisure Research, 20,* 289-304.

Martin, J.J., & Cutler, K. (2002). An exploratory study of flow and motivation in theater actors. *Journal of Applied Sport Psychology, 14,* 344-352.

Moneta, G.B. (2004). The flow model of intrinsic motivation in Chinese: Cultural and personal moderators. *Journal of Happiness Studies, 5,* 181-217.

Mullan, E., & Markland, D. (1997). Variations in self-determination across the stages of change for exercise in adults. *Motivation and Emotion, 21,* 342-362.

Ntoumanis, N. (2001). A self-determination approach to the understanding of motivation in physical education. *British Journal of Educational Psychology, 71,* 225-242.

Oman, R.F., & McAuley, E. (1993). Intrinsic motivation and exercise behavior. *Journal of Health Education, 24,* 232-238.

Pelletier, L.G., Fortier, M.S., Vallerand, R.J., & Brière, N.M. (2001). Associations among perceived autonomy support, forms of self-regulation, and persistence: A prospective study. *Motivation and Emotion, 25,* 279-306.

Pelletier, L.G., Fortier, M.S., Vallerand, R.J., Tuson, K.M., Brière, N.M., & Blais, M.R. (1995). Toward a new measure of intrinsic motivation, extrinsic motivation, and amotivation in sports: The Sport Motivation Scale (SMS). *Journal of Sport and Exercise Psychology, 17,* 35-53.

Prochaska, J.O., & DiClemente, C.C. (1983). Stages and processes of self-change of smoking: Toward an integrative model of change. *Journal of Consulting and Clinical Psychology, 51,* 390-395.

Prochaska, J.O., & DiClemente, C.C. (1986). Toward a comprehensive model of change. In W.R. Miller & N. Heather (Eds.), *Addictive behaviors: Processes of change* (pp. 3-27). New York: Plenum Press.

Prochaska, J.O., & Velicer, W.F. (1997). The Transtheoretical Model of health behavior change. *American Journal of Health Promotion, 12,* 38-48.

Rose, E.A., Parfitt, G., & Williams, S. (2005). Exercise causality orientations, behavioural regulation for exercise and stage of change for exercise: Exploring their relationships. *Psychology of Sport and Exercise, 6,* 399-414.

Ryan, R.M., & Deci, E.L. (2000). Self-determination theory and the facilitation of intrinsic motivation, social development, and well-being. *American Psychologist, 55,* 68-78.

Ryan, R.M., Frederick, C.M., Lepes, D., Rubio, N., & Sheldon, K. (1997). Intrinsic motivation and exercise adherence. *International Journal of Sport Psychology, 28,* 335-354.

Sallis, J.F., & Owen, N. (1999). *Physical activity and behavioral medicine.* Thousand Oaks, CA: Sage.

Sallis, J.F., & Owen, N. (2002). Ecological models of health behaviour. In *Health behaviour and health education theory, research, and practice* (3rd ed., pp. 462-484). San Francisco: Jossey-Bass.

Sarrazin, P., Vallerand, R., Guillet, E., Pelletier, L., & Cury, F. (2002). Motivation and dropout in female handballers: A 21-month prospective study. *European Journal of Social Psychology, 32*, 395-418.

Sénécal, C., Nouwen, A., & White, D. (2000). Motivation and dietary self-care in adults with diabetes: Are self-efficacy and autonomous self-regulation complementary or competing constructs? *Health Psychology, 19*, 452-457.

Sheeran, P., Norman, P., & Orbell, S. (1999). Evidence that interactions based on attitudes better predict behaviour than intentions based on subjective norms. *European Journal of Social Psychology, 29*, 403-406.

Sheldon, K.M., Ryan, R.M., Deci, E.L., & Kasser, T. (2004). Independent effects of goal contents and motives on well-being: It's both what you pursue and why you pursue it. *Personality and Social Psychology Bulletin, 30*, 475-486.

Sheldon, K., Williams, G., & Joiner, T. (2003). *Motivating physical and mental health: Applying self-determination theory in the clinic.* New Haven, CT: Yale University Press.

Standage, M., Duda, J.L., & Ntoumanis, N. (2003). A model of contextual motivation in physical education: Using constructs from self-determination theory and achievement goal theories to predict physical activity intentions. *Journal of Educational Psychology, 95*, 97-110.

Stein, G.L., Kimiecik, J.C., Daniels, J., & Jackson, S.A. (1995). Psychological antecedents of flow in recreational sport. *Personality and Social Psychology Bulletin, 21*, 125-135.

Sutton, S. (2000). Interpreting cross-sectional data on stages of change. *Psychology and Health, 15*, 163-171.

Trost, S.G., Bauman, A.E., Sallis, J.F., & Brown, W. (2002). Correlates of adults' participation in physical activity: Review and update. *Medicine and Science in Sports and Exercise, 34*, 1996-2001.

Tulloch, H., Fortier, M., & Hogg, W. (in press). Physical activity counseling in primary care: Who has and who should counsel? *Patient Education and Counseling.*

Vallerand, R.J. (1997). Toward a hierarchical model of intrinsic and extrinsic motivation. In M.P. Zanna (Ed.), *Advances in experimental social psychology* (Vol. 29, pp. 271-360). New York: Academic Press.

Vallerand, R.J. (2001). A hierarchical model of intrinsic and extrinsic motivation in sport and exercise. In G.C. Roberts (Ed.), *Advances in motivation in sport and exercise* (pp. 263-320). Champaign, IL: Human Kinetics.

Vallerand, R.J., & Losier, G.F. (1994). Self-determined motivation and sportsmanship orientations: An assessment of their temporal relationship. *Journal of Sport and Exercise Psychology, 16*, 229-245.

Vallerand, R.J., & Losier, G.F. (1999). An integrative analysis of intrinsic and extrinsic motivation in sport. *Journal of Applied Sport Psychology, 11*, 142-169.

Vansteenkiste, M., Simons, J., Lens, W., Sheldon, K.M., & Deci, E.L. (2004). Motivating learning, performance, and persistence: The synergistic effects of intrinsic goal contents and autonomy-supportive contexts. *Journal of Personality and Social Psychology, 87*, 246-260.

Waterman, A.S., Schwartz, S.J., Goldbacher, E., Green, H., Miller, C., & Philip, S. (2003). Predicting the subjective experience of intrinsic motivation: The roles of self-determination, the balance of challenges and skills, and self-realization values. *Personality and Social Psychology Bulletin, 29,* 1447-1458.

White, R.W. (1959). Motivation reconsidered: The concept of competence. *Psychological Review, 66,* 297-333.

Williams, G. (2002). Improving patients' health through supporting the autonomy of patients and providers. In E.L. Deci & R.M. Ryan (Eds.), *Handbook of self-determination research* (pp. 233-254). Rochester, NY: University of Rochester Press.

Williams, G., Cox, E., Kouides, R., & Deci, E. (1999). Presenting the facts about smoking to adolescents: The effects of an autonomy supportive style. *Archives of Pediatrics and Adolescent Medicine, 153,* 959-964.

Williams, G.C., Gagné, M., Ryan, R.M., & Deci, E.L. (2002). Facilitating autonomous motivation for smoking cessation. *Health Psychology, 21,* 40-50.

Williams, G.C., Grow, V.M., Freedman, Z.R., Ryan, R.M., & Deci, E.L. (1996). Motivational predictors of weight loss and weight-loss maintenance. *Journal of Personality and Social Psychology, 20,* 115-126.

Williams, G.C., McGregor, H.A., Zeldman, A., Freedman, Z.R., & Deci, E.L. (2004). Testing a self-determination theory process model for promoting glycemic control through diabetes self-management. *Health Psychology, 23,* 58-66.

Wilson, P.M., & Rodgers, W.M. (2004). The relationship between perceived autonomy support, exercise regulations and behavioral intentions in women. *Psychology of Sport and Exercise, 5,* 229-242.

Wilson, P.M., Rodgers, W.M., Blanchard, C.M., & Gessell, J. (2003). The relationship between psychological needs, self-determined motivation, exercise attitudes, and physical fitness. *Journal of Applied Social Psychology, 33,* 2373-2392.

CHAPTER 8

Allen, J.B., & Howe, B.L. (1998). Player ability, coach feedback, and female adolescent athletes' perceived competence and satisfaction. *Journal of Sport and Exercise Psychology, 20,* 280-299.

Ames, C. (1984). Competitive, cooperative and individualistic goal structure: A motivational analysis. In R. Ames & C. Ames (Eds.), *Research on motivation in education: Vol. I. Student motivation* (pp. 177-207). New York: Academic Press.

Amorose, A.J., & Horn, T.S. (2000). Intrinsic motivation: Relationships with collegiate athletes' gender, scholarship status, and perceptions of their coaches' behavior. *Journal of Sport and Exercise Psychology, 22,* 63-84.

Amorose, A.J., & Smith, P. (2003). Feedback as a source of physical competence information: Effects of age, experience and type of feedback. *Journal of Sport and Exercise Psychology, 25,* 341-359.

Amorose, A.J., & Weiss, M.R. (1998). Coaching feedback as a source of information about perceptions of ability: A developmental examination. *Journal of Sport and Exercise Psychology, 20,* 395-420.

Anderssen, N. (1993). Perception of physical education classes among young adolescents: Do physical education classes provide equal opportunities to all students? *Health Education Research, 8,* 167-179.

Bakker, C. (1999). Psychological outcomes of physical education. In Y.V. Auweele, F.B. Bakker, S. Biddle, M. Durand, & R. Seiler (Eds.), *Psychology for physical education* (pp. 69-72). Champaign, IL: Human Kinetics.

Baron, R.M., & Kenny, D.A. (1986). The moderator-mediator variable distinction in social psychological research: Conceptual, strategic and statistical considerations. *Journal of Personality and Social Psychology, 51,* 1173-1182.

Black, S.J., & Weiss, M.R. (1992). The relationship among perceived coaching behaviors, perceptions of ability, and motivation in competitive age-group swimmers. *Journal of Sport and Exercise Psychology, 14,* 309-325.

Deci, E.L., & Ryan, R.M. (1985). *Intrinsic motivation and self-determination in human behavior.* New York: Plenum Press.

Deci, E.L., & Ryan, R.M. (1991). A motivational approach to self. Integration in personality. In R.A. Dienstbier (Ed.), *Nebraska symposium on motivation: Perspectives on motivation* (Vol. 38, pp. 237-288). Lincoln, NE: University of Nebraska Press.

Deci, E. L., & Ryan, R. M. (2000). The "what" and "why" of goal pursuits: Human needs and the self-determination of behavior. *Psychological Inquiry, 11,* 227-268.

Dweck, C.S., & Leggett, E.L. (1988). A social-cognitive approach to motivation and personality. *Psychological Review, 95,* 256-273.

Ferrer-Caja, E., & Weiss, M.R. (2000). Predictors of intrinsic motivation among adolescent students in physical education. *Research Quarterly for Exercise and Sport, 71,* 267-279.

Ferrer-Caja, E., & Weiss, M.R. (2002). Cross-validation of a model of intrinsic motivation with students enrolled in high school elective courses. *Journal of Experimental Education, 71,* 41-65.

Goudas, M., Dermitzaki, I., & Bagiatis, K. (2001). Motivation in physical education is correlated with participation in sport after school. *Psychological Reports, 88,* 491-496.

Hagger, M.S., Biddle, S.J.H., & Wang, C.K.J. (2005). Physical self-perceptions in adolescence: Generalizability of a multidimensional, hierarchical model across gender and grade. *Educational and Psychological Measurement, 65,* 297-322.

Hagger, M.S., Chatzisarantis, N.L.D., Barkoukis, V., Wang, C.K.J., & Baranowski, J. (2005a). Perceived autonomy support in physical education and leisure-time physical activity: A cross-cultural evaluation of the trans-contextual model. *Journal of Educational Psychology, 97,* 287-301.

Hagger, M.S., Chatzisarantis, N., Culverhouse, T., & Biddle, S.J.H. (2003). The processes by which perceived autonomy support in physical education promotes leisure-time physical activity intentions and behavior: A trans-contextual model. *Journal of Educational Psychology, 95,* 784-795.

Hagger, M.S., Chatzisarantis, N.L.D., & Harris, J. (2006). From psychological need satisfaction to intentional behavior: Testing a motivational sequence in two behavioral contexts. *Personality and Social Psychology Bulletin, 32,* 131-138.

Hagger, M.S., Chatzisarantis, N.L.D., Hein, V., Pihu, M., Soós, I., & Karsai, I. (2005b). Teacher, peer, and parent autonomy support in physical education and leisure-time physical activity: A trans-contextual model of motivation in three cultures. Unpublished manuscript, University of Nottingham, Nottingham, UK.

Harter, S. (1978). Effectance motivation reconsidered: Toward a development model. *Human Development, 21*, 34-64.

Harter, S. (1981). A model of intrinsic mastery motivation in children: Individual differences and developmental change. In W.A. Collins (Ed.), *The Minnesota symposium on child psychology* (Vol. 14, pp. 215-255). Hillsdale, NJ: Erlbaum.

Hein, V., Müür, M., & Koka, A. (2004). Intention to be physically active after school graduation and its relationship to three types of intrinsic motivation. *European Physical Education Review, 10*, 5-19.

Horn, T.S., Glenn, S.D., & Wentzell, A.B. (1993). Sources of information underlying personal ability judgements in high school athletes. *Pediatric Exercise Science, 5*, 263-274.

Koka, A., & Hein, V. (2003). Perceptions of teacher's feedback and learning environment as predictors of intrinsic motivation in physical education. *Psychology of Sport and Exercise, 4*, 333-346.

Koka, A., & Hein, V. (2005). The effect of perceived teacher feedback on intrinsic motivation in physical education. *International Journal of Sport Psychology, 36*, 91-106.

Mancini, V.H., & Wuest, D.A. (1989). Self-Assessment Feedback Instrument (SAFI). In P.W. Darst & B. Dorothy (Eds.), *Analyzing physical education and sport instruction* (pp. 143-147). Champaign, IL: Human Kinetics.

Marsh, H.W. (1989). Age and sex effects in multiple dimensions of self-concept: Preadolescence to early adulthood. *Journal of Educational Psychology, 81*, 417-430.

Martens, R. (1987). *Coaches guide to sport psychology.* Champaign, IL: Human Kinetics.

McAuley, E., Duncan, T., & Tammen, V.V. (1989). Psychometric properties of the Intrinsic Motivation Inventory in a competitive sport setting: A confirmatory factor analysis. *Research Quarterly for Exercise and Sport, 60*, 48-58.

Nicholls, J.G. (1984). Achievement motivation: Conceptions of ability, subjective experience, task choice, and performance. *Psychological Review, 91*, 328-346.

Nicholls, J.G. (1989). *The competitive ethos and democratic education.* Cambridge, MA: Harvard University Press.

Ntoumanis, N. (2001). A self-determination approach to the understanding of motivation in physical education. *British Journal of Educational Psychology, 71*, 225-242.

Peterson, P., & Swing, S. (1982). Beyond time on task: Students' reports of their thought processes during classroom instruction. *Elementary School Journal, 82*, 481-491.

Peterson, P.L., Swing, S.R., Stark, K.D., & Waas, G.A. (1984). Students' cognitions and time on task during mathematics instruction. *American Educational Research Journal, 21*, 487-515.

Prochaska, J.J., Sallis, J.F., Slymen, D.J., & McKenzie, T.L. (2003). A longitudinal study of children's enjoyment of physical education. *Pediatric Exercise Science, 15*, 170-178.

Ryan, R.M., & Deci, E.L. (2000). Self-determination theory and the facilitation of intrinsic motivation, social development, and well-being. *American Psychologist, 55*, 68-78.

Smith, R.E., Smoll, F.L., & Hunt, E.B. (1977). A system for the behavioural assessment of athletic coaches. *Research Quarterly, 48*, 401-407.

Vallerand, R.J. (1997). Toward a hierarchical model of intrinsic and extrinsic motivation. In M.P. Zanna (Ed.), *Advances in experimental social psychology* (Vol. 29, pp. 271-360). New York: Academic Press.

Van Wersch, A.V., Trew, K., & Turner, I. (1992). Post-primary school pupils' interest in physical education: Age and gender differences. *British Journal of Educational Psychology, 62,* 56-72.

Yukelson, D. (1998). Communicating effectively. In J.M. Williams (Ed.), *Applied sport psychology: Personal growth to peak performance* (3rd ed., pp. 142-157). Mountain View, CA: Mayfield.

CHAPTER 9

Alexandris, K., Tsorbatzoudis, C., & Grouios, G. (2002). Perceived constraints on recreational sport participation: Investigating their relationship with intrinsic motivation, extrinsic motivation and amotivation. *Journal of Leisure Research, 34,* 233-252.

Amabile, T.M. (1996). *Creativity in context.* Boulder, CO: Westview Press.

Amiot, C.E., Gaudreau, P., & Blanchard, C.M. (2004). Self-determination, coping, and goal attainment in sport. *Journal of Sport and Exercise Psychology, 26,* 396-411.

Beauchamp, P.H., Halliwell, W.R., Fournier, J.F., & Koestner, R. (1996). Effects of cognitive-behavioral psychological skills training on the motivation, preparation, and putting performance of novice golfers. *Sport Psychologist, 10,* 157-170.

Blais, M.R., Sabourin, S., Boucher, C., & Vallerand, R.J. (1990). Toward a motivational model of couple happiness. *Journal of Personality and Social Psychology, 59,* 1021-1031.

Brière, N.M., Vallerand, R.J., Blais, M.R., & Pelletier, L.G. (1995). Développement et validation d'une mesure de motivation intrinsèque et extrinsèque et d'amotivation en contexte sportif: L'Echelle de Motivation dans les Sports (EMS). *International Journal of Sport Psychology, 26,* 465-489.

Brunel, P.C. (1999). Relationships between achievement goal orientations and perceived motivational climate on intrinsic motivation. *Scandinavian Journal of Medicine and Science in Sports, 9,* 365-374.

Chantal, Y., Guay, F., Dobreva-Martinova, T., Vallerand, R.J. (1996). Motivation and elite performance: An exploratory investigation with Bulgarian athletes. *International Journal of Sport Psychology, 27,* 173-182.

Chantal, Y., Robin, P., Vernat, J.-P., & Bernache-Assolant, I. (2005). Motivation, sportspersonship, and athletic aggression: A mediational analysis. *Psychology of Sport and Exercise, 6,* 233-249.

Chatzisarantis, N.L.D., Hagger, M.S., Biddle, S.J.H., Smith, B., & Wang, J.C.K. (2003). A meta-analysis of perceived locus of causality in exercise, sport, and physical education contexts. *Journal of Sport and Exercise Psychology, 25,* 284-306.

Conroy, D.E. (2004). The unique psychological meanings of multidimensional fears of failing. *Journal of Sport and Exercise Psychology, 26,* 484-491.

Cresswell, S.L., & Eklund, R.C. (2005). Motivation and burnout among top amateur rugby players. *Medicine and Science in Sports and Exercise, 37,* 469-477.

Deci, E.L., Eghrari, H., Patrick, B.C., & Leone, D.R. (1994). Facilitating internalization: The self-determination theory perspective. *Journal of Personality, 62,* 119-142.

Deci, E.L., & Ryan, R.M. (1985). *Intrinsic motivation and self-determination in human behavior.* New York: Plenum Press.

Deci, E.L., & Ryan, R.M. (2000). The "what" and "why" of goal pursuits: Human needs and the self-determination of behavior. *Psychological Inquiry, 11,* 227-268.

Doganis, G. (2000). Development of a Greek version of the Sport Motivation Scale. *Perceptual and Motor Skills, 90,* 505-512.

Gagné, M., Ryan, R.M., & Bargmann, K. (2003). Autonomy support and need satisfaction in the motivation and well-being of gymnasts. *Journal of Applied Sport Psychology, 15,* 372-390.

Georgiadis, M.M., Biddle, S.J.H., & Chatzisarantis, N.L.D. (2001). The mediating role of self-determination in the relationship between goal orientations and physical worth in Greek exercisers. *European Journal of Sport Science, 1,* 1-9.

Goudas, M., Biddle, S.J.H., & Fox, K. (1994). Perceived locus of causality, goal orientations and perceived competence in school physical education classes. *British Journal of Educational Psychology, 64,* 453-463.

Gould, D., Udry, E., Tuffey, S., & Loehr, J. (1996). Burnout in competitive junior tennis players: I. A quantitative psychological assessment. *Sport Psychologist, 10,* 322-340.

Green-Demers, I., Pelletier, L.G., & Ménard, S. (1997). The impact of behavioral difficulty on the saliency of the association between self-determined motivation and environmental behaviors. *Canadian Journal of Behavioral Science/Revue canadienne des sciences du comportement, 29,* 157-166.

Green-Demers, I., Pelletier, L.G., Stewart, D.G., & Gushue, N.R. (1998). Coping with the less interesting aspects of training: Toward a model of interest and motivation enhancement in individual sports. *Basic and Applied Social Psychology, 20,* 251-261.

Guay, F., Mageau, G.A., & Vallerand, R.J. (2003). On the hierarchical structure of self-determined motivation: A test of top-down, bottom-up, reciprocal, and horizontal effects. *Personality and Social Psychology Bulletin, 29,* 992-1004.

Hagger, M.S., Chatzisarantis, N.L.D., & Harris, J. (2006). From psychological need satisfaction to intentional behavior: Testing a motivational sequence in two behavioral contexts. *Personality and Social Psychology Bulletin, 32,* 131-138.

Hamer, M., Karageorghis, C.I., & Vlachopoulos, S.P. (2002). Motives for exercise participation as predictors of exercise dependence among endurance athletes. *Journal of Sports Medicine and Physical Fitness, 42,* 233-238.

Härdle, W., & Simar, L. (2003). *Applied multivariate statistical analysis.* Berlin: Springer-Verlag.

Jackson, S.A., Kimiecik, J.C., Ford, S.K., & Marsh, H.W. (1998). Psychological correlates of flow in sport. *Journal of Sport and Exercise Psychology, 20,* 358-378.

Koestner, R., & Losier, G.F. (2002). Distinguishing three types of being highly motivated: A closer look at introjection, identification, and intrinsic motivation. In E.L. Deci & R.M. Ryan (Eds.), *Handbook of self-determination research* (pp. 101-122). Rochester, NY: University of Rochester Press.

Kowal, J., & Fortier, M.S. (2000). Testing relationships from the hierarchical model of intrinsic and extrinsic motivation using flow as a motivational consequence. *Research Quarterly for Exercise and Sport, 71,* 171-181.

Li, F.Z. (1999). The Exercise Motivation Scale: Its multifaceted structure and construct validity. *Journal of Applied Sport Psychology, 11*, 97-115.

Li, F., & Harmer, P. (1996). Testing the simplex assumption underlying the sport motivation scale. *Research Quarterly for Exercise and Sport, 67*, 396-405.

Lin, C.- Y., & Chi, L.- K. (2003). Development of the Sport Motivation Scale: Analysis of reliability and validity. *Psychological Bulletin for Sport and Experience Psychology of Taiwan, 2*, 15-32.

Mallett, C.J. (2003). Elite athletes: What makes the fire burn so brightly? Unpublished PhD thesis, University of Queensland, Australia.

Martens, M.P., & Webber, S.N. (2002). Psychometric properties of the sport motivation scale: An evaluation with college varsity athletes from the US. *Journal of Sport and Exercise Psychology, 24*, 254-270.

Martin, J.J., & Cutler, K. (2002). An exploratory study of flow and motivation in theater actors. *Journal of Applied Sport Psychology, 14*, 344-352.

Mullen, E., Markland, D., & Ingledew, D.K. (1997). A graded conceptualisation of self-determination in the regulation of exercise behavior: Development of a measure using confirmatory factor analytic procedures. *Personality and Individual Differences, 23*, 745-752.

Ntoumanis, N. (2001). Empirical links between achievement goal theory and self-determination theory in sport. *Journal of Sports Sciences, 19*, 397-409.

Ntoumanis, N. (2002). Motivational clusters in a sample of British physical education classes. *Psychology of Sport and Exercise, 3*, 77-194.

Otis, N., Grouzet, F.M., & Pelletier, L.G. (2005). The latent motivational change in academic setting: A three-year longitudinal study. *Journal of Educational Psychology, 97*, 170-183.

Pelletier, L.G., Dion, S.C., Slovinec-D'Angelo, M., & Reid, R.D. (2004). Why do you regulate what you eat? Relationships between forms of regulation, eating behaviors, sustained dietary behavior change, and psychological adjustment. *Motivation and Emotion, 28*, 245-277.

Pelletier, L.G., Fortier, M.S., Vallerand, R.J., & Brière, N. (2001). Associations among perceived autonomy support, forms of self-regulation, and persistence: A prospective study. *Motivation and Emotion, 25*, 279-306.

Pelletier, L.G., Fortier, M.S., Vallerand, R.J., Tuson, K.M., Brière, N.M., & Blais, M.R. (1995). Toward a new measure of intrinsic motivation, extrinsic motivation, and amotivation in sports: The Sport Motivation Scale (SMS). *Journal of Sport and Exercise Psychology, 17*, 35-53.

Pelletier, L.G., & Kabush, D. (2005). The Sport Motivation Scale: Revision and addition of the integrated regulation subscale. Manuscript in preparation. University of Ottawa.

Pelletier, L.G., Tuson, K.M., Green-Demers, I., Noels, K., & Beaton, A.M. (1998). Why are you doing things for the environment? The Motivation toward the Environment Scale (MTES). *Journal of Applied Social Psychology, 28*, 437-468.

Pelletier, L.G., Tuson, K.M., & Haddad, N.K. (1997). Client motivation for therapy scale: A measure of intrinsic motivation, extrinsic motivation, and amotivation for therapy. *Journal of Personality Assessment, 68*, 414-435.

Petherick, C.M., & Weigand, D.A. (2002). The relationship of dispositional goal orientations and perceived motivational climates on indices of motivation in male and female swimmers. *International Journal of Sport Psychology, 33,* 218-237.

Raedeke, T.D., & Smith, A.L. (2001). Development and preliminary validation of an athlete burnout measure. *Journal of Sport and Exercise Psychology, 23,* 281-306.

Ryan, R.M. (1995). Psychological needs and the facilitation of integrative processes. *Journal of Personality, 63,* 397-427.

Ryan, R.M., & Connell, J.P. (1989). Perceived locus of causality and internalization: Examining reasons for acting in two domains. *Journal of Personality and Social Psychology, 57,* 749-761.

Ryan, R.M., & Deci, E.L. (2000). Self-determination theory and the facilitation of intrinsic motivation, social development, and well-being. *American Psychologist, 55,* 68-78.

Sarrazin, P., Vallerand, R., Guillet, E., Pelletier, L.G., & Cury, F. (2002). Motivation and dropout in female handballers: A 21-month prospective study. *European Journal of Social Psychology, 32,* 395-418.

Vallerand, R.J. (1997). Toward a hierarchical model of intrinsic and extrinsic motivation. *Advances in Experimental Social Psychology, 29,* 271-360.

Vallerand, R.J., Fortier, M.S., & Guay, F. (1997). Self-determination and persistence in a real-life setting: Toward a motivational model of high school dropout. *Journal of Personality and Social Psychology, 72,* 1161-1176.

Vallerand, R.J., & Losier, G.F. (1994). Self-determined motivation and sportsmanship orientations: An assessment of their temporal relationship. *Journal of Sport and Exercise Psychology, 16,* 229-245.

Vallerand, R.J., & Losier, G.F. (1999). An integrative analysis of intrinsic and extrinsic motivation in sport. *Journal of Applied Sport Psychology, 11,* 142-169.

Wang, C.K.J., & Biddle, S.J.H. (2001). Young people's motivational profiles in physical activity: A cluster analysis. *Journal of Sport and Exercise Psychology, 23,* 1-22.

Weiss, W.M., & Weiss, M.R. (2003). Attraction- and entrapment-based commitment among competitive female gymnasts. *Journal of Sport and Exercise Psychology, 25,* 229-247.

CHAPTER 10

Baron, R.M., & Kenny, D.A. (1986). The moderator-mediator variable distinction in social psychological research: Conceptual, strategic, and statistical considerations. *Journal of Personality and Social Psychology, 51,* 1173-1182.

Brière, N.M., Vallerand, R.J., Blais, M.R., & Pelletier, L.G. (1995). Dèvelopement et validation d'une measure de motivation intrinsèque, extrinsèque, et d'amotivation en contexte sportif: L'échelle de Motivation dans les Sports (ÉMS). [On the development and validation of the French form of the Sport Motivation Scale.] *International Journal of Sport Psychology, 26,* 465-489.

Chantal, Y., Guay, F., Dobreva-Martinova, T., & Vallerand, R.J. (1996). Motivation and elite performance: An exploratory investigation with Bulgarian athletes. *International Journal of Sport Psychology, 27,* 173-182.

Chirkov, V. I., & Ryan, R. M. (2001). Parent and teacher autonomy support in Russian and U.S. adolescents: Common effects on well-being and academic motivation. *Journal of Cross-Cultural Psychology, 32*, 618-635.

Cresswell, S.L., & Eklund, R.C. (2005). Motivation and burnout among top amateur rugby players. *Medicine and Science in Sports and Exercise, 37*, 469-477.

Csikszentmihalyi, M. (1975). *Beyond boredom and anxiety.* San Francisco: Jossey-Bass.

Csikszentmihalyi, M. (1990). *Flow: The psychology of optimal performance.* New York: Harper Perennial.

deCharms, R. (1968). *Personal causation: The internal affective determinants of behavior.* New York: Academic Press.

Deci., E.L., & Moller, A.C. (2005). The concept of competence: A starting place for understanding intrinsic motivation and self-determined extrinsic motivation. In A.J. Elliot & D.S. Dweck (eds.), *Handbook of competence and motivation* (pp. 579-597). New York: Guilford Press.

Deci, E.L., & Ryan, R.M. (1985). *Intrinsic motivation and self-determination in human behavior.* New York: Plenum Press.

Duda, J.L., & Treasure, D.C. (2001). Toward optimal motivation in sport: Fostering athletes' competence and sense of control. In J. Williams (Ed.), *Applied sport psychology: Personal growth to peak performance* (4th ed., pp. 43-62). Mountain View, CA: Mayfield.

Freudenberger, H.J. (1980). *Burnout: The high cost of high achievement.* Garden City, NY: Anchor Press.

Gagné, M., Ryan, R.M., & Bargmann, K. (2003). Autonomy support and need satisfaction in the motivation and well-being of gymnasts. *Journal of Applied Sport Psychology, 15*, 372-390.

Gold, Y., & Roth, R. (1993). *Teachers managing stress and preventing burnout: The professional health solution.* London: Falmer Press.

Gould, D. (1996). Personal motivation gone awry: Burnout in competitive athletes. *Quest, 48*, 275-289.

Gould, D., & Dieffenbach, K. (2002). Overtraining, under recovery, and burnout in sport. In M. Kellmann (Ed.), *Enhancing recovery: Preventing underperformance in athletes* (pp. 25-35). Champaign, IL: Human Kinetics.

Gould, D., Tuffey, S., Udry, E., & Loehr, J. (1996). Burnout in competitive junior tennis players: II. Qualitative analysis. *Sport Psychologist, 10*, 341-366.

Gould, D., Udry, E., Tuffey, S., & Loehr, J. (1996). Burnout in competitive junior tennis players: I. A quantitative psychological assessment. *Sport Psychologist, 10*, 322-340.

Green-Demers, I., Pelletier, L.G., Stewart, D.G., & Gushue, N.R. (1998). Coping with the less interesting aspects of training: Toward a model of interest and motivation enhancement in individual sports. *Basic and Applied Social Psychology, 20*, 251-261.

Hall, H.K., Cawthraw, I.W., & Kerr, A.W. (1997). Burnout: Motivation gone awry or a disaster waiting to happen? In R. Lidor & M. Bar-Eli (Eds.), *Innovations in sport psychology: Linking theory and practice. Proceedings of the IX World Congress in Sport Psychology: Part 1* (pp. 306-308). Netanya, Israel: Ministry of Education, Culture and Sport.

Kellmann, M. (2002). Psychological assessment of underrecovery. In M. Kellmann (Ed.), *Enhancing recovery: Preventing underperformance in athletes* (pp. 37-55). Champaign, IL: Human Kinetics.

Klinger, E. (1975). Consequences of commitment to and disengagement from incentives. *Psychological Review, 82*, 1-25.

Kowal, J., & Fortier, M.S. (1999). Motivational determinants of flow: Contributions from self-determination theory. *Journal of Social Psychology, 139*, 355-368.

Krane, V., Greenleaf, C.A., & Snow, J. (1997). Reaching for gold and the practice of glory: A motivational case study of an elite gymnast. *Sport Psychologist, 11*, 53-71.

Lemyre, P.-N., Kuczka, K.K., Treasure, D.C., & Roberts, G.C. (2005). Overtraining and burnout: Elite athletes telling their stories. Paper presented at the Association for the Advancement of Applied Psychology annual conference, Vancouver, Canada.

Lemyre, P-N., Treasure, D.C., & Roberts, G.C. (2006). Influence of variability of motivation and affect on elite athlete burnout susceptibility. *Journal of Sport and Exercise Psychology, 28*, 32-48.

Mallett, C.J., & Hanrahan, S.J. (2004). Elite athletes: Why does the "fire" burn so brightly? *Psychology of Sport and Exercise, 5*, 183-200.

Nicholls, J.G. (1989). *The competitive ethos and democratic education.* Cambridge, MA: Harvard University Press.

Pelletier, L.G., Fortier, M.S., Vallerand, R.J., & Brière, N.M. (2001). Associations among perceived autonomy support, forms of self-regulation, and persistence: A prospective study. *Motivation and Emotion, 25*, 279-306.

Pelletier, L.G., Fortier, M., Vallerand, R.J., Tuson, K.M., Brière, N.M., & Blais, M.R. (1995). The Sports Motivation Scale (SMS): A measure of intrinsic motivation, extrinsic motivation and amotivation in sports. *Journal of Sport and Exercise Psychology, 17*, 35-53.

Raedeke, T.D. (1997). Is athlete burnout more than just stress? A sport commitment perspective. *Journal of Sport and Exercise Psychology, 19*, 396-417.

Raglin, J.S., & Wilson, G.S. (2000). Overtraining in athletes. In Y.L. Hanin (Ed.), *Emotions in sport* (pp. 191-207). Champaign, IL: Human Kinetics.

Reeve, J. (1998). Autonomy support as an interpersonal motivating style: Is it teachable? *Contemporary Educational Psychology, 23*, 312-330.

Reeve, J. (2002). Self-determination theory applied to educational settings. In E.L. Deci & R.M. Ryan (Eds.), *Handbook of self-determination research.* Rochester, NY: University of Rochester Press.

Ryan, R.M., & Deci, E.L. (2000). Self-determination theory and the facilitation of intrinsic motivation, social development, and well-being. *American Psychologist, 55*, 68-78.

Sarrazin, P., Vallerand, R.J., Guillet, E., Pelletier, L.G., & Cury, F. (2002). Motivation and dropout in female handballers: A 21-month prospective study. *European Journal of Social Psychology, 32*, 395-418.

Silva, J.M. (1990). An analysis of the training stress syndrome in competitive athletics. *Journal of Applied Sport Psychology, 2*, 5-20.

Smith, R. (1986). Toward a cognitive-affective model of athletic burnout. *Journal of Sport Psychology, 8*, 36-50.

Steinacker, J.M., & Lehmann, M. (2002). Clinical findings and mechanisms of stress and recovery in athletes. In M. Kellmann (Ed.), *Enhancing recovery: Preventing underperformance in athletes* (pp. 103-118). Champaign, IL: Human Kinetics.

Treasure, D.C., Standage, M., Lemyre, P.N., & Ntoumanis, N. (2004). A longitudinal examination of motivation orientation and basic needs satisfaction in a sample of elite level swimmers. Paper presented at the Second International Conference on Self-Determination Theory, Ottawa, Ontario.

Vallerand, R.J. (1997). Toward a hierarchical model of intrinsic and extrinsic motivation. In M.P. Zanna (Ed.), *Advances in experimental social psychology* (pp. 271-359). New York: Academic Press.

CHAPTER 11

Arndt, J., Solomon, S., Kasser, T., & Sheldon, K.M. (2004). The urge to splurge: A terror management account of materialism and consumer behavior. *Journal of Consumer Psychology, 14*, 198-212.

Chirkov, V.I., & Ryan, R.M. (2001). Parent and teacher autonomy support in Russian and U.S. adolescents: Common effects on well-being and academic motivation. *Journal of Cross-Cultural Psychology, 32*, 618-635.

Crocker, J., & Park, L.E. (2004). The costly pursuit of self-esteem. *Psychological Bulletin, 130*, 392-414.

Deci, E.L., Eghrari, H., Patrick, B.C., & Leone, D.R. (1994). Facilitating internalization: The self-determination perspective. *Journal of Personality, 62*, 119-142.

Deci, E.L., & Ryan, R.M. (1985). *Intrinsic motivation and self-determination in human behavior.* New York: Plenum Press.

Deci, E.L., & Ryan, R.M. (1995). Human autonomy: The basis for true self-esteem. In M. Kernis (Ed.), *Efficacy, agency, and self-esteem* (pp. 31-49). New York: Plenum Press.

Deci, E.L., & Ryan, R.M. (2000). The "what" and "why" of goal pursuits: Human needs and the self-determination of behavior. *Psychological Inquiry, 11*, 227-268.

Duriez, B., Vansteenkiste, M., Soenens, B., & De Witte, H. (2005). The social costs of extrinsic versus intrinsic goal pursuits: Their relation with right-wing authoritarianism, social dominance, and racial prejudice. Manuscript submitted for publication.

Eccles, J.S., & Wigfield, A. (2002). Motivational beliefs, values, and goals. *Annual Review of Psychology, 53*, 109-132.

Feather, N.T. (1992). Values, valences, expectations, and actions. *Journal of Social Issues, 48*, 109-124.

Frederick, C.M., & Ryan, R.M. (1993). Differences in motivation for sport and exercise and their relationships with participation and mental health. *Journal of Sport Behavior, 16*, 125-145.

Guay, F., Mageau, G.A., & Vallerand, R.J. (2003). On the hierarchical structure of self-determined motivation: A test of top-down, bottom-up, reciprocal, and horizontal effects. *Personality and Social Psychology Bulletin, 29*, 992-1004.

Hagger, M.S., Chatzisarantis, N.L.D., Barkoukis, V., Wang, C.K.J., & Baranowski, J. (2005). Perceived autonomy support in physical education and leisure-time physical activity: A cross-cultural evaluation of the trans-contextual model. *Journal of Educational Psychology, 97*, 287-301.

Kasser, T. (2002). *The high price of materialism.* London: MIT Press.

Kasser, T., & Ahuvia, A.C. (2002). Materialistic values and well-being in business students. *European Journal of Social Psychology, 32,* 137-146.

Kasser, T., & Ryan, R.M. (1993). A dark side of the American dream: Correlates of financial success as a central life aspiration. *Journal of Personality and Social Psychology, 65,* 410-422.

Kasser, T., & Ryan, R.M. (1996). Further examining the American dream: Differential correlates of intrinsic and extrinsic goals. *Personality and Social Psychology Bulletin, 22,* 280-287.

Kasser, T., & Ryan, R.M. (2001). Be careful what you wish for: Optimal functioning and the relative attainment of intrinsic and extrinsic goals. In P. Schmuck & K.M. Sheldon (Eds.), *Life goals and well-being* (pp. 116-131). Seattle, Toronto, Bern, Göttingen: Hogrefe & Huber.

Kasser, T., Ryan, R.M., Couchman, C.E., & Sheldon, K.M. (2004). Materialistic values: Their causes and consequences. In T. Kasser & A.D. Kanfer (Eds.), *Psychology and consumer cultures: The struggle for a good life in a materialistic world* (pp. 11-28). Washington, DC: American Psychological Association.

Kernis, M. (2003). Toward a conceptualization of optimal self-esteem. *Psychological Inquiry, 14,* 1-26.

Kim, Y., Kasser, T., & Lee, H. (2003). Self-concept, aspirations, and well-being in South-Korea and the United States. *Journal of Social Psychology, 143,* 277-290.

Kuhl, J., & Beckmann, J. (1994). *Volition and personality: Action versus state orientation.* Göttingen, Germany: Hogrefe.

Lens, W., Simons, J., & Dewitte, S. (2001). Student motivation and self-regulation as a function of future time perspective and perceived instrumentality. In S. Volet & S. Järvelä (Eds.), *Motivation in learning contexts: Theoretical advances and methodological implications* (pp. 223-248). New York: Pergamon.

Lens, W., Simons, J., & Dewitte, S. (2002). From duty to desire: The role of students' future time perspective and instrumentality perceptions for study motivation and self-regulation. In F. Pajares & T. Urdan (Eds.), *Academic motivation of adolescents* (pp. 221-245). Greenwich, CT: Information Age.

Markland, D., Ryan, R.M., Tobin, V.J., & Rollnick, S. (in press). Motivational interviewing and self-determination theory. *Journal of Consulting and Clinical Psychology.*

McHoskey, J.W. (1999). Machiavellianism, intrinsic versus extrinsic goals, and social interest: A self-determination analysis. *Motivation and Emotion, 23,* 267-283.

Miller, R.B., & Brickman, S.J. (2004). A model of future-oriented motivation and self-regulation. *Educational Psychology Review, 16,* 9-33.

Miller, W.R., & Rollnick, S. (1991). *Motivational interviewing: Preparing people to change addictive behavior.* New York: Guilford Press.

Miller, W.R., & Rollnick, S. (2002). *Motivational interviewing.* New York: Guilford Press.

National Agriculture Library. (2005). Nutrition.gov: Smart nutrition starts here. United States Department of Agriculture. Retrieved August 1, 2005, from www.nutrition. gov.

Prochaska, J.O., & DiClemente, C.C. (1982). Transtheoretical therapy: Toward a more integrative model of change. *Psychotherapy: Theory, Research, and Practice, 19*, 276-288.

Prochaska, J.O., DiClemente, C.C., & Norcross, J.C. (1992). In search of how people change: Applications to addictive behaviors. *American Psychologist, 47*, 1102-1114.

Richins, M.L., & Dawson, S. (1992). A consumer value orientation for materialism and its measurement: Scale development and validation. *Journal of Consumer Research, 19*, 303-316.

Ryan, R.M., Chirkov, V.I., Little, T.D., Sheldon, K.M., Timoshina, E., & Deci, E.L. (1999). The American dream in Russia: Extrinsic aspirations and well-being in two cultures. *Personality and Social Psychology Bulletin, 25*, 1509-1524.

Ryan, R.M., Frederick, C.M., Lepes, D., Rubio, N., & Sheldon, K.M. (1997). Intrinsic motivation and exercise adherence. *International Journal of Sport Psychology, 28*, 335-354.

Ryan, R.M., Sheldon, K.M., Kasser, T., & Deci, E.L. (1996). All goals were not created equal: An organismic perspective on the nature of goals and their regulation. In P.M. Gollwitzer & J.A. Bargh (Eds.), *The psychology of action: Linking motivation and cognition to behavior* (pp. 7-26). New York: Guilford Press.

Shaw, J., & Waller, G. (1995). The media's impact on body image: Implications for prevention and treatment. *Eating Disorders: The Journal of Treatment and Prevention, 3*, 115-123.

Sheldon, K.M., & Kasser, T. (1995). Coherence and congruence: Two aspects of personality integration. *Journal of Personality and Social Psychology, 68*, 531-543.

Sheldon, K.M., Ryan, R.M., Deci, E.L., & Kasser, T. (2004). The independent effects of goal contents and motives on well-being: It's both what you pursue and why you pursue it. *Personality and Social Psychology Bulletin, 30*, 475-486.

Simons, J., Vansteenkiste, M., Lens, W., & Lacante, M. (2004). Placing motivation and future time perspective theory in a temporal perspective. *Educational Psychology Review, 16*, 121-139.

Sirgy, M.J. (1998). Materialism and quality of life. *Social Indicators Research, 43*, 227-260.

Stice, E., & Shaw, H.E. (1994). Adverse effects of the media portrayed thin-ideal on women and linkages to bulimic symptomatology. *Journal of Social and Clinical Psychology, 13*, 288-308.

Vallerand, R.J. (1997). Toward a hierarchical model of intrinsic and extrinsic motivation. In M.P. Zanna (Ed.), *Advances in experimental social psychology* (pp. 271-360). San Diego: Academic Press.

Vallerand, R.J., & Ratelle, C.F. (2002). Intrinsic and extrinsic motivation: A hierarchical model. In E.L. Deci & R.M. Ryan (Eds.), *Handbook of self-determination research* (pp. 37-64). Rochester, NY: University of Rochester Press.

Vansteenkiste, M., Duriez, B., Simons, J., & Soenens, B. (in press). Materialistic values and well-being among business students: Further evidence for their detrimental effect. *Journal of Applied Social Psychology.*

Vansteenkiste, M., Lens, W., & Deci, E.L. (2006). Intrinsic versus extrinsic goal-contents in self-determination theory: Another look at the quality of academic motivation. *Educational Psychologist.*

Vansteenkiste, M., Neyrinck, B., Niemic, C., Soenens, B., & De Witte, H. (2005a). Examining the relations among extrinsic versus intrinsic work value orientations, basic need satisfaction, and job experience: A self-determination theory approach. Manuscript resubmitted for publication.

Vansteenkiste, M., & Sheldon, K.M. (2006). There is nothing more practical than a good theory: Integrating motivational interviewing and self-determination theory. *British Journal of Clinical Psychology.*

Vansteenkiste, M., Simons, J., Braet, C., Bachman, C., & Deci, E.L. (2005b). Promoting maintained weight loss through healthy lifestyle changes among obese children: An experimental test of self-determination theory. Manuscript submitted for publication.

Vansteenkiste, M., Simons, J., Lens, W., Sheldon, K.M., & Deci, E.L. (2004a). Motivating persistence, deep level learning and achievement: The synergistic role of intrinsic-goal contents and autonomy-supportive contexts. *Journal of Personality and Social Psychology, 87,* 246-260.

Vansteenkiste, M., Simons, J., Lens, W., Soenens, B., & Matos, L. (2005c). Examining the impact of extrinsic versus intrinsic goal framing and internally controlling versus autonomy-supportive communication style upon early adolescents' academic achievement. *Child Development, 2,* 483-501.

Vansteenkiste, M., Simons, J., Lens, W., Soenens, B., Matos, L., & Lacante, M. (2004b). Less is sometimes more: Goal-content matters. *Journal of Educational Psychology, 96,* 755-764.

Vansteenkiste, M., Simons, J., Soenens, B., & Lens, W. (2004c). How to become a persevering exerciser: The importance of providing a clear, future goal in an autonomy-supportive way. *Journal of Sport and Exercise Psychology, 26,* 232-249.

Vansteenkiste, M., Soenens, B., & Vandereycken, W. (2005). Motivation to change in eating disorder patients: A conceptual clarification on the basis of self-determination theory. *International Journal of Eating Disorders, 37,* 1-13.

Vitousek, K., Watson, S., & Wilson, G.T. (1998). Enhancing motivation for change in treatment-resistant eating disorders. *Clinical Psychology Review, 18,* 391-420.

Wankel, L.M. (1993). The importance of enjoyment to adherence and psychological benefits from physical activity. *International Journal of Sport Psychology, 24,* 151-169.

Williams, G.C., Cox, E.M., Hedberg, V.A., & Deci, E.L. (2000). Extrinsic life goals and health-risk behaviors among adolescents. *Journal of Applied Social Psychology, 30,* 1756-1771.

Wood, J.V., & Wilson, A.E. (2003). How important is social comparison? In M.R. Leary & J.P. Tangney (Eds.), *Handbook of self and identity* (pp. 344-366). New York: Guilford Press.

CHAPTER 12

Atkinson, J.W. (1957). Motivational determinants of risk-taking behavior. *Psychological Review, 64,* 359-372.

Bandura, A. (1997). *Self-efficacy: The exercise of control.* New York: Freeman.

Baumeister, R., & Leary, M.R. (1995). The need to belong: Desire for interpersonal attachments as a fundamental human motivation. *Psychological Bulletin, 117*, 497-529.

Conroy, D.E. (2001). Progress in the development of a multidimensional measure of fear of failure: The Performance Failure Appraisal Inventory (PFAI). *Anxiety, Stress, and Coping, 14*, 431-452.

Conroy, D.E. (2003). Representational models associated with fear of failure in adolescents and young adults. *Journal of Personality, 71*, 757-783.

Conroy, D.E. (2004). The unique psychological meanings of multidimensional fears of failing. *Journal of Sport and Exercise Psychology, 26*, 484-491.

Conroy, D.E., & Coatsworth, J.D. (2004). The effects of coach training on fear of failure in youth swimmers: A latent growth curve analysis from a randomized, controlled trial. *Journal of Applied Developmental Psychology, 25*, 193-214.

Conroy, D.E., & Elliot, A.J. (2004). Fear of failure and achievement goals in sport: Addressing the issue of the chicken and the egg. *Anxiety, Stress, and Coping, 17*, 271-285.

Conroy, D.E., Elliot, A.J., & Hofer, S.M. (2003). A 2×2 achievement goals questionnaire for sport: Evidence for factorial invariance, temporal stability, and external validity. *Journal of Sport and Exercise Psychology, 25*, 456-476.

Crocker, J., & Park, L.E. (2004). The costly pursuit of self-esteem. *Psychological Bulletin, 130*, 392-414.

Cury, F., Da Fonséca, D., Rufo, M., Peres, C., & Sarrazin, P. (2003). The trichotomous model and investment in learning to prepare for a sport test: A mediational analysis. *British Journal of Educational Psychology, 73*, 529-543.

Cury, F., Da Fonséca, D., Rufo, M., & Sarrazin, P. (2002a). Perceptions of competence, implicit theory of ability, perception of motivational climate, and achievement goals: A test of the trichotomous conceptualization of endorsement of achievement motivation in the physical education setting. *Perceptual and Motor Skills, 95*, 233-244.

Cury, F., Elliot, A., Sarrazin, P., Da Fonséca, D., & Rufo, M. (2002b). The trichotomous achievement goal model and intrinsic motivation: A sequential mediational analysis. *Journal of Experimental Social Psychology, 38*, 473-481.

deCharms, R. (1968). *Personal causation: The internal affective determinants of behavior.* New York: Academic Press.

Deci, E.L., & Ryan, R.M. (1985). *Intrinsic motivation and self-determination in human behavior.* New York: Plenum Press.

Duda, J.L. (1989). The relationship between task and ego orientation and the perceived purpose of sport among male and female high school athletes. *Journal of Sport and Exercise Psychology, 11*, 318-335.

Dweck, C., & Bempechat, J. (1983). Children's theories of intelligence: Consequences from learning. In S. Paris, G. Olsen, & H. Stevenson (Eds.), *Learning and motivation in the classroom* (pp. 239-256). Hillsdale, NJ: Erlbaum.

Elliot, A.J. (1997). Integrating the "classic" and "contemporary" approaches to achievement motivation: A hierarchical model of approach and avoidance achievement motivation. In M. Maehr & P. Pintrich (Eds.), *Advances in motivation and achievement* (Vol. 10, pp. 143-179). Greenwich, CT: JAI Press.

Elliot, A.J. (1999). Approach and avoidance motivation and achievement goals. *Educational Psychologist, 34,* 169-189.

Elliot, A.J. (2005). A conceptual history of the achievement goal construct. In A.J. Elliot & C.S. Dweck (Eds.), *A conceptual history of the achievement goal construct* (pp. 52-72). New York: Guilford Press.

Elliot, A.J., & Church, M.A. (1997). A hierarchical model of approach and avoidance achievement motivation. *Journal of Personality and Social Psychology, 72,* 218-232.

Elliot, A.J., & Conroy, D.E. (2005). Beyond the dichotomous model of achievement goals in sport and exercise psychology. *Sport and Exercise Psychology Review, 1,* 17-25.

Elliot, A.J., & Harackiewicz, J.M. (1996). Approach and avoidance achievement goals and intrinsic motivation: A mediational analysis. *Journal of Personality and Social Psychology, 70,* 968-980.

Elliot, A.J., & McGregor, H.A. (1999). Test anxiety and the hierarchical model of approach and avoidance achievement motivation. *Journal of Personality and Social Psychology, 76,* 628-644.

Elliot, A.J., & McGregor, H.A. (2001). A 2 × 2 achievement goal framework. *Journal of Personality and Social Psychology, 80,* 501-519.

Elliot, A.J., McGregor, H.A., & Thrash, T.M. (2002). The need for competence. In E.L. Deci & R.M. Ryan (Eds.), *Handbook of self-determination research* (pp. 361-387). Rochester, NY: University of Rochester Press.

Elliot, A.J., & Reis, H.T. (2003). Attachment and exploration in adulthood. *Journal of Personality and Social Psychology, 85,* 317-331.

Elliot, A.J., & Thrash, T.M. (2004). The intergenerational transmission of fear of failure. *Personality and Social Psychology Bulletin, 30,* 957-971.

Epstein, J.L. (1989). Family structures and student motivation: A developmental perspective. In C. Ames & R. Ames (Eds.), *Research on motivation in education: Goals and cognitions* (pp. 259-295). San Diego, CA: Academic Press.

Feltz, D.L., & Lirgg, C.D. (2001). Self-efficacy beliefs of athletes, teams, and coaches. In R.N. Singer, H.A. Hausenblas, & C.M. Janelle (Eds.), *Handbook of sport psychology* (2nd ed., pp. 340-361). New York: Wiley.

Flett, G.L., & Hewitt, P.L. (2001). *Perfectionism: Theory, research, and treatment.* Washington, DC: American Psychological Association.

Gernigon, C., d'Arippe-Longueville, F., Delignières, D., & Ninot, G. (2004). A dynamical systems perspective on goal involvement states in sport. *Journal of Sport and Exercise Psychology, 26,* 572-596.

Greenfeld, N., & Teevan, R.C. (1986). Fear of failure in families without fathers. *Psychological Reports, 59,* 571-574.

Harter, S. (1983). Developmental perspectives on the self-system. In E.M. Hetherington (Ed.), *Handbook of child psychology. Vol. 4. Socialization, personality and social development* (4th ed., pp. 275-386). New York: Wiley.

Harter, S. (1999). *The construction of the self: A developmental perspective.* New York: Guilford Press.

Harwood, C.G. (2002). Assessing achievement goals in sport: Caveats for consultants and a case for contextualization. *Journal of Applied Sport Psychology, 14,* 106-119.

Heckhausen, H. (1984). Emergent achievement behavior: Some early developments. In J. Nicholls & M. Maehr (Eds.), *Advances in motivation and achievement* (Vol. 3, pp. 1-32). Greenwich, CT: JAI Press.

Hermans, H.J.M., ter Laak, J.J.F., & Maes, P.C.J.M. (1972). Achievement motivation and fear of failure in family and school. *Developmental Psychology, 6,* 520-528.

Horn, T.S. (2004). Developmental perspectives on self-perceptions in children and adolescents. In M.R. Weiss (Ed.), *Developmental sport and exercise psychology: A lifespan perspective* (pp. 101-143). Morgantown, WV: Fitness Information Technology.

Krohne, H.W. (1992). Developmental conditions of anxiety and coping: A two-process model of child-rearing effects. In K.A. Hagtvet & T.B. Johnsen (Eds.), *Advances in test anxiety research* (Vol. 7, pp. 143-155). Amsterdam: Swets & Zeitlinger.

Masten, A.S., & Coatsworth, J.D. (1998). The development of competence in favorable and unfavorable environments: Lessons from research on successful children. *American Psychologist, 53,* 205-220.

McAuley, E., Peña, M.M., & Jerome, G.J. (2001). Self-efficacy as a determinant and an outcome of exercise. In G.C. Roberts (Ed.), *Advances in motivation in sport and exercise* (pp. 235-261). Champaign, IL: Human Kinetics.

McClelland, D.C. (1958). The importance of early learning in the formation of motives. In J.W. Atkinson (Ed.), *Motives in fantasy, action, and society* (pp. 437-452). Princeton, NJ: Van Nostrand.

McClelland, D.C., Atkinson, J.W., Clark, R.A., & Lowell, E.L. (1953). *The achievement motive.* East Norwalk, CT: Appleton-Century-Crofts.

Nicholls, J.G. (1984). Achievement motivation: Conceptions of ability, subjective experience, task choice, and performance. *Psychological Review, 91,* 328-346.

Nicholls, J.G., Patashnick, M., Cheung, P., Thorkildsen, T., & Lauer, J. (1989). Can achievement motivation succeed with only one conception of success? In F. Halisch & J. Van den Beroken (Eds.), *Competence considered* (pp. 185-193). Lisse, The Netherlands: Swets & Zeitlinger.

Pelletier, L.G., Dion, S., Tuson, K., & Green-Demers, I. (1999). Why do people fail to adopt environmental behaviors? Toward a taxonomy of environmental amotivation. *Journal of Applied Social Psychology, 29,* 2481-2504.

Pelletier, L.G., Fortier, M.S., Vallerand, R.J., Tuson, K.M., Brière, N.M., & Blais, M.R. (1995). Toward a new measure of intrinsic motivation, extrinsic motivation, and amotivation in sports: The Sport Motivation Scale (SMS). *Journal of Sport and Exercise Psychology, 17,* 35-53.

Puca, R.M., & Schmalt, H.D. (1999). Task enjoyment: A mediator between achievement motives and performance. *Motivation and Emotion, 23,* 15-29.

Roberts, B.W., Bogg, T., Walton, K.E., Chernyshenko, O.S., & Stark, S.E. (2004). A lexical investigation of the lower-order structure of conscientiousness. *Journal of Research in Personality, 38,* 164-178.

Rosen, B.C., & D'Andrade, R. (1959). The psychosocial origins of achievement motivation. *Sociometry, 22*, 185-218.

Ryan, R.M., & Deci, E.L. (2002). An overview of self-determination theory: An organismic-dialectical perspective. In E.L. Deci & R.M. Ryan (Eds.), *Handbook of self-determination research* (pp. 3-33). Rochester, NY: University of Rochester Press.

Schmalt, H.D. (1982). Two concepts of fear of failure motivation. In R. Schwarzer, H.M. van der Ploeg, & C.D. Spielberger (Eds.), *Advances in test anxiety research* (Vol. 1, pp. 45-52). Lisse, The Netherlands: Swets & Zeitlinger.

Singh, S. (1992). Hostile press measure of fear of failure and its relation to child-rearing attitudes and behavior problems. *Journal of Social Psychology, 132*, 397-399.

Teevan, R.C. (1983). Childhood development of fear of failure motivation: A replication. *Psychological Reports, 53*, 506.

Teevan, R.C., & McGhee, P. (1972). Childhood development of fear of failure motivation. *Journal of Personality and Social Psychology, 21*, 345-348.

Thrash, T.M., & Elliot, A.J. (2002). Implicit and self-attributed achievement motives: Concordance and predictive validity. *Journal of Personality, 70*, 729-755.

Vallerand, R.J. (2001). A hierarchical model of intrinsic and extrinsic motivation in sport and exercise. In G.C. Roberts (Ed.), *Advances in motivation in sport and exercise* (pp. 263-319). Champaign, IL: Human Kinetics.

White, R.W. (1959). Motivation reconsidered: The concept of competence. *Psychological Review, 66*, 297-333.

Winterbottom, M.R. (1958). The relation of need for achievement to learning experiences in independence and mastery. In J.W. Atkinson (Ed.), *Motives in fantasy, action, and society* (pp. 453-478). Princeton, NJ: Van Nostrand.

CHAPTER 13

Ames, C. (1992a). Achievement goals, motivational climate, and motivational processes. In G.C. Roberts (Ed.), *Motivation in sport and exercise* (pp. 161-176). Champaign, IL: Human Kinetics.

Ames, C. (1992b). Classrooms: Goals, structures, and student motivation. *Journal of Educational Psychology, 84*, 261-271.

Bandura, A. (1986). *The foundations of thought and action.* Englewood Cliffs, NJ: Prentice Hall.

Biddle, S.J.H. (1997). Cognitive theories of motivation and the physical self. In K.R. Fox (Ed.), *The physical self: From motivation to well-being.* Champaign, IL: Human Kinetics.

Biddle, S.J.H. (1999). The motivation of pupils in physical education. In C.A. Hardy & M. Mawer (Eds.), *Learning and teaching in physical education* (pp. 105-125). London: Falmer Press.

Biddle, S.J.H., Gorely, T., & Stensel, D.J. (2004). Health-enhancing physical activity and sedentary behaviour in children and adolescents. *Journal of Sports Sciences, 22*, 679-701.

Biddle, S., Soós, I., & Chatzisarantis, N. (1999). Predicting physical activity intentions using goal perspectives and self-determination theory approaches. *European Psychologist, 4*, 83-89.

Biddle, S.J.H., & Wang, C.K.J. (2003). Motivation and self-perception profiles and links with physical activity in adolescent girls. *Journal of Adolescence, 26,* 687-701.

Biddle, S.J.H., Wang, C.K.J., Chatzisarantis, N.L.D., & Spray, C.M. (2003). Motivation for physical activity in young people: Entity and incremental beliefs concerning athletic ability. *Journal of Sports Sciences, 21,* 973-989.

Biddle, S.J.H., Wang, C.K.J., Kavussanu, M., & Spray, C.M. (2003). Correlates of achievement goal orientations in physical activity: A systematic review of research. *European Journal of Sport Science, 3,* 1-20.

Butler, R. (1987). Task-involving and ego-involving properties of evaluation: Effects of different feedback conditions on motivational perceptions, interest, and performance. *Journal of Educational Psychology, 79,* 474-482.

De Bourdeaudhuij, I., & Van Oost, P. (1999). A cluster-analytical approach toward physical activity and other health related behaviors. *Medicine and Science in Sports and Exercise, 31,* 605-612.

Deci, E.L., & Flaste, R. (1995). *Why we do what we do: Understanding self-motivation.* New York: Penguin.

Deci, E.L., & Ryan, R.M. (1985). *Intrinsic motivation and self-determination in human behavior.* New York: Plenum Press.

Deci, E.L., & Ryan, R.M. (1987). The support of autonomy and the control of behavior. *Journal of Personality and Social Psychology, 53,* 1024-1037.

Deci, E.L., & Ryan, R.M. (1991). A motivational approach to self: Integration in personality. In R.A. Dienstbier (Ed.), *Nebraska symposium on motivation* (pp. 237-288). Lincoln, NE: University of Nebraska Press.

Deci, E.L., & Ryan, R.M. (2000). The "what" and "why" of goal pursuits: Human needs and the self-determination of behavior. *Psychological Inquiry, 11,* 227-268.

Dorobantu, M., & Biddle, S. (1997). The influence of situational and individual goals on the intrinsic motivation of Romanian adolescents towards physical education. *European Yearbook of Sport Psychology, 1,* 148-165.

Duda, J.L. (1989). Goal perspectives, participation and persistence in sport. *International Journal of Sport Psychology, 20,* 42-56.

Duda, J.L., Chi, L., Newton, M., Walling, M., & Catley, D. (1995). Task and ego orientation and intrinsic motivation in sport. *International Journal of Sport Psychology, 26,* 40-63.

Duda, J.L., & Nicholls, J.G. (1992). Dimensions of achievement motivation in schoolwork and sport. *Journal of Educational Psychology, 84,* 290-299.

Dweck, C.S. (1986). Motivational processes affecting learning. *American Psychologist, 41,* 1040-1048.

Dweck, C.S. (1999). *Self-theories: Their role in motivation, personality, and development.* Philadelphia: Taylor & Francis.

Dweck, C.S., & Leggett, E. (1988). A social-cognitive approach to motivation and personality. *Psychological Review, 95,* 256-273.

Epstein, J. (1989). Family structures and student motivation: A developmental perspective. In C. Ames & R. Ames (Eds.), *Research on motivation in education* (Vol. 3, pp. 259-295). New York: Academic Press.

Fox, K.R., & Corbin, C.B. (1989). The Physical Self Perception Profile: Development and preliminary validation. *Journal of Sport and Exercise Psychology, 11*, 408-430.

Fox, K., Goudas, M., Biddle, S., Duda, J., & Armstrong, N. (1994). Children's task and ego goal profiles in sport. *British Journal of Educational Psychology, 64*, 253-261.

Freedman, D.S., Srinivasan, S.R., Valdez, R.A., Williamson, D.F., & Berenson, G.S. (1997). Secular increases in relative weight and adiposity among children over two decades: The Bogalusa Heart Study. *Pediatrics, 99*, 420-426.

Hagger, M.S., Chatzisarantis, N., & Biddle, S.J.H. (2002). The influence of autonomous and controlling motives on physical activity intentions within the Theory of Planned Behaviour. *British Journal of Health Psychology, 7*, 283-297.

Hagger, M.S., Chatzisarantis, N.L.D., & Harris, J. (2006). From psychological need satisfaction to intentional behavior: Testing a motivational sequence in two behavioral contexts. *Personality and Social Psychology Bulletin, 32*, 131-138.

Hair, J.F.J., Anderson, R.E., Tatham, R.L., & Black, W.C. (1998). *Multivariate data analysis* (5th ed.). Englewood Cliffs, NJ: Prentice Hall.

Harwood, C.G., Hardy, L., & Swain, A.J.B. (2000). Achievement goals in sport: A critique of conceptual and measurement issues. *Journal of Sport and Exercise Psychology, 22*, 235-255.

Hong, Y., Chiu, C., & Dweck, C.S. (1995). Implicit theories of intelligence: Reconsidering the role of confidence in achievement motivation. In M.H. Kernis (Ed.), *Efficacy, agency, and self-esteem* (pp. 197-216). New York: Plenum Press.

Lintunen, T., Valkonen, A., Leskinen, E., & Biddle, S.J.H. (1999). Predicting physical activity intentions using a goal perspectives approach: A study of Finnish youth. *Scandinavian Journal of Medicine and Science in Sports, 9*, 344-352.

Nicholls, J.G. (1984). Achievement motivation: Conceptions of ability, subjective experience, task choice, and performance. *Psychological Review, 91*, 328-346.

Nicholls, J.G. (1989). *The competitive ethos and democratic education.* Cambridge, MA: Harvard University Press.

Ntoumanis, N. (2001). Empirical links between achievement goal theory and self-determination theory in sport. *Journal of Sports Sciences, 19*, 397-409.

Ommundsen, Y., & Roberts, G.C. (1999). Effect of motivational climate profiles on motivational indices in team sport. *Scandinavian Journal of Medicine and Science in Sports, 9*, 389-397.

Rawsthorne, L.J., & Elliot, A.J. (1999). Achievement goals and intrinsic motivation: A meta-analytic review. *Personality and Social Psychology Review, 3*, 326-344.

Roberts, G.C. (1992). Motivation in sport and exercise: Conceptual constraints and convergence. In G.C. Roberts (Ed.), *Motivation in sport and exercise* (pp. 3-29). Champaign, IL: Human Kinetics.

Rowlands, A.V., Eston, R.G., & Ingledew, E.K. (1997). Measurement of physical activity in children with particular reference to the use of heart rate and pedometry. *Sports Medicine, 24*(4), 258-272.

Ryan, R.M., & Connell, J.P. (1989). Perceived locus of causality and internalization: Examining reasons for acting in two domains. *Journal of Personality and Social Psychology, 57*, 749-761.

Ryan, R.M., & Deci, E.L. (2000a). Intrinsic and extrinsic motivations: Classic definitions and new directions. *Contemporary Educational Psychology, 25,* 54-67.

Ryan, R.M., & Deci, E.L. (2000b). Self-determination theory and the facilitation of intrinsic motivation, social development and well-being. *American Psychologist, 55,* 68-78.

Sallis, J.F., & Owen, N. (1999). *Physical activity and behavioral medicine.* Thousand Oaks, CA: Sage.

Sallis, J.F., Prochaska, J.J., & Taylor, W.C. (2000). A review of correlates of physical activity of children and adolescents. *Medicine and Science in Sports and Exercise, 32,* 963-975.

Sarrazin, P., Biddle, S.J.H., Famose, J.-P., Cury, F., Fox, K., & Durand, M. (1996). Goal orientations and conceptions of the nature of sport ability in children: A social cognitive approach. *British Journal of Social Psychology, 35,* 399-414.

Treasure, D.C., & Roberts, G.C. (1995). Applications of achievement goal theory to physical education: Implications for enhancing motivation. *Quest, 47,* 475-489.

Twisk, J.W.R., Kemper, H.C.G., van Mechelen, W., & Post, G.B. (1997). Tracking of risk factors for coronary heart disease over a 14-year period: A comparison between lifestyle and biologic risk factors with data from the Amsterdam growth and health study. *American Journal of Epidemiology, 145,* 888-898.

Vallerand, R. J. (1997). Towards a hierarchical model of intrinsic and extrinsic motivation. In M. P. Zanna (Ed.), *Advances in experimental social psychology* (pp. 271-359). New York: Academic Press.

Vallerand, R.J., & Ratelle, C.F. (2002). Intrinsic and extrinsic motivation: A hierarchical model. In E.L. Deci & R.M. Ryan (Eds.), *Handbook of self-determination research* (pp. 37-63). Rochester, NY: University of Rochester Press.

Wang, C.K.J., & Biddle, S.J.H. (2001). Young people's motivational profiles in physical activity: A cluster analysis. *Journal of Sport and Exercise Psychology, 23,* 1-22.

Wang, C.K.J., Chatzisarantis, N.L.D., Spray, C.M., & Biddle, S.J.H. (2002). Achievement goal profiles in school physical education: Differences in self-determination, sport ability beliefs, and physical activity. *British Journal of Educational Psychology, 72,* 433-445.

Wang, C.K.J., Liu, W.C., Sun, Y., & Biddle, S.J.H. (2003). Female secondary students' sport ability beliefs and regulatory styles: Relationships with enjoyment, effort and boredom. *Journal of Tianjin Institute of Physical Education, 18,* 13-18.

Weiner, B. (1992). *Human motivation: Metaphors, theories, and research.* Newbury Park, CA: Sage.

Weiss, M.R., Ebbeck, V., & Horn, T.S. (1997). Children's self-perception and sources of physical competence information: A cluster analysis. *Journal of Sport and Exercise Psychology, 19,* 52-70.

Welk, G.J., Corbin, C.B., & Dale, D. (2000). Measurement issues in the assessment of physical activity in children. *Research Quarterly for Exercise and Sport, 71,* 59-73.

CHAPTER 14

Ames, C. (1992). Achievement goals, motivational climate, and motivational processes. In G.C. Roberts (Ed.), *Motivation in sport and exercise* (pp. 161-176). Champaign, IL: Human Kinetics.

Amorose, A.J., & Horn, T.S. (2000). Intrinsic motivation: Relationships with collegiate athletes' gender, scholarship status, and perceptions of their coaches' behavior. *Journal of Sport and Exercise Psychology, 22*, 63-84.

Amorose, A.J., & Horn, T.S. (2001). Pre- to post-season changes in the intrinsic motivation of first year college athletes: Relationships with coaching behavior and scholarship status. *Journal of Applied Sport Psychology, 13*, 355-373.

Amorose, A.J., & Weiss, M.R. (1998). Coaching feedback as a source of information about perceptions of ability: A developmental examination. *Journal of Sport and Exercise Psychology, 20*, 395-420.

Baard, P.P. (2002). Intrinsic need satisfaction in organizations: A motivational basis of success in for-profit and not-for-profit settings. In E.L. Deci & R.M. Ryan (Eds.), *Handbook of self-determination research* (pp. 255-276). Rochester, NY: University of Rochester Press.

Barnett, N.P., Smoll, F.L., & Smith, R.E. (1992). Effects of enhancing coach-athlete relationships on youth sport attrition. *Sport Psychologist, 6*, 111-127.

Black, S.J., & Weiss, M.R. (1992). The relationship among perceived coaching behaviors, perceptions of ability, and motivation in competitive age-group swimmers. *Journal of Sport and Exercise Psychology, 14*, 309-325.

Boggiano, A.K., Flink, C., Shields, A., Seelbach, A., & Barrett, M. (1993). Use of techniques promoting students' self-determination: Effects on students' analytic problem-solving skills. *Motivation and Emotion, 17*, 319-336.

Chelladurai, P. (1993). Leadership. In R.N. Singer, M. Murphy, & L.K. Tennant (Eds.), *Handbook of research on sport psychology* (pp. 647-671). New York: Macmillan.

Chelladurai, P., & Saleh, S.D. (1980). Dimensions of leader behavior in sports: Development of a leadership scale. *Journal of Sport Psychology, 2*, 34-45.

Chelladurai, P., & Trail, G. (2001). Styles of decision making in coaching. In J.M. Williams (Ed.), *Applied sport psychology: Personal growth to peak performance* (4th ed., pp. 107-119). Palo Alto, CA: Mayfield.

d'Arripe-Longueville, F., Fournier, J.F., & Dubois, A. (1998). The perceived effectiveness of interactions between expert French judo coaches and elite female athletes. *Sport Psychologist, 12*, 317-332.

Deci, E.L., Koestner, R., & Ryan, R.M. (2001). Extrinsic rewards and intrinsic motivation in education: Reconsidered once again. *Review of Educational Research, 71*, 1-27.

Deci, E.L., & Ryan, R.M. (1985). *Intrinsic motivation and self-determination in human behavior.* New York: Plenum Press.

Deci, E.L., & Ryan, R.M. (1987). The support of autonomy and the control of behavior. *Journal of Personality and Social Psychology, 53*, 1024-1037.

Duda, J. (1996). Maximizing motivation in sport and physical education among children and adolescents: The case for greater task involvement. *Quest, 48*, 290-302.

Duda, J.L., & Hall, H. (2001). Achievement goal theory in sport: Recent extensions and future directions. In R.N. Singer, H.A. Hausenblas, & C.M. Janelle (Eds.), *Handbook of sport psychology* (2nd ed., 417-443). New York: Wiley.

Gagné, M., Ryan, R.M., & Bargmann, K. (2003). Autonomy support and need satisfaction in the motivation and well-being of gymnasts. *Journal of Applied Sport Psychology, 15*, 372-389.

Graham, S. (1990). Communicating low ability in the classroom: Bad things that good teachers sometimes do. In S. Graham & V.S. Folkes (Eds.), *Attribution theory: Applications to achievement, mental health, and interpersonal conflict* (pp. 17-36). Hillsdale, NJ: Erlbaum.

Grolnick, W.S., & Apostoleris, N.H. (2002). What makes parents controlling? In E.L. Deci & R.M. Ryan (Eds.), *Handbook of self-determination research* (pp. 161-182). Rochester, NY: University of Rochester Press.

Hagger, M.S., & Chatzisarantis, N.L.D. (2005). *The social psychology of exercise and sport.* Buckingham, UK: Open University Press.

Hagger, M.S., Chatzisarantis, N.L.D., & Harris, J. (2006). From psychological need satisfaction to intentional behavior: Testing a motivational sequence in two behavioral contexts. *Personality and Social Psychology Bulletin, 32,* 131-138.

Hardy, L. (1997). The Coleman Roberts Griffith address: Three myths about applied consultancy work. *Journal of Applied Sport Psychology, 9,* 277-294.

Harwood, C.G., Hardy, L., & Swain, A. (2000). Achievement goals in sport: A critique of conceptual and measurement issues. *Journal of Sport and Exercise Psychology, 22,* 235-255.

Henderlong, J., & Lepper, M.R. (2002). The effects of praise on children's intrinsic motivation: A review and synthesis. *Psychological Bulletin, 128,* 774-795.

Hollembeak, J., & Amorose, A.J. (2005). Perceived coaching behaviors and college athletes' intrinsic motivation: A test of self-determination theory. *Journal of Applied Sport Psychology, 17,* 20-36.

Horn, T.S. (1987). The influence of teacher-coach behavior on the psychological development of children. In D. Gould & M.R. Weiss (Eds.), *Advances in pediatric sport sciences. Vol. 2: Behavioral issues* (pp. 121-142). Champaign, IL: Human Kinetics.

Horn, T.S. (2002). Coaching effectiveness in the sport domain. In T.S. Horn (Ed.), *Advances in sport psychology* (pp. 309-354). Champaign, IL: Human Kinetics.

Horn, T.S., & Harris, A. (2002). Perceived competence in young athletes: Research findings and recommendations for coaches and parents. In F.L. Smoll & R.E. Smith (Eds.), *Children and youth in sport* (pp. 435-464). Dubuque, IA: Kendall/Hunt.

Horn, T.S., Lox, C.L., & Labrador, F. (2001). The self-fulfilling prophecy theory: When coaches' expectations become reality. In J.M. Williams (Ed.), *Applied sport psychology: Personal growth to peak performance* (4th ed., pp. 63-81). Palo Alto, CA: Mayfield.

Lewin, K. (1951). Problems of research in social psychology. In D. Cartwright (Ed.), *Field theory in social science: Selected theoretical papers.* New York: Harper & Row.

Mageau, G.A., & Vallerand, R.J. (2003). The coach-athlete relationship: A motivational model. *Journal of Sports Sciences, 21,* 883-904.

Markland, D. (1999). Self-determination moderates the effects of perceived competence on intrinsic motivation in an exercise setting. *Journal of Sport and Exercise Psychology, 21,* 351-361.

McArdle, S., & Duda, J.K. (2002). Implications of the motivational climate in youth sports. In F.L. Smoll & R.E. Smith (Eds.), *Children and youth in sport* (pp. 409-434). Dubuque, IA: Kendall/Hunt.

Murry, M.C., & Mann, B.L. (2001). Leadership effectiveness. In J.M. Williams (Ed.), *Applied sport psychology: Personal growth to peak performance* (4th ed., pp. 82-106). Palo Alto, CA: Mayfield.

Newton, M., Duda, J.L., & Yin, Z. (2000). Examination of the psychometric properties of the Perceived Motivational Climate in Sport Questionnaire-2 in a sample of female athletes. *Journal of Sports Sciences, 18,* 275-290.

Pelletier, L.G., Séguin-Lévesque, C., & Legault, L. (2002). Pressure from above and pressure from below as determinants of teachers' motivation and teaching behavior. *Journal of Educational Psychology, 94,* 186-196.

Pelletier, L.G., & Vallerand, R.J. (1996). Supervisors' beliefs and subordinates' intrinsic motivation: A behavioural confirmation analysis. *Journal of Personality and Social Psychology, 71,* 331-340.

Pintrich, P.R. (2003). A motivational science perspective on the role of student motivation in learning and teaching contexts. *Journal of Educational Psychology, 95,* 667-686.

Reeve, J. (2002). Self-determination theory applied to educational settings. In E.L. Deci & R.M. Ryan (Eds.), *Handbook of self-determination research* (pp. 161-182). Rochester, NY: University of Rochester Press.

Reinboth, M., Duda, J.L., & Ntoumanis, N. (2004). Dimensions of coaching behavior, need satisfaction, and the psychological and physical welfare of young athletes. *Motivation and Emotion, 28,* 297-313.

Roberts, G.C. (2001). Understanding the dynamics of motivation in physical activity: The influence of achievement goals and motivational processes. In G.C. Roberts (Ed.), *Advances in motivation in sport and exercise* (pp. 1-50). Champaign, IL: Human Kinetics.

Ryan, R.M., & Deci, E.L. (1989). Bridging the research traditions of task/ego involvement and intrinsic/extrinsic motivation: Comment on Butler (1987). *Journal of Educational Psychology, 81,* 265-268.

Ryan, R.M., & Deci, E.L. (2000). Self-determination theory and the facilitation of intrinsic motivation, social development, and well being. *American Psychologist, 55,* 68-78.

Ryan, R.M., & Deci, E.L. (2002). An overview of self-determination theory: An organismic-dialectical perspective. In E.L. Deci & R.M. Ryan (Eds.), *Handbook of self-determination research* (pp. 3-33). Rochester, NY: University of Rochester Press.

Ryan, R.M., Koestner, R., & Deci, E.L. (1991). Ego-involved persistence: When free-choice behavior is not intrinsically motivated. *Motivation and Emotion, 15,* 185-205.

Ryan, R.M., & Powelson, C.L. (1991). Autonomy and relatedness as fundamental to motivation and education. *Journal of Experimental Education, 60,* 49-66.

Sarrazin, P., Vallerand, R., Guillet, E., Pelletier, L., & Cury, F. (2002). Motivation and dropout in female handballers: A 21-month prospective study. *European Journal of Social Psychology, 32,* 395-418.

Seifriz, J.J., Duda, J.L., & Chi, L. (1992). The relationship of perceived motivational climate to intrinsic motivation and beliefs about success in basketball. *Journal of Sport and Exercise Psychology, 14,* 375-391.

Smoll, F.L., & Smith, R.E. (2002). Coaching behavior research and intervention in youth sport. In F.L. Smoll & R.E. Smith (Eds.), *Children and youth in sport* (pp. 211-231). Dubuque, IA: Kendall/Hunt.

Smoll, F.L., Smith, R.E., Barnett, N.P., & Everett, J.J. (1993). Enhancement of children's self-esteem through social support training for youth sport coaches. *Journal of Applied Psychology, 78,* 602-610.

Theeboom, M., De Knop, P., & Weiss, M.R. (1995). Motivational climate, psychosocial responses, and motor skill development in children's sport: A field-based intervention study. *Journal of Sport and Exercise Psychology, 17*, 294-311.

Treasure, D.C. (2001). Enhancing young people's motivation in youth sport: An achievement goal approach. In G.C. Roberts (Ed.), *Advances in motivation in sport and exercise* (pp. 79-100). Champaign, IL: Human Kinetics.

Vallerand, R.J., & Losier, G.F. (1999). An integrative analysis of intrinsic and extrinsic motivation in sport. *Journal of Applied Sport Psychology, 11*, 142-169.

Vallerand, R.J., & Ratelle, C.F. (2002). Intrinsic and extrinsic motivation: A hierarchical model. In E.L. Deci & R.M. Ryan (Eds.), *Handbook of self-determination research* (pp. 37-64). Rochester, NY: University of Rochester Press.

Vallerand, R.J., & Reid, G. (1984). On the causal effects of perceived competence on intrinsic motivation: A test of cognitive evaluation theory. *Journal of Sport Psychology, 6*, 94-102.

Vansteenkiste, M., Simons, J., Sheldon, K.M., Lens, W., & Deci, E.L. (2004). Motivating learning, performance, and persistence: The synergistic effects of intrinsic goal contents and autonomy-supportive contexts. *Journal of Personality and Social Psychology, 87*, 246-260.

Weiss, M.R., & Ferrer-Caja, E. (2002). Motivational orientations and sport behavior. In T.S. Horn (Ed.), *Advances in sport psychology* (2nd ed., pp. 101-184). Champaign, IL: Human Kinetics.

Weiss, M.R., & Williams, L. (2004). The why of youth sport involvement: A developmental perspective on motivational processes. In M.R. Weiss (Ed.), *Developmental sport and exercise psychology: A lifespan perspective* (pp. 223-268). Morgantown, WV: Fitness Information Technology.

Whitehead, J., & Corbin, C. (1991). Youth fitness testing: The effect of percentile-based evaluative feedback on intrinsic motivation. *Research Quarterly for Exercise and Sport, 62*, 225-231.

CHAPTER 15

Ajzen, I., & Fishbein, M. (1980). *Understanding attitudes and predicting social behavior.* Englewood Cliffs, NJ: Prentice Hall.

Ames, C. (1992). Achievement goals, motivational climate, and motivational processes. In G. Roberts (Ed.), *Motivation in sport and exercise* (pp. 161-176). Champaign, IL: Human Kinetics.

Boggiano, A.K. (1998). Maladaptive achievement patterns: A test of a diathesis-stress analysis of helplessness. *Journal of Personality and Social Psychology, 74*, 1681-1695.

Brière, N.M., Vallerand, R.J., Blais, M.R., & Pelletier, L.G. (1995). Développement et validation d'une mesure de motivation intrinsèque, extrinsèque et d'amotivation en contexte sportif: L'Echelle de Motivation dans les Sports (EMS). *International Journal of Sport Psychology, 26*, 465-489.

Brustad, R.J., Babkes, M.L., & Smith, A.L. (2001). Youth in sport: Psychological considerations. In R.N. Singer, H.A. Hausenblas, & C.M. Janelle (Eds.), *Handbook of sport psychology* (2nd ed., pp. 604-635). New York: Wiley.

Chatzisarantis, N.L.D., & Biddle, S.J.H. (1998). Functional significance of psychological variables that are included in the theory of planned behaviour: A self-determination theory approach to the study of attitudes, subjective norms, perceptions of control and intentions. *European Journal of Social Psychology, 28,* 303-322.

Chatzisarantis, N.L.D., Biddle, S.J.H., & Meek, G.A. (1997). A self-determination theory approach to the study of intentions and the intention-behaviour relationship in children's physical activity. *British Journal of Health Psychology, 2,* 434-360.

Chatzisarantis, N.L.D., Hagger, M.S., Biddle, S.J.H., Smith, B., & Wang, J.C.K. (2003). A meta-analysis of perceived locus of causality in exercise, sport, and physical education contexts. *Journal of Sport and Exercise Psychology, 25,* 284-306.

Clark, D.G., & Blair, S.N. (1988). Physical activity and the prevention of obesity in childhood. In N.A. Krasneger, G.D. Grane, & N. Kretchnar (Eds.), *Childhood obesity: A biobehavioral perspective* (pp. 121-142). Caldwell, NJ: Telford.

Deci, E.L., & Ryan, R.M. (1985). *Intrinsic motivation and self-regulation in human behavior.* New York: Plenum Press.

Deci, E.L., & Ryan, R.M. (2000). The "what" and "why" of goal pursuits: Human needs and the self-determination of behavior. *Psychological Inquiry, 11,* 227-268.

Duda, J.L., & Hall, H. (2001). Achievement goal theory in sport: Recent extensions and future directions. In R.N. Singer, H.A. Hausenblas, & C.M. Janelle (Eds.), *Handbook of sport psychology* (2nd ed., pp. 417-443). New York: Wiley.

Gagné, M., Ryan, R., & Bargmann, K. (2003). Autonomy support and need satisfaction in the motivation and well-being of gymnasts. *Journal of Applied Sport Psychology, 15,* 372-390.

Hagger, M.S., Biddle, S.J.H., & Wang, C.K.J. (2005). Physical self-perceptions in adolescence: Generalizability of a multidimensional, hierarchical model across gender and grade. *Educational and Psychological Measurement, 65,* 297-322.

Harter, S. (1985). *Manual for the self-perception profile for children.* Denver: University of Denver Press.

Hodge, K., & Petlichkoff, L. (2000). Goal profiles in sport motivation: A cluster analysis. *Journal of Sport and Exercise Psychology, 22,* 256-272.

Hollembeak, J., & Amorose, A.J. (2005). Perceived coaching behaviors and college athletes' intrinsic motivation: A test of self-determination theory. *Journal of Applied Sport Psychology, 17,* 1-17.

Lindner, K.J., Johns, D.P., & Butcher, J. (1991). Factors in withdrawal from youth sport: A proposed model. *Journal of Sport Behavior, 14*(1), 4-18.

Mageau, G.A., & Vallerand, R.J. (2003). The coach-athlete relationship: A motivational model. *Journal of Sports Sciences, 21,* 883-904.

Ministry for Youth and Sport (2006). *Ministère de la jeunesse des sports et de la vie associative.* Retrieved November 1, 2006, from the World Wide Web: http://www.jeunesse-sports.gouv.fr/

Nicholls, J.G. (1989). *The competitive ethos and democratic education.* Cambridge, MA: Harvard University Press.

ObÉpi. (2003). Troisième enquête épidémiologique nationale sur l'obésité et le surpoids en France. Paris, France: Inserm-Institut Roche de l' Obésité.

Pelletier, L.G., Fortier, M.S., Vallerand, R.J., Tuson, K.M., & Brière, N.M. (2001). Association among perceived autonomy support, forms of self-regulation, and persistence: A prospective study. *Motivation and Emotion, 25,* 279-306.

Pelletier, L.G., Fortier, M.S., Vallerand, R.J., Tuson, K.M., Brière, N.M., & Blais, M.R. (1995). Toward a new measure of intrinsic motivation, extrinsic motivation and amotivation in sports: The Sport Motivation Scale (SMS). *Journal of Sport and Exercise Psychology, 17,* 35-53.

Perkins, D.F., Jacobs, J.E., Barber, B.L., & Eccles, J.S. (2004). Childhood and adolescent sports participation as predictors of participation in sports and physical fitness activities during young adulthood. *Youth and Society, 35,* 495-520.

Reinboth, M., Duda, J.L., & Ntoumanis, N. (2004). Dimensions of coaching behavior, need satisfaction, and the psychological and physical welfare of young athletes. *Motivation and Emotion, 28,* 297-313.

Ryan, R.M., & Deci, E.L. (2000). Self-determination theory and the facilitation of intrinsic motivation, social development, and well-being. *American Psychologist, 55,* 68-78.

Ryan, R.M., & Deci, E.L. (2002). On assimilating identities to the self: A self-determination perspective on integration and integrity with cultures. In M.R. Leary & J.P. Tangney (Eds.), *Handbook of self and identity* (pp. 253-272). New York: Guilford Press.

Sarrazin, P., Guillet, E., & Cury, F. (2001). The effect of coach's task- and ego-involving climate on the changes in perceived competence, relatedness and autonomy among girl handballers. *European Journal of Sport Science, 1,* 1-9.

Sarrazin, P.G., Vallerand, R.J., Guillet, E., Pelletier, L.G., & Cury, F. (2002). Motivation and dropout in female handballers: A 21-month prospective study. *European Journal of Social Psychology, 32,* 395-418.

Scanlan, T.K., Simons, J.P., Carpenter, P.J., Schmidt, G.W., & Keeler, B. (1993). The sport commitment model: Measurement and development for the youth sport domain. *Journal of Sport and Exercise Psychology, 15,* 16-38.

Sénécal, C., Julien, E., & Guay, F. (2003). Role conflict and academic procrastination: A self-determination perspective. *European Journal of Social Psychology, 33,* 135-145.

Swann, W.B. (2005). The self and identity negotiation. *Interaction Studies, 6,* 69-83.

Vallerand, R.J. (1997). Toward a hierarchical model of intrinsic and extrinsic motivation. In M.P. Zanna (Ed.), *Advances in experimental social psychology* (pp. 271-359). New York: Academic Press.

Vallerand, R.J., & Bissonnette, R. (1992). Intrinsic, extrinsic and amotivational styles as predictors of behavior: A prospective study. *Journal of Personality, 60,* 599-620.

Vallerand, R.J., Fortier, M.N., & Guay, F. (1997). Self-determination and persistence in a real-life setting: Toward a motivational model of high school dropout. *Journal of Personality and Social Psychology, 72,* 1161-1176.

Vallerand, R.J., Pelletier, L.G., Blais, M.R., Brière, N.M., Sénécal, C., & Vallières, E.F. (1992). The Academic Motivation Scale: A measure of intrinsic, extrinsic and amotivation in education. *Educational and Psychological Measurement, 52,* 1003-1017.

Vansteenkiste, M., Simons, J., Lens, W., Sheldon, K.M., & Deci, E.L. (2004). Motivating learning, performance, and persistence: The synergistic effects of intrinsic goal contents and autonomy-supportive contexts. *Journal of Personality and Social Psychology, 87,* 246-260.

CHAPTER 16

Amiot, C.E., Gaudreau, P., & Blanchard, C.M. (2004). Self-determination, coping, and goal attainment in sport. *Journal of Sport and Exercise Psychology, 26,* 396-411.

Blanchard, C.M., Amiot, C., Vallerand, R.J., & Provencher, P. (2005). Team cohesion and the satisfaction of basic psychological needs. Manuscript submitted for publication.

Brière, N.M., Vallerand, R.J., Blais, M.R., & Pelletier, L.G. (1995). Développement et validation d'une mesure de motivation intrinsèque, extrinsèque et d'amotivation en contexte sportif: l'Échelle de motivation dans les sports (EMS). [On the development and validation of the French form of the Sport Motivation Scale.] *International Journal of Sport Psychology, 26,* 465-489.

Bryk, A.S., & Raudenbush, S.W. (1992). *Hierarchical linear models: Applications and data analysis methods.* Newbury Park, CA: Sage.

Carron, A.V., Brawley, L.R., & Widmeyer, W.N. (1990). The impact of group size in an exercise setting. *Journal of Sport and Exercise Psychology, 12,* 376-387.

Chantal, Y., & Bernache-Assollant, I. (2003). A prospective analysis of self-determined sport motivation and sportspersonship orientations. *Athletic Insight: Online Journal of Sport Psychology, 5.*

Csikszentmihalyi, M. (1990). *Flow: The psychology of optimal experience.* New York: Harper Perennial.

Deci, E.L., & Ryan, R.M. (2000). The "what" and "why" of goal pursuits: Human needs and the self-determination of behavior. *Psychological Inquiry, 11,* 227-268.

Deci, E.L., & Ryan, R.M. (2002). *Handbook of self-determination research.* Rochester, NY: University of Rochester Press.

Diener, E., Emmons, R.A., Lausen, R.J., & Griffin, S. (1985). The Satisfaction with Life Scale. *Journal of Personality, 49,* 71-75.

Duda, J.L., & Nicholls, J.G. (1992). Dimensions of achievement motivation in school-work and sport. *Journal of Educational Psychology, 84,* 290-299.

Endler, N.S., & Parker, J.D.A. (1994). Multidimensional assessment of coping: A critical evaluation. *Journal of Personality and Social Psychology, 58,* 844-854.

Frederick, C.M., & Ryan, R.M. (1993). Differences in motivation for sport and exercise and their relations with participation and mental health. *Journal of Sport Behavior, 16,* 124-137.

Gagné, M., Ryan, R.M., & Bargmann, K. (2003). The effects of parent and coach autonomy support on the need satisfaction and well-being of gymnasts. *Journal of Applied Sport Psychology, 15,* 372-390.

Gaudreau, P. (2005). Does it really hurt to be a perfectionist? Examining change in life-satisfaction and the mediating role of motivation and coping. Unpublished manuscript, University of Montreal, Montreal, Canada.

Gauvin, L., & Rejeski, W.J. (1993). The Exercise-Induced Feeling Inventory: Development and initial validation. *Journal of Sport and Exercise Psychology, 15,* 403-423.

Gauvin, L., & Szabo, A. (1992). Application of the experience sampling method to the study of the effects of exercise withdrawal on well-being. *Journal of Sport and Exercise Psychology, 14,* 362-374.

Kowal, J., & Fortier, M. (2000). Testing relationships from the hierarchical model of intrinsic and extrinsic motivation using flow as a motivational consequence. *Research Quarterly for Exercise and Sport, 71,* 171-181.

Krane, V., Greenleaf, C.A., & Snow, J. (1997). Reaching for gold and the price of glory: A motivational case study of an elite gymnast. *Sport Psychologist, 11*, 53-71.

Lazarus, R.S., & Folkman, S. (1984). *Stress, appraisal, and coping.* New York: Springer.

McAuley, E., & Courneya, K.S. (1994). The Subjective Exercise Experiences Scale (SEES): Factorial validity and effects of acute exercise. *Journal of Sport and Exercise Psychology, 16*, 163-177.

Ntoumanis, N., & Biddle, S.J.H. (1998). Affect and achievement goals in physical activity: A meta-analysis. *Scandinavian Journal of Medicine and Science in Sports, 8*, 120-124.

Ntoumanis, N., & Biddle, S.J.H. (1999). A review of motivational climate in physical activity. *Journal of Sports Sciences, 17*, 643-665.

Raedeke, T.D., & Smith, A.L. (2001). Development and preliminary validation of an athlete burnout measure. *Journal of Sport and Exercise Psychology, 24*, 281-306.

Reinboth, M., Duda, J.L., & Ntoumanis, N. (2004). Dimensions of coaching behavior, need satisfaction, and the psychological and physical welfare of young athletes. *Motivation and Emotion, 28*, 297-313.

Ryan, R.M., & Deci, E.L. (2001). On happiness and human potentials: A review of research on hedonic and eudaimonic well being. In S. Fiske (Ed.), *Annual review of psychology* (Vol. 52, pp. 141-166). Palo Alto, CA: Annual Reviews.

Ryff, C.D., & Keyes, C.L.M. (1995). The structure of psychological well-being revisited. *Journal of Personality and Social Psychology, 69*, 719-727.

Ryff, C., & Singer, B. (1998). The contours of positive human health. *Psychological Inquiry, 9*, 1-28.

Ryff, C., & Singer, B. (2000). Interpersonal flourishing: A positive health agenda for the new millennium. *Personality and Social Psychology Review, 4*, 30-44.

Seggar, J.F., Pedersen, D.M., Hawkes, N.R., & McGown, C. (1997). A measure of stress for athletic performance. *Perceptual and Motor Skills, 84*, 227-236.

Skinner, E.A., Edge, K., Altman, J., & Sherwood, H. (2003). Searching for the structure of coping: A review and critique of category systems for classifying ways of coping. *Psychological Bulletin, 129*, 216-269.

Vallerand, R.J. (1997). Toward a hierarchical model of intrinsic and extrinsic motivation. In M.P. Zanna (Ed.), *Advances in experimental social psychology* (Vol. 29, pp. 271-360). San Diego: Academic Press.

Vallerand, R.J., Brière, N., Blanchard, C.M., & Provencher, P. (1997). On the development and validation of a new measure of sportsmanship: The multidimensional sportsmanship orientation scale (MSOS). *Journal of Sport and Exercise Psychology, 19*, 197-206.

Vallerand, R.J., & Losier, G.F. (1994). Self-determined motivation and sportsmanship orientations: An assessment of their temporal relationship. *Journal of Sport and Exercise Psychology, 16*, 229-245.

Vallerand, R.J., & Losier, G.F. (1999). An integrative analysis of intrinsic and extrinsic motivation in sport. *Journal of Applied Sport Psychology, 11*, 142-169.

CHAPTER 17

Abramson, L.Y., Seligman, M.E.P., & Teasdale, J.D. (1978). Learned helplessness in humans: Critique and reformulation. *Journal of Abnormal Psychology, 87,* 49-74.

Amabile, T.M. (1985). Motivation and creativity: Effects of motivational orientation on creative writers. *Journal of Personality and Social Psychology, 48,* 393-399.

Amiot, C.E., Gaudreau, P., & Blanchard, C.M. (2004). Self-determination, coping, and goal attainment in sport. *Journal of Sport and Exercise Psychology, 26,* 396-411.

Amorose, A.J., & Horn, T.S. (2001). Pre- to post-season changes in the intrinsic motivation of first year college athletes: Relationships with coaching behavior and scholarship status. *Journal of Applied Sport Psychology, 13,* 355-373.

Assor, A., Roth, G., & Deci, E.L. (2004). The emotional costs of parents' conditional regard: A self-determination theory analysis. *Journal of Personality, 72,* 47-88.

Bargh, J.A., & Ferguson, M.J. (2000). Beyond behaviorism: On the automaticity of higher mental processes. *Psychological Bulletin, 126,* 925-945.

Baumeister, R.F., & Leary, M.R. (1995). The need to belong: Desire for interpersonal attachments as a fundamental human motivation. *Psychological Bulletin, 117,* 497-529.

Blais, M.R., Vallerand, R.J., Gagnon, A., Brière, N.M., & Pelletier, L.G. (1990). Significance, structure, and gender differences in life domains of college students. *Sex Roles, 22,* 199-212.

Blais, M.R., Vallerand, R.J., Pelletier, L.G., & Brière, N.M. (1994). Construction et validation de l'Inventaire des Motivations Interpersonnelles. [Construction and validation of the Interpersonal Motivations Inventory.] Unpublished manuscript, University of Quebec at Montreal.

Blanchard, C.M., Amiot, C., Saint-Laurent, E., Vallerand, R.J., & Provencher, P. (2005a). An analysis of the bi-directional effects between contextual and situational motivation in a natural setting. Manuscript submitted for publication.

Blanchard, C.M., Amiot, C., Vallerand, R.J., & Provencher, P. (2005b). Team cohesion and the satisfaction of basic psychological needs. Manuscript submitted for publication.

Brière, N.M., Vallerand, R.J., Blais, M.R., & Pelletier, L.G. (1995). Développement et validation d'une mesure de motivation intrinsèque, extrinsèque et d'amotivation en contexte sportif: L'échelle de Motivation dans les Sports (ÉMS). [On the development and validation of the French form of the Sport Motivation Scale.] *International Journal of Sport Psychology, 26,* 465-489.

Brunel, P., & Vallerand, R.J. (2005). On the relative effects of contextual motivation and situational factors on situational motivation as a function of time. Manuscript submitted for publication.

Chantal, Y., & Bernache-Assollant, I. (2003). A prospective analysis of self-determined sport motivation and sportspersonship orientations. *Athletic Insight: Online Journal of Sport Psychology, 5.*

Chantal, Y., Robin, P., Vernat, J.-P., & Bernache-Assollant, I. (2005). Motivation, sportspersonship, and athletic aggression: A mediational analysis. *Psychology of Sport and Exercise, 6,* 233-249.

Chatzisarantis, N.L.D., Biddle, S.J.H., & Meek, G.A. (1997). A self-determination theory approach to the study of intentions and the intention-behaviour relationship in children's physical activity. *British Journal of Health Psychology, 2,* 343-360.

Chatzisarantis, N.L.D., Hagger, M.S., Biddle, S.J.H., Smith, B., & Wang, J.C.K. (2003). A meta-analysis of perceived locus of causality in exercise, sport, and physical education contexts. *Journal of Sport and Exercise Psychology, 25,* 284-306.

Connell, J.P., & Wellborn, J.G. (1991). Competence, autonomy, and relatedness: A motivational analysis of self-esteem processes. In M.R. Gunnar & L.A. Sroufe (Eds.), *The Minnesota symposium on child psychology: Self-processes in development* (Vol. 23, pp. 43-77). Hillsdale, NJ: Erlbaum.

Cresswell, S.L., & Eklund, R.C. (2005). Motivation and burnout among top amateur rugby players. *Medicine and Science in Sports and Exercise, 37,* 469-477.

deCharms, R.C. (1968). *Personal causation: The internal affective determinants of behavior.* New York: Academic Press.

Deci, E.L. (1971). Effects of externally mediated rewards on intrinsic motivation. *Journal of Personality and Social Psychology, 18,* 105-115.

Deci, E.L. (1975). *Intrinsic motivation.* New York: Plenum Press.

Deci, E.L. (1980). *The psychology of self-determination.* Lexington, MA: Heath.

Deci, E.L., Eghrari, H., Patrick, B.C., & Leone, D.R. (1994). Facilitating internalization: The self-determination theory perspective. *Journal of Personality, 62,* 119-142.

Deci, E.L., & Ryan, R.M. (1980). The empirical exploration of intrinsic motivational processes. *Advances in experimental social psychology* (Vol. 11, pp. 30-80). New York: Academic Press.

Deci, E.L., & Ryan, R.M. (1985). *Intrinsic motivation and self-determination in human behavior.* New York: Plenum Press.

Deci, E.L., & Ryan, R.M. (1991). A motivational approach to self: Integration in personality. In R. Dienstbier (Ed.), *Nebraska symposium on motivation: Perspectives on motivation* (Vol. 38, pp. 237-288). Lincoln, NE: University of Nebraska Press.

Deci, E.L., & Ryan, R.M. (2000). The "what" and "why" of goal pursuits: Human needs and the self-determination of behavior. *Psychological Inquiry, 11,* 227-268.

Deci, E. L., & Ryan, R. M. (2002). Self-determination research: Reflections and future directions. In E. L. Deci & R. M. Ryan (Eds.), *Handbook of self-determination research* (pp. 431-441). Rochester, NY: University of Rochester Press.

Deci, E.L., Vallerand, R.J., Pelletier, L.G., & Ryan, R.M. (1991). Motivation and education: The self-determination theory perspective. *Educational Psychologist, 26,* 325-346.

Donahue, E., Vallerand, R.J., Miquelon, P., Valois, P., Buist, A., Goulet, P., & Côté, M. (2005). A motivational model of steroid use in sport. Manuscript submitted for publication.

Edwards, Y. V., Portman, T. A. A., & Bethea, J. (2002). Counseling student computer competency skills: Effects of technology course in training. *Journal of Technology in Counseling.* Retrieved November 4, 2006 from http://jtc.colstate.edu/Vol2_2/edwards.htm

Emmons, R.A. (1995). Levels and domains in personality: An introduction. *Journal of Personality, 63*, 341-364.

Fairchild, A.J., Horst, S.J., Finney, S.J., & Barron, K.E. (2005). Evaluation existing and new validity evidence for the Academic Motivation Scale. *Contemporary Educational Psychology, 30*, 331-358.

Ferrer-Caja, E., & Weiss, M.R. (2000). Predictors of intrinsic motivation among adolescent students in physical education. *Research Quarterly for Exercise and Sport, 71*, 267-279.

Fitzsimons, G.M., & Bargh, J.A. (2004). Automatic self-regulation. In R.F. Baumeister & K.D. Vohs (Eds.), *Handbook of self-regulation: Research, theory, and applications* (pp. 151-170). New York: Guilford Press.

Fortier, M.S., & Grenier, M.N. (1999). Les déterminants personnels et situationnels de l'adhérence à l'exercise: Une étude prospective. [Personal and situational determinants of exercise adherence.] *STAPS, 48*, 25-37.

Fortier, M.S., Vallerand, R.J., & Guay, F. (1995). Academic motivation and school performance: Toward a structural model. *Contemporary Educational Psychology, 20*, 257-274.

Gagné, M., & Deci, E.L. (2005). Self-determination theory and work motivation. *Journal of Organizational Behavior, 26*, 331-362.

Gagné, M., Ryan, R.M., & Bargmann, K. (2003). Autonomy support and need satisfaction in the motivation and well-being of gymnasts. *Journal of Applied Sport Psychology, 15*, 372-390.

Goudas, M., Biddle, S.J.H., & Fox, K.R. (1994). Perceived locus of causality, goal orientations, and perceived competence in school physical education classes. *British Journal of Educational Psychology, 64*, 453-563.

Grolnick, W. S., & Apostoleris, N.H. (2002). What makes parents controlling? In E.L. Deci & R.M. Ryan (Eds.), *Handbook of self-determination research* (pp. 161-181). Rochester, NY: University of Rochester Press.

Grolnick, W. S., & Ryan, R.M. (1987). Autonomy in children's learning: An experimental and individual difference investigation. *Journal of Personality and Social Psychology, 52*, 890-898.

Grouzet, F.M.E., Vallerand, R.J., Thill, E.E., & Provencher, P.J. (2005). From environmental factors to outcomes: A test of a motivational causal sequence. *Motivation and Emotion, 28*, 331-346.

Guay, F., Blais, M.R., Vallerand, R.J., & Pelletier, L.G. (1999). The Global Motivation Scale. Unpublished manuscript, University of Quebec at Montreal.

Guay, F., Mageau, G.A., & Vallerand, R.J. (2003). On the hierarchical structure of self-determined motivation: A test of top-down, bottom-up, reciprocal, and horizontal effects. *Personality and Social Psychology Bulletin, 29*, 992-1004.

Guay, F., Vallerand, R.J., & Blanchard, C. (2000). On the assessment of situational intrinsic and extrinsic motivation: The situational motivation scale (SIMS). *Motivation and Emotion, 24*, 175-213.

Hagger, M.S., & Chatzisarantis, N.L.D. (2005). *The social psychology of exercise and sport.* Buckingham, UK: Open University Press.

Hagger, M.S., Chatzisarantis, N., Barkoukis, V., Wang, C.K.J., & Baranowski, J. (2005). Perceived autonomy support in physical education and leisure-time physical activity: A cross-cultural evaluation of the trans-contextual model. *Journal of Educational Psychology, 97*, 287-301.

Hagger, M.S., Chatzisarantis, N., Culverhouse, T., & Biddle, S.J.H. (2003). The processes by which perceived autonomy support in physical education promotes leisure-time physical activity intentions and behaviour: A trans-contextual model. *Journal of Educational Psychology, 95,* 784-795.

Harter, S. (1978). Effectance motivation reconsidered: Toward a developmental model. *Human Development, 1,* 34-64.

Heatherton, T.F., Nichols, P., Mahamedi, F., & Keel, P. (1995). Body weight, dieting, and eating disorder symptoms among college students. *American Journal of Psychiatry, 152,* 1623-1629.

Hein, V., Müür, M., & Koka, A. (2004). Intention to be physically active after school graduation and its relationship to three types of intrinsic motivation. *European Physical Education Review, 10,* 5-19.

Hodgins, H., Yacko, H.A., & Gottlieb, E. (2005). Autonomy and nondefensiveness. Manuscript submitted for publication.

Hollembeak, J., & Amorose, A.J. (2005). Perceived coaching behaviours and college athletes' intrinsic motivation: A test of self-determination theory. *Journal of Applied Sport Psychology, 17,* 20-36.

Jackson, S.A., Ford, S.K., Kimiecik, J.C., & Marsh, H.W. (1998). Psychological correlates of flow in sport. *Journal of Sport and Exercise Psychology, 4,* 358-378.

Joussemet, M., Koestner, R., Lekes, N., & Houlfort, N. (2004). Introducing uninteresting tasks to children: A comparison of the effects of rewards and autonomy support. *Journal of Personality, 72,* 139-166.

Koestner, R., Bernieri, F., & Zuckerman, M. (1992). Self-determination and consistency between attitudes, traits, and behaviors. *Personality and Social Psychology Bulletin, 18,* 52-59.

Kowal, J., & Fortier, M.S. (1999). Motivational determinants of flow: Contributions from self-determination theory. *Journal of Social Psychology, 139,* 355-368.

Kowal, J., & Fortier, M.S. (2000). Testing relationships from the hierarchical model of intrinsic and extrinsic motivation using flow as a motivational consequence. *Research Quarterly for Exercise and Sport, 71,* 171-181.

Lepper, M.R., & Cordova, D.I. (1992). A desire to be taught: Instructional consequences of intrinsic motivation. *Motivation and Emotion, 16,* 187-208.

Lévesque, C., & Pelletier, L.G. (2003). On the investigation of primed and chronic autonomous and heteronomous motivational orientations. *Personality and Social Psychology Bulletin, 29,* 1570-1584.

Li, F. (1999). The Exercise Motivation Scale: Its multifaceted structure and construct validity. *Journal of Applied Sport Psychology, 11,* 97-115.

Li, F., & Harmer, P. (1996). Testing the simple assumption underlying the Sport Motivation Scale: A structural equation modeling analysis. *Research Quarterly for Exercise and Sport, 67,* 396-405.

Mageau, G.A., & Vallerand, R.J. (2003). The coach-athlete relationship: A motivational model. *Journal of Sports Sciences, 21,* 883-904.

Mullan, E., Markland, D., & Ingledew, D.K. (1997). A graded conceptualisation of self-determination in the regulation of exercise behaviour: Development of a measure using confirmatory factor analytic procedures. *Personality and Individual Differences, 23,* 745-752.

Ntoumanis, N. (2001). Empirical links between achievement goal theory and self-determination theory in sport. *Journal of Sports Sciences, 19*, 397-409.

Ntoumanis, N. (2005). A prospective study of participation in optional school physical education using a self-determination theory framework. *Journal of Educational Psychology, 97*, 444-453.

Ntoumanis, N., & Blaymires, G. (2003). Contextual and situational motivation in education: A test of the specificity hypothesis. *European Physical Education Review, 9*, 5-21.

Ntoumanis, N., Pensgaard, A-M., Martin, C., & Pipe, K. (2004). An idiographic analysis of amotivation in compulsory school physical education. *Journal of Sport and Exercise Psychology, 26*, 197-214.

Parfitt, G., & Gledhill, C. (2004). The effect of choice of exercise mode on psychological responses. *Psychology of Sport and Exercise, 5*, 111-117.

Pelletier, L.G., Dion, S., & Lévesque, C. (2004). Can self-determination help protect women against sociocultural influences about body image and reduce their risk of experiencing bulimic symptoms? *Journal of Social and Clinical Psychology, 23*, 61-88.

Pelletier, L.G., Dion, S.C., Slovinec-D'Angelo, M., & Reid, R.D. (2004). Why do you regulate what you eat? Relationships between forms of regulation, eating behaviors, sustained dietary behavior change, and psychological adjustment. *Motivation and Emotion, 28*, 245-277.

Pelletier, L.G., Fortier, M.S., Vallerand, R.J., & Brière, N.M. (2001). Associations among perceived autonomy support, forms of self-regulation, and persistence: A prospective study. *Motivation and Emotion, 25*, 279-306.

Pelletier, L.G., Fortier, M.S., Vallerand, R.J., Tuson, K.M., Brière, N.M., & Blais, M.R. (1995). Toward a new measure of intrinsic motivation, extrinsic motivation, and amotivation in sports: The Sport Motivation Scale (SMS). *Journal of Sport and Exercise Psychology, 17*, 35-53.

Pelletier, L.G., & Kabush, D. (2005). The Sport Motivation Scale: Revision and addition of the integrated regulation subscale. Unpublished manuscript, University of Ottawa.

Pelletier, L.G., Vallerand, R.J., Green-Demers, I., Blais, M.R., & Brière, N.M. (1996). Vers une conceptualisation motivationnelle multidimensionnelle du loisir: Construction et validation de l'Échelle de Motivation vis-à-vis des Loisirs (EML). [Construction and validation of the Leisure Motivation Scale.] *Loisir et Société, 19*, 559-585.

Raedeke, T.D. (1997). Is athlete burnout more than just stress? A sport commitment perspective. *Journal of Sport and Exercise Psychology, 19*, 396-417.

Ratelle, C.F., Baldwin, M., & Vallerand, R.J. (2005). On the cued activation of situational motivation. *Journal of Experimental Social Psychology, 41*, 482-487.

Ratelle, C.F., Sénécal, C., Vallerand, R.J., & Provencher, P.J. (2005). The relationship between school-leisure conflict and poor educational and mental health indices: A motivational analysis. *Journal of Applied Social Psychology, 35*, 1800-1823.

Ratelle, C.F., Vallerand, R.J., Chantal, Y., & Provencher, P. (2004). Cognitive adaptation and mental health: A motivational analysis. *European Journal of Social Psychology, 34*, 459-476.

Reinboth, M., Duda, J.L., & Ntoumanis, N. (2004). Dimensions of coaching behavior, need satisfaction, and the psychological and physical welfare of young athletes. *Motivation and Emotion, 28*, 297-313.

Richer, S., & Vallerand, R.J. (1998). Construction et validation de l'Échelle du senti-ment d'appartenance sociale. [Construction and validation of the Relatedness Feeling Scale.] *Revue européenne de psychologie appliquée/European Journal of Applied Psychology*, *48*, 129-137.

Ryan, R.M. (1993). Agency and organization: Intrinsic motivation, autonomy and the self in psychological development. In R. Dienstbier (Ed.), *Nebraska symposium on motivation* (Vol. 40, pp. 1-56). Lincoln, NE: University of Nebraska Press.

Ryan, R.M., & Connell, J.P. (1989). Perceived locus of causality and internalization: Examining reasons for acting in two domains. *Journal of Personality and Social Psychology*, *57*, 749-761.

Ryan, R.M., Connell, J.P., & Grolnick, W.S. (1992). When achievement is not intrinsi-cally motivated: A theory and assessment of self-regulation in school. In A.K. Boggiano & T.S. Pittman (Eds.), *Achievement and motivation: A social-developmental perspective* (pp. 167-188). Cambridge, MA: Cambridge University Press.

Ryan, R.M., Deci, E.L., & Grolnick, W.S. (1995). Autonomy, relatedness, and the self: Their relation to development and psychopathology. In D. Cicchetti & D.J. Cohen (Eds.), *Developmental psychology, Vol. 1: Theory and methods* (pp. 618-655). New York: Wiley.

Ryan, R.M., Frederick, C.M., Lepes, D., Rubio, N., & Sheldon, K.M. (1997). Intrinsic motivation and exercise adherence. *International Journal of Sport Psychology*, *28*, 335-354.

Ryan, R.M., Koestner, R., & Deci, E.L. (1991). Ego-involved persistence: When free-choice behavior is not intrinsically motivated. *Motivation and Emotion*, *15*, 185-205.

Sarrazin, P., Vallerand, R.J., Guillet, E., Pelletier, L.G., & Cury, F. (2002). Motivation and dropout in female handballers: A 21-month prospective study. *European Journal of Social Psychology*, *57*, 749-761.

Sénécal, C., Vallerand, R.J., & Guay, F. (2001). Antecedents and outcomes of work-family conflicts: Toward a motivational model. *Personality and Social Psychology Bulletin*, *27*, 176-186.

Simons, J., Dewitte, S., & Lens, W. (2003). Don't do it for me. Do it for yourself! Stressing the personal relevance enhances motivation in physical education. *Journal of Sport and Exercise Psychology*, *25*, 145-160.

Standage, M., Duda, J.L., & Ntoumanis, N. (2003). Predicting motivation regulations in physical education: The interplay between dispositional goal orientations, motivational climate and perceived competence. *Journal of Sports Sciences*, *21*, 631-647.

Standage, M., & Treasure, D.C. (2002). Relationship among achievement goal orienta-tions and multidimensional situational motivation in physical education. *British Journal of Educational Psychology*, *72*, 87-103.

Stice, E. (2001). Risk factors for eating pathology: Recent advances and future directions. In R. Striegel-Moore & L. Smolak (Eds.), *Eating disorders: Innovative directions in research and practice* (pp. 51-74). Washington, DC: American Psychological Association.

Thøgersen-Ntoumani, C., & Ntoumanis, N. (2006). The role of self-determined moti-vation to the understanding of exercise-related behaviours, cognitions and physical self-evaluation. *Journal of Sports Sciences*, *24*, 393-404.

Vallerand, R.J. (1997). Toward a hierarchical model of intrinsic and extrinsic motivation. In M.P. Zanna (Ed.), *Advances in experimental social psychology* (Vol. 29, pp. 271-360). New York: Academic Press.

Vallerand, R.J. (2001). A hierarchical model of intrinsic and extrinsic motivation in sport and exercise. In G. Roberts (Ed.), *Advances in motivation in sport and exercise* (2nd ed., pp. 263-319). Champaign, IL: Human Kinetics.

Vallerand, R.J. (in press). Intrinsic and extrinsic motivation in sport and physical activity: A review and a look at the future. In G. Tenenbaum & E. Eklund (Eds.), *Handbook of sport psychology* (3rd ed.). New York: Wiley.

Vallerand, R.J., & Bissonnette, R. (1992). Intrinsic, extrinsic, and amotivational styles as predictors of behavior: A prospective study. *Journal of Personality, 60,* 599-620.

Vallerand, R.J., Blais, M.R., Brière, N.M., & Pelletier, L.G. (1989). Construction et validation de l'Échelle de motivation en éducation (EME). [On the construction and validation of the French form of the Academic Motivation Scale.] *Canadian Journal of Behavioural Science, 21,* 323-349.

Vallerand, R.J., Brière, N.M., Blanchard, C., & Provencher, P. (1997). Development and validation of the Multidimensional Sportspersonship Orientations Scale. *Journal of Sport and Exercise Psychology, 19,* 197-206.

Vallerand, R.J., Chantal, Y., Guay, F., & Brunel, P. (2005). On the influence of motivational orientations on situational motivation: A test of the top-down specificity hypothesis. Manuscript submitted for publication.

Vallerand, R.J., Deshaies, P., Cuerrier, J.-P., Brière, N.M., & Pelletier, L.G. (1996). Toward a multidimensional definition of sportsmanship. *Journal of Applied Sport Psychology, 8,* 89-101.

Vallerand, R.J., & Fortier, M.S. (1998). Measures of intrinsic and extrinsic motivation in sport and physical activity: A review and critique. In J. Duda (Ed.), *Advancements in sport and exercise psychology measurement* (pp. 83-100). Morgantown, WV: Fitness Information Technology.

Vallerand, R.J., Fortier, M.S., & Guay, F. (1997). Self-determination and persistence in a real-life setting: Toward a motivational model of high school dropout. *Journal of Personality and Social Psychology, 72,* 1161-1176.

Vallerand, R.J., Guay, F., Mageau, G., Blanchard, C.M., & Cadorette, I. (2005b). Self-regulatory processes in human behavior: A test of the hierarchical model of intrinsic and extrinsic motivation. Manuscript submitted for publication.

Vallerand, R.J., & Losier, G.F. (1994). Self-determined motivation and sportsmanship orientations: An assessment of their temporal relationship. *Journal of Sport and Exercise Psychology, 16,* 229-245.

Vallerand, R.J., & Losier, G.F. (1999). An integrative analysis of intrinsic and extrinsic motivation in sport. *Journal of Applied Sport Psychology, 11,* 142-169.

Vallerand, R.J., O'Connor, B.P., & Hamel, M. (1995). Motivation in later life: Theory and assessment. *International Journal of Aging and Human Development, 41,* 221-238.

Vallerand, R.J., Pelletier, L.G., Blais, M.R., Brière, N.M., Sénécal, C., & Vallières, E.F. (1992). The Academic Motivation Scale: A measure of intrinsic, extrinsic, and amotivation in education. *Educational and Psychological Measurement, 52,* 1003-1019.

Vallerand, R.J., Pelletier, L.G., Blais, M.R., Brière, N.M., Sénécal, C., & Vallières, E.F. (1993). On the assessment of intrinsic, extrinsic, and amotivation in education:

Evidence on the concurrent and construct validity of the Academic Motivation Scale. *Educational and Psychological Measurement, 53,* 159-172.

Vallerand, R.J., & Perreault, S. (1999). Intrinsic and extrinsic motivation in sport: Toward a hierarchical model. In R. Lidor & M. Bar-Eli (Eds.), *Sport psychology: Linking theory and practice* (pp. 191-212). Morgantown, WV: Fitness Information Technology.

Vallerand, R.J., & Ratelle, C.F. (2002). Intrinsic and extrinsic motivation: A hierarchical model. In E.L. Deci & R.M. Ryan (Eds.), *Handbook of self-determination research* (pp. 37-64). Rochester, NY: University of Rochester Press.

Vallerand, R.J., & Reid, G. (1984). On the causal effects of perceived competence on intrinsic motivation: A test of cognitive evaluation theory. *Journal of Sport Psychology, 6,* 94-102.

Vallerand, R.J., & Rousseau, F.L. (2001). Intrinsic and extrinsic motivation in sport and exercise: A review using the hierarchical model of intrinsic and extrinsic motivation. In R. Singer, H. Hausenblas, & C. Janelle (Eds.), *Handbook of sport psychology* (2nd ed., pp. 389-416). New York: Wiley.

Weiss, M.R., & Smith, A.L. (2002). Friendship quality in youth sport: Relationship to age, gender, and motivation variables. *Journal of Sport and Exercise Psychology, 24,* 420-437.

White, R.W. (1959). Motivation reconsidered: The concept of competence. *Psychological Review, 66,* 297-333.

Williams, G.C., Grow, V.M., Freedman, Z.R., Ryan, R.M., & Deci, E.L. (1996). Motivational predictors of weight loss and weight-loss maintenance. *Journal of Personality and Social Psychology, 70,* 115-126.

Wilson, P.M., & Rodgers, W.M. (2004). The relationship between perceived autonomy support, exercise regulations and behavioral intentions in women. *Psychology of Sport and Exercise, 5,* 229-242.

Wilson, P.M., Rodgers, W.M., Fraser, S.N., Murray, T.C., & McIntyre, C.A. (2004). The relationship between psychological need satisfaction and self-perceptions in females. *Journal of Sport and Exercise Psychology, 26,* S200.

CONCLUSION

Amorose, A.J., & Horn, T.S. (2000). Intrinsic motivation: Relationships with college athletes' gender, scholarship status, and perceptions of their coaches behavior. *Journal of Sport and Exercise Psychology, 22,* 63-84.

Amorose, A.J., & Horn, T.S. (2001). Pre- and post-season changes in the intrinsic motivation of first year college athletes: Relationships with coaching behavior and scholarship status. *Journal of Applied Sport Psychology, 13,* 355-373.

Brière, N., Vallerand, R.J., Blais, N., & Pelletier, L. (1995). Development and validation of a measure of intrinsic, extrinsic, and amotivation in sports: The Sport Motivation Scale (SMS). *International Journal of Sport Psychology, 26,* 465-489.

Chantal, Y., Guay, F., Dobreva-Martinova, T., & Vallerand, R.J. (1996). Motivation and elite performance: An exploratory investigation with Bulgarian athletes. *International Journal of Sport Psychology, 27,* 173-182.

Chatzisarantis, N. L. D., & Hagger, M. S. (2006). Effects of a brief intervention based on the trans-contextual model on leisure time physical activity participation. Manuscript submitted for publication.

Csikszentmihalyi, M. (1990). *Flow: The psychology of optimal experience.* New York: Harper & Rowe.

Cury, F., Elliot, A.J., Sarrazin, P., Da Fonséca, D., & Rufo, M. (2002). The trichotomous achievement goal model and intrinsic motivation: A sequential mediational analysis. *Journal of Experimental Social Psychology, 38,* 473-481.

Deci, E.L., Eghrari, H., Patrick, B.C., & Leone, D.R. (1994). Facilitating internalization: The self-determination theory perspective. *Journal of Personality, 62,* 119-142.

Deci, E.L., & Ryan, R.M. (1985). *Intrinsic motivation and self-determination in human behavior.* New York: Plenum Press.

Deci, E.L., & Ryan, R.M. (1987). The support of autonomy and the control of behavior. *Journal of Personality and Social Psychology, 53,* 1024-1037.

Deci, E.L., & Ryan, R.M. (2000). The "what" and "why" of goal pursuits: Human needs and the self-determination of behavior. *Psychological Inquiry, 11,* 227-268.

Deci, E.L., Vallerand, R.J., Pelletier, L.G., & Ryan, R.M. (1991). Motivation in education: The self-determination perspective. *Educational Psychologist, 26,* 325-346.

Duda, J.L., & Tappe, M.K. (1989). The personal incentives for exercise questionnaire: Preliminary development. *Perceptual and Motor Skills, 68,* 1122.

Edmunds, J.K., Ntoumanis, N., & Duda, J.L. (2006). A test of self-determination theory in the exercise domain. *Journal of Applied Social Psychology, 36,* 2240-2265.

Elliot, A.J. (1999). Approach and avoidance motivation and achievement goals. *Educational Psychologist, 34,* 169-189.

Elliot, A.J., & Conroy, D.E. (2005). Beyond the dichotomous model of achievement goals in sport and exercise psychology. *Sport and Exercise Psychology Review, 1,* 17-25.

Elliot, A.J., & Reis, H.T. (2003). Attachment and exploration in adulthood. *Journal of Personality and Social Psychology, 85,* 317-331.

Gagné, M., Ryan, R.M., & Bargmann, K. (2003). Autonomy support and need satisfaction in the motivation and well-being of gymnasts. *Journal of Applied Sport Psychology, 15,* 372-390.

Guay, F., Mageau, G.A., & Vallerand, R.J. (2003). On the hierarchical structure of self-determined motivation: A test of top-down, bottom-up, reciprocal, and horizontal effects. *Personality and Social Psychology Bulletin, 29,* 992-1004.

Hagger, M.S., & Chatzisarantis, N.L.D. (2005). *The social psychology of exercise and sport.* Buckingham, UK: Open University Press.

Hagger, M.S., Chatzisarantis, N.L.D., Barkoukis, V., Wang, C.K.J., & Baranowski, J. (2005). Perceived autonomy support in physical education and leisure-time physical activity: A cross-cultural evaluation of the trans-contextual model. *Journal of Educational Psychology, 97,* 376-390.

Hagger, M.S., Chatzisarantis, N.L.D., Culverhouse, T., & Biddle, S.J.H. (2003). The processes by which perceived autonomy support in physical education promotes leisure-time physical activity intentions and behavior: A trans-contextual model. *Journal of Educational Psychology, 95,* 784-795.

Hagger, M.S., Chatzisarantis, N.L.D., & Harris, J. (2006). From psychological need satisfaction to intentional behavior: Testing a motivational sequence in two behavioral contexts. *Personality and Social Psychology Bulletin, 32,* 131-138.

Iyengar, S.S., Ross, L., & Lepper, M.R. (1999). Independence from whom? Interdependence with whom? Cultural perspectives on in-groups versus out-groups. In D. Miller (Ed.), *Cultural divides: Understanding and overcoming group conflict.* New York: Sage.

Li, F. (1999). The Exercise Motivation Scale: Its multifaceted structure and construct validity. *Journal of Applied Sport Psychology, 11,* 97-115.

Maehr, M.L., & Braskamp, L.A. (1986). *The motivation factor: A theory of personal investment.* Lexington, MA: Lexington Books.

Markland, D., & Hardy, L. (1993). The Exercise Motivations Inventory: Preliminary development and validity of a measure of individuals' reasons for participation in regular physical exercise. *Personality and Individual Differences, 15,* 289-296.

Markland, D., & Ingledew, D.K. (1997). The measurement of exercise motives: Factorial validity and invariance across gender of a revised Exercise Motivations Inventory. *British Journal of Health Psychology, 2,* 361-376.

Markland, D., Ryan, R.M., Tobin, V.J., & Rollnick, S. (2005). Motivational interviewing and self-determination theory. *Journal of Social and Clinical Psychology, 24,* 785-805.

Markland, D., & Tobin, V. (2004). A modification to the Behavioural Regulation in Exercise Questionnaire to include an assessment of amotivation. *Journal of Sport and Exercise Psychology, 26,* 191-196.

Nicholls, J.G. (1989). *The competitive ethos and democratic education.* Cambridge, MA: Harvard University Press.

Pelletier, L.G., Fortier, M.S., Vallerand, R.J., & Brière, N.M. (2001). Associations among perceived autonomy support, forms of self-regulation, and persistence: A prospective study. *Motivation and Emotion, 25,* 279-306.

Pelletier, L.G., Fortier, M.S., Vallerand, R.J., Tuson, K.M., Brière, N.M., & Blais, M.R. (1995). Toward a new measure of intrinsic motivation, extrinsic motivation and amotivation in sport: The Sport Motivation Scale (SMS). *Journal of Sport and Exercise Psychology, 17,* 35-53.

Ryan, R.M., & Connell, J.P. (1989). Perceived locus of causality and internalization: Examining reasons for acting in two domains. *Journal of Personality and Social Psychology, 57,* 749-761.

Ryan, R.M., Frederick, C.M., Lepes, D., Rubio, N., & Sheldon, K.M. (1997). Intrinsic motivation and exercise adherence. *International Journal of Sport Psychology, 28,* 335-354.

Sarrazin, P., Vallerand, R.J., Guillet, E., Pelletier, L.G., & Cury, F. (2002). Motivation and dropout in female handballers: A 21-month prospective study. *European Journal of Social Psychology, 32,* 395-418.

Sheldon, K.M., & Elliot, A.J. (1999). Goal striving, need satisfaction, and longitudinal well-being: The self-concordance model. *Journal of Personality and Social Psychology, 76,* 482-497.

Sheldon, K.M., & Kasser, T. (1995). Coherence and congruence: Two aspects of personality integration. *Journal of Personality and Social Psychology, 68,* 531-543.

Silberstein, L.R., Striegel-Moore, R.H., Timko, C., & Rodin, J. (1988). Behavioral and psychological implications of body dissatisfaction: Do men and women differ? *Sex Roles, 19*, 219-232.

Smoll, F.L., Smith, R.E., Barnett, N.P., & Everett, J.J. (1993). Enhancement of children's self-esteem through social support training for youth sport coaches. *Journal of Applied Psychology, 78*, 602-610.

Vallerand, R.J. (1997). Towards a hierarchical model of intrinsic and extrinsic motivation, In: M.P. Zanna (Eds.), *Advances in experimental social psychology* (pp. 271-359). New York: Academic Press

Vallerand, R.J., & Losier, G.F. (1994). Self-determined motivation and sportsmanship orientations: An assessment of their temporal relationship. *Journal of Sport and Exercise Psychology, 16*, 229-245.

Vallerand, R.J., & Ratelle, C. (2002). Intrinsic and extrinsic motivation: A hierarchical model. In E.L. Deci & R.M. Ryan (Eds.), *Handbook of self-determination research* (pp. 37-63). Rochester, NY: University of Rochester Press.

Vallerand, R.J., & Reid, G. (1984). On the causal effects of perceived competence on intrinsic motivation: A test of cognitive evaluation theory. *Journal of Sport Psychology, 6*, 94-102.

Vansteenkiste, M., & Sheldon, K.M. (2006). "There's nothing more practical than a good theory": Integrating motivational interviewing and self-determination theory. *British Journal of Clinical Psychology, 45*, 63-82.

Waterman, A.S. (1993). The two conceptions of happiness: Contrasts of personal expressiveness (eudaimonia) and hedonic enjoyment. *Journal of Personality and Social Psychology, 64*, 678-691.

Williams, G.C. (2002). Improving patients' health through supporting the autonomy of patients and providers. In E.L. Deci & R.M. Ryan (Eds.), *Handbook of self-determination research* (pp. 233-254). Rochester, NY: University of Rochester Press.

Wilson, P.M., Rodgers, W.M., Blanchard, C.M., & Gessell, J. (2003). The relationship between psychological needs, self-determined motivation, exercise attitudes, and physical fitness. *Journal of Applied Social Psychology, 33*, 2373-2392.

INDEX

Page numbers followed by an italicized f or t refer to the figure or table on that page, respectively.

Martin S. Hagger, PhD, is a chartered psychologist and reader in social and health psychology in the School of Psychology at the University of Nottingham, United Kingdom. He has authored more than 50 research articles, book chapters, and books on motivation, including *Social Psychology of Exercise and Sport* with Nikos Chatzisarantis. He was commissioned to edit *Advances in Self-Determination Theory Research in Exercise and Sport,* a special issue of the peer-reviewed scholarly journal *Psychology of Exercise and Sport.* He is coeditor of *Psychology and Health,* associate editor of *Psychology of Sport and Exercise,* and on the international advisory board of *British Journal of Health Psychology.*

Nikos L.D. Chatzisarantis, PhD, is a principal lecturer in the School of Psychology at University of Plymouth, United Kingdom. Since 1995 he has been researching human motivation and decision-making processes from a self-determination theory perspective. He has been published in peer-reviewed journals of both mainstream psychology and exercise psychology. He earned a PhD in education and a master's degree in sport and exercise psychology from the University of Exeter. He is a member of the advisory boards of *International Journal of Sport Psychology, Psychology and Health,* and *Research Quarterly for Exercise and Sport.*